HOW TO BE YOUR OWN LAWYER
(SOMETIMES)

Also by Howard Eisenberg:

HOW TO BE YOUR OWN DOCTOR (SOMETIMES)
WITH KEITH SEHNERT, M.D.

HOW TO BE YOUR OWN LAWYER
SOMETIMES

Walter L. Kantrowitz, J.D., LL.M. and Howard Eisenberg

A Perigee Book

Perigee Books
are published by
G. P. Putnam's Sons
200 Madison Avenue
New York, New York 10016

Library of Congress Cataloging in Publication Data

Kantrowitz, Walter L
    How to be your own lawyer (sometimes)

    Includes index.
    1. Law—United States—Popular works.   I. Eisenberg,
Howard, joint author.   II.   Title.
[KF387.K34   1980]   340'.0973   79–20685
ISBN 0–399–50457–5 pbk.

First Perigee Printing, 1980

Printed in the United States of America

CONTENTS

LIST OF FORMS

HE AND SHE: AN APOLOGY AND EXPLANATION

The law is complex enough. To complicate it even further by ponderously inserting "he or she" or "herself and himself" everywhere in this manuscript that these alternatives occur would make the legal thickets we have sought to penetrate on the reader's behalf unconscionably thicker.

So, for purposes of clarity, we fall back upon this ancient—if somewhat cowardly—contractual legal device:

Grammatical usage

In construing this document, feminine or neuter pronouns shall be substituted for those masculine in form and vice versa in any place in which the context so requires.

When we use the masculine pronoun, then, we are in no way taking the position that women cannot be their own lawyers. As the growing numbers and high ranking of women in law schools today demonstrate, women law students and lawyers are proving to be every bit as good as men in the profession—and often better.

INTRODUCTION

More Than Just a Band-aid

It came as a surprise to almost no one on Lomond Avenue when we decided to collaborate on a book to be titled *How to Be Your Own Lawyer (Sometimes)*. One of us had been a lawyer for twenty years. The other had just finished co-authoring with Keith Sehnert, M.D., *How to Be Your Own Doctor (Sometimes)*. Since we are next-door neighbors, the combination seemed as natural as law and order.

The first time we sat down to discuss the project, we weren't at all certain we could safely recommend enough self-help law to fill even a very short book. Two years later, new subject areas are still suggesting themselves, but we wistfully deflect them. Every book has its "pub date," and we have passed ours twice already.

We're not sorry we took so long. We firmly believe that *How to Be Your Own Lawyer (Sometimes)* will be as valuable in cutting legal bills and eliminating unnecessary visits to the lawyer as readers report *How to Be Your Own Doctor (Sometimes)* has been in paring medical expenses and curbing unnecessary trips to the doctor.

The need for a book that reduces dependence on lawyers—by taking you step-by-programmed-step through do-it-yourself management of the most commonly encountered legal problems—seems clearly foreshadowed in statements by two Chief Justices of the U.S. Supreme Court.

It was Mr. Justice Warren Burger who said: "The notion that most people want black-robed judges, well-dressed lawyers and fine paneled courtrooms as the setting to resolve their disputes is not correct. People with problems, like people with pains, want relief, and they want it as quickly and inexpensively as possible." Lawyers, he added, "may be a handicap" in trying to resolve minor disputes.

In a separate (though earlier) opinion, the late Chief Justice Earl Warren concurred: "The consumer is demanding reasonably priced legal services. And he will get them. Not only does he feel forgotten, he feels wounded and betrayed by the legal profession."

How to Be Your Own Lawyer (Sometimes) can help to bind the wounds. Used thoughtfully and with care, it will be more than just a Band-Aid.

A few rare individuals, of course, will want the whole roll of gauze. A lawyer friend of ours told us of one such man whom he represented in bitter litigation with a former employer over a matter of severance pay. The client—let's call him Richard Resolute—became deeply involved in his case. He bombarded the attorney with questions and phone calls, and spent hours in law libraries researching fine points and seeking precedents to suggest. When it was time for the EBTs—examinations before trial—he arrived with a valise full of notes and documents, and afterward earnestly declared to his attorney the wish to join him at the counsel table when his trial came up.

"I was about to say OK," recalls his lawyer, "when an image of Richard sitting resolutely beside me whispering sudden thoughts and suggestions sotto voce in my ear all during the trial flashed into my mind. I quickly asked if he remembered seeing the railing that divides a courtroom. Of course he had. 'You've heard the expression being admitted to the bar? Well, that's the bar. Only lawyers can sit at the table on the other side of the railing.'

"That little white lie didn't faze Resolute one bit. 'When,' he inquired, 'will my case come up?'

"'The calendar's pretty crowded,' I said. 'It could be two or three years.' He nodded and left with what seemed to me a particularly resolute look on his face, even for him. About a month later, I learned its meaning when he phoned exultantly to say, 'I've been accepted by Columbia Law School. Save me a seat at the counsel table.'"

Concluded my attorney friend, "Resolute made it through law school with straight As and passed his bar exam the first time around. Boy, was I glad I managed to settle his case before he got his diploma!"

Not too many readers of this book will want to go quite so far as Resolute. But while you're deciding if you, too, want to sit at the counsel table, you should be able to get quite a decent elementary legal education in the pages ahead.

One of the best things about writing a book in collaboration is that you are never alone. When Author A can't parse another paragraph, Author B spurs him on. Facing the typewriter together helped, but there were other helping hands and minds as well.

Leading all the rest was Jack E. Horsley, a courtly trial lawyer from Lincoln country, sometimes introduced at legal conventions as "one of the great ones," and himself co-author (with John Carlova) of *Your Family and the Law* and *Testifying in Court: the Advanced Course.* Graciously good-natured Jack is easy to exploit. But he made so many excellent comments and suggestions in his reading of the manuscript—many of them incorporated into the final text—that, we must confess, we're glad we took advantage of him. My weight-lifting law partner Paul Goldhamer merits honorable mention for cheerfully carrying more than his share of the office load in the more than a year that this work was in progress.

Both our families got into the act. Arlene Eisenberg (Howard's marriage and writing associate) took time off from a mammoth writing project of her own to skillfully sift through great masses of material to rough-draft a number of particularly difficult chapters; son Evan contributed research from Harvard's law library and, when deadlines pressed, made preliminary drafts of several chapters as well. Future law partner Barry Kantrowitz (at seventeen it's a little early for the official announcement) "clerked" on the project and made himself generally invaluable. Paralegals Gary Graifman and Judith Anderson researched and gathered material for a number of subject areas. Gary must have liked what he saw—he has since enrolled in law school.

Christine Russo (chapter 1) and Stanley Gornish (chapters 9 through 11) eloquently recounted personal *pro se* adventures. This book is the richer and more useful for their reports and perceptions. Others—judges, attorneys, laypersons—contributed individual courtroom and other legal experiences or observations: Milton Blackstone, Kenneth Becker, Louis Narotsky, A. J. Vogl, Irv Adler, Harry Paxton, Jack Lavin, Rhoda Naidus, Phillips Huston, Ed Whitney, Tom McGill, Jack Angel, Steve Enright, David Kull, Pat Pavese, and Joel Goldberg among them. Not all were used, but all were appreciated. That last can certainly be said as well of Robert Blumberg of the firm of Julius Blumberg, Inc., producers of thousands of law blanks and forms, a number of which—though certainly not all—are reproduced by permission in this book.

Can we omit the name of our editor, Ned Chase? Hardly, for without his enthusiasm and appreciation, our original outline might

15

CHAPTER I

You Don't Have to Go to Law School

Chris Russo didn't know whether to sob or smile when the process server handed her the Summons and Complaint form:

> . . . in that the defendant, Christine Russo, harbors two vicious canines . . . that said animals are a clear and present menace to society . . . that on or about June 12, 1975, said savage animals did attack plaintiff with the intention of doing him bodily harm, and said dogs did bite plaintiff causing grievous wounds and injury to his person and property (viz., clothing) . . . that for such injury, pain and suffering plaintiff sustained damages and demands judgment in the sum of . . .
>
> $10,000.00.

The judge in Manhattan Civil Court frowned when Chris appeared in court. "Young lady," he warned, "a $10,000 lawsuit is a very serious matter. I advise you to get yourself an attorney." Chris stood her ground. "Your Honor," she said stubbornly, "I refuse to dignify these ridiculous charges by hiring a lawyer."

We begin this book with Chris Russo's story because it reflects an interesting and significant trend—the ultimate act of faith in the do-it-yourself creed: the decision, with a ruinous lawsuit hanging like a concrete slab from a construction crane over your head—to be your own lawyer.

Time was when the legal profession scornfully dismissed self-representing *pro se* appearances as the aberrations of cranks and crackpots. The automatic learned-in-law-school response was to shrug one's shoulders ruefully, shake one's head wisely and intone: "The lawyer who represents himself has a fool for a client."

Inference clear. No further translation needed. If a trained lawyer shouldn't plead his own cause, how much more perilous that course for the untrained average citizen? Which is our cue to return to the case at hand.

Chris Russo's story begins at the curb on 36th Street between Park and Lexington avenues in Manhattan, walking her beloved black poodles, Gigi (height 10 1/2 inches, age 15, deaf, nearly blind, dull of tooth and arthritic of movement) and Penny (age 10, going deaf, cataract in one eye and "so loving she could lick you to death").

"About halfway down the block," Chris remembers, "I noticed a little old man who had stopped and was looking at me strangely. I thought to myself, this man must be afraid of dogs, and drew Gigi and Penny closer to the curb so he'd have the sidewalk to himself. The dogs were busily sniffing about the base of the tree, and I had my eyes on them, when suddenly this man came between me and them, tangled in the leash, tripped, and practically fell on his face. He turned, looked up and angrily accused: 'Your dog bit me!' "

The man then lifted his pants leg, pointing at a red mark on his calf, then quickly scrambled to his feet, took Chris's address and limped dramatically offstage.

A month later, there was an attorney's letter in Chris's mailbox, followed shortly thereafter by a phone call. "My client," the attorney announced, "is willing to settle for $100. That will cover his medical expenses and the cost of a suit to replace the one your dogs ruined. It's a very generous offer."

"I'm not convinced that my dogs bit him," Chris replied, "but I'll consider it. Meanwhile, I'd appreciate a chance to see what I'm paying for. Please send me a copy of the medical bill and report."

The medical papers and a notice from the Board of Health arrived in the same mail. "That did it," says Chris. "The medical report read, 'puncture wound, left great toe—dog bite (?), varicose veins.' And the only prescribed treatment was a soak—no precautionary injections, no nothing. I thought, Who is this man kidding? There were just too many contradictions. If the dog bit through the shoe, how in heaven's name could his pants be ripped? And the red mark he'd showed me was on the lower calf. With that I resolved, 'Mister, I'm not paying you one red cent! and I'll see you in court!' "

Two months later, a process server thoughtfully provided the opportunity. Chris telephoned the court clerk, learned that anyone may file a *pro se* answer, typed a statement explaining that her dogs were aging, placid, loving house-pet poodles, not vicious attack Dobermans, and delivered it to the courthouse at 111 Centre Street. There a sympathetic clerk supplied her with the appropriate form to attach. "Anything else I have to do between now and the trial?" Chris asked. "Just one thing, lady," was the reply. "Get ready."

Chris, like most Americans today, is a lot more court-savvy than our parents and grandparents were. Years of exposure to TV courtroom dramas—to *Perry Mason* and *Petrocelli*, to *The Defenders* and *Owen Marshall*—has given a surface familiarity with court procedures to millions. Tapemeasure in hand, Chris measured the street, the width of the sidewalk, the base of the tree the dogs had been sniffing, and the combined length of her arm and the leash. She diagrammed the scene—buildings, street and all—and that was when she realized that the man had had six feet of clearance. Why then had he chosen to walk between the tree and the dogs? If he had been bitten—and Chris now refused to accept that—he had only his own negligence to blame.

A Notice of Trial Date arrived soon after, and at the courthouse the lawyer offered Chris another chance to settle—this time for $250.

"Even then," Chris remembers, "I was tempted. The nuisance of a trial didn't appeal to me one bit. But every time I thought of paying that extortion money, I said, 'No way!'

"The plaintiff didn't show," Chris continues. "His lawyer gave the judge some excuse or other and won a 30-day postponement. But a few weeks later, he showed up at my house, walked the dogs with me for three blocks and tried to persuade me, 'friend to friend,' that the smartest thing I could do was settle on the spot: 'I'd hate to see a nice lady like you get stuck with a $10,000 judgment.' I told him indignantly that what he was doing was perfectly stinking, that if he'd told the truth I might have settled at the start, but that I had no intention of letting him get away with permanently branding my dogs as vicious public malefactors."

Thoroughly convinced at last that she meant business, the attorney had a subpoena served summoning Chris to his office for the taking of a deposition. She ignored it—her first legal mistake. Several days after the deposition date, another paper was served—this time by the court ordering her to appear.

"Your Honor," Chris explained, "this young man came to my

19

home. He has been hounding me. I thought this was just some new kind of harassment. Also, I was unaware that his request to go to his office to give a deposition had the force of a court order."

The judge softened. "You're willing to give the deposition now?"

"Yes."

"Well," he said, turning to the attorney, "set up a new date for deposition. I want you all in court ready for trial in 30 days."

The old man was not there the third time, the fourth or the fifth. Each time his attorney was ready with an excuse, but it seemed to Chris that it was all part of the pattern of harassment—annoy her, waste her mornings, make her lose time from her job and, exasperated, she'd finally settle. But she was not about to yield, and by the sixth nonappearance, it was the judge who'd had enough.

"This lady," he told the lawyer angrily, "has been here every time we've called her. She has given you everything you wanted. Now it's time your client showed up. No more excuses. Get him down here—now, or I'll dismiss!" Within an hour, the "sick" plaintiff was there, and a judge and courtroom had been assigned. Chris agreed to waive the jury, got the judge's permission to bring her dogs to court ("They're my best defense, your Honor") and the following morning the trial of Gigi and Penny began.

The plaintiff's attorney called Chris as the first witness, while her girlfriend Peggy held the tethered dogs. After a number of establishing questions, the lawyer posed the one on which he fully expected to win the case: "Ms. Russo, is it not true, as you admitted in deposition, that your dog Gigi has a history of biting people— that, in fact, she bit your own brother?"

Surprised, the judge interrupted. "Ms. Russo," he said impatiently, "you might as well settle this case. If you've already made that kind of damaging admission, this matter is a waste of the court's time."

"Your Honor," Chris replied, "it may sound as though the dog is guilty—but there are a lot of extenuating circumstances, and a lot of things that don't add up. For one thing, Gigi did nip my brother twelve years ago, but only because he pretended to rough me up. She just came to my defense."

"Really?" said the judge. "Only one nip in the past twelve years? Well then, let's continue testimony after lunch."

An important point about the dogs had already been indirectly

20

established: how completely and unflappably harmless they were. While her mistress was on the stand, Penny had amiably and repeatedly licked the opposing attorney's hand. When the two dogs restlessly strained at their leashes, barking for Chris, the judge had signaled to Peggy to release them.

Recalls Chris: "It was a crazy scene. Penny is deaf and couldn't hear me call her. Gigi is blind and was unable to see me. They were marvelous defense witnesses. Not once did they snap at anybody—not even when Gigi's leash wound around the court reporter's stand and practically knocked it over. Finally, they sniffed me out, and both went quietly to sleep in my lap."

Chris now had the opportunity to cross-examine the old man. She got him to admit that he walks with his head down and doesn't always look where he is going. She brought out, too, that the rip in his trousers was not six inches long, not even an inch or two, but that it was "a tooth hole." At that point the judge interrupted again: "Are you going to ask him the obvious question? If you won't, I will. Where are the pants?" Replied the plaintiff, "I couldn't wear them. I threw them away." This from a thrifty old man who had already admitted in court that one reason he walked with his eyes on the ground was to look for lost coins.

Chris then put Peggy on the stand to testify that, when walked, the dogs always make a beeline for the curb. "You see, your Honor," Chris exclaimed, "he walked between me and the curb, looking down at the ground for coins, and that's how he got entangled in the leash."

By now the judge, thoroughly enjoying himself, was imperceptibly beginning to help lawyerless Chris. "So, Perry Mason," he said, "now you want to make a motion that the case be dismissed on grounds of contributory negligence? Well, I'll take that under advisement. Meanwhile, please continue." The plaintiff's lawyer jumped to his feet. "Your Honor," he said, "all this is irrelevant and immaterial. My client's medical report clearly establishes the defendant's liability."

"Oh, yes," said Chris, "thank you for reminding me about the medical report. Your Honor, I'd like to recall the plaintiff. Now," she said, turning to him, "where were you bitten?" The old man pulled up both pants legs. "You saw it," he said peevishly. "I already showed it to you when your dogs bit me." He pointed once more to his lower calf. "See?"

"I see it," said Chris, "but I'm challenging it. The strange thing is your medical report reads, 'puncture wounds left great toe, dog bite (?), varicose veins.'"

The judge jumped up. "I don't believe you!" he said. "Let me see that report!" Somewhat shaken, Chris obliged and waited as he examined the paper. "By gosh," the judge exclaimed explosively, "you're right. Young lady, you're a darned good cross-examiner. Your old dog would have had to bite through his shoe to do what this claims she did."

Now it was time for summation. "This poor woman," declaimed the opposing lawyer, "hasn't any children of her own. Hence, she treats her dogs as though they were children. Like a mother whose children can do no wrong, her dogs can do no wrong."

When he finished, Chris was steaming. She turned to the attorney. "You don't know me," she retorted angrily, "and you are drawing conclusions you have no right to draw. I happen to have 24 nieces and nephews, and if my dogs ever bit one of them, I assure you the dogs would be the first to go."

The judge's decision was not long in coming. "Case dismissed," he said. "Insufficient evidence and possible contributory negligence."

Chris exchanged exultant glances with Peggy. She'd hung tough. Without benefit of counsel, she'd defeated her adversary. She'd saved herself legal fees and possibly $10,000 to boot.

Chris Russo won her case. Does that mean that you, with no formal legal training, can successfully be your own lawyer, too? That you can defend yourself in court, write your own will, start your own business, file your own bankruptcy, handle your own divorce? The answer is yes—sometimes. To find out when, read on.

CHAPTER 2

Pro Se: Taking the Law into Your Own Hands

If you were beginning your freshman year in law school, the urbane silver-haired dean might assemble you and your fellow students in the auditorium and deliver a few thousand preliminary words of caution and counsel.

It seems fitting as you begin this book—a kind of home study course in do-it-yourself law—that I appoint myself dean and do the same.

It started with Socrates. The idea of *pro se*, a phrase in Latin meaning "for oneself," or "self-representation"—in effect, taking the law into your own hands—sounds radical but it has an old and honorable history.

In ancient Athens, every citizen was required to plead his own cause in courts which were run from judge to jury by nonprofessionals. Juries compared in size to ours as the Mormon Tabernacle Choir does to a barbershop quartet—normally, 201 members for a civil case and 501 for a criminal matter, with an astonishing 6,000-man jury recorded once by whoever kept the Greek edition of the *Guinness Book of Records.* This very massiveness contributed to the emergence of the third-oldest profession—perhaps informally known to local fourth century A.D. critics as chariot-chasers—lawyers.

Before Athens invented trial by jury, a magistrate chosen by lot decided each matter, and arguing one's case was relatively unintimidating. But when the accused had to appear before a cast of thousands—with banishment or a hemlock cocktail a distinct possibility if words failed you—pleading one's own cause became an awesome responsibility.

Litigants began to purchase speeches from professional orators, or to beg a particularly eloquent friend or relative to speak for them. Attempts to outlaw ghost writers and stand-ins were notably unsuccessful, and so the legal profession was born.

23

Whether or not that was a good thing for civilization can be argued pro and con ad infinitum. In any case, there has been of late a return to the ways of the early Greeks: a dazzling and to some lawyers alarming, do-it-yourself law renaissance throughout the United States. Every day, thousands of Americans appear *pro se*, chiefly in Small Claims Courts but in higher courts as well. Tens of thousands, particularly in trend-making states like California and New York, have successfully and inexpensively guided their own marital separations and divorces, often with follow-the-numbers "divorce kits." (Some, of course, have messed up—like a woman who used a kit to divorce her husband of nineteen years and ten months. She found out too late something that a good lawyer would have told her—that if she'd waited just two more months, she would have been eligible upon his death for widow's Social Security benefits.) In states like Wisconsin and Michigan, simplified probate procedures have made it possible for self-reliant widows and heirs to collectively save themselves hundreds of thousands of dollars in legal fees by processing small estates without benefit of counsel.

It seems possible that today's teenagers will be even more *pro se*–minded than their parents, thanks to a slowly growing movement toward teaching elementary law courses in our public school systems—as with an Ohio course, called "Practical Law for the Peanut-Butter-and-Pizza Set."

Self-lawyering: suddenly it's very Main Street. The Era of the Expert, though not dead, is badly wounded. In my father's day, lawyers were respected and admired members of the community—which is one reason he encouraged me to go to law school. But today once unchallenged professionals are under fire on many fronts: physicians who perform doubtful surgery, educators who don't teach Johnny to read, engineers whose dams crumble and bridges buckle, chemists and other scientists who assured us that progress was our most important product but rarely warned of its by-products of poisons and pollution, architects whose arena domes collapse. When disappointed consumers take target practice, we lawyers, too, occasionally find ourselves at the center of the bullseye. Even Ralph Nader and his associate Mark Green, attorneys themselves, have not spared the rod on the legal profession.

There's no room in this book to get into that debate. It won't teach you to write a will or start a business. It's enough for present purposes to say that most attorneys do a pretty good job. Some do a great job; a few don't do a job at all and are a disgrace to the profession. One problem from the consumer's point of view—and it's another important reason for the flowering of self-lawyering—is that almost all of us do an expensive job. As a Washington attorney ruefully remarked at a cocktail party recently, "We lawyers are pricing ourselves out of the market."

The whereas and heretofore factor. The achievements of members of my profession in administering the law—and in government and industry as well—are many. Lawyers and the law played a key role in giving the vote to women, a seat in the front of the bus to American blacks and early retirement to Richard Nixon. Still it sometimes seems that attorneys are only slightly more popular than a state trooper behind a roadside billboard with a radar gun.

But then we of the lawbook are accustomed to being unloved. In every age there has been some uneasiness about us. Plato labeled lawyers (in company with physicians) as "the pests of a country." King Ferdinand of Spain went so far as to warn colonists about to embark for the Indies not to "carry along . . . law-students, for fear lest [law] suits should get a footing in that new world . . ." And Sir Thomas More, in picturing Utopia, reserved no place in it for lawyers. "Let them in," he seemed to be saying, "and there goes the neighborhood!"

Why can't we ever win a popularity poll now and then? The answer seems, at least in part, to be guilt by association—a general impression that the law is designed more to entrap than to enlighten, more to confuse than to codify, more to impoverish widows and orphans than to protect them. Many people perceive the law as intricate and entangling, a spider's web of whereases and heretofores, respecting property more than persons, which, once entered, traps the unwary (often the wary as well) in silk-steel strands of torts and testimony. They retain lawyers as expensive but necessary guides through the labyrinth.

Often, of course, we *are* necessary. The law is full of specialties—maritime, bankruptcy, space, negligence, foreign trade, criminal, anti-trust, insurance, corporation. Long study and still longer experience are required to master them. And who has the time? Except for those serving it—like Clifford Irving, the hoax-autobiographer of Howard Hughes, who whiled away the long penitentiary days and nights by researching the law on an I.R.S. claim against him for $120,000 in back taxes, then argued and won his case in court—usually only lawyers.

But many legal matters are far less complex. In a modern lawyer's office, they are, in fact, often routinely handled by paralegals or secretaries. An uncomplicated will or separation agreement is needed for a client? An attorney dictates brief instructions: "Use paragraph 91, 93, 96. Close with paragraph 117C." The secretary feeds names and other details into a computerized typewriter, dials the ordered program, and the typewriter hums, clicks and produces an elegant and eminently legal document at 540 words per minute.

It is upon these comparatively easy-to-handle areas of the law, involving everyday, simply structured legal problems, that the following chapters concentrate. You may not get the job done as fast as that $600-a-month automatic typewriter, but you can do it. And you'll be able to accomplish a lot more than Supertypewriter, merely by following the step-by-step instructions, explanations and legal forms in the pages ahead.

Throwing the book at you. This book is designed to demystify the law, and to mark the main roads through the maze, so that whether you plan to travel alone or with an attorney, your familiarity with methods and procedures will get you there more easily, less expensively. You won't find any dense legal jargon here, nor will you need to hire a lawyer to help you read and understand it. Our honorable intention has been to inform and educate, not to produce a 400-page sleeping pill. To avoid that unfortunate result, we've tried to enliven and illuminate the text by making as many points as possible with stories and case experiences—my own and those of friends and colleagues.

We've asserted that this book should be helpful. We would be less than candid if we failed to add that being your own lawyer may not be all Elberta peaches and cream. It will help if you're spunky, determined, intelligent, and patient.

Stubbornness counts. So does the ability to puzzle things out. When you were a kid, did you not only take the family alarm clock apart but manage to put it back together? When your bathroom faucet drips, can you change the washer? And, above all, do you have that quality known as true grit? You may need it, because the course of true *pro se* representation will not always run smooth.

You may be tripped up now and then by unfamiliar rules and procedures—as Stanley Gornish was, a time or two (in chapters 9, 10, and 11), in handling his own divorce. But Stanley bounced right back up. So can you.

You may run into mild hostility from initially reluctant judges

—as (in chapter 1). Christine Russo did. Judges are accustomed to *pro se* litigants in Small Claims Court, but less so in higher courts. After all, judges were lawyers before they were fitted for black robes. An occasional judge may resent *pro se* parties, in subconscious sympathy for attorneys who may thereby lose a fee. *Pro se* may clog the assembly line just a bit. Rules have to be explained, frozen procedures thawed. But *pro se* cases are becoming so common that this problem will fade. The vast majority of judges will go out of their way to sympathetically explain, and now and then even lend a helping hand.

You can expect some confusion, some occasional bafflement. What is called the Superior Court in California is the Supreme Court in New York, District Court in Texas, and the Circuit Court in Florida. Even Small Claims Courts go under different names— Justice Court in one jurisdiction, Municipal Court in another. To list the variations would more than double the length (and price) of this book and halve its readability.

The law is generally divided into two parts: substantive and procedural. *Example:* Substantive law tells you that if your spouse commits adultery, you are entitled to a divorce. Procedural law tells you how to get it, using adultery as your grounds. We've sought in this book to set forth sufficient substantive law to provide you with a basic understanding of your rights and obligations relative to common problems you may encounter. Our chief objective, however, has been to focus on practice and procedures: the how-you-can-do-it half of the law.

Thick law-for-the-layperson books designed to be more encyclopedic than this one abound in public libraries. We urge you to refer to them if the need for some piece of substantive law should arise: a definition, a statute, a complete state-by-state listing of bankruptcy exemptions for the debtor, or of the grounds for divorce in the state of Illinois.

You can expect to run around a lot—and get the runaround at least a little. But so do beginning lawyers. The first proposed separation decree I ever prepared came back in the mail with a note from the court clerk scrawled on the first page: "Wrong—see Rule 192." I made the fix, mailed it back. It returned again, this time with a note on the second page: "See Rule 197." I repaired the damage, but the third time hand-carried it to the clerk and asked him to check it for errors all the way to the end while I waited.

To err now and then is part of the learning process. You'll ask the legal stationery supply clerk for the wrong form and have to go back again. You'll forget to bring a certified check to court—the only kind they'll accept from a nonlawyer. You'll make a mistake on a form and be forced to return for another copy. (Avoid that eventuality, by the way, by immediately photocopying several extra copies of any forms you purchase, so you'll not only have the original for submission but spares for your files and for worksheets as well.)

Legal geography may occasionally inconvenience you in using this book, as it did us in writing it. It would have been easier to publish in Monaco or Liechtenstein where one set of rules applies. State, county, and town courts in this country are not so marvelously monolithic. We have 50 states, but far more than 50 different sets of rules and forms, often with variations from one judicial district to the next in the very same state. So again, a little library legwork may periodically be in order, a little courage mustered to ask the occasional advice of your local court clerk.

When not to be your own lawyer. This book will give you a respectable smattering of the law, but by no means will make you a lawyer—nor make lawyers obsolete. The law is complex. It is alive; it meanders, doubles back, reverses itself, varies jurisdictionally. In *Oliver Twist*, the violently lawyer-phobic Charles Dickens puts these heated words in the mouth of Mr. Bumble: "The law is a ass." That may be. But it can also very quickly make "a ass" out of the novice who gets in too deep.

That's where the *Sometimes* in our title comes in—in letters ten feet tall. It is designed to remind the reader to stay in safe waters— knee-deep in the law but no deeper. In general, I believe you should not represent yourself when: 1) you are charged with a crime; 2) you are the plaintiff or defendant in a lawsuit involving a substantial sum of money; or 3) you are insecure.

Being your own lawyer in a criminal case can be particularly hazardous. It's been done, of course. In Massachusetts, a grade-school dropout indicted for murder effectively argued 45 pretrial motions *pro se*. (For the actual trial, yielding to the judge's suasion, he reluctantly accepted an attorney.) But the results are more likely to be catastrophic, like the case of a Chicago man who sealed his own fate when he rashly asked a key witness, "Isn't it true that I was wearing a ski mask when I held up your store?"

As attorneys denouncing *pro se* law are fond of remarking, "Everyone has the constitutional right to make a fool of himself." An attorney indicted in Louisiana proved their point. Convicted and sentenced to a prison term, he appealed. His grounds? Having served as his own lawyer, he had been "inadequately and incompetently represented."

There are, then, times when even lawyers need lawyers. Part II of this book is dedicated to such moments—when it's clear that you're over your head and need an attorney to throw you a life preserver. The final three chapters will help you find the right lawyer, evaluate his credentials, and keep your legal bills to a minimum. Hourly "time billing" is rapidly becoming the most prevalent method of determining legal fees. The person who arrives at his attorney's office well-prepared requires less time and attention and will be more likely to beat the clock.

Being your own attorney is not only possible in the situations discussed in this book, but it is your legal right. In *Faretta v. California*, the U.S. Supreme Court confirmed that the right to counsel guaranteed by the Constitution includes the right to serve as one's own counsel. This does not, however, confer upon you the right to act as someone else's counsel, which would be practicing law without a license. You can handle your own divorce, prepare your own will and file your own bankruptcy, but—do the same for a friend, a relative, or a stranger and you'll be committing a crime.

End of caveats and dire warnings—which, as dean of this one-volume law school, I felt obliged to present. Actually, I have high hopes for you. As you embark on your *pro se* career, I wish you only happy cases, quickly and favorably resolved.

PART I

HOW TO BE YOUR OWN LAWYER

CHAPTER 3

The Bargaining Table: Settling out of Court

•Your next-door neighbor decides to fell a tree in his backyard that's been blocking the sun from his swimming pool. You have no objections—until the tree topples with a resounding crash on your roof. His homeowner's insurance company will be glad to pay for patching the hole. But the repairman you consult warns that the roof has been so weakened by the blow that you really need a whole new section, to the tune of $800. The insurance company won't sing along.

•Your $500 floor-to-ceiling drapes, pride of your living room, are due for freshening, and you take them to a local dry cleaner, whose clerk blithely assures you that they can handle the job. You pick them up next day, hang them, and are dismayed to discover that they're so badly shrunken your two-year-old can press his nose against the glass patio door without moving the drapes. Your indignant phone calls are met with a frosty "Sorry, but we're not responsible for shrinkage." Your angry demands for the owner's name and address are met with yawns and "Sorry, but that information is confidential."

•You stop for a light on Main Street, but the car behind you keeps going. A body shop estimates $350 and says you're getting off easy. But the other driver neither sends your estimate and claim to his insurance company, nor answers your half-dozen phone calls.

Take cases like these to a lawyer, and you may find yourself taken even less seriously by counsel ("You've got a case, but I can't afford to handle it") than by the people whose moneybelts you want to pry open. With such relatively small sums at stake (likely to be reduced even further by settlement), there's no way a lawyer can be compensated for his time on your case, unless one threatening letter will do the job. If he's your business lawyer, who regularly represents you in more lucrative matters, he'll probably handle your case as an accommodation. But ordinarily, "hungry" lawyers are hard to find. Many new law grads would rather clerk for an established firm than try to eke out a living in the peanut gallery. Young lawyers quickly learn they can barely pay their rent on nickel-and-dime cases. On borderline cases edging into four figures, a lawyer may swallow his pride and accept, but chances are that he and court costs will swallow most of your recovery as well.

THE FIRST STEP:
CONSIDER OTHER THAN LEGAL ALTERNATIVES

If you've been stung by a businessman, this could be the moment to try hitting him in his reputation—at the cost of a phone call and a follow-up postage stamp. Call the local Better Business Bureau (which might be able to seduce him into arbitration), file a complaint with a consumer fraud agency (usually listed in the phone book's white pages as part of the state attorney-general's office), or write to the nearest newspaper with a consumer action column. If you're dealing with a large corporation, don't waste time with subordinates, who are paid to give you as little as possible. Go right to the top with a strong, reasoned and well-documented letter to the corporation's president.

If these tactics fail, only two reasonable options remain. Forget the whole thing. Or be your own lawyer in courts all over the nation expressly designed to make it relatively easy to represent yourself. There's no lack of precedent. As far back as 1516, describing his ideal in *Utopia*, Sir Thomas More fantasized a world in which, "They have no lawyers among them, for they consider them as a sort of people whose profession it is to disguise matters . . . therefore, they think it is much better that every man should plead his own cause and trust it to the judge . . . By this means, they both cut off many delays, and find out truth more certainly."

THE SECOND STEP:
WHO IS THE ENEMY?

The first truth for you to find out is just who the enemy is. Where a well-established corporation is concerned—a department store, a chain operation, a local firm of good repute and long standing—it's no problem at all. A look at a sales slip, or a phone call to the company will tell you all you need to know for preparation and service of your papers. But smaller, less financially secure or fly-by-night firms sometimes guard their identities as jealously as a Leavenworth escapee. Fortunately, there are some simple measures to smoke out the man behind the corporate mask.

Names on the plate glass like "Joe's Dry Cleaners" or "Calgary & Co." don't on their face tell you who the actual owner is. You can sue Joe's or Calgary & Co., but it's better practice to sue "Joseph Calgary, doing business as Joe's Dry Cleaners." Just about every state requires someone operating a business under a fictitious or partnership name to file a D/B/A (Doing Business As) certificate, listing the names and addresses of the actual owners. Failure to file such a certificate is a crime in some states.

Corporations, too, must register—in some states only with the secretary of state in the capital, as with sole proprietors and partners, but in others a copy is also sent to the clerk of the county in which the firm operates. Often the names of those listed as incorporators are dummies—the lawyer who drafted the incorporation papers, for example. But since you've learned the corporate name, you can sue under that name.

If you don't have the address, you're still not stymied. You simply serve the papers on the secretary of state—in some states you can do this by mail, in others you'll have to pay a small fee to have them served. He, in turn, will mail the papers to whoever is listed as registered agent for that corporation, or to the person on whom such process has been designated to be served.

If it's an individual who must bear your legal wrath, be sure to get the name right as well as complete, because if you win your case, a judgment against that person is filed "officially of record" in the county or court clerk's office. That being the first place a credit manager checks out, it will become a black mark against his credit, if he ever wishes to make a loan or major purchase. If you're dealing with a person of property, the filing of a judgment ordinarily becomes a lien against his home (more on how to do this in chapter 6) or other real property, which he'll have to reckon with (and clear) if he ever tries to sell it. If you don't know who you're dealing with—all you have is a license plate number—you can write to the state motor vehicle bureau, and for a modest fee ($5 in New Jersey) they'll send you the owner's name and address and often the name of his insurance company.

Though Jones caused your injury, you may have the right to sue Smith as well—if Jones drove the car that hit you, but borrowed it from owner Smith. (If Jones stole the car, Smith would be guiltless, unless he carelessly left the keys in the car.) Similarly, if the timberjack who cut down that tree was hired by your neighbor, you have the right to sue both. And if an independent contractor picked up and delivered your drapes to the incompetent dry cleaner, you may sue him too. The name of the game is to tag a culprit with the ability to pay.

THE THIRD STEP:
CAN YOU COLLECT?

The attorney asks three questions—and so should you—before deciding to sue: 1) Is the person you sue responsible for your personal injury or property damage? 2) Did you, in fact, sustain an injury or damage? 3) Does the person who caused your injury or damage—or is responsible for it—have the financial means to pay for the damages? If the answer to any of the three questions is "no," you may be wasting your time. I say *may* not *will*, because the person you win the judgment against may be broke today, but rich five years from now. And judgments in some jurisdictions are valid for ten years or more.

THE FOURTH STEP:
HOW MUCH SHOULD YOU CLAIM?

In a personal injury case, the answer to that is often ridiculous—as when an attorney recently took the case of a gas station attendant whose leg was broken by a motorist when her car lurched forward at a gasoline pump. The injury was "worth" several thousand dollars, which is what he eventually settled for. But he scared the young couple half to death when he filed suit against them for $2 million.

In a property claim, you must be more realistic. The value is relatively easy to determine, and you must be able to establish the extent of your loss before you can proceed. Clear photographs—of your shrunken drapes hanging in place, of the crumbled rear fender of your car, of the heavy tree branch resting on your roof—will help to prove your claim. A witness will serve the same purpose—a good neighbor summoned to look at the damage and willing to testify in court or give you a written (and later notarized) statement of what he's seen.

You'll help your case with receipted bills to prove repairs you've already paid for, or written estimates to support your claims of work required. If you're in the habit of neatly filing receipts for all expensive purchases—or even if you just jumble them in a drawer somewhere—in the case of the drapes, you should be able to come up with evidence of their cost. If your drapes were totally ruined, you're entitled to their original cost less reasonable depreciation. If, like the car, they can be repaired, you're entitled to the total cost of that repair. If the car was demolished, you'd sue for its current value. That's easy to determine in the used-car Blue Book, which is updated monthly, and which any friendly car dealer (is there any other kind?) will be happy to let you examine. Photocopy the appropriate page. Use the edition for the month in which the accident occurred. (There are, incidentally, regional editions. You'll find a Japanese import listed at a higher value in the eastern edition than in the western and, conversely, a German import valued higher in the western edition. The reason: greater transportation costs.)

THE FIFTH STEP:
PUTTING THE DEFENDANT ON NOTICE

You've loaded your gun. Now fire it into the air to get their attention. That's done with a sternly worded and businesslike letter—I just keep a carbon, but you may feel more comfortable sending it certified with a return receipt requested—putting the other side on notice that you intend to press your claim.

It should read something like this:

Form No. 1

Dear ———:

I intend to represent myself in my claim against you for the damages I suffered as a result of your negligence in:
a) allowing your tree to fall on my roof on (date);
b) in failing to take due and proper care of my drapes when I brought them to your shop for cleaning, on (date), and by shrinking and otherwise damaging them, so as to have made them of no use or value to me.
c) careless and reckless operation of your car, with the result that it collided into the rear of mine on (date), at (place).

If you are insured, please turn this letter over to your insurance company. If you are not, please contact me directly, so we may discuss a settlement of my claim.

If I do not hear from you or your insurance company within one week of the date of this letter, I will have no alternative but to commence suit against you without further notice.

One week is actually too short a time to expect an insurance company, in all its bureaucratic glory, to react. So despite your stated deadline, there's no point in initiating suit for several weeks. If your letter bomb then fails to produce an unconditional surrender—or even a "so sue me!" shrug—it's time to roll out the heavy artillery. Skip the next several steps in negotiating, and move on to those preparatory to actually instituting suit. If, however, the enemy runs up the white flag, proceed to the next step.

THE SIXTH STEP: PREPARING TO NEGOTIATE

This step, for which you'll need to thoroughly marshal your evidence, simultaneously readies your case for negotiation and courthouse. You're aiming your gun, even if you hope you won't have to fire it. And your best ammunition is the facts, especially if they're in your favor. To prove the facts, you must present your evidence: photographs, diagrams, witnesses or their statements, estimates or paid bills, or demonstrative evidence such as the shrunken drapes.

If you expect to settle, the adjuster will want—and, since you want him to foot the bill, he's entitled—to see how you arrived at the damages you claim. Close-up photos of the damage to your car will be useful, a look at the car itself—if it hasn't yet been repaired—would be even better. Your estimate of, or the paid bill for, the cost of roof or car repair, or your original bill for the drapes, will help convince him of the value of your case. A diagram of the street, with measurements to curbs and corners will not only be helpful to your auto damage case but, re-examined later, will refresh your memory and help you in court when it's time to testify.

It is usually foolish to argue. Raising your voice only raises the temperature. Simply state what you expect to prove, and display photographs or other exhibits that help to prove it. If the opposition wants to argue, politely remind him that the meeting was scheduled not as a debate, but as an attempt to reach common ground leading to settlement.

THE SEVENTH STEP:
STRENGTHENING YOUR CASE WITH LIVE EVIDENCE—
WITNESSES

I saw a cartoon once that eloquently summed up a problem lawyers sometimes encounter in dealing with an eyewitness who could clinch—or, at least, strongly fortify—their case. It showed a jury filing back into the courtroom and the judge asking, "Have you reached a verdict?" The jury foreman replies: "We have, your Honor. We decided we didn't want to get involved."

The apathetic eyewitness who sees, hears and speaks no evil is more common in criminal trials, where the fear—real or imagined—of gangland retribution lurks, than in minor civil matters like "The Case of the Battered Bumper." If you find a witness to your fender-bender—a man waiting for a bus, a shopkeeper standing at his store entrance—ask if he would mind giving you a statement on what he saw. Keep it simple and straightforward, in his own words, either dictated to you or written on a pad, the back of an envelope, anything at all—something like, "My name is Charles DeVito. I reside at 12 Chestnut Street, Chicago, Illinois. On the morning of March 12, 1978, at approximately 10:15 A.M., I witnessed an auto accident on the corner of Michigan Boulevard and Huron Street. This is what happened . . ."

If things are hectic, you might settle for name, address, and phone number, and a promise to let you meet him next morning to take the statement. Normally, the attorney sends an investigator to get the statement or, if it's a key piece of testimony, arranges to take it himself. But if you're a reasonably friendly and empathetic person, you should be able to handle it yourself. If you hear that old line "I'd rather not get involved," try to get the other person to put himself in your shoes. ("How would you feel if *you* had the accident, and needed the witness?") Conclude by telling your witness that you will try hard to settle so he will not have to go to court, that you intend to be reasonable with the other side, and that court will be your last resort. You might add that his written statement may well be enough to convince the other side to settle. If it's strong enough, this may, in fact, be the case.

Occasionally, you run across the greedy witness, who sniffs an opportunity to turn your misfortune into his good fortune. Such witnesses are happily rare. Most people are willing to testify upon subpoena with reimbursement for actual loss of time. But an attorney I know tried a case in which his client was struck and killed by a police car while crossing the street. The police insisted that the man was drunk and had walked into the side of their car as they drove by. My friend was nevertheless confident. He had an eyewitness who—though unwilling to give a statement in writing—told the investigator that he had seen the front end of the police car strike the man as he crossed. On the eve of the trial, my friend phoned to tell the witness the time and place. "Sure," said his eyewitness. "I'll be there with bells on. But only if you're willing to guarantee me a $10,000 fee for my time and trouble." To serve him with a subpoena would have been useless. A man of this stamp would vengefully testify for the other side. Damned if he yielded to extortion and damned if he didn't, my attorney friend didn't and lost the case.

Is there anything you can do if this happens to you? Sometimes, with a bit of luck, such a situation can be turned to your advantage. Make a careful memorandum immediately after your witness issues his ultimatum. Then go ahead and subpoena him anyway. If he won't tell the truth, you are entitled to claim "surprise," cross-examine him as a hostile witness, and expose his venal demand. It's a maneuver that just might win your case.

You'll have no such difficulty getting your mother-in-law to bear witness for you, if she happened to be keeping you company when you brought in your drapes. Members of your family, spouse included, may freely testify. The court may, however, discount their testimony slightly, depending on how much sincerity they project.

THE EIGHTH STEP:
NEGOTIATING A SETTLEMENT

Seeking a settlement is not a sign of weakness, but rather of common sense. At the end of every trial, there is one happy person and one unhappy one; and—as Boileau's droll parable, versified by Alexander Pope, made clear two centuries ago—half an oyster is better than none.

Once (says an author, where I need not say),
Two travelers found an oyster in their way:
Both fierce, both hungry, the dispute grew strong;
While, scale in hand, dame Justice passed along.
Before her each with clamor pleads the laws,
Explain'd the matter, and would win the cause.
Dame Justice, weighing long the doubtful right,
Takes, opens, swallows it before their sight.
The cause of strife removed so rarely well,
'There, take (says Justice), take ye each a shell.
We thrive at Westminster on fools like you:
'Twas a fat oyster—live in peace—Adieu.'

Suppose one of the disputants had been awarded *both* shells. He would have the satisfaction of a moral victory—and an empty stomach. Wouldn't he have done better to try and settle before Dame Justice arrived on the scene? Presidents, as well as Popes, agree: "Discourage litigation," urged Abe Lincoln. "Persuade your neighbors to compromise whenever you can. Point out to them how the nominal winner is often a real loser—in fees, expenses and waste of time."

My Aunt Fannie—yes, I really do have an Aunt Fannie, and a warm and good-hearted lady she is, too—discovered the advantages of settlement when, chewing a tasty morsel of bread still warm from the local bakery, she felt a sudden sharp pain in the roof of her mouth, and, removing the chunk of bread, found the dough pink with her blood. Fingering the bread, she found a quarter-inch sliver of glass inside. After her dentist had treated her, she urged me to seek damages from the bakery—mostly, I think, because she was angered by the baker's flat denial of responsibility.

I wrote a claim letter to the bakery owner—along the lines of the one on page 37—and several weeks later an adjuster phoned to tell me he didn't think much of our case. A dental bill for treatment of a cut in the mouth was not, he said, proof that the cut had been incurred biting into his client's bread. I agreed, of course. It was no more proof of liability than your going to the doctor to cast your broken arm would prove that you had tripped on my living-room rug.

He changed his mind, however, when I told him that I'd asked my aunt to save the chunk of bloody bread with the glass splinter still in it, and he agreed to settle for $400 if I could produce that evi-

41

dence. I gave him directions to the house, and phoned ahead to tell my Uncle Matty to have Exhibit A ready. Eager to display it, Matty removed it from the freezer, and waited on the front lawn for the adjuster's arrival. When he drove up, my uncle proudly opened the foil—and the glass sliver fell out of the packet into the grass, never to be seen again. P.S. The case was settled, but for $100 less.

I recently heard of a case in which a woman successfully negotiated a rather large settlement entirely without benefit of counsel. A year earlier, she had been in an auto accident that had resulted in serious leg injuries and several operations. She never thought of suing until her doctor suggested it. Then, still uncomfortable with the idea of going to court, she phoned the insurance company and told them that she planned to sue but would prefer to settle before consulting a lawyer. "Send us your medical reports," they suggested.

Two weeks later, an adjuster called. "How much," he asked, "do you want?" "Fifty-thousand," she said, holding her breadth. "Too much," he declared, "but we'll give you $25,000." She refused, but when he called back in several weeks, raising the offer to $35,000, she accepted. Would an experienced attorney have gotten her more? Quite possibly. But his 33 1/3 percent of the settlement might have netted her less. In any event, her happily negotiated ending was spoiled. She invested the money in her brother's business—which, shortly thereafter, went into bankruptcy.

Settlement should be sought at every step of the game: before the summons is issued, before the case comes to trial, before the judgment. Often a lawsuit is filed with the specific goal of reaching a settlement. Once litigation has begun, various legal maneuvers ostensibly designed to further the pursuit of justice can be used to pressure, intimidate, bluff, or simply wear down your opponent into settling. If you're up against a large firm represented by an experienced lawyer, you're more likely to find yourself victim than wielder of such weapons. "You don't have a case," he'll say, and send you a demand for a bill of particulars, requiring you to produce the specifics of your case.

If the court you're suing in permits jury trials, you have a potent weapon in your arsenal, especially if you're a private individual tackling a corporation. The jury member's sympathy for the common person, especially the accident victim, is well-known. Often company lawyers will settle small cases where they know the law is on their side, just to avoid trying the case. But eloquent lawyers sway juries, so a jury trial could backfire against you.

THE NINTH STEP:
ARM WRESTLING WITH THE ADJUSTER

If you expect the adjuster to be hatchet-faced, gimlet-eyed, and icy, you may be in for a surprise when this easygoing, amiable gentleman shows up to discuss your case. Don't let him lead you down the garden path. There's a slaughterhouse at the other end of it and a skinning knife in a shoulder holster under his jacket. After he's sympathetically heard your tale of woe, winning your confidence with appropriate interjections of "What a shame!" and "How unfortunate!" comes the effort to skewer and make shish kebab of you. "The way my client tells it, you were backing up at the time he hit you." Or, "Can you prove your drapes weren't damaged before you brought them in?"

Don't spoil your beautiful new friendship by holding that against him. He's only doing his job, which is to save his company as much as he can. There'll be times, when it's to his or the company's advantage, when he'll surprise you with his generosity. Such endearing moments usually follow a speech from his supervisor that morning: "Hey, you've got a helluva backlog of cases, Fred. How come you haven't settled any lately?" Or, if you're lucky, your encounter may come up the day after the circulation of a company-wide memo urging the closing of as many cases as possible, so they won't be carried on the books into the next fiscal year.

I remember early in my practice when my partner and I had a personal injury case we thought was worth $10,000 to $12,000. When the adjuster made contact with me and asked what we'd take to settle, I replied $15,000. He said "You've got a deal," and I wanted to kick myself. Instantly, the thought ran through my head, "He knows something I don't know." But perhaps not. Insurance companies are required to set aside a reserve for each claim. My figure may simply have coincided with his reserve.

At various points in negotiations, the adjuster may legitimately request certain information from you. Don't be afraid to send him copies of estimates, paid bills, and canceled checks relating to your damages. You can tell him you have witnesses, and, if pressed, even be willing to read part of their statements to establish that, yes, you do indeed have a case. Your ultimate concession—if he says his supervisor has some doubts about settling, and all it would take would be some convincing evidence to push him over the line—might be to send him one or more witness statements.

But be sure to block out witness names and addresses, or you're giving your adversary the opportunity to subtly intimidate your witnesses into changing their story. Not forcefully—simply by asking over and over again, "Are you sure?" and "Do you know the penalty for perjury?" Frequently, the attempt to destroy the foundation of your case may be so polite as to disarm you: "Oh, by the way, may I have the names and addresses of your witnesses?" Your answer should be an equally polite, "I'll be happy to give them to you for your files if you agree to settle the case. Otherwise, no—unless ordered by the court."

Always ask for the maximum amount that your bills or estimates warrant, but be prepared at this stage to take a little less. An early settlement at less than full value will save you the time and effort involved in going to court and proving your case. It will also give you the cash to repair your car or roof, or you can put it in the bank and start earning interest on it. Too, your original estimates may be higher than the actual cost of repair—especially if you bargain with the repair man or shop around.

Once you've made contact with the adjuster, keep on his back until you either have the case settled, or it's clear that going to court will be necessary. The crossroad—the moment when it can go either way—will come when he declares, "Give me a written statement and I'll see if I can settle your case." That's not good enough. Don't sign anything until he tells you that he *will* settle if you sign on the bottom line. Otherwise, he's free to take your signed statement and use it against you in court.

When, after several meetings and phone calls, settlement is still distant, it's time to formally start your suit. If, however, your mini-Geneva Conference has worked, the adjuster will ask you for a general release.

The Tenth Step:
The General Release

The individual or insurance company is entitled to something for his or their money, and that something is a document releasing them from any and all claims you may have against them. If there's any possibility you may have other dealings with this person that might end in a dispute (like a loan not yet repaid), make sure the release applies only to the matter being settled. Do this by saying, "This document is intended to release Mr. X from liability relating to the automobile accident that took place between his auto and mine on (date) and (place)." Or, ". . . relating to the tree that fell on my roof on (date)."

For your part, you ought to get a release from him. On an intersection collision, for example, after you've settled with his insurance company for damage to your car, he might still bring a separate claim against you for his damages. In order to wrap up the package and put a bow on it, it's a good idea to ask to "exchange" releases—such as the general release form that follows:

Form No. 2

B 110—General Release—Individual: 6-76

JULIUS BLUMBERG, INC., LAW BLANK PUBLISHERS
80 EXCHANGE PL. AT BROADWAY, N. Y. C. 10004

To all to whom these Presents shall come or may Concern, Know That

(YOUR NAME HERE), residing at (YOUR ADDRESS HERE)

as RELEASOR,

in consideration of the sum of   (The amount you are to receive here)

($),

received from   (THE PERSON AGAINST WHOM YOU ARE MAKING THE

CLAIM HERE)

as RELEASEE,

receipt whereof is hereby acknowledged, releases and discharges (THE PERSON AGAINST WHOM

YOU ARE MAKING THE CLAIM HERE)

the RELEASEE, RELEASEE'S heirs, executors, administrators, successors and assigns from all actions, causes of action, suits, debts, dues, sums of money, accounts, reckonings, bonds, bills, specialties, covenants, contracts, controversies, agreements, promises, variances, trespasses, damages, judgments, extents, executions, claims, and demands whatsoever, in law, admiralty or equity, which against the RELEASEE, the RELEASOR, RELEASOR'S heirs, executors, administrators, successors and assigns ever had, now have or hereafter can, shall or may, have for, upon, or by reason of any matter, cause or thing whatsoever from the beginning of the world to the day of the date of this RELEASE.

(If you may have any other dealings with the person you are

releasing, limit the release here.)

Whenever the text hereof requires, the use of singular number shall include the appropriate plural number as the text of the within instrument may require.

This RELEASE may not be changed orally.

In Witness Whereof, the RELEASOR has hereunto set RELEASOR'S hand and seal on the   (Date)
day of   19   .

In presence of

....(You sign here)...L.S.
Type or print your name here

STATE OF   , COUNTY OF   ss.:
On   (date)   19   before me
personally came   (Your Name)

to me known, and known to me to be the individual(s) described in, and who executed the foregoing RELEASE, and duly acknowledged to me that   he   executed the same.

......................................(NOTARY PUBLIC SIGNS HERE)...........................

If the party making payment is not the same as the party released, delete words "as RELEASEE" and add names of parties released after the word "discharges."

46

The Final Step:
Collecting Your Check

Insurance companies may have deep pockets and short arms, but their word *is* their bond. So once the adjuster has agreed to a settlement for a specific amount, unless the company goes bankrupt—which once actually happened to me in a case settled for $1,500—it's money in the bank. (Even in that case, we did collect part of the settlement many years later, when the State Insurance Department liquidated the company's assets.)

No need then to feel skittish about giving the adjuster the signed release he requests. He doesn't carry the company's checkbook with him, and your payment will be in the mail soon. How soon? Two to three weeks' wait is not unusual. If the bureaucracy's wheels seem to have developed a flat tire, a phone call to the adjuster should help speed up the bookkeeping process. The check for your car, drapes or roof replacement will reach you eventually. Just don't spend the money on something else before it arrives.

CHAPTER 4

Preparing for Court

You were for peace, but they were for war. The adjuster stalled, dragged both feet, led you on, and then offered you such a pittance in settlement that the only road left was the one leading to the courthouse.

Before you go, be sure you're 101 percent ready. When Francis Bacon was chancellor of England, there was a rogue named Hogg brought before him for sentencing who argued, "Your Honor should release me. Everyone knows Hogg is kin to Bacon." Lord Bacon glowered down from the bench. "Not," he said, "until it's hung."

You may have the best case in the world. But you'll be hung for sure if you don't do your homework—carefully considering and assembling all the evidence and presenting it in the best possible light, in the appropriate court.

THE FIRST STEP:
SELECTING THE COURT

Small Claims Courts are also called—depending on the state— Magistrate's Court, Justice of the Peace Court, Municipal Court, and Justice Court. The last and most common alternate name suggests the goal—not always achieved: the dispensing of justice with a minimum of technical delay. You are not only allowed, but expected, and in some states (e.g., Idaho) required, to eliminate the middleman, and be your own lawyer.

The maximum claim in these "people's courts" varies from $200 (Georgia and Mississippi) to $2,000 (New Mexico), or even $2,500 in Florida, where small claims are handled in county court. If your claim exceeds the maximum jurisdiction, you'll have to take it to the next highest court. But you'll still be within the family of courts accustomed to dealing with the *pro se* litigant pleading his own cause. In California, for example, the Small Claims Court roof of $500 is the floor of the Municipal Court, which in turn ceilings at $5,000. In Connecticut the $750 limit on Small Claims Court is succeeded by the Court of Common Pleas with a maximum jurisdiction of $15,000.

A telephone call to the local courthouse will acquaint you with the court and dollar boundaries in your state. But note that "local" here may not necessarily refer to your own locale, but rather that of the party you're suing. The place to file is in a court in the county where the defendant lives, works or has a place of business. In an auto accident, the place where the collision occurred is an acceptable venue (appropriate court), even though neither party resides there. If you live in Ohio but collide with a driver from Georgia in California, either Georgia or California would be the place for you to file suit—unless you can in some way connect the defendant with your home state. If, for example, you are hit by a company car owned by General Motors, you may be able to sue in your home state of Ohio, because GM does business in all 50 states.

I recently wrote a 30-page brief on a question of jurisdiction, so I can tell you the issue can be as complicated as an octopus wrestling match.

THE SECOND STEP:
PREPARING A SUMMONS AND COMPLAINT

The *pro se* clerk found in most Small Claims Courts is everybody's friend. It's his job to help the plaintiff prepare his "summons and complaint" (the document notifying your foe that he has just become a defendant) and later to help the defendant submit his "answer and counterclaim," if any. He may simply ask you for the information he needs to fill out the papers, or in a busy court situation he may give you an information sheet to fill out and save him some time. To save yourself some time, find out in advance the cost of an index number (officially filing your case and identifying it from this time forth and forevermore), and have the cash (no personal checks, please) with you. Have a small mailing fee ready, too, because in some courts the clerk mails the summons and complaint for you. Be sure you have the defendant's correct address. If the letter bounces because of incorrect address—or is refused—the

50

clerk may suggest you hire a process server to do that dirty work for you.

THE THIRD STEP:
SERVING THE SUMMONS

In my first few months of private practice, I found it necessary to serve a summons on a man who, as good luck would have it, had his office just a block away from where my new bride worked. "Daisy," I said, "this is a contingency case—no money until I win, and meanwhile I pay expenses out of pocket. I have a summons to serve, and a professional process server will cost me $5. If you serve it, I'll take you out to dinner instead."

I had made her an offer she couldn't refuse—not even on the torrentially rainy day this turned out to be. Dutifully, on her lunch hour, my young bride went to the man's Empire State Building office. But I'll let her tell the story:

I stood there soaked and disheveled, intimidated by the elegance of the office. Everybody was rushing around, and nobody paid the slightest attention to me. Finally, someone took pity on me and directed me to the man I had to serve. I handed him the summons—at which point Walter had assumed I'd know enough to make a fast getaway. Instead, I just stood there like a Western Union boy waiting for a tip. Sensing my ignorance, the man shrewdly exploited it. "Oh," he said, after reading the paper, "you're in the wrong place. You have to serve this paper at our other office, at 200 West 48th Street." He handed it back to me, and left. I retreated to the nearest phone booth, called Walter and said, "Please—don't ever give me this job again!"

I haven't. It cost me the $5 to hire a process server—but I took her out to dinner anyway. Ever since then, we've had a family joke that ends with Daisy saying, "You don't want the summons, mister? OK, I'll take it back."

If you know the rules of the game—which unfortunately I had not explained adequately to Daisy—anyone can play. Legally, all you have to do is tag the recipient with the summons. He can throw up his arms and let it fall to the floor. Too late. He's been served.

As party to the suit, you are not allowed to serve the summons yourself. But a friend or relative can. If they're not exactly ecstatic at the prospect of a nip in the shin from an aroused German shepherd, or a punch in the mouth from a surly character who's been drinking beer all day, you can hire a process server for $2 to $25 through the Yellow Pages.

In some states, if the professional—or your friend—goes to someone's home and repeatedly finds them absent, he's allowed to give the summons to someone of "reasonable age and discretion" (no fair taping it to a baby carriage on the front porch), and then go home and mail a duplicate copy. Or he can, in extremis, use nail-and-mail—that is nail (or cellophane tape) it to the front door, then mail another one. If the defendant appears and fights the case, there's no question but that he was served. If he doesn't and you obtain a default judgment, he could later challenge, saying you used "sewer service." In cases where the quarry is elusive, it's best to hire a professional—he'll know how to handle the situation better than ("no offense, beloved wife") Daisy did.

I know of no state where you may serve your own papers. Your case might, indeed, be literally laughed out of court if you did. And in many states (though neither New York nor some others), it would have been equally unacceptable for Daisy to serve them—not because of what she is (my wife), but because of what she is not (a deputy sheriff, constable or other official court officer).

Once this necessary evil of the service of the summons has been accomplished, you must file an affidavit of service with the clerk of the court, since this notifies him that the action has now been commenced. A hired gun will have his own affidavit form. Sometimes the court routinely furnishes one. You can buy one at that legal stationery store you're keeping so busy, or just type one yourself, following the rough form of the sample below. It's nothing more than a sworn statement (another way of saying it's been notarized) giving the name, address, and sometimes a rudimentary description of the person served, and the date and place of service. (See sample that follows.)

State of ____

         ss:

County of ____

____ being duly sworn, deposes and says: I am over 18 years of age and not a party to this action. On ____, at ____, I served the summons and complaint on ____, known to me to be the defendant mentioned therein, by delivering the summons and complaint to and leaving the same with the said defendant in person.

Sworn to before me this ____
day of ____, 1978   (signed) ____

_____

Notary public

A Small Claims Court summons often specifies the trial date, notifying the defendant that he must either appear on that date or a default judgment will be entered against him, unless he obtains an adjournment. In higher courts, the defendant ordinarily has a certain number of days to answer, appearing in person or by attorney. If he elects to be his own lawyer, he will visit the same *pro se* clerk you did for help in preparing his denial or defenses. But there may not be much help needed. The most common answer: a general repudiation that simply denies "each and every allegation." Now, with all precincts heard from, the clerk automatically sets a trial date and notifies both sides by mail.

When you find a summons staring at you, you have three alternatives: default, defend, or settle. A default is almost always the wrong choice. Even if you don't think you have much of a defense, there's always the chance that the plaintiff will bungle his case and present evidence so inadequate that you can move for dismissal without presenting any defense. Or you may come up with enough extenuating evidence so that the judge awards the plaintiff less than he demands. One way to gather such evidence is through the fishing expedition known as "discovery."

THE FOURTH STEP:
PRETRIAL DISCOVERY

"The growing emphasis on pretrial procedures," wrote Justice Bernard Botein, "is eliminating much of the element of surprise which made the trial a game of chance, and put a premium on the lawyer's adroitness. Now many more cases are won by thorough, painstaking preparation than by brilliant coups in the courtroom.''

Judge Botein was, of course, thinking of bigger trout than your dry cleaner. But the principle is the same, and in lower courts which permit it—and not many Small Claims Courts do—three commonly used devices can help you prepare and win your case: a Demand for a Bill of Particulars, EBT (an examination before trial: also known as oral deposition), and written interrogatories. Unless the other side is represented by an attorney—or, like you, has read this book—you're not likely to encounter any of these discovery devices. Still, it doesn't hurt to know about them, or, where permitted, use them to your advantage. Again, let your court clerk be your guide.

The Demand for a Bill of Particulars is probably most common, especially in auto accident cases, and, like the other two, it is made possible by our justice system's requirement that all parties know what the other side claims prior to trial. In effect, the accused must know of what he is accused, but the right is reciprocal. In an auto accident, the defendant is entitled to know when and where you claim the accident took place, the extent of your damage or physical injuries, and what you claim to be his negligence. The questions are submitted to you in the form of a Demand (see following page), and you are required to reply by mail within a prescribed time period: say, ten or fifteen days. Failure to reply allows the delighted defendant to apply to dismiss your complaint, or block your offering of evidence in the areas of the questions asked. Since they are always key questions, ignoring the Demand could instantly wipe out your case.

Well, not instantly. Our courts are liberal in offering a second chance to the delinquent. Most of the time, they'll order the complaint dismissed only if you don't serve the Bill of Particulars on or before a certain extended date. So you get that last chance to cure your failure to comply.

A demand for a Bill of Particulars comes with a fence built around it. If it asks irrelevant questions, you can ask the court to strike the demand. In some states, you can selectively ignore those questions you consider unrelated, and if your opponent makes application to dismiss, you can point out to the court the ''irrelevant and immaterial'' queries. But in other jurisdictions, ignoring questions may be dangerous. You will, in effect, be accepting your adversary's version of the facts.

54

Form No. 4

form of demand for bill of particulars in personal injury action.

SUPREME COURT ___COUNTY

[Title of cause]   }   Notice
                Index No.__

PLEASE TAKE NOTICE, that the defendant hereby demands that the plaintiff furnish said defendant with a written verified bill of particulars of his claims against said defendant within 10 days after the service of this notice, specifying in detail:

1. The date and approximate time of day of the occurrence complained of in the complaint herein:

2. The location of the occurrence complained of.

3. An itemized and detailed statement of each and every act of negligence which plaintiff will charge against the said defendant.

4. Whether the notice of the alleged defective condition of defendant's premises claimed to have caused the accident was actual notice or constructive notice and if actual notice is claimed, a statement of when and to whom such notice was given.

5. An itemized and detailed statement of each and every injury suffered by the plaintiff.

6. An itemized and detailed statement of each and every injury which the plaintiff claims will be permanent, specifying the character, degree and cause of the permanency.

7. The length of time it will be claimed that the plaintiff was totally disabled, and also the length of time it will be claimed that the plaintiff was partially disabled.

8. The length of time that plaintiff was confined to the hospital, his bed and his home, specifying each separately.

9. The nature of plaintiff's business or occupation, specifying the name and address of his employer, the amount of wages or salary per day, week, or month and the length of time plaintiff was prevented from performing said business or occupation and the wages lost thereby.

10. An itemized and detailed statement of each and every expense incurred or to be incurred, for medical and hospital or other care or treatment of the plaintiff, specifying the names and addresses of the persons with whom such expenses have been incurred, or is to be incurred, and the reasons for the same.

Dated____,19__.

                            _____

                            Attorney for Defendant
Office, P.O. Address, and Telephone Number

Open any busy trial attorney's calendar book and you'll find it liberally sprinkled with the letters "EBT"—examination before trial. This pretrial maneuver, the equivalent of sending a reconnaissance satellite over enemy territory, begins with the receipt of a notice from the opposing attorney directing you to appear at the courthouse, or his office, at a particular time and date for the taking of your oral deposition. It's all perfectly legal, and not something about which you have a choice.

You may be asked any question relating to the accident and your damages or injury, as well as anything else that may shed light on the accident's cause. Normally, these depositions are recorded by a court reporter, and a transcript must be submitted to you to give you a chance to correct any stenographic errors. You can't correct your own, though—changing answers at this point is not just bad form, it's impossible. Sometimes the deposition is taped, even videotaped and you can bring your own tape recorder and do likewise. You are, of course, free to interrogate your adversary by examining him before trial. This offers yet another opportunity for settlement. I've found that these examinations—with both parties, and usually their attorneys, sitting across the table—are an ideal time to negotiate. At such times, I've settled many a case on the spot.

You're not likely to run into written interrogatories in minor cases; they're most often used in complex commercial litigation. Similar to a demand for a bill of particulars, they may be so detailed that the questions sometimes run on for 40 or 50 pages. They require a lawyer experienced in the defusing of legal booby traps.

THE FIFTH STEP:
THE COUNTERCLAIM

Of all weapons available to the defendant in a civil suit, perhaps the most powerful is the counterclaim. Based on the principle that the best defense is a good offense, it's a table-turner that makes the plaintiff a defendant and the defendant a plaintiff. Although it has no legal effect on the original claim, it may strongly influence how much is collected. If, for example, you're sued by a bricklayer for the $500 balance you owe him for your patio, you might counterclaim for the $1,000 it cost you to have it ripped up and properly relaid. The counterclaim serves to remind the person who throws the first brick that his glass house is not shatterproof. Even if the original plaintiff thinks he can rebut your counterclaim, he probably began the suit without bargaining for the trouble of preparing a defense as well as an offense, and the counterclaim may induce him to consider a settlement. An equilibrium of claims may even lead to a judicial decision that cancels out both. Routinely, for example, landlords' suits against tenants who've just moved out, attempting to recover the final month's rent, end when the tenant counterclaims for his security deposit.

A high-powered and somewhat risky variation on the strategy of using a counterclaim to discourage the original plaintiff involves counterclaiming for an amount beyond the jurisdiction of the Small Claims Court where the suit began. This means that the entire process has to be transferred to the next highest court, which in turn may mean more effort and expense than the plaintiff had originally anticipated.

It's a good idea to call the courthouse and find out the local procedure for instituting a counterclaim. It may involve visiting the clerk before the trial, or you may be allowed to make the counterclaim at the trial itself. In the latter case, the original plaintiff will no doubt get an adjournment to prepare his response.

Counterclaims are often more malicious than meritorious. In a recent small claims case, a landscaper sued a wealthy woman who refused to pay him $100 for trimming her extensive hedges and $40 for pruning her oak tree. Rather than pay, she counterclaimed for $2,000, alleging that he had irreparably damaged the oak by removing several live branches. The unfortunate gardener was furious and resolved not to yield no matter what the cost. But he was forced to hire a lawyer, retain an expert witness, and spend $400 to collect his $140. He might have been better advised to forget it— or, better yet, be his own lawyer.

Interposing a counterclaim varies so much from one jurisdiction to another that your best bet is to get the courthouse clerk to guide you to the right form for your area, and help you fill it out.

THE SIXTH STEP:
GETTING THE RELUCTANT WITNESS (AND OTHER EVIDENCE)
TO COURT

Paying witnesses is perfectly legal—but only if they are experts whose testimony you need to establish the extent of personal injury or property damage. You could, if the matter were worth enough, even import them from another country: one successful

Maryland malpractice attorney regularly flies in British physicians, whose testimony he has found particularly effective. But you cannot pay a nonexpert for testifying. This is the same as buying evidence. In addition to being unethical and illegal, if it comes out that you are paying your witnesses (other than the statutory witness fee), it could blow your case to the moon. Employees of government agencies—policemen, for example—may, as a matter of law or policy, require a subpoena before they'll appear in court. A polite request will ordinarily suffice for friends, or for people stimulated by the prospect of starring in a real live trial.

For the cynical and the indifferent and those who won't or normally can't take time off from work a subpoena may be necessary. A subpoena, like a summons, summons its recipient to court "under penalty" (in Latin, *sub poena*) of fine or imprisonment for contempt of court, and of liability for damages to the litigant who needs his testimony and might lose his case without it. It is a stern document, and before resorting to it you should always try a personal request. Otherwise you risk giving offense and ending up with a hostile witness on the stand. But if a witness is crucial to your case, subpoena him anyway.

Few people are likely to risk the sometimes harsh penalties for lying under oath. Perjury penalties, though common enough in criminal cases, are, in fact, rarely imposed in civil actions—and for good reason. When it's one man's word against another's, it's often next to impossible to know who is telling the truth. I have a case right now with $60,000 at stake, in which my client's testimony is so diametrically opposite to that of our adversary that it's as though they were describing life on two different planets. One of the two is lying. (I'm sure it's not my client.) Only God knows, but a jury will have to decide.

A subpoena can be prepared by any officer of the court. In some states, a lawyer qualifies. He simply has the document filled out in his office, and served by one of his clerks. Presumably you're not an officer of the court, but you can enlist the aid of the court clerk, who is. She'll either give you a copy of the court's subpoena form, or tell you where to buy a standard form. She'll help you fill out the very simple document—name of witness, name of case, name of judge, on whose behalf testimony is required, when and where to appear—and put her Jane Hancock at the bottom. Sometimes that's not enough. In some courts, the judge's signature is required to make the subpoena enforceable. Thereafter, it's your baby: the subpoena must be served personally, and, as with a summons, you have the choice of using a friend or a professional to do the job. With a subpoena, there is a small additional expense. It's valid only if accompanied by a witness fee, out of your pocket, of from $2 to $10, depending on the distance the witness lives from the courthouse.

Testimony of witnesses is not the only evidence to be marshaled before trial. Consider whether you want to present evidence that, in effect, makes the judge an eyewitness for your side. You might, for example, bring in the drapes the cleaner ruined. If you feel particularly daring, you might pull a Perry Mason, dramatically scattering dirt on the courtroom floor to show how badly your new and fully guaranteed vacuum cleans. (Don't forget to bring an extension cord long enough to reach an electrical outlet, or your demonstration may fizzle.) Even Perry Mason might consider having your wrecked car towed to the bench going a bit too far, but photos of the vehicle or of the scene of the accident would serve nobly.

Documentary evidence is something else to think about. Canceled checks to show payment, rubber checks to show nonpayment, copies of contract or leases, warning letters, registered mail receipts, promissory notes, business and official records—in short, any written evidence bearing on your case—should be painstakingly gathered for possible presentation in court. Records and documents in someone else's possession may be obtained by issuing a *subpoena duces tecum* —a form of subpoena specifying not only the individual, but also the materials he's ordered to bring to court: hospital or motor vehicle records, business books or pages from a police blotter, for example.

THE SEVENTH STEP:
CHECKING OUT THE LAW

It's not enough to have the facts on your side; you need the law there, too. You may have three witnesses to testify that Don Deadbeat personally guaranteed to repay the loan you gave his brother Jon. But the law requires that a guarantee ("a promise to pay the debt, default or obligation of another") be in writing. If it isn't, I can personally guarantee that your case will be thrown out of court. That's the law.

It's two weeks since you sold your old car to the sixteen-year-old who answered your ad. The $250 he gave you has already been paid out as part of the down payment on your new car. But there's no point in fighting his sudden claim for a refund. The law is clear that infants—in most states that's the term for anyone under age eighteen—have a right to repudiate a contract. That's the law.

The legal shelves of your local library are chock-full of plump volumes on "law for the layman" that cover a great deal of basic ground. Look through a few on the specific points at issue. You may not even have to go that far. Our chapters in this book on bankruptcy, wills, divorce, starting a business, etc., may tell you all you need to know. If they don't, a call to the Legal Aid Society, a visit to the law library in your courthouse, or even a short conference with a local attorney should clear up the point of law troubling you and may provide just what you need to clinch your case.

THE EIGHTH STEP:
WHAT TO WEAR IN COURT

Back in law school, an eon or two ago, I had a professor who warned my class never to wear a red tie or otherwise flashy clothes, lest we offend a judge or juror. Of all members of the bar, Wall Street lawyers seem to tuck that advice closest to heart. Rarely have I seen one garbed in anything but the classic uniform of dark suit, button down white or blue oxford shirt, conservative tie and wingtip shoes. But a few months ago, I almost dropped my attaché case, when I walked into court on a warm summer's day to find the judge robeless and tieless on the bench, looking like a golf pro in slacks and a sport shirt. I've never been personally courageous enough to wear anything but a conservative suit and tie. Civil liberties notwithstanding, there is still an occasional judicial curmudgeon of the old school who flies into a tirade if a lady lawyer comes in wearing a floppy hat or a pants suit, or, heat wave notwithstanding, a male lawyer appears without a tie.

In Small Claims Court the contesting parties usually appear dressed as though for work, which, if it's a daytime session, is where they'll be headed afterward. If you're your own lawyer, I'd say that though courts have loosened up considerably on dress codes since Clarence Darrow's day, neatness still counts. That remarkable defense attorney used to illustrate the point with the story of a client accused of burglary, for whom Darrow plea-bargained the minimum two-year sentence in an informal conference with the judge, in return for a guilty plea. Darrow was taken aback, though, when the poor, rough laborer was led into the courtroom, and he realized he had neglected to warn the man to shave and wear his Sunday clothes. He recalled:

I could see that the judge was inspecting George, looking at . . . the stubble on his face, the tobacco juice on his dirty shirt; poor collarless, loyal, sweaty George! I had muffed it; I knew it, but was helpless. The judge looked him over again, asked him to stand up, voiced a few remarks about the case, then said, very slowly, and haltingly, "I sentence you to the penitentiary for two years—and—" (taking another look at George) "and—six months."

THE NINTH STEP:
THE JUDGE AS NEGOTIATOR

If the parties differ radically in their perceptions of the strengths of their cases, a third party may have to step in to restore perspective. The role of intermediary may not be filled until the case is called before the judge himself, either for trial, or during an informal discussion at a calendar call.

The judge—or in some courts, his secretary or clerk who is deputized to try to settle cases before trial—will size up arguments on both sides, then suggest a compromise figure somewhere between what the plaintiff demands and the defendant is willing to offer: a figure unacceptable to either. You were hit in the rear by another car, and you're suing for the $400 your mechanic tells you it'll cost for repairs. The judge suggests $250 as a settlement. You are outraged; why should you have to shell out $150 for something that wasn't your fault? Strange to say, the insurance company's lawyer is equally indignant; he can prove that the driver he's representing was guiltless. The judge, unimpressed, calls each of you to the bench in turn for a private parley. He points out to you that your Chevy is eight years old, and not worth a whole lot more than you're asking for repairs. Besides, the defendant has a witness who'll testify that your back fender was already well-wrinkled before the accident. He assures the opposing counsel that in nineteen out of twenty cases he's seen, the judgment has gone against the man driving behind, and the award tends to be pretty close to what's asked.

Now, if he'd accidentally told you what he meant to tell the lawyer, and vice versa, both of you would come out roaring for blood and judgment. But as it is, both of you emerge chastened, thoughtful and ready for corridor compromise.

When the circumstances dictate, most of us are willing, if reluctantly, to soften our demands. Benjamin Franklin illustrates that in his autobiography with the story of the man who, on purchasing an ax from a smith, insisted that the entire surface of the ax-head be polished till it glistened. The smith agreed, provided that his customer turn the wheel. The man turned, while the smith bore down heavily on the stone with the ax face. From time to time, the customer, red-faced and perspiring, stopped turning to examine the ax. Finally, at one such moment, he declared, "I'm satisfied." "No," said the smith, "turn on, turn on; we shall have it bright by-and-by; as yet, it is only speckled." The customer sighed. "Yes," he said, "but I think I like a speckled ax best."

CHAPTER 5

Trying Your Case

Appellate Justice Bernard Botein recalled in his autobiography how, as a brand-new judge on the morning of his first charge to a jury, he arrived in the robing room at 10:15. "I'll apologize to the jurors and counsel for keeping them waiting," he said, as he was being helped into his robe. "Judge," said his clerk, "I hope you won't think I'm speaking out of turn. But when you've been here as long as I have, you'll know that no matter what time the judge enters the courtroom, it's 10 o'clock."

THE FIRST STEP: THE CALENDAR CALL

No matter what time the judge enters the courtroom, a roomful of people who have nursed their legal grudges through months or years of adjournments, delays and postponements as they waited impatiently for justice to triumph—for them—settle into nervous attention as the judge declares the court in session. The clerk calls the calendar, intoning, in the order in which they are scheduled to be heard, anywhere from several to several hundred cases, in the form: *Joe Doakes* vs. *Jane Doe.*

If you're Joe, you're the plaintiff. When you hear your case called, stand up and sound off: "Plaintiff is ready." In urban areas, where justice is necessarily mass-produced, the calendar judge may order, "Go to Room 4 and try your case." Or you may find that in this Small Claims, Justice, or County Court that to help clear clogged dockets, cases are being tried by a supporting cast of arbitrators—generally lawyers who volunteer without pay as a service to the community. They have the same duties and powers as a judge, but informal, in business suit or dress rather than black robe, they are stripped of some of the judicial mystique and are referred to as Mr. or Ms. Arbitrator. Their decisions are nonetheless binding and usually nonappealable.

You are, of course, free to insist on going before a judge ("Plaintiff ready; trial by the court only"). That way, in a complex or, to you, important case, you can request a stenographic record of the proceedings and, if it later seems necessary, may appeal. But it's unlikely that you'd tackle the complexities of an appeal without counsel. Furthermore, in some Small Claims Courts, you automatically waive your right of appeal. And a transcript of a stenographic record may be a souvenir that could cost you as much as a lawyer. Transcripts run from $1.50 to $3.00 per page, margins on all four sides are wide as sidewalks, every "yes" or "no, sir" stands on a line by itself, and the typist may use a legal ratchet—an ingenious device on a typewriter that widens the spaces between lines so as to fit three or four *fewer* lines on every transcript page you buy.

So you're ready. But all your readiness—factual and psychological—may go for nought if your opponent requests that mixed blessing and curse of the judicial procedure: an adjournment. As a young attorney, I was the resident adjournment specialist for the first law office that I ever worked for. I was wisely deemed too inexperienced to try a case myself, but my boss had a lot of confidence in me and was sure I could find my way to the courthouse. When he was tied up on a more important case, I was invariably assigned to await the calendar call, then rise to heights of eloquence as I declaimed, "Application for adjournment."

Judges vary, but most will grant a few adjournments as a matter of course. Not, of course, without spirited resistance from the same attorney who is ready and eager to begin this case, though yesterday he cheerfully requested and received adjournments on two others. "Your Honor," he will insist, "this man is a deadbeat. I gave him an adjournment last time when he called my office and said he was suffering from gout. I request a judgment, subject to his proving he had a valid reason for not appearing."

After the first few adjournments ("My star witness is out-of-town" . . . "My mother-in-law is ill"), you can insist on trying the case, or win by default if the other side fails to appear. In the unlikely event that this offends your sense of fair play, you can ask for a peremptory adjournment. That means that the next time they either show or lose. Magnanimity in these matters, however, walks on quicksand. When your star witness has a conflicting dental appointment and you innocently ask for equal adjournment time, you may become party to an unhappy dialogue like this:

THE JUDGE:
There have already been five adjournments of this case. If you're not ready to proceed, I'm dismissing.
YOU:
But, your Honor, the defendant asked for all the adjournments up till now, not me!
THE JUDGE: *(EMPHATICALLY):*
Sorry. Proceed—or the case will be dismissed.

Missing the calendar call—because you circled the block so many times looking for a parking space that you felt like an Apache attacking a wagon train—doesn't automatically hold you in default. In some courts, you can phone in to the court clerk (have case name, time, and docket number handy) to say you'll be late, or to ask for an adjournment. And after the first calendar call, there is often a second one to give latecomers another chance.

Nevertheless, the judge's patience can wear thin. The other day, my partner waited two hours with three witnesses for a defendant who, though into his third adjournment and having received two notices, failed to appear. The judge declared him in default and awarded judgment to our side. As everyone left the courtroom, a clerk met us breathlessly. "Judge," she said, "the defendant is on the phone. He's hung up in New City waiting for a witness." Responded the judge tartly, "Tell him he's already been hung."

Even if both sides are ready, the judge, bogged down in an unexpectedly lengthy case, may not be. You may sit around anxiously until two o'clock, only to be told: "Come back tomorrow at ten."

If your case is only halfway down the list, you have the option of going out for a cup of coffee. But if you've never seen this judge in action—and it's a good idea to size him up the day before—you'd do better to stay and watch. Things may get a bit dull at times, especially when the litigants approach the bench for an informal discussion with the judge—perhaps about a possible settlement—and you can't hear a thing. Neither side, by the way, has the right to confer privately with the judge unless the judge requests it. Ordinarily, if one side approaches the bench, the other side has the right to join in the conference. While waiting for your case to be called, don't conspicuously read your newspaper or chat with a fellow spectator. The judge may not gavel for order; he may just take his pique out on you when your case comes up.

THE SECOND STEP:
WHILE YOU WAIT, NEGOTIATE

A compromise settlement is often a victory for both sides. But too many parties make no attempt to negotiate once the lawsuit is started. After the case is tried, one party will be very unhappy with the verdict—and it could be you. I believe in the direct approach. I invite my opponent to step out in the corridor and simply ask, "Do you think we can work out a settlement?" If he says, "No," I've lost nothing. If he says, "What do you have in mind?" I'm ready with a proposal.

At that point, compromise is often the most sensible way to go. In a settlement, you can't expect the full recovery that comes with winning your case. But something is better than nothing, and a partial settlement beats going home empty-handed, with your pockets picked for interest and court costs as well.

THE THIRD STEP:
HONOR HIS HONOR

Your case is called at last. Whatever opinion you may have formed of the judge, address him as "your Honor"—unless he is not a judge and tells you to call him "Mr. Arbitrator"—and stand when you address him. Judges are attorneys. They went to law schools. They belong to bar associations, and political clubhouses. They've made many friends among their colleagues along the way. But you've got something going for you, too. Judges know that periodically, they—or whoever appointed them—must face the electorate. They want to carve out a pro-people record to stand on. Still, their education, associations, and sympathies often tend to make them pro-lawyer, and you may be up against an attorney who has worked with the judge for years. You may even note subtle signs of what you suspect is favoritism. You can be friendly, too, but don't try to get chummy; familiarity breeds contempt citations.

Don't approach the judge out of court—in the corridor or a restaurant during the lunch break—unless you have a specific procedural question. Not whether the judge and your brother went to college together. That can boomerang badly—as in the story that's told of a judge who was approached by an unctuous litigant in a case he was trying.

"I've been asking around, your Honor, because we both have the same last name, and it seems possible we're related."

"Is that so?" replied the judge, polite but somewhat nettled. "I'm glad you told me. I'll withdraw from the case: I certainly can't sit on a suit in which a relative of mine is involved."

Imagining the problems and postponements this would cause, the man quickly backed off. After several questions about the judge's family and origins, he said, "I guess I was a bit hasty. Seems we're not related after all."

"I'm sure glad to hear that," said the judge coolly. "I'd certainly hate to be related to someone low enough to try to influence a judge."

In court or out, keep your opinions of the judge's ability and character to yourself. You're hardly in a position to follow the example of Tom Marshall, the keen nineteenth-century Kentucky lawyer who once, citing authority after authority in a vain attempt to convince an unlettered backwoods judge that he'd made the wrong decision on a point of law, finally declared:

"Will your Honor please fine me $10 for contempt of court?"

"What for?" exclaimed the astonished justice. "You have committed no contempt of court."

"But I assure you," Marshall replied, "that I have an infernal contempt for it."

THE FOURTH STEP:
THE TRIAL BEGINS

The judge or arbitrator will order every witness—either altogether or individually as each comes up—to take the oath, just as you've seen it done in Perry Mason's courts. Unless you have religious objections and explain them to the judge, you'll be sworn in to testify.

You'll most likely be your own first witness. But since you're also your own lawyer, the traditional form of testimony—the witness replying to the lawyer's questions—would look and sound somewhat inane. So tell your story in narrative form instead—just as it happened. Be brief, but not at the expense of important facts. It makes sense to prepare an outline for yourself, for insurance in case you should get flustered or confused. A sharp attorney on the other side might ask that you not refer to notes, but chances are that the judge would be unsympathetic to that objection, and you'll probably get away with glancing from time to time at an inconspicuous note pad on your lap to refresh your memory and make sure you've covered significant points.

The first move with any witness is identification, so there'll be no confusion about who's who. Give your name and address. Then launch right in. Let's say you're the plaintiff in an automobile damage case. Your testimony—a series of helpful verbal snapshots—would go something like this:

My name is Charlie Channing. I live at 12 Madison Street, Central City. At about 3:00 P.M. on December 17, 1976, I was in my car and I had just left the Sears & Roebuck parking lot. I was driving along Main Street, and when I got to the corner of Main and Grand I noticed a red light. I applied my brakes and stopped. There was one car in front of me. I was in the right hand lane. I was looking straight ahead, when all of a sudden my car was hit in the rear. Both I and the person driving behind me pulled over to the side of the road. I got out of the car and we exchanged driver information, ownership information and insurance company information. I examined the back of my car and noticed a dent in the fender. We didn't talk much about how it happened, but Mr. Martin, the other driver, said he must have been thinking about something else.

That's it: straight, simple, without fireworks or dramatics. The best advice I can give you, as your own lawyer or witness, is to be yourself. Imitate a high-powered attorney you've seen in a courtroom drama and you're likely to fall flat on your case.

Courts today are more structured and less tolerant than they were in ancient Athens. Then, an advocate named Hyperides, sensing as the trial progressed that desperate measures were called for if he was to save the life of the beautiful courtesan Phryne against a charge of impiety, suddenly stripped his client to the buff—whereupon the admiring jury rendered an acquittal.

Like dramatics, wit has its place in the courtroom, but not a very large place—a lesson learned the hard way by a Broadway personality who came before Judge Botein in a dispute over song rights. Lounging in the witness stand as if it were the set of the *Tonight* show, he seemed more interested in wisecracking ("Your Honor, it must be unconstitutional to make theatre people get up this early in the morning") than in winning his case. Under cross-examination, asked to describe a certain transaction, he launched into a colorful monologue that convulsed the courtroom. The opposing lawyer shrewdly asked the court reporter to read back the witness's last answer, which he did—in a flat, uninflected stenographer's drone that would have made a Woody Allen script sound like an electronics parts catalogue. The witness listened in obvious pain.

"Do you think that was funny?" asked the counsel.

"Well, I don't see . . ."

"Will the stenographer please read back the witness' answer again?"

"Oh, no, not again!" cried the witness. His testimony thereafter was sobriety itself.

Continuing your own sober testimony:

I then went home, and the next day I took my car to Bob Wilson at the Friendly Garage. He inspected it and gave me a written estimate saying it would cost $600 to repair. Since I needed the car, I had the work done, and he gave me this bill, which is marked paid. And here is my canceled check, in full payment of the repair. Your Honor, I'd like to offer these documents in evidence.

THE FIFTH STEP:
YOUR EXPERT WITNESS

If you haven't yet made the repair—or where large sums are involved, even if you have renovated the vehicle—you may have to get the mechanic to go to court with you and testify as to the extent of damage and the cost of repair. In some states, an affidavit from an expert witness like a doctor or a mechanic is accepted as evidence of damage or injury up to a certain dollar limit—$1,000 in New York. Elsewhere, or where larger sums are involved, you may have to pay your expert witness to testify, unless the opposing attorney consents in writing to accept an affidavit or deposition. Most likely he won't. It would mean giving up the chance to cross-examine, and to see you confronted with an expense that might make it unprofitable for you to continue.

Your mechanic may agree to testify for $25 or $50—or just for kicks—but not if he has to wait around in court all day. It takes some nervous juggling, but the best approach if he works nearby is to phone him half an hour before you expect your case to be called. If it comes up sooner than anticipated, you can say "I'm waiting for a witness, your Honor; he'll be here in half an hour," and generally the judge will push your case back. Some high-priced experts, like a $750-an-appearance orthopedic surgeon I know, will only testify on an "on call" basis: you call him when the case comes up, and he testifies as soon as he gets to court. In general, judges are understanding about witnesses who have to get back to work. If a busy witness shows up when another who's in no special hurry has just begun to testify, chances are good that you'll be permitted to insert the new arrival out of order.

The expense of expert testimony, like legal fees, won't be added on to the judgment, if you win. So, if you can afford it, and you're confident of your case, you'll come out ahead if you pay for repairs yourself and then try to recover the money rather than hire an expert to appraise them in court.

If you do have an expert witness, it's your job as your own lawyer to question him and draw out the testimony needed to make your case. Before putting him on the stand, you should have thoroughly and carefully discussed with him the questions you intend to ask, and the answers you expect him to give. In outline, the questioning might go like this:

1. Identify him. Ask your witness' name and address—unless the clerk has already done that for you.

2. Ask his place of employment and whether he owns his own garage or works for someone else.

3. Establish his expertise. Ask him to describe the nature of his work. His answer should be that his job is to estimate the costs of making repairs on automobiles, to purchase the parts and to perform or supervise the repairs. You've now accomplished your first objective: identifying him as an authority on the cost of repairing an automobile.

4. Ask him whether he actually examined your vehicle—a 1976 Chevrolet four-door, color blue, Ohio license plate JOE-723. The answer had better be yes.

5. Did he check the parts book to determine the actual cost of the parts? Did he come up with an estimate of the total cost of repairing the particular damage done by defendant—namely, to the rear bumper, trunk and related areas? Yes, and yes again.

6. The final question: "Would you please tell the court what it will cost to make the necessary repairs?" Once he states that figure, you have no further questions, and the witness may

now be cross-examined by opposing counsel, whose objective will be to subtly try to cast doubt on his qualifications and on the figure he's quoted. If asked whether he is being paid to testify, and how much, the witness needn't be embarrassed to answer honestly. He is, after all, losing time from work to appear. If it's a jury trial, the lawyer may adopt an indignant tone: "Isn't it a fact that you are being paid for testifying today?"—as if there were something intrinsically evil in the practice, which he frequently uses himself, of paying an expert witness to appear. To steal the artificial thunder from this routine trick, you might earlier make the point yourself in direct questioning, so that the jury will take the innocent fact in stride.

THE SIXTH STEP:
OTHER WITNESSES

I trust it's no longer true today, but in freewheeling earlier days in America, it was as easy to buy a witness as to buy a five-cent cigar. One of my favorite stories of those days is of the scoundrel who went from lawyer to lawyer trying to get someone to defend him. He was so patently guilty that no one would take the case. Finally, someone recommended a West Coast shyster with a reputation for handling the dregs of the underworld. The accused wrote him a desperate letter, and was overjoyed several days later to receive this telegram: WILL TAKE CASE. ARRIVING FRIDAY WITH TWO WITNESSES.

Whether or not you use an expert, you may want to present an eyewitness: a friend who was in the car with you, a shopkeeper who was looking out the window, a policeman standing on the corner. Again, it's crucial to discuss the events with your witness ahead of time to make sure that your accounts coincide—and that you want him as your witness. On the stand, ask him if he was a witness to an accident on that particular day; where he was standing; whether he observed the occurrence. Then ask him to describe in his own words exactly what happened.

Under cross-examination, your witnesses may be subjected to that old trial lawyer's trick of asking whether they've reviewed or discussed their testimony with the attorney—in this case, you—at any time before the trial. Many witnesses, suspecting a trick, but not the right one, will answer "no." They will thereby tell a lie and, what's worse, a possibly damaging one. Warn your witnesses that it's as proper to rehearse a case before trial as a cast before a Broadway opening.

I always advise my clients and their witnesses that if they know the answer to a question, they should give it promptly and briefly. If they don't know the answer, they should say so candidly. If they don't understand the question, they should ask to have it clarified or restated.

The cross-examining attorney may try to bully, finesse, or double talk your witnesses (and you) into confusion, contradiction or uncertainty about street names, which way you were driving, how fast, how much of the damage to your car occurred *prior* to the accident. If you're reasonably sure you remember correctly, don't let him hammer in that wedge of doubt. Don't be afraid to show detailed knowledge of the subject. In a rural court, the story goes, a witness in an assault case was asked by the opposing counsel, "How far were you from the parties when the alleged assault took place?"

"Four feet, five and one-half inches," was the instant reply.

"Aha!" cried the lawyer, sensing an opening. "A bit peculiar, isn't it, that you should happen to know the distance precisely?"

"Not at all," answered the unflappable witness. "I expected that some confounded fool would ask me, so I went and measured it."

THE SEVENTH STEP:
THE PLAINTIFF RESTS

When all your witnesses have testified, and you've handed up to the judge all your documents—bills, canceled checks, affidavits, and so on—and asked that they be entered as evidence in the record of the trial, you're ready to utter those satisfying words: "The plaintiff rests." But no matter how mind-weary you are, don't rest until you've offered sufficient evidence to make out a prima facie ("in the first view") case—enough so that, if the defendant didn't offer any evidence in his defense, you'd win the case.

If you haven't made out a prima facie case, the other side may successfully move: "Your Honor, the plaintiff has failed to make a prima facie case. I move to dismiss." If the judge disagrees, it's the defendant's turn to put forth his case. Once that presentation has been made, you may go forward to rebut it if you wish to do so. Let's say you lent someone $1,000 and got a note promising to pay in 90 days. If the 90 days go by and it hasn't been paid, all you have to do to make out a prima facie case in court is to hand the judge the note and say you haven't been paid. If the defendant says nothing (or doesn't show), you get the judgment. If his defense says, "Two weeks ago I sent a check for $1,000 in full payment," you have to be ready to come forward and say, "Here's his check—it bounced."

THE EIGHTH STEP:
THE DEFENDANT'S CASE—AND YOUR OBJECTIONS TO IT

The attorney for the defendant will probably begin by calling his client to tell his own version of the story. Chances are they're going to produce an account that will differ appreciably from yours—especially in the matter of who was at fault. As your own lawyer, you have the right to object to certain questions the lawyer may ask and certain answers the witness may give.

There's no way to compress a year-long school course on evidence into a few pages. But I will try to give you an idea of some of the grounds for objection:

HEARSAY: A witness can testify only to things he's actually seen, not to things someone else saw and told him about. Hearsay evidence—what's "heard said"—is inadmissable because not only does it distort, it is also irresponsible and immune to cross-examination. So if the witness says that he didn't actually see what happened, but a bystander did and told him you were backing up when the other car hit you, stand up and say, "Objection, your Honor. Hearsay." The judge will sustain the objection, and the testimony will be stricken.

IRRELEVANT AND IMMATERIAL. Another ground for objection is that testimony is irrelevant and immaterial to the issues before the court. The lawyer can't parade his client's spotless traffic record by asking him whether he's ever been involved in an accident before. That has nothing to do with the specific question of who's to blame in this case. Neither can he introduce evidence that you've been involved in a prior accident.

BEST EVIDENCE: There are also objections you can make to written evidence. According to the "best evidence" rule, you can object if an unsigned carbon is introduced instead of the original document. The lawyer can get around this by showing it to the witness and asking him if he's ever compared the carbon to the origi-

73

nal. The answer will be, "Yes, it's an exact duplicate." Then, "Do you have the original?" "No, it's lost." The carbon may now be submitted as the best evidence available. By the same rule, an oral account of the contents of a written communication may be introduced only if the paper itself is unavailable.

RECORDS: Business record entries, too, are objectionable, unless first shown to have been made in the regular course of business. Someone who's suing you for payment for merchandise he's sold you, can't simply submit his ledger and point to the balance due. First he has to introduce testimony from the person who made the entry or was in charge of its being made, to prove it wasn't trumped up for the occasion. He himself may say, "These were made by my bookkeeper in the regular course of business, under my supervision."

A friend who's been practicing law for twenty years has a very simple rule. Any time a question is asked by the opposing counsel, and he knows the answer to that question is going to be damaging to his case, he jumps up and says, "Objection." At this point, the judge will say one of three things: 1) "Objection sustained"—in which case my friend is pleasantly surprised; 2) "Objection overruled"—in which case the witness can answer the question, but the interruption may have confused him or derailed his train of thought; or, 3) "On what grounds?"—in which case my friend, having had a few seconds to think, offers whatever grounds come closest to the situation.

It's unlikely that you'll be able to come up with a plausible reason as easily as an experienced attorney. But you'll find that you can go a long way with "Irrelevant and immaterial." And if you're stuck, there's always the candid approach: "Well, as you know, your Honor, I'm no lawyer, but it just doesn't sound fair for that to be used as evidence."

Discreet use of your right to object, besides barring potentially damaging testimony, may impress your opponent that you've done your homework and intimidate him into settlement. But don't imitate my friend's calisthenic bouncing up and down at anything vaguely objectionable; that in itself can become objectionable. Faced with transparent delaying tactics, I've heard judges say, "Sit down—I'll tell you when to object."

Restraint is especially important if you're your own lawyer, doubly so if you're the defendant, and even more so in a jury trial. Even the legendary Clarence Darrow, commanding his own defense against trumped-up charges of conspiring to bribe jurors in the 1911 McNamara case—the dynamiting of the *Los Angeles Times* building—found this to be true. At one point in the trial, his chief lawyer was taken ill, and Darrow took his place. "But this was not easy," he recalled in his autobiography. "It is all very well to object to evidence and so-called evidence where someone else is concerned, but it looks bad if one is the defendant and has (personally) to rise up and protest against letting something in." To paraphrase another literary figure, "The defendant may protest too much."

THE NINTH STEP:
CROSS-EXAMINATION

When you're not objecting, you should be taking notes—especially on statements that strike you as half-truths or untruths—for use in your cross-examination. It rarely pays to berate, bully or be rude to a witness during cross-examination. "Didn't you lie when you said that I was backing up?" only yields indignant or unproductive answers like, "No, I didn't lie!"

When you cross-examine, keep in mind two rules pounded into the head of every law student who's ever taken a "Trial Advocacy" course. First, never ask a question of any importance unless you're pretty darned sure you know—from prior homework—what the answer is going to be. Second, avoid asking any question in the "Why?" family. A witness may not volunteer information; he can only respond to your specific questions. You must serve as helmsman, steering the witness in the direction you choose. A broad question like "Would you explain that, please?" turns the wheel over to the witness. There's no telling where his answer will take your case—very possibly right into the rocks.

Cross-examination is a subtle art. It requires a series of innocent-sounding, suspicion-lulling questions leading the witness down the path into ambush, at which point you hit him with the question that will force him to change his story.

Serjeant Ballantine, a great English barrister of the last century, was interrupted during a cross-examination by a magistrate, who objected: "Really, this is a long way from the point."

"I am aware of that, your Lordship," responded Ballantine. "If I were to begin any closer, the witness would discover my object."

In cross-examining the defendant's expert witness—say, an auto mechanic who has also examined your car—a good leading question might be whether he's employed by the insurance company, and isn't it his job to come up with the lowest possible estimates? (Exception: a jury trial, where reference to insurance could conceivably influence the jury.) Then you might try to find out whether he actually repairs cars or only gives estimates. When was the last time he actually performed labor of this kind on a car? Haven't costs gone up since then? How much does he allow per hour for labor? (It may be half the $15 an hour your regular shop charges.) Does he know how long it will take to repair the car? What parts book does he use? Has he used retail prices (the only ones available to you) or wholesale? On a small claim, the insurance company probably won't bother to bring an expert witness, but if they do, you should be prepared to cross-examine him, show him your original estimate and compare it item for item with his to make sure he hasn't "absent-mindedly" omitted something.

THE TENTH STEP: SUMMATION

When both sides have concluded their cases, you can ask the judge for permission to make a short summation of your argument. You may not have to ask. When litigants appear in person, the judge or arbitrator will usually inquire, "Do you have anything to add?" This is your big moment. As the trial or hearing progressed, you should have briefly outlined your strongest evidence, and noted your opponent's weakest evidence. Conclude by asking the judge for a favorable decision: "Your Honor, I ask that judgment be entered for the plaintiff in the amount of $400."

Don't expect an immediate verdict: you may have to endure anywhere from a day's to a week's suspense first. The judge may already have made up his mind, but he's witnessed too many unpleasant scenes—disappointed litigants screaming at or even attacking their grinning, victorious opponents—to want the winners and losers game played in his court. So he will most likely "reserve decision"—which means that, after a restless night, you can probably phone his clerk for the good or bad news first thing in the morning.

In a complex case, with many law books and precedents to be consulted, the wait may, of course, be much longer—as it was in a

grueling three-week trial involving a businessman of doubtful reputation. At trial's end, at which time the judge reserved decision, the
finagling financier immediately boarded his private jet for a much-
needed vacation in his favorite tax haven, the Bahamas. Three
days later, returning from eighteen holes of golf, he found a cable
from his elated lawyer at the front desk. Opening it with trembling
fingers, he read a terse message: JUSTICE HAS TRIUMPHED.

The outraged businessman dashed off an incensed reply: APPEAL
IMMEDIATELY.

CHAPTER 6

Collecting Judgment:
How to Get the Money in Your Pocket

In the third book of *Gargantua and Pantagruel,* by Rabelais, it comes suddenly and scandalously to light that the learned and lovable Judge Bridlegoose has for 50 years been deciding cases by throwing dice. Called to account before a panel of his peers, he explains his innovative approach to dispensing justice:

> Having well and exactly . . . reviewed, recognized, read, and read over again, turned and tossed over, seriously perused and examined the bills of complaint, accusations, impeachments, indictments, warnings, citations, summonings . . . instructions, proofs, allegations, depositions, cross speeches, contradictions, rejoinders, replies, confirmations . . . issues, exceptions, dilatory pleas, demurs, compositions, injunctions, reliefs, reports, returns, confessions, acknowledgements . . . both at the one and the other side as a good judge ought to do . . . I give out sentence in his favour unto whom hath befallen the best chance by dice . . .

Asked why, since he leaves the decision purely to chance, he bothers to accept pleas and evidence and hear testimony, he replies:

> . . . First, for formality-sake . . . Secondly . . . in lieu of some other honest and healthful exercise. Thirdly . . . I defer, protract, delay, prolong, intermit, surcease, pause, linger, suspend . . . and shift off the time of giving a definitive sentence, to the end that the suit or process, being . . . sifted, searched and examined . . . argued, disputed, and debated, may . . . come at last to its full ripeness and maturity. By means whereof, when the fatal hazard of the dice ensueth

thereupon, the condemned parties will, with much greater patience . . . endure and bear up the disastrous load of their misfortune than if they had been sentenced at their first arrival unto the court . . .

The sixteenth-century French physician and satirist may be forgiven for his lack of faith in the judicial process: his father, a lawyer, is said to have wasted much of the family's substance in lengthy, costly litigation with a neighbor over water rights. But even today, the loser will swear that Judge Bridlegoose is alive and well and living in the robes of the man who heard his case. In such a mood, he may not bear his misfortune with the lamblike meekness so prized by Judge Bridlegoose. Should the disgruntled litigant you've defeated attempt to escape his fate, here's how you can compel him to accept it.

THE FIRST STEP:
LEARNING IF—AND WHAT—YOU'VE WON OR LOST

The day after trial you phone the clerk's office, and learn that you don't have to appeal, because justice *has* triumphed. Celebrate your victory, but don't spend the money yet. First, you have to collect it.

In some cases, the plaintiff wins interest and court costs as well. Court costs are unlikely to cover your actual expenses. "Costs" often amount to $5–10 per $100 awarded, but they could be a flat $25, or something entirely different, depending upon the rules of the particular court. The defendant is obliged to reimburse you for such disbursements as your filing and process-serving fees as well. The cost of transcript or judgment and the sheriff's fee are sometimes tacked on, too.

The amount of the award gathers interest from the time the plaintiff became legally entitled to it—for example, the day the services were rendered. It continues to earn interest after the judgment is entered, until finally paid. In most jurisdictions, personal-injury and property-damage claims are an exception to this. They don't start to bear interest until the case is proven and judgment entered. There is, however, a movement to have such judgments include interest from the time of the occurrence. The argument: This could encourage insurance companies to settle before trial, thereby helping unclog court dockets.

If the witness tables are turned and the defendant wins his counterclaim, interest, costs and disbursements will help to fatten his award. But if you are so naive as to think court costs include reimbursement for your attorney's fees, you probably still think the stork brings babies. About the only way you stand any chance of getting that back is the way a client of the late celebrated criminal lawyer Sam Leibowitz did. "Here," said the petty criminal, handing Leibowitz a $100 bill as a retainer to defend him against a charge of pickpocketing, "but I want you to know, I was framed. I been a pro for 24 years, and nobody ain't ever felt my hand in his pocket yet." After his client left, Leibowitz felt in his pocket for his fee. It was gone. He had turned over half his desk drawers when his client returned. "I want you to have your heart in this case," he said, handing Leibowitz the $100 bill. "Now you *know* I was framed!"

The courts award legal fees only where they are explicitly specified as a penalty, either by law or by the provisions of a contract. A loan agreement with a bank may warn that if it must hire a lawyer to collect, the bank is entitled to an additional 15–25 percent for legal fees. In at least one state, the landlord would be liable for attorney's fees as part of punitive damages if he intentionally and wrongfully withheld his tenant's security deposit; and in some cases federal anti-trust laws provide for the defendant's payment of treble damages plus legal fees.

On the face of it then, a judgment would seem to be a taste of ashes for the loser, of caviar for the winner. But a judgment has two faces. As one county court judge put it, "It's a beautiful piece of paper, but if you can't collect it, what's the good of it?" In New York City, which may be no worse than many other jurisdictions in this regard, 40 percent of all small claims judgments are never collected. The exultant plaintiff sometimes finds that with a favorable judgment, he's only won Round One. Round Two may be only the beginning of a long struggle to collect.

THE SECOND STEP:
DOCKETING THE JUDGMENT

That beautiful piece of paper, the transcript of judgment (prepared for you in most cases by the clerk), can nevertheless be a formidable weapon, and one that, unlike most modern armaments, may last for as long as twenty years. Once the judgment is docketed, it becomes a lien on all the judgment debtor's real property within that county.

Sometimes the clerk dockets the judgment for you. If your inquiry reveals that it's up to you, obtain a transcript of the judgment (while you wait) and mail or take it to the county clerk's office in every county where you know or suspect the debtor owns property. After you've established the cost of filing with a preliminary phone call, send the transcript and your certified check or money order along with a self-addressed postcard and your request that the clerk acknowledge receipt.

If ever your quarry tries to sell his house, apply for a loan, or get a mortgage on a new home, the credit investigator will inevitably come across the judgment, and any deal will have to wait until it's paid. I've had cases where five, six, even ten years after giving up on collecting a judgment I receive a telephone call from the old judgment debtor who informs me that the bank won't consider making a loan until he's paid up. It always restores my faith in mankind to observe the touching attack of conscience that ensues.

THE THIRD STEP:
MAKING SURE THE DEFENDANT KNOWS HE'S LOST

If the other side is represented by an insurance company attorney, you should get an extra copy of the judgment and mail it to him. Within three or four weeks, assuming no appeal, you will almost certainly get a check in the mail.

The court may mail a copy of the judgment directly to the defendant. But to be on the safe side, mail him a copy yourself, along with a letter something like this:

Enclosed please find a judgment that has been entered against you on (date). Please be advised that I will wait five days to receive full payment from you.

In the event that I do not receive it, I will have no alternative but to turn the matter over to the sheriff for execution against your property.

The last line may sound a bit stern for a matter of a few hundred dollars. The words "sheriff" and "execution" conjure up images of six-guns and hanging judges. But in real life, the sheriff (sometimes called marshal) is much less harsh and, in general, much less effective because of the legal handcuffs he wears, carefully constructed by a society determined to prevent any possible abuse of his historically sometimes oppressive office.

THE FOURTH STEP:
ATTEMPTING TO REVERSE THE JUDGMENT-APPEAL

The loser's second thought when he hears the decision (the first may be unprintable) is, "Well, dammit, I'll appeal!" Easy to say, not as easy to do. The appeals process is lengthy, requires extensive research, and—except among jailhouse lawyers with time on their hands—is rarely done *pro se*. It's not surprising, then, that most Small Claims Courts do not provide for an appeals process.

An appeal from any court is an expensive venture, since purchase of the trial record is required—a cost which may be recovered only if the appeal is successful. An appeal from Small Claims Court is further complicated by the fact that there is no verbatim record—no court reporter. Further, the appeals process is complex and technical, and may reduce even the most ardent champion of self-advocacy to consulting, or even retaining, a lawyer.

First, you must serve the other party with a notice of appeal and, ordinarily, file it (there is a small fee) with the court whose decision you're appealing and the appellate court—all this usually within 30 days after you were notified of the judgment. (Consider that your move gives your adversary a countermove. The right to file a cross-appeal. If, for example, he was awarded only $200 of his $1,000 claim, your appeal gives him the chance for a second bite at the apple and the possibility of recovering more than he was awarded in the lower court.) Nevertheless, you elect to take your chances. Your next step, then, is to "settle and establish the record on appeal"—reproducing all documents (the summons, the complaint, etc.), testimony, evidence and the court's decision for review by the next highest court, according to its specific (and you'd have to check them) rules. When the record is filed with the appropriate appellate court, the case officially enters that court's jurisdiction.

Now comes the hard part. You must write and serve on your adversary an appeals brief—a summary of the facts based on the record of the case, and the reasons you believe justice has not been done. It won't be much of an argument if you can't cite chapter and verse of the law, so it's best either to consult a lawyer or live in a law library for a day or so to locate a telling precedent or two.

A great deal may depend on trivial technicalities. As someone once put it: "A flaw in a brief, like one in a boiler, leaves everyone in hot water." But remember that a brief is supposed to be brief. Judges nowadays are likely to be less offended by verbosity than was Thomas Egerton, Lord Keeper of the Great Seal in Queen Elizabeth's time. When Richard Mylward, a greenhorn barrister, submitted a replication (a legal pleading) of 120 pages, the Lord Keeper commanded that:

> The Warden of the Fleet shall take the said Richard Mylward into his custody . . . and then and there shall [put] a hole in the myddest of the . . . replication . . . and put the said Richard's head through the same hole . . . and then . . . shall lead the same Richard, bareheaded and barefaced, round about Westminster Hall whilst the courts are sitting, and show him at the bar of every of the three Courts within the Hall, and then shall . . . keep him prisoner until he shall have paid £10 to her Majesty for a fine . . . for the abuse aforesaid."

Upon receipt of your brief, the other side must respond with a brief, the arguments of which you should attempt to rebut in yet another document—your reply brief. Both parties should appear on the date set for the case on the appellate court calendar, at which time they may have the choice of allowing the court to decide on the basis of all the papers before it or of arguing the case orally. The court will often go beyond the submitted briefs, doing independent research to reach a decision that either affirms the lower court's judgment, reverses it, modifies it, or orders a new trial.

The delay inherent in an appeal would seem to make it tempting to the reluctant judgment debtor, but it's actually no help in keeping his money in his pocket. An appeal does not stay the execution of a judgment, unless the appellant puts up a costly appeals bond (something like putting money in escrow) to pay the judgment if the appeal fails.

The Fifth Step:
Opening Default—You Lost But Nobody Let You Know

You get a judgment in the mail one day saying you owe $400, and you're as indignant as the art collector who has just noticed his prize Picasso is signed with two "c's" and one "s". Perhaps you never got the summons, because it was served on a garbage can. Or maybe you were in the hospital, asked your brother-in-law to go to court to get you an adjournment and he plumb forgot about it.

But all is not lost. You can apply to open your default—in effect, reopen the case. You prepare an affidavit either stating that the summons was never received or giving good reasons why you didn't appear. You must show, too, that you have a good and meritorious defense against the plaintiff's claim. You submit this form to the judge along with an Order to Show Cause or a Notice of Motion. Such orders are different in every state, but you should be able to persuade the clerk to show you one from a case that's already public record, which you can have photocopied and then use as a model for your own.

If the judge is convinced by your affidavit, he'll sign the Show Cause Order, making provision for service upon the other party and setting a hearing date. The order stays, or delays, execution on the original judgment until both sides have argued the application before the judge. If your application is granted, the original judgment will be vacated—sometimes conditioned upon posting of a bond—and the case restored to the calendar. If not, the judgment stands and enforcement may proceed apace.

The Sixth Step:
Your Local Sheriff Supports You

The law is on your side as, with a copy of the transcript of judgment furnished you by the court clerk and a fee (sometimes as little as $1) in hand, you enter the door down the hall marked Sheriff's Office.

This long arm of the court carries out such sometimes nasty duties as arresting spouses in alimony arrears or evicting tenants who haven't paid their rent, but in this case collecting your judgment by executing on (seizing and selling) your debtor's property. The sheriff is sometimes on salary, sometimes an independent contractor earning fees on evictions and commissions (5 percent is not unusual) on collections.

Within a reasonable time after you visit him, he or one of his deputies should pay a visit to your debtor. The sheriff has the right to enter the target's home, take inventory of any salable valuables (paintings, antiques, jewelry) and advertise an auction sale. Proof that this happens may be found on the bulletin board of almost any county courthouse, where such auctions are usually advertised. My personal experience is, however, that although sheriffs don't hesitate to do this where a business is involved, they are often reluctant to enter someone's home and auction off personal property. For one thing, the pickings are usually slim, the effort involved considerable. For another, the rules about property exempt from execution are fairly complex, and include such things as essential furniture, appliances and fixtures, wedding rings, tools, clothing, and the family Bible. Moreover, it's more convenient to attach someone's stocks, bonds, and bank account than a 50-pound TV set—but the TV set is all the sheriff sees when he enters the house. So, unless the debtor has a business, a busy sheriff (and these are the only kind found in urban areas) may simply serve the notice and, if he hears nothing further, forget it.

THE SEVENTH STEP:
LOCATING HIS ASSETS

A harried sheriff—especially one working on a commission—is unlikely to waste time trying to collect your judgment without detailed information about the debtor's assets, income, employer, and the like. It's your not-always-easy job to get that information. You may accomplish this if you are willing to pay for a private credit check—possibly through your banker. If you know where your debtor banks (from a check you've seen, or through discreet inquiries) or if it's a small-town situation with only a handful of banks, you could serve them all with a restraining notice, subpoena, and questionnaire. That package asks if the debtor has an account with the bank, how much money is in it, the account number and the branch. The papers (50¢ in New York) can often be served by mail and sometimes require a token payment to the bank.

Just last month, my office obtained a $1,500 judgment against an individual but hadn't the faintest clue as to where he banked. We knew that there were fourteen banks in his home town and felt certain that he had an account in one of them. Using the shotgun method, we mailed (certified, with return receipt requested) a restraining notice and questionnaire subpoena to all fourteen. We got a direct hit. One of the banks informed us that the debtor maintains a safe deposit vault. We won't know its contents until the sheriff opens the vault. With luck, the family jewels or stocks and bonds squirreled away will yield enough to satisfy our client's judgment. If our luck isn't that good, we'll find a pair of cuff links and a collar button.

After you've won your judgment, you have the right to require the judgment debtor to appear in court for questioning, in what is sometimes called "Proceedings Supplemental to Judgment" or "Supplementary Proceedings." You must serve the recalcitrant debtor with a subpoena compelling him to appear and answer your questions. It's also possible to subpoena third parties such as banks, employers, or people who owe him money. If the debtor doesn't show—and many deadbeats don't—the next step is to ask the court to hold him in contempt. You'll fill out another form usually called a "Motion for Contempt for Failure to Appear in Supplementary Proceedings," to which you attach the original subpoena, on which the clerk will have noted the delinquent's default for failure to appear. The debtor will be served with an order to appear in court and show cause why he should not be punished for contempt. At this hearing, the judge will probably issue a conditional contempt order, assigning a new date on which he must appear for questioning or else be held in contempt. If he shows up at the hearing, the judge may direct him to answer your questions then and there.

If he defaults a second time, you can apply for a warrant directing the sheriff to arrest him and bring him to court. There the judge will present him with the alternative of answering your questions immediately or going to jail.

Once you've got him in court, be prepared to sound like a military interrogator: "Do you have a bank account? Where? Any jewelry? Does your landlord have a security deposit from you?" You may be able to buy a form questionnaire. Julius Blumberg in Manhattan sells this one for 25¢:

Form No. 5

W 451—Questions: spaces for judgment debtor to answer—use with information subpoena (Blumbergs No. 407 or 417). Blank Ct.: 4-64

COPYRIGHT 1964 BY JULIUS BLUMBERG, INC., LAW BLANK PUBLISHERS
80 EXCHANGE PLACE AT BROADWAY, NEW YORK

COURT

COUNTY OF _____

Index No. _____

against		
	Plaintiff	QUESTIONS AND ANSWERS in connection with INFORMATION SUBPOENA regarding
	Defendant	.... *Judgment Debtor*

STATE OF NEW YORK, COUNTY OF _____ *ss.:*

_____ being duly sworn deposes and says; that deponent is the * Judgment Debtor above named and the recipient of an information subpoena herein and of the original and a copy of questions accompanying said subpoena. Deponent makes the following answers (each answer immediately following the question to which it responds) in compliance with the subpoena.

1. Q. What is your full name? A.
2. Q. Have you ever been known by any other name? A.
3. Q. What is your occupation or profession? A.
4. Q. Where do you live and with whom? A.

5. Q. Do you occupy an apartment or house? A.
6. Q. What is the landlord's name and address? A.

7. Q. Have you a written lease? A.
8. Q. Who pays the rent? A.
9. Q. How is the rent paid, by check or cash? A.
10. Q. When is the rent payable? A.
11. Q. Do you get receipts for the rent from your landlord? A.
12. Q. How much is the rent? A.
13. Q. For how long a time have you lived in the premises you now occupy? A.
14. Q. How much security do you have on deposit with your landlord? A.
15. Q. Are you married? A.
16. Q. What is your spouse's full name? A.
17. Q. Are you the owner of the household furnishings in your home? A.
18. Q. Did you buy said furnishings on the installment plan? A.
19. Q. Are said furnishings covered by a security agreement such as a chattel mortgage or conditional sale contract? A.
20. Q. Are said furnishings insured? A.
21. Q. If so, in whose name, and in what company? A.

22. Q. How many children have you, and what are their ages? A.

23. Q. Are any of your children employed? A.
24. Q. Is your spouse engaged in an independent business? A.
25. Q. What is the name and address of the business? A.

26. Q. What is the nature of the business? A.
27. Q. Is your spouse employed? A.
28. Q. What is the name and address of the employer? A.

29. Q. What is the nature of the occupation? A.
30. Q. What salary is paid to your spouse? A.
31. Q. Does your spouse own any real estate or have any interest in real estate? A.

32. Q. Does your spouse hold any chattel mortgages or security agreements? A.

33. Q. Does your spouse own an automobile, airplane or boat? A.
34. Q. Is the same covered by a chattel mortgage, conditional sale or other security agreement? A.

35. Q. Has your spouse a bank, check or savings account? A.

36. Q. Has your spouse any jewelry? A.
37. Q. Describe each item of jewelry and give approximate values? A.

38. Q. Is your spouse an officer, director or stockholder in any corporation? A.

39. Q. Does your spouse own any stocks, bonds, defense bonds or other securities? A.
40. Q. Identify each such item? A.

41. Q. Are any of your children officers, directors or stockholders in any corporation? A.

* Excerpt from CPLR section 5224 (a) 3. "...... Answers shall be made in writing under oath by the person upon whom served. if an individual, or by an officer, director, agent or employee having information, if a corporation. partnership or sole proprietorship. Each question shall be answered separately and fully and each answer shall refer to the question to which it responds. Answers shall be returned together with the original of the questions within seven days after receipt." If space is insufficient, use last page to answer, giving number of the question answered.

42. *Q.* Are you engaged in business in an individual, partnership or corporate form? *A.*

43. *Q.* If engaged in business give your business address and name of your firm? *A.*

44. *Q.* If employed give your employer's name and address? *A.*

45. *Q.* What share or interest have you in the firm with which you are connected? *A.*
46. *Q.* In what capacity are you employed? *A.*
47. *Q.* Are you employed under a written contract? *A.*
48. *Q.* For how long a time have you worked with your present employer? *A.*
49. *Q.* What salary do you receive? *A.*
50. *Q.* When is your salary payable? *A.*
51. *Q.* Is your salary payable by check or in cash? *A.*
52. *Q.* Do you receive any bonus or emolument other than your salary? *A.*
53. *Q.* Have you a drawing account? *A.*
54. *Q.* What amount of income have you received from your trade or profession during each of the two years immediately preceding the entry of judgment in this action? *A.*
55. *Q.* What amount of income have you received from other sources during each of these two years? *A.*

56. *Q.* Have you a bank, check or savings account? *A.*
57. *Q.* If so, give names and addresses of banks where you have accounts? *A.*

58. *Q.* Have you closed any bank account since the summons in this action was served on you? *A.*

59. *Q.* If so give name and address of bank. *A.*

60. *Q.* How much was on deposit at time the account was closed? *A.*

61. *Q.* Give date, name and address of payee of the last check you drew. *A.*

62. *Q.* What was the amount of said check and the consideration therefor? *A.*

63. *Q.* Is the payee related to you, or to any member of your family? *A.*
64. *Q.* Have you any life, accident, health or any other kind of insurance? *A.*
65. *Q.* If so, what are the names of the companies and the numbers and amounts of each policy? *A.*

66. *Q.* Who are the beneficiaries in each policy? *A.*

67. *Q.* Were the beneficiaries changed? If so, when? *A.*
68. *Q.* Do you own an automobile, airplane or boat? *A.*
69. *Q.* Is it covered by a chattel mortgage, conditional sale or other security agreement? *A.*

70. *Q.* Was it bought on the installment plan? *A.*
71. *Q.* Where do you keep the automobile? *A.*
72. *Q.* Have you any jewelry or diamonds? *A.*
73. *Q.* Describe each item and give approximate values? *A.*

74. *Q.* Do you own any interest in real estate? *A.*

75. *Q.* Do you have shares or proprietory lease in a cooperative or condominium? *A.*

76. *Q.* Do you own any chattel or real estate mortgages? *A.*

77. *Q.* Do you hold any participating interest in any real estate or chattel mortgage? *A.*

78. *Q.* Do you receive any income from trust funds? *A.*

79. *Q.* Do you own any stocks, bonds, defense bonds or other securities? *A.*
80. *Q.* Describe each item? *A.*

81. *Q.* Are you an officer, director or shareholder in any corporation? *A.*

82. *Q.* Do you own a piano, phonograph, radio, television set, horses, carriages, trucks, paintings or silverware? *A.*

83. *Q.* Do you own any rugs or tapestries? If so, describe them. *A.*

84. *Q.* Have you a library, collection of curios, coins, stamps, antiques or statuary? *A.*

85. *Q.* Do you receive royalties from any patent, copyright or invention? *A.*

86. *Q.* Do you own a seat in any stock, cotton, produce, commercial or other exchange? *A.*

87. *Q.* Are you a trustee, executor or administrator under any will or testament, insurance policy or trust agreement? *A.*

88. *Q.* Have you any property in pawn? *A.*

89. *Q.* Did you ever borrow money and pledge or deposit as collateral security any property, real or personal? *A.*

90. *Q.* If so, state names and addresses of persons with whom such security was deposited. *A.*

91. *Q.* Have you made a last will and testament? *A.*
92. *Q.* Have you one or more safe deposit boxes? *A.*
93. *Q.* If so, give the location of each and the names of all persons having access to each box? *A.*

94. *Q.* Do you have access to any other safe deposit box? *A.*

95. *Q.* Are you a beneficiary under any trust or last will? *A.*

96. *Q.* Are you a lessee of any real estate? *A:*
97. *Q.* If so, where is the property located. *A.*

98. *Q.* Have you an interest in any mortgage, mechanics lien or other lien on real property? *A.*

99. *Q.* Have you any judgments in your favor? *A.*
100. *Q.* If so, state details and amounts. *A.*

101. *Q.* Does anybody owe you money? *A.*
102. *Q.* If so, give details? *A.*

103. *Q.* Are there any judgments against you? *A.*
104. *Q.* If so, state details and amounts. *A.*

105. *Q.* Have you ever before been examined by a judgment creditor? *A.*

106. *Q.* Have you any right or interest in any action now pending in any court? *A.*

107. *Q.* Are you a party to any action now pending in any court? *A.*

108. *Q.* Have you sold, conveyed or assigned any of your property real or personal within the past 2 years? *A.*

109. *Q.* Have you made a gift of any of your real or personal property to anyone since the summons in the above entitled action was served on you? *A.*

110. *Q.* Are you named as beneficiary under a life insurance policy issued to some other person? *A.*

111. *Q.* Have you received any money or property under any will or by inheritance? *A.*

112. *Q.* Was a receiver of your property ever appointed? *A.*

113. *Q.* How do you pay for your living expenses? *A.*

114. *Q.* What is the source of your income which you use to support yourself? *A.*

115. *Q.* Do you receive any money from others to help support yourself? *A.*
116. *Q.* If so, give names and addresses of such persons. *A.*

117. *Q.* Give the amounts that such persons contribute for your support. *A.*

118. *Q.* Do you receive such monies by check or in cash? *A.*
119. *Q.* What deposits have you with any utility company? *A.*

120. *Q.* Do you receive or are you entitled to receive money from trust or pension funds? *A.*

121. *Q.* Have you any sources of income other than as testified to? *A.*

122. *Q.* Where did you file your Federal and State income tax returns for the past 2 years? *A.*

123. *Q.* Are you entitled to any refund for Federal or State income taxes paid? *A.*

124. *Q.* Does anyone hold any property or money in trust for you? *A.*

125. *Q.* Do you keep any records relating to your income and expenses? *A.*
126. *Q.* Do you employ an accountant? *A.*
127. *Q.* Have you borrowed money from any bank or other lending institution within the past 2 years? *A.*

128. *Q.* Do you have an interest in insurance or other claims now pending? *A.*
129. *Q.* If so, give details? *A.*

90

THE EIGHTH STEP:
HOLDING UP THE BANK—AND OTHER WAYS OF CONFISCATING YOUR DEBTOR'S ASSETS

If you discover that assets owed or owned by the debtor are held by a third party such as a bank—and you've tied them up by serving a restraining notice—enter the sheriff with an execution or levy on the account. The bank pays him—adding his fee, or poundage—and, deducting his fee, he pays you. Surgery being completed, the debtor's account, or what's left of it, is once more open for business. Approximately the same strategy applies to anyone else who owes money to the man who owes you: the landlord who holds his security, the homeowner whose roof he just repaired (you know about that because you saw his truck outside for two days).

If he has a car, you may find that someone has a lien on it already, perhaps the bank that loaned him the money to buy it. In this case, if the sheriff attaches and auctions the car, the prior lien will have to be satisfied, which may not leave you with much of the proceeds. Income executions—or garnishments—are another often used device. They empower the sheriff to collect either from the debtor or from his employer—usually by mail, monthly or quarterly—a certain percentage of his salary until the debt is paid. But this can be done only if the salary is above a certain minimum, varying from state to state. In Minnesota, the first 75 percent of earnings or 40 times federal minimum hourly wage, whichever is greater, cannot be attached, garnisheed, or levied upon. In New York, up to 10 percent may be garnisheed but only from a salary above $85 a week.

Only one garnishee can be placed on a salary at one time; you may have to wait in line until a previous debt is paid off. Federal law—with penalties of one year's imprisonment, $1,000 or both—prohibits an employer from willfully firing an employee who's being garnisheed—which many companies used to do to avoid the annoyance and cost of the extra bookkeeping.

This first-claim-first-served principle applied to income executions may allow a wily debtor to evade a judgment almost indefinitely. A sharpy who knows that a creditor is going to succeed in obtaining a judgment against him may, before the case comes up, say to a friend:

"You know that $20,000 I owe you? (*WINK*) Well, I want you to sue me for it." His accomplice files suit, the summons goes unanswered, and within a few weeks, the sheriff has an order to garnishee the conspirator's wages—maybe $30 a week on a $300 salary, or $1,500 a year. When the genuine creditor finally gets his judgment, he has to wait in line, with no end in sight.

But this stratagem can sometimes be foiled by a vigilant creditor. Once, trying to collect on a judgment, I asked in my supplementary proceedings if there were any other judgments against the debtor. He said there was one, for $10,000. I asked who the judgment creditor was, and he gave the name. On a hunch, I asked if they were related, and, reddening, he said, "Yes, my uncle . . . he lent me money." After further investigation, I brought an action to set aside that judgment on grounds of fraud, and asked for copies of all the underlying documents—canceled checks, promissory notes, etc. Result: a respectable settlement of my client's claim.

THE NINTH STEP:
SOMETHING IS BETTER THAN NOTHING

A settlement after judgment may not be a half-bad idea if you're dealing with someone who's shown a talent for weaving and bobbing. Such good folks have a knack for staying two steps ahead of the sheriff. And where the sum involved is relatively small, even with full information, the sheriff may feel it isn't worth his time and trouble (5 percent of $200 hardly makes it worthwhile to leave his office), and he may just put your judgment at the bottom of the pile. When you corner an escape artist, you may be able to make a deal that would be less than you'd get if you made pursuing him a full-time project. But you may be better off with a certified check in the hand rather than a deadbeat in the bush. So if he says, "Look, I owe you $1,000. If you leave me alone, I'll give you $700 right now," consider that seriously. It could prove far better than an agreement to pay you $20 a week for 50 weeks. That may sound like more, but it won't be if he changes jobs or leaves town, leaving you with $20 a week for only five weeks.

THE LAST STEP:
SATISFACTION OF JUDGMENT

Judgments do get satisfied, difficult as the process may sometimes be. If the sheriff has collected the debt—or enough of it so you're willing to call it quits—he'll file a paper with the court called the Satisfaction of Judgment. If you've dealt directly, the debtor should ask for—or you can offer—the same paper. (See form on pages 94–95.)

When it comes to collecting your judgment, ingenuity coupled with true grit can't hurt. Take the case of Jones, the collection manager, who tried for ten years to collect the $200 owed his firm by Smith, a notorious deadbeat more skilled in evasive action than the Red Baron. After sending collection letters ranging in tone from polite formality to indignant wrath, getting a judgment, and pestering the frustrated sheriff with phone calls, Jones finally cornered Smith in a neighborhood bar. Harangued for two hours with threats, insults, pleas, and a final, impassioned appeal to his personal integrity and self-esteem, Smith at last broke down and wrote out a check for $200.

Elated, Jones practically flew to Smith's bank, and asked the teller to certify the check. The teller scanned his books briefly, then said, "Sorry. Insufficient funds." Crushed, Jones turned away dejectedly. Suddenly he brightened. "How much is in his account?"

"A hundred and fifty."

"Here," said Jones crisply, drawing two twenties and a ten from his wallet, "deposit this in Smith's account, and cash this check."

Form No. 6

B 242—Whole or Partial Satisfaction of Judgment.
    Blank Court.

COPYRIGHT 1973 BY JULIUS BLUMBERG, INC., LAW BLANK PUBLISHERS
80 EXCHANGE PL. AT BROADWAY, N.Y.C. 10004

COURT

COUNTY OF

Index No.

Plaintiff(s)

against

SATISFACTION OF
JUDGMENT

Defendant(s)

WHEREAS, a judgment was entered in the above entitled action on   19
in the   Court of   County of
in judgment book   page No.   in favor of

and against

for the sum of $ which judgment was docketed on   19
in the office of the Clerk of the County of   in judgment book   page No.

and said judgment has been   paid and the sum of $ remains unpaid.

AND it is certified that there are no outstanding executions with any Sheriff or Marshal within the State
of New York,

THEREFORE,   satisfaction of said judgment is hereby acknowledged, and the said
Clerks are hereby authorized and directed to make an entry of   satisfaction on the docket of
said judgment.

Dated:

....
The name signed must be printed beneath

STATE OF NEW YORK, COUNTY OF   ss.:

On the   day of   19   , before me personally came

to me known and known to me to be the
in the above entitled action, and to be the same person   described in and who executed the within satisfaction
of judgment and acknowledged to me that   he   executed the same.

94

State of

County of $\left.\right\}$ *ss.:*

On the   day of   , *nineteen hundred and*
before me personally came
to me known, who, being by me duly sworn, did depose and say that   *he resides at* **No.**

that   *he is the*   *of*

the corporation described in, and which executed, the foregoing instrument; that   *he knows the seal of*
said corporation; that the seal affixed to said instrument is such corporate seal; that it was so affixed
by order of the board of   *of said corporation; and that*   *he signed h*
name thereto by like order.

State of

County of $\left.\right\}$ *ss.:*

On the   day of   , *nineteen hundred and*
before me personally came
personally known to me and to me known to be a member of the firm of

and to me known to be the person described in and who executed the foregoing satisfaction of judgment
in the firm name of   *and*   *he acknowledged*
that   *he executed same as the act and deed of said firm for the uses and purposes therein mentioned.*

CHAPTER 7

Where There's a Will

Tell the lawyer next door (and at the rate law schools are churning out graduates these days, there may soon be a lawyer next door to everyone) that you are thinking of preparing your own will, and he will likely reward you with a patronizing chuckle.

Making your own will can, of course, be moderately risky. Lawyers may even profess to be happy to see you do it: If they lose a fee in the short run, they may gain much more when employed to contest your will in the long run, as witness this "Song of the Barristers" from the old English Inns of Court:

Now this festive occasion our spirit unbends,
Let us never forget the profession's best friends,
So we'll send the wine round and a nice bumper fill,
To the jolly testator who makes his own will.

That attitude hasn't changed much over the years. Almost every attorney-authored book I've ever read on law for the layman, every article I've ever read about wills and estates, every pamphlet on the subject published by state bar associations emphasizes that you should *not* prepare your own will, that it's a job that only a lawyer can adequately handle.

Now, it's easy to conclude that this viewpoint is akin to that of the service station operator who warns darkly that if you change your points and sparkplugs yourself, your motor is sure to burn up by nightfall. Perhaps there is a little of that. Lawyers are only human.

I think, though, that a larger reason for lawyers to urge themselves upon people in the matter of wills is the conviction that the poorly informed layman will make a mess of what can be a fairly complex matter, with the result that—as the "Song of the Barristers" suggests—his will will be thwarted and his heirs will be the

97

poorer. That does happen, but I think the relevant phrase is "poorly informed." If you're well-informed, if you carefully, diligently, and intelligently follow the steps I'm about to outline, and if you have a reasonably simple estate, there is no reason why you can't successfully draw up and execute your own will.

DRAWING YOUR WILL

STEP ONE:
WHEN *NOT* TO DRAW YOUR OWN WILL

But—Department of Fair Warning—there are situations in which you should no more consider being your own lawyer than being your own open-heart surgeon.

1. Retain a lawyer if you are a person of wealth and property whose large estate will be subject to federal inheritance taxes. Skilled legal and tax advice and estate planning may measurably reduce, possibly even—unfair as this may sound—entirely eliminate such taxes. What constitutes a "large" estate? A Rockefeller or du Pont would be amused, but we're talking about $250,000 or more where the spouse is beneficiary, or more than $120,000 where there is no spouse. A sum of $250,000 or less left to a spouse is currently exempt from federal taxation, and $120,000 is exempted no matter who is the heir.* If what's involved is less than these amounts, you can be your own lawyer.

2. Get a lawyer if you plan to write your will in such a way that you'll leave behind unhappy or quarrelsome relatives. If you anticipate that one or more will try to set aside the will, it makes sense to retain an attorney. Two reasons: Not only will you have someone trained to handle complexities, but you'll have an out-

---

*Thus, a surviving spouse may inherit up to $370,000 without paying federal estate taxes.

side, disinterested witness to whom you've expressed your real desires and who'll be able to testify, if need be, to your intent.

That's exactly what happened in a case I handled several years ago on behalf of two women whose elderly sister had died, leaving her entire estate of about $100,000 to her attorney. Since she had, in effect, disinherited her other living sisters, with the possibility of the attorney's having exercised undue influence for personal aggrandizement, it made sense to challenge the will.

However, at the preliminary hearing before the Surrogate, the attorney testified under oath that he had known his client for 35 years, that he had handled her husband's estate upon his death, that he and his wife had long and warm social relationships with the widow, and that she had confided to him that she had not seen any of her sisters in twenty years and felt abandoned by them. When she expressed the desire to make him her heir, he had insisted—quite wisely as it turned out—on bringing in another firm of lawyers to draw up the will.

He had demanded that they carefully interrogate her to be sure that her act was voluntary, that she was of sound mind, and that she knew what she wanted. The lawyers had then not only witnessed the will, but prepared affidavits setting forth her feelings, expressed to them, of abandonment by her family. Convinced that we could not win a court fight and that it would drag on several years and simply eat up the estate in legal costs, I proposed a settlement, to which the widow's heirs promptly agreed: in return for withdrawing objections, $2,500 as a token payment to each sister.

3. Get a lawyer if you want advice to help you create a complicated trust, naming a bank or trust company executor and trustee. The Irving Trust Company of New York, for example, currently won't accept trusteeship of an estate of less than $300,000. Many people, under the impression that banks welcome any and all trusts, have been posthumously disappointed when the bank renounced the appointment. I recall one well-meaning husband who, thinking he had a friend at Chase Manhattan and wanting to give his wife "the best advice money can buy" named the bank cotrustee with his spouse, of a trust created for her benefit. But when all his debts were paid, it quickly became apparent that he didn't have the money to buy it. The bottom line on his estate analysis read only $60,000—including their $40,000 home. The estate was simply too tiny to tolerate Chase's minimum fee of several thousand dollars a year, so the bank politely "renounced." After much

unnecessary delay, the Surrogate Judge agreed that another rela-tive—who agreed to waive any fee—could act as co-trustee, and the probate process marched on.

STEP TWO:
CONSULT YOUR SPOUSE

Even in this so-called age of women's liberation, many husbands thoughtlessly draw up wills that will affect their wives' futures tremendously without even consulting them. Sometimes it's the husband who ignores the wife, sometimes it's a male-chauvinist-in-a-hurry attorney. Either way, the result is often a resentful, em-bittered widow who discovers after her husband's death that she has been deprived of effective control of her own life, because of some Scrooge-trustee banker who handles her money as though it were his—or as if he were next in line to inherit.

Frequently, only one spouse—usually the husband—comes to my office for the initial conference on the proposed will. When the matter of trusts or guardians for young children comes up, and the man gives me his choices—his brother or sister—I ask if he has dis-cussed it with his wife. Often he'll say, "Don't worry about it. Just prepare the will. There'll be no problem with Carol." I mail a copy of the will to his home for review before the signing in my office, and then sit back to wait for the inevitable embarrassed phone call from the man: "Carol wants her mother to be the children's guard-ian if we both die in a plane crash. You'll have to give us a day or two to work it out." The point is clear: Consult with your partner before consigning your decision to paper.

STEP THREE:
LEARN THE LEGAL REQUIREMENTS FOR A WILL IN YOUR STATE

A friendly Surrogate (in some states, Probate) Judge's clerk can be helpful if you have any questions. What makes a will valid var-ies from state to state in only three respects: (1) the minimum age at which it can be drawn; (2) the number of witnesses required (two or three); (3) whether or not the state accepts a holographic will (handwritten, often without witnesses).

The requirements of a legal will common to all states include:
1. In general, wills must be in writing. Oral (or noncupative)

100

wills, except in the case of someone on his deathbed or military personnel on active duty—like the paratrooper about to jump into combat who says, "Charlie, make sure my mom gets the $1,000 I won in the crap game last night!"—are not acceptable. Noncupative wills are a fascinating phenomenon. But they are so rare, witness and other requirements differ so sharply in those states accepting them, and you are so unlikely to deliver yourself of one that there is no point in discussing them further here.

Preferably, a will should be typed. I've handwritten a few for clients myself—but it's a stopgap measure, something that isn't taught in law school and that I never would have thought of doing if I hadn't known a physician I'll call Dr. Pepper. The doctor was in his late 60s when he called upon me to prepare wills for him and for his wife, his longtime housekeeper whom he'd married only a year or so earlier. Their wills were reciprocal—he leaving everything to her and she to him—except that upon the death of the survivor, the entire estate passed to his favorite charity.

A few years later, the wife entered the hospital, and that week, at home alone, the husband died in bed. When the wife's relatives learned of the husband's death, they called in another lawyer and, with the wife's consent, instructed him to prepare a new will, cutting off the husband's charity and leaving the $50,000 estate to her family. The lawyer talked to her, went back to his office to have it typed, and returned next day for her signature. Too late. She had died during the night. Did conscience qualms contribute? I don't know. I do know that the few times since then that I've been called to a hospital, I've made it a point to write the will out in longhand and have it properly executed (the lawyer's code word for "signed") and witnessed then and there. Such wills are not considered holographic because they are not in the testator's own handwriting.

Unwitnessed holographic wills are accepted in fewer than half the states, which makes them a bad gamble. But some strange ones have been probated—including one penciled on the wall of his New Jersey cell by a prisoner just before he hanged himself.

2. The testator—or person making the will—must be of age: at least 14 to 21, depending on the state.

3. The person must be mentally competent—"of sound mind and memory"—to dispose of his property. Many court battles are fought over this specification, and, with fortunes at stake, experts often bitterly disagree over what constitutes competence and sani-

ty. Essentially, the testator must know and understand the nature and consequences of his acts.

4. The testator must act of his or her own free will, without undue outside influence. In a case several years ago, two lawyers were accused of undue influence over an elderly immigrant who was "forgetful, eccentric, and whose mental acuities were waning." The deceased man's daughter declared in the Surrogate Court, when the will was offered for probate, that her father had originally appointed a bank as his executor, but later decided to save that fee by appointing his daughter instead. He had called in the two attorneys to change his will to that effect, and, said the daughter, they persuaded him to add them as executors.

The undue influence they had exerted would have given each of them a fat and undeserved executor's commission and legal fee, since the estate was over $100,000, at which magic number, instead of executors *sharing* a 4 to 5 percent fee, each receives a 4 to 5 percent fee of his own. Such fraudulent conduct, said the Surrogate Judge, should certainly not be rewarded. He ordered the will admitted to probate with the exception of article eight, the clause appointing them as co-executors.

The fact that the document must express the wishes of the person making it is deemed so important that when a careful lawyer makes the will, he routinely asks the testator at the time the will is executed, "Does this will express your wishes?"

5. There must be witnesses to the signature. In most states a minimum of two witnesses is required, but using one more than required is a sensible idea. Three are mandated in Connecticut, Louisiana, Massachusetts, Maine, South Carolina, New Hampshire, and Vermont.

6. It must be signed by the person making it, and the signature *must* be at the end of the will, with nothing following it but the attestation clause (see no. 7) and the signatures of the witnesses. Anything written below the signature is invalid—although it does not invalidate what is written before it. Surrogates tell me this is a common mistake. A will, handsomely typed and drafted by an attorney, correct in all details, is submitted for probate by the deceased's family. And there, below his signature, is a postscript roughly typed or handwritten in much later, which the lawyer never saw. It's a last wish that simply cannot be granted by the court.

7. Although there is no absolute requirement for a formal attestation clause, I have never seen a will prepared by an attorney

without one. This clause appears before the witnesses' signatures and states that the document was signed and declared by the maker to be his will in the presence of the witnesses, and that the witnesses were acting at his request. Although not every state requires that the will be signed in the witnesses' presence, it is always best to do it that way. It's wisest, too, to assemble all the witnesses at the same time for the "ceremony," so that in effect they are witnessing each other.

STEP FOUR:
THE FORM AND LANGUAGE OF THE WILL

In spite of the elaborate legal language of many wills, no special form is required. Something as simple as this (though I'm not urging its use) can be admitted to probate as a last will and testament:

After I die I want everything I
own to be given to my brother Jason.

January 6, 1971   (signed) Bradley Brown

John Kent
Barbara Fink
Witnesses

A wedding is as legal and binding when the bride wears a bikini as when she wears a formal white gown. An informally worded will is every bit as legal as one couched in lofty legalese. The father of Princess Grace of Monaco was a bricklayer before he became a millionaire, and he retained some of the casual ways and sense of humor of his youth. In spite of its relaxed tone, John B. Kelly's will was carefully reviewed by his attorneys and was as legal as running a green light. But he had fun writing its introduction and it has become a much quoted classic:

For years I have been reading Last Wills and Testaments, and I have never been able to clearly understand any of them at one reading.

Therefore, I will attempt to write my own Will with the hope that it will be understandable and legal. Kids will be called "kids" and not "issue," and it will not be cluttered up with "parties of the first part," "per stirpes," "perpetuities," "quasijudicial," "to wit" and a lot of other terms that I am sure are only used to confuse those for whose benefit it is written.

This is my Last Will and Testament and I believe I am of sound mind. (Some lawyers will question this when they read my Will, however, I have my opinion of some of them, so that makes it even.) I revoke any and all previous Wills made before by me.

Where once it was customary to do wills formally on 8½ x 14 legal paper, many courts now routinely accept ordinary 8½ x 11 typing paper. But, in a pinch, they have accepted wills for probate on the back of an envelope, scrawled across a paper restaurant placemat or on the back of a dunning letter from a creditor. A will on the back of a hospital chart, casually disposing of six million dollars, was successfully probated.

STEP FIVE:
PREPARING TO MAKE YOUR WILL—A WORKABLE WORKSHEET

ANSWER THE FOLLOWING BASIC QUESTIONS ABOUT YOURSELF, YOUR FAMILY AND HOW YOU WANT TO DISTRIBUTE YOUR PROPERTY AFTER DEATH:

1. What is your full legal name?
2. What is your principal legal place of residence?
   a) Street address
   b) County
   c) City
   d) State
3. Have you ever had a will before? (If this will revokes a prior one, it's a good idea to physically destroy any prior wills when the new one has been completed and properly signed.)
4. Are you single or married? (If you are legally separated or divorced, consider yourself single).
5. Do you desire to leave any specific property, such as a piece

of jewelry, clothing, furniture, or pet to a particular person? (See Step 7, p. 108).

5a.   If the answer to 5 is yes, set down the name of each person that you want to receive a specific item, with the item or items next to their names.

6.   Do you wish to leave to any particular person any specific amount of cash or percentage of your estate—the property, real or personal, in which you have a right or interest? (See Step 7).*

6a.   If the answer to 6 is yes, set down the name of each person that you want to receive a specific amount (or percentage) along with the amount (or percentage).

7.   What is the name of your spouse (husband or wife)?

8a.   What are the names of your children, if any?

8b.   What are the ages of your children?

9.   If any of the children are minors (under the age of eighteen years), put down the name of the person or persons whom you would want to take care of them, if both you and your spouse were to pass away. (Clear this with the individual in advance; also provide the name of an alternate, in case the first person is unable to serve as guardian at the time of your death.)

10.   Do you believe that your spouse will be capable of handling the affairs of your estate after you are gone? (If there is no spouse and the children are major beneficiaries, will one or more of them be able to handle your affairs?) In most estates of modest amounts, it's common to name your spouse as executor or executrix of the estate.

11.   What person other than your spouse or child (children) would you trust to handle your affairs and carry out your wishes after your death? This question is to determine an alternate executor in case your spouse is, for any reason, unable to assume the duties of executor. You may want to name your oldest child, if he or she is over the age of eighteen.

---

*You can't will somebody something that you have, in a sense, otherwise assigned. Where money is held in a joint account with rights of survivorship, you have already provided that on your death it will automatically pass to the survivor. Likewise, in cases where the assignee or beneficiary is named, money deposited in trust for another, life insurance, and pension plans and accounts (Keogh plans, I.R.A. accounts, et al.) will find their way to the person named without so much as a mention in your will.

Form No. 7
LAST WILL AND TESTAMENT

OF

(*your name*)

I, (*your name*), residing at (*street address*) in the County of (*county*) City of (*city*), State of (*state*), do hereby make, publish and declare this to be my Last Will and Testament revoking all wills and codicils by me at any time heretofore made, and do intend by this instrument to dispose of all property which, at my death, I own or have the power to dispose of:

FIRST: I direct that all my just debts, funeral expenses, and expenses in connection with the administration of my estate be paid as soon as practicable after my death.

SECOND: After the payment of my just debts and funeral expenses, I give, bequeath, and devise all the rest, residue, and remainder of my estate, of whatever kind and description, to (fill in: *to my wife or husband or name of person to whom you are leaving your estate*) provided that (s)he shall survive me.

THIRD: If (*my wife, husband, or name of other person*) shall predecease me, or if (s)he and I shall die simultaneously, or under such circumstances as to render it difficult or impossible to determine with certainty whether (s)he survived me, then, and in any of said events, I give, bequeath and devise the rest, residue, and remainder of my estate to (*my children*), [*name*] and [*name*] *or others you may name*) in equal shares, *per stirpes.* *

FOURTH: I appoint (*my wife, husband, or name of other person*) executor of this last will and testament, and if (s)he predeceases me, or for any reason fails or ceases to act as such executor, I appoint (*name of substitute*) as substitute executor.

---

*If any of the children predecease the testator, the share that they would have received shall go to their descendants, if any.

I hereby direct that my executor (or substitute) herein shall not be required to furnish any bond or any other undertaking for the performance of their duties.

FIFTH: I give my Executor (or substitute) the fullest power and authority in all matters and questions and to do all acts which I might or could do if living, including, without limitation, complete power and authority to sell (at public or private sale, for cash or credit with or without security), mortgage, lease and dispose of and distribute in kind, all property, real and personal, at such times as (s)he (or substitute) may determine, all without Court order.

IN WITNESS WHEREOF, I have hereunto, set my hand this — day of——19—.

———(L.S.)*
(type name here)

SUBSCRIBED, SEALED, PUBLISHED, AND DECLARED by the above-named Testator as and to be his Last Will and Testament, in the presence of each of us, all present at the same time, who at his request in his presence and in the presence of each other, have hereunto subscribed our names as attesting witnesses, the day and year last above written.

——————————————residing at ————————————

——————————————residing at ————————————

——————————————residing at ————————————

Before you begin to type the will, read the form over carefully. Make sure that you have the information required for each blank. If the answer on your page is not filled in, or is a negative answer, the paragraph in question does not belong in your will. Check off those paragraphs that will be needed in your will. Read these paragraphs carefully before you begin to fill in the blanks. If you wish

---

Locus sigilli; in Latin, literally "the place of the seal"—where in medieval days the nobleman (who else had anything to bequeath?) applied his signet ring in hot wax to formalize and authenticate the document.

to give additional gifts in your will, go on to Step Seven. If not, proceed to Step Eight.

STEP SEVEN:
MAKING OTHER BEQUESTS

Personal effects. What will happen to your watch, valuable jewelry, paintings, antiques, old books, and so on after you are gone? If you care, you will determine this before your death. This can be done in three ways, each of which has some advantages and some drawbacks: 1. Physically and permanently give the item to the recipient while you are still alive, as a gift (a possible tax savings since gift taxes have certain exemptions). 2. Specify exactly what goes to whom in your will. This assures the items going to the right person, but there is the danger that a long list of bequests might complicate probate proceedings. A later change of heart about who gets what could mean changing the entire will, or at least drawing up an official addition, or codicil. 3. You can leave everything to one person—usually a spouse or close relative—and simply leave a special letter designating how the items are to be distributed. Since such a letter is not binding, it had better be someone you trust.

Following are samples of clauses to insert—above your signature, of course—if you decide to leave personal effects to anyone:

I give to my son (*name*) the *gold watch and chain* which I inherited from my father.

or

I give to my daughter (*name*) any automobile that I may own at the time of my death.

Specific bequests of money. Here are some sample clauses enabling you to give a specific amount of money or a percentage of your estate:

I give to my (son, daughter, friend)————, the sum of $5,000.00, if he shall survive me.

or

After the payment of my just debts and funeral expenses, I give, bequeath and devise all the rest, residue, and remainder of my estate as follows:

A. 50% to my wife
B. 25% to my son
C. 25% to my daughter

If any of the foregoing shall predecease me I give their share to their descendants, if any. If they have no descendants, then their share shall be given to the survivors.

Business bequests. If you are in business, either solo or with a partner, you will certainly want to think about whose name goes on the door when yours comes down. If it's a single ownership, do you think it best for the business to be liquidated, or should it be continued by your spouse and/or someone else? If the business is a partnership, if one partner dies, have provisions been made for the other to buy out his shares? Do you want to leave an interest in the business to your son, your wife, a faithful employee—or all of the above? If it's a single ownership and you have only one possible heir, you can pass it on simply enough with this provision:

> I hereby give my business and everything identified with it including accounts receivable, fixtures and all other properties of my business to my wife, Virginia. If my executors have to use part of the assets of the business to pay my debts and expenses, I then give to my wife, Virginia, whatever remains out of the assets of my business.

The Ethical Will. You don't have to have vast sums of money in order to leave something of value to your family or loved ones. What money you leave may soon be gone, but your parting words of wisdom can become a permanent family treasure to be recalled and fondly quoted by generations to come. In the Old Testament, Issac simply but beautifully blessed his sons before his death. Pope John XXIII's will left no material possessions, only five poignant pages of blessings and reiterations of his faith. Jack Kelly's will left millions in money and property and some sound advice on business and personal life as well.

> I want you all to understand that U.S. Government Bonds are the best investment even if the return is small . . . As the years gather, you will meet some pretty good salesmen who will try to sell you everything from stock in a copper or gold

mine to some patent that they will tell you will bring you millions, but remember, that for every dollar made that way, millions have been lost. I have been taken by this same gentry . . . In this document I can only give you things, but if I had the choice to give worldly goods or character, I would give you character. The reason I say that is with character you will get worldly goods because character is loyalty, honesty, ability, sportsmanship and, I hope, a sense of humor.

If I don't stop soon, this will will be as long as *Gone With the Wind*, so just remember, when I shove off for greener pastures or whatever it is on the other side of the curtain, that I do it unafraid and if you must know, a little curious.

STEP EIGHT:
DISINHERITING RELATIVES

This difficult maneuver requires a lawyer, but there are things you should know before discussing or considering it. Simply omitting someone from your will should automatically mean he or she will not receive part of your estate, right? Wrong. A spouse, child, parent, or, in the absence of these, even a distant relative may go to court, start a "will contest" and claim that the deceased person simply forgot to mention them, and successfully demand the state-prescribed portion of the estate. The only way to be sure a relative you dislike does not get to dine at Maxim's on you after you're gone is to clearly and specifically disinherit that person by name in your will. It isn't even necessary to give a token bequest—a dollar, an old Nixon bumper sticker, a paperback copy of *How To Be Your Own Best Friend*—but it is advisable to explain briefly *why* you have not left a bequest.

Benjamin Franklin willed his son his lands in Nova Scotia (then, of course, neither accessible nor very valuable), as well as "my books and papers which he has in his possession, and all debts standing against him on my account books . . ." The reason Franklin gave: "The part he acted against me in the late war, which is of public notoriety, will account for my leaving him no more of an estate he endeavored to deprive me of."

Some 200 years later, a U.S. businessman disinherited his sisters even more pungently. He wrote: "I leave nothing to my two sisters Hazel and Katherine as they revere Franklin D. Roosevelt, and the

110

taxes caused by him more than equaled their share." Not all omissions are vindictive. If you think your kids, even those over 18, aren't sophisticated or experienced enough to handle large sums wisely, and you feel the pursestrings will be safest in Mom's hands, you can simply add something like the following to your will: "I intentionally make no provision for my children Philip and Betty because I know their Mother will well provide for them."

But if your marriage proved more vinegar and gall than sweetness and light, you might want to attempt an outright disinheriting of your spouse this way:

> I make no provision for my wife (husband)___(name)___
> since (s)he has abandoned me and we have been living separate
> and apart since ___(approximate date)___. It is my wish that my
> said wife (husband) receive no part of my estate.

In the real world, "My spouse having left my bed and board and abandoned me, I leave her (him) nothing" is easier said than accomplished. It may, in fact, result in a bitter estate-wasting court battle for an elective share—the amount he or she may be entitled to receive by state statute if there is no will. Instead of disinheriting your wife, you may want to leave her the minimum mandated by your state, and tie up her elective share in trust for her life so she can only use the income, with the principal going to the children on her death. Let's say, for example, that in your state a wife's elective share (what she elects to take if she refuses what you have left her in your will—presumably a lesser amount, or nothing at all) is 1/3 of your estate (with the other 2/3 shared by your children according to statute). If your estate is $60,000, then her mandated elective share would be $20,000—which, if you have not been on the best of terms, it might grieve you deeply to see her receive. Depending on the size of her elective share, she is entitled to receive up to $10,000 in cash outright. However, you would have the right to write your will so that anything over that—in this case another $10,000—was placed in a trust, giving her only the income from that trust for life. Thus, she would receive perhaps 7 percent of the $10,000, or $700 a year income, but the principal would be preserved by the trust, to be divided among your children upon her death. But, take care; this can get as sticky as taffy in August, and a lawyer should be consulted.

Step Nine:
Controlling Use of Funds (Trusts)

If you are concerned that a profligate beneficiary, whom you nevertheless love, may waste in months the substance you earned in a lifetime, and you'd like to exercise some posthumous control, feel free to attach strings to your bequests. A wealthy Englishman who died without sons left each of his nephews a sizable annuity but stipulated:

> As (they) are fond of indulging themselves in bed in the morning, and as I wish them to prove to the satisfaction of my executors that they have got out of bed in the morning and either employed themselves in business or taken exercise in the open air, from five to eight o'clock every morning from the fifth of April to the tenth of October . . . this is to be done for seven years . . . to the satisfaction of my executors, who may excuse them in case of illness, but the task must be made up when they are well, and if they will not do this, they shall not receive any share of my property. Temperature makes the faculties clear, and exercise makes them rigorous.

You may not wish to inflict such conditions upon your heirs, but you may want to protect them from the temptations of sudden wealth by seeing to it that the principal of your estate is paid out to them over a period of years. This may be done by including a trust clause in your will. That, as the word implies, involves selecting some person or institution you trust implicitly, but—unless the individual is a close relative—it will probably involve payment of an annual trustee's fee. A sample trust clause:

> If my son, Randolph, survives me, I give $50,000.00 to my Trustee, in trust, for the following purposes:

> (a) My Trustee shall hold, manage, invest and reinvest the principal, and shall collect the income therefrom. So much of the net income as my Trustee shall deem proper shall be applied to the support, maintenance or education of my son during his minority, and any balance of such net income shall be accumulated during his minority to be paid to him when he attains 21 years of age. Thereafter, the entire net income shall be paid to my son during his life in semiannual installments.

(b) Upon the death of my son, the principal of the trust shall be paid *per stirpes* to his descendants; or, if there be none, *per stirpes* to my descendants then living.

But that's the simplest of samples. Creating a trust and getting the most out of it for your heirs becomes more complicated with each new tax reform bill. The technicalities thrive and grow: Must the trustee account for the proceeds of every transaction? Is the duration of the trust sufficient to satisfy statutory requirements on the time during which administration must be concluded? For tax purposes, do you want to create the trust on a "generation skipping" basis—so the value of the property will be fixed at the time you die, and its benefits will go to your child (or children) until he (or she, or they) die, and then to the grandchild (or grandchildren) and be taxable on the basis of its worth at the time of your death?

Clearly, this is no job for the do-it-yourselfer. Get yourself a good lawyer.

STEP TEN:
TYPING THE WILL

After selecting the will paragraphs that meet your needs, type them in double-space format. When you are finished, but before signing, copy the witness paragraph (attestation clause) as set forth at the end of the form will, on page 107, directly beneath the place provided for your signature. Then, because casebooks of the law are replete with cases where wills were "doctored," take these precautions:

- In typing the will avoid erasures that could later be considered suspicious—especially in numerals, amounts of money, or changing "or" to "and," or "and" to "or."
- Spell out amounts of money and percentages in both words and figures. For example: five thousand dollars ($5,000.00); forty percent (40%); twenty (20) shares of stock.
- All paragraphs should be numbered. Type neatly, with ample margins. Double-space, numbering each page at bottom center, and do not leave any long blank spaces where additional paragraphs could be fraudulently inserted.
- Make sure the signature does not start a new page. Some part of the body of the will should be on the signature page, even if

only one line, so that no fraudulent pages can be inserted between the prior page and your signature.

- Staple the completed will on top (upper left and right) before the signing and witnessing ceremony. Some of our loftier law offices use rivets and colored ribbon, but such elegant accouterments do more to enhance the fee than the will's legality. Make sure the pages are in the proper order before you staple them together, so there's no need to pluck them out and restaple. To be sure there's been no hanky-panky—no pages pulled out and others substituted—the surrogate's clerk will often hold the will up to the light to check for tell-tale staple holes.

No will should be signed until all pages are stapled and in good order. I remember witnessing one will some years ago, when the lawyer had the will's pages spread out on his desk, pulled out the bottom one, had his client sign it and didn't assemble and staple the will until the man had left. This is bad practice at best and opens the door to suspicion of fraud at worst.

STEP ELEVEN:
YOUR SPOUSE'S RECIPROCAL WILL

Some people say, "My wife doesn't need a will—everything is in my name." But if both of you were on the *Titanic* at the same time, and it was proven that she, having made it into a lifeboat that later swamped, survived you by minutes, she would die intestate. As a result, a brother-in-law you both despised could become guardian of your children and administrator of your estate.

That need not be so if you have reciprocal wills, or travel on separate planes. If you and your spouse agree on beneficiaries, guardians, executors, and alternates, doing reciprocal wills is a simple matter of a typewriter sex change.

Just photocopy the first will, cross out husband's name and insert the wife's (or vice versa), replace "he" with "she" and "his" with "hers," and then have it all retyped.

STEP TWELVE:
EXECUTING THE WILL

The act of signing a will, like the act of purchasing a cemetery plot, is a confession of mortality that none of us particularly enjoys making. Probably because of that, there's a lot of heavy-handed levity on such occasions. Executing the will properly is, however, serious business, for the way you sign your will is very important in determining whether it will in the end be adjudged a valid document. At least two witnesses (three in some states) must be present during the signing. They should be responsible adults, preferably people who know you and will be able to testify that you knew what you were doing at the time you made your will. They should, preferably, be not much older than you are, so that there's a good possibility they'll be around at the probating.

They don't have to be, however. Their signatures are presumed authentic unless contested. I've probated wills without any living witnesses—you get death certificates. In some jurisdictions, witnesses are required to appear in court to testify to the circumstances surrounding the signing of the will. Sometimes affidavits are sufficient. Avoid using as a witness someone who is either a beneficiary or the intimate of a beneficiary. This can raise suspicion about the possibility of coercion or "undue influence," and in some cases can cause the witness to lose his inheritance.

All witnesses must be present at the signing and must remain for the entire period. Each should witness the other's signing as well as yours. You must specifically tell them that you would like them to act as witnesses to your will. It is not necessary for them to read your will. Just show them the document and tell them it is your last will and testament. If you have ever had a prior will, tell them that when you sign this will you intend it to revoke and replace that prior will. Tell them that you prepared the will yourself and that it expresses all your wishes. But sign only the original. Don't make the mistake of signing copies as well. If you should make a new will at a future time and a forgotten signed copy of the old will is produced by a disgruntled beneficiary, a classic—and costly—battle of attorneys could ensue.

At this point, sign the will in the place provided. If the will is more than one page long, initial each page on the lower left-hand corner. Make sure that the will is dated correctly—the date of your signing. Now, ask the witnesses to sign their names and addresses under the witness clause, after first reading the clause silently or aloud. After they have signed, examine their signatures to make sure their names are legible. If not, ask them to print their names under their signatures. Your will is now official. Now what do you do with it?

STEP THIRTEEN:
PUT THE WILL IN A SAFE PLACE

From Nancy Drew to Agatha Christie, mystery novel fans have been entertained by variations on the Case of the Missing Will. But it's no fun for your family if the will that's missing is yours. So not only should your will be kept in a safe place but your named executor and a substitute should know where it is. If your will cannot be found, the surrogate will be forced to conclude that you died without one. Even if it is known that you previously made a will, if it cannot be found the presumption is that you destroyed it. In many states, you can file the original will in the probate court for safekeeping. It is a good idea to give a copy to your executor though. If you change your mind, you can simply file another, starting off with "I revoke my prior will."

Your bank safe deposit box seems a wise choice, but even that can create problems, unless the box is in your spouse's name so that he or she can get into the vault after your death. Vaults are sealed on death and it will be necessary for your representatives to obtain a court order to open it—in the presence of the state tax commissioner, who doesn't trust anyone.

I have always suggested to my clients that they leave their original will in my safe. This assures its availability without court order; if the attorney loses the will, the presumption of revocation does not follow, and a copy can be introduced to prove the existence of the will. But if you don't have an attorney, you might consider his and hers safety deposit boxes, with his will in her box and her will in his—allowing quick and easy access for the survivor.

STEP FOURTEEN:
LEAVE A COMPLETE LIST OF DOCUMENTS (AND THEIR WHEREABOUTS) WITH YOUR SPOUSE OR A TRUSTED RELATIVE

You could start from scratch, but the easy way to compile this list is by filling out a Documents Inventory similar to the one below:

Form No. 8
VALUABLE DOCUMENTS INVENTORY
AS OF:_____

NAME_____

ADDRESS_____

SOCIAL SECURITY #_____

DRIVER'S LICENSE #_____

BANK ACCOUNTS: I HAVE ACCOUNTS IN THE FOLLOWING BANKS:

_____

_____

_____

LIFE INSURANCE: A LIST OF MY LIFE INSURANCE POLICIES (INCLUDING EMPLOYER GROUP LIFE COVERAGE ALONG WITH NAME OF CO. POLICY NUMBERS AND TYPE) IS LOCATED AT:
_____

THE POLICIES ARE KEPT IN:_____

DISABILITY INSURANCE: I AM COVERED BY THE FOLLOWING BENEFIT PLANS:
_____

AND PERSONAL HEALTH INSURANCE ISSUED BY:
_____
(include policy numbers)

BIRTH CERTIFICATES FOR (LIST FAMILY MEMBERS)

_____ , _____

_____ , _____

_____ , _____

KEPT AT:_____
_____

INVESTMENTS: I OWN THE FOLLOWING SECURITIES:

$____ U.S. SAVINGS BONDS, HELD AT:_____
_____

$____ CORPORATE OR MUNICIPAL BONDS, HELD AT:
_____
_____ shares of _____
Stock_____
_____ shares of _____
Stock_____

STOCK CERTIFICATES ARE HELD AT:_____

MY INVESTMENT BROKER IS:_____

PHONE #_____

RECORD OF PURCHASE AND SALE IS KEPT AT:
_____

117

A SEPARATE LIST OF THESE INVESTMENTS IS ATTACHED WITH SERIAL NUMBERS OR CERTIFICATE NUMBERS.

REAL ESTATE:

LOCATION:_____

TITLE IN NAME(S) OF: _____

_____

THERE IS A MORTGAGE DUE, HELD BY:

_____

THE DEED, MORTGAGE, SURVEYS, TITLE INSURANCE POLICY, TAX RECEIPTS AND CONTRACTS ARE KEPT AT:

_____

OTHER REAL ESTATE I OWN OR HAVE AN INTEREST IN IS LOCATED AT:

_____

MARRIAGE CERTIFICATE KEPT AT:

_____

MILITARY RECORDS KEPT AT:_____

_____

SOCIAL SECURITY NUMBERS (LIST FAMILY MEMBERS)

_____,_____

_____,_____

KEPT AT _____

CREDIT CARDS (LIST COMPANY AND #)

_____,_____

_____,_____

_____,_____

INCOME TAX: COPIES OF INCOME TAX RETURNS, ALONG WITH ALL RECEIPTS, ARE KEPT AT:

_____

MY ACCOUNTANT IS: _____

PHONE # _____

THE KEY TO MY SAFETY DEPOSIT BOX IS IN:

_____

MY BOX IS RENTED FROM:

_____

AUTOMOBILE REGISTRATION NOS.:

_____YEAR:_____

MAKE:_____

LIST OF VALUABLE PERSONAL JEWELRY:

_____

_____

MY PROPERTY IS COVERED BY FIRE, THEFT OR LIABILITY INSURANCE ISSUED BY:_____

_____

POLICY #_____

118

PERSONAL OBLIGATIONS:
I OWE MONEY TO: _____
_____

THE FOLLOWING OWE
MONEY TO ME: _____
_____

WILL:
( ) I have executed a will.
Date of Will: _____
The original copy is kept at:
_____

MY ATTORNEY IS: _____

PHONE # _____

FUNERAL
ARRANGEMENTS:
I own a cemetery plot in
_____

THE DEED TO THE PLOT IS
KEPT AT:
_____

I HAVE PREPARED WRIT-
TEN INSTRUCTIONS RE-
GARDING FUNERAL AR-
RANGEMENTS, A COPY OF
WHICH IS KEPT AT:
_____

It is recommended you make several photocopies of this inventory: keep the original in your safety deposit box, one copy in a safe place at home and perhaps give a copy to your attorney, a trusted friend or advisor. Along with this list you can leave a letter with specific instructions relating to funeral, burial, or anything else that might occur before the reading of the will. You should also leave specific instructions if you wish to donate body organs for medical use.

II: Re-evaluating Your Will

A will made when you are 25 may not represent your feelings, wishes, or circumstances when you are 40, 50 or 60. So a will should be reviewed regularly. Whenever there is a significant change in your circumstances, it's re-evaluation time.

Step One:
Review Your Circumstances

Have there been any significant changes since your will was drawn? For example:
- in income or other assets?
- in family size or circumstances—new children, death, divorce, or separation?

119

- in how you feel about your bequests—is there someone you wish to add or delete?
- in where you live, if you've moved to another state? If your will is valid in the state where you drew it, it's probably OK, since each state gives full faith and credit to the laws of all the other states. However, an executor may not be acceptable if he lives in another state, unless he is a blood relative.
- changes in health or other status of beneficiaries?
- in federal or state tax laws? These may lead you to change some provisions of your will.

STEP TWO:
IF MINOR CHANGES ARE NEEDED, DRAW UP A CODICIL

A codicil is a written document that amends the will.

It refers to the will specifically. It must be prepared and executed with the same formalities, and in the manner of a will. All the requirements needed in a will—testator's signature, witnesses, and the rest—are also needed for drawing up a codicil. The changes you want to make in the original will must be made very clear so as not to create problems of interpretation later on. If the changes are substantial, it is better to prepare a new will in order to avoid problems later.

The following is a sample of a first codicil to a will:

Form No. 9
CODICIL

I, ——, now residing in ——, do hereby make, publish and declare this instrument to be the First Codicil to my Last Will and Testament, which bears the — day of —, 19-.

FIRST: I hereby delete Article — of my said Last Will and Testament and substitute, in lieu thereof, a new Article — as follows:

(insert new clause)

or

I hereby amend Article — of my said Last Will and Testament by adding, at the end thereof, additional paragraphs as follows:

(insert new clause)

120

or

I hereby add a new Article — to my said Last Will and Testament, as follows:

(insert new clause)

SECOND: In each and every respect, except as herein modified and except as it is inconsistent with this First Codicil, I hereby ratify, confirm and republish my said Last Will and Testament, which bears date the — day of —,19–.

IN WITNESS WHEREOF, I have hereunto set my hand and seal this —, in the year One Thousand Nine Hundred and —

——(L.S.)

SUBSCRIBED, SEALED, PUBLISHED AND DECLARED by the above-named Testator (your name here) as and to be his First Codicil to his Last Will and Testament, in the presence of each of us, all present at the same time, who at his request in his presence and in the presence of each other, have hereunto subscribed our names as attesting witnesses, the day and year last above written.

_____ residing at _____

_____ residing at _____

_____ residing at _____

Remember, the same formalities as the original will are required. The codicil should be kept with the original will and copies furnished to those who have copies of the will.

STEP THREE:
WRITE A NEW WILL IF CHANGES ARE TO BE EXTENSIVE

Recently, I was appointed guardian to several infants who are the great-grandchildren of a man who made a will in 1926, and in 1927 and 1928 made three codicils to the will. The second codicil completely changed the disposition of a trust that was for the benefit of his daughter for her life. A third codicil changed the executor, but then reaffirmed the will and first codicil without men-

121

tioning the second codicil. Fifty years later, upon the daughter's death, a long-drawn-out—and expensive—proceeding was required in order to determine the testator's intent. This could have been avoided if he had drawn a new will rather than three codicils that left things so confused.

While a codicil can be used for adding to a will and revoking a portion of a will, if you wish to revoke a legacy or reduce the sum of a bequest, it may be a good idea to draw up a new will. Codicils are presented with the will, and publicly revoking a legacy might prove embarrassing to the eliminated legatee and be an incentive to contest the codicil. Follow all the procedures outlined earlier in this chapter in making your new will.

CAVEATS

- A will may seem like a good place to get in the last word, but avoid the temptation. A libel suit against your estate can reduce it considerably.
- Get legal counsel if you need it.
- Be sure to follow all steps exactly; if the will is not valid you will die intestate.
- Be sure all language is clear and can't be interpreted in any other way.
- Be sure there is flexibility: give your executor enough authority so he doesn't have to get court permission every time he has to sell stock.

CHAPTER 8

How to Enjoy Probate (and Administer an Estate)

"The meek may inherit the earth, but you can be sure there'll be a lawyer there to handle probate." That line from a popular TV show mirrors the general national impression that the only thing as certain as death and taxes is the need to hire a lawyer to deal with the problems they create.

For many years, that's been all too true. It's been, "Grandpa's dead. Call the undertaker and the lawyer." But it need be true no more. With a road map to follow—and I'm about to draw that now—handling probate and administration of small-to-medium estates may be challenging but need not be overwhelming.

The client who is his own lawyer can save a substantial sum—in some states and situations as much as 5 percent or more of the estate's value. The lawyer's fee today is more often computed by the hour than by a percentage, but the larger the estate, the more hours its administration will entail. The expenses of the probate system were never more vividly summed up than by the Ohio judge who, after closing the docket on a particularly lucrative estate, sarcastically congratulated the lawyers upon the handsome fees they had pocketed and concluded drily, "The heirs should never be permitted to loot an estate."

The attorney's first task—and it's yours *pro se*—is to determine if there is, indeed, an estate that requires processing through the courts. It was in pursuit of this duty that I found myself one morning in the home of an elderly physician who had died earlier in the week. With his niece, who'd been named executrix of his estate, I went through the house from top to bottom. At the top, we made a most peculiar discovery: an attic crammed with a treasure trove of brand-new merchandise still in its original cartons. There must have been a dozen electric clocks, a half-dozen electric blankets, box after box of china, pots, transistor radios. When we found a shoebox full of canceled bankbooks, I understood.

The doctor had been a bank-gift junkie. Any time a New York

123

area savings bank announced free gifts for opening new accounts, he trotted to the bank, deposited $25 or $50, and happily hauled his dividend back to his attic squirrel-nest. Later, we discovered a counterpart shoebox in his desk, this one crammed with current bankbooks, and with a master chart identifying the dates on which each account could properly be closed, so that he could start a new gift account somewhere else.

To him it was a hobby. To me it was a headache. Later, in administering the estate, we had to fill out withdrawal slips for some 50 different banks and supply each with a death certificate and a court certificate of authority in order to withdraw the funds.

If the lawyer determines that a court proceeding is necessary (as it certainly was in the case of the Bankbook Junkie), his next job (again, yours if you are your own lawyer) is to have the will admitted to probate and an executor appointed, or if there is no will, an administrator. There are many important steps ahead: marshaling assets, paying debts, preparing and filing inheritance tax returns (an accountant can help here), distributing assets to heirs, and preparing a final accounting of everything that went on along the way. That sounds like quite an attaché caseful, and it is, but it's nothing a reasonably intelligent and resourceful person can't handle, one careful step at a time.

If there are no assets in the name of the deceased, or the assets—a home, for instance—are all jointly owned "with rights of survivorship," court proceedings may not be necessary. Such assets can usually be transferred easily to the survivor by merely paying any inheritance taxes that may be due.

We hear of cases where the heirs run to the bank while the body is still warm to clean out the vault or to use a power of attorney that had legally expired with the deceased to empty bank accounts. This is, however, strictly against the law, and in most states a crime. If there are assets in the deceased's name—bank accounts, art, jewelry—they can only be legally transferred to the heirs by a court-appointed representative of the estate.

Pro se probate is easier in some states than in others. A simplified Uniform Probate Act has been adopted by at least a dozen states, and in 1973 Wisconsin pioneered the next logical step: a do-it-yourself probate law that works so well that not one of the first 400 cases processed—by quite ordinary citizens—resulted in litigation. "No longer," said Governor Patrick Lucey, "is the citizen required, in effect, to pay a legal tax amounting to hundreds or

124

thousands of dollars for a service he wants to perform for himself.''

No matter what the state, in general the steps to follow are the same.

THE FIRST STEP:
DETERMINING IF THERE IS A WILL

The next-of-kin, attorney, or accountant should know if there's a will and where to find it. But some otherwise quite sensible people seem so afraid that making a will on Monday will cause a heart attack on Tuesday that they never get around to it. And others, like the late Howard Hughes, are so secretive about their affairs that when they die so many authentic wills turn up that the American dream of full employment is gloriously achieved for a small army of handwriting experts.

The most likely place to look for a will after a fruitless ransacking of old tin boxes and bureau drawers is in Grandpa's safe deposit box. If the vault is in the late Mr. Jones's name, it will probably be sealed by the bank (which regularly checks obituary notices) and a court order will be needed to open it. That's easier to get than it sounds: a simple matter of filling out a Probate (sometimes called Surrogate) Court application. Once the news is out, opening that vault is no longer a family matter. A gentleman from the state tax department will insist on being invited to make sure that when Grandpa Jones's worldly possessions are divided, a beneficent government's share is not overlooked.

The deposit box's contents should be carefully inventoried and then neatly tucked away once more, pending determination of who is entitled to what. If a will is found, the next step is to apply to have it admitted to probate—formally accepted as Grandpa Jones's last will and testament—and to have the "executor" named in it officially appointed. If there is no will, an "administrator" should be appointed. The nouns are different. Their duties are identical.

THE SECOND STEP:
PROBATING THE WILL

It is the responsibility of whoever is named as executor—in this preliminary proceeding known as "the proponent"—to deliver the

125

will to the Probate Court clerk. Don't delay. Many states require delivery within 30 days of death. Ask the court that: 1) the will be admitted to probate; and 2) he or she be appointed executor, or (the female of the species) executrix. This is accomplished by presenting a printed form petition obtainable either from the court or from a local legal stationer.

The petition requires information about the decedent (name, last address, date and place of death), about the proponent (name, address, relationship, age, citizenship), and about the will (date executed, names of witnesses, name, address, relationship and age of anyone named in the will as beneficiary, executor or trustee). Finally, the petition requires the same information for any relatives who would have been entitled to receive a portion of the estate if no will existed. An estimate of the value of the real and personal property involved will be needed, too, since filing fees are usually based on the size of the estate.

Each interested party (all potential heirs) must be notified of the pending probate proceeding, sometimes by process server, sometimes by mail, depending upon the requirements of that particular court. There's another way. The executor can arrange to have each sign a waiver and consent ("I waive service of notice and consent that the will be admitted to probate and that Sara Jones be named executrix").

In some states, living witnesses to the will must be located and asked to sign affidavits stating that the will was properly signed in their presence, that the testator acted of his own free will, and that they knew him to be of sound mind at the time. In some stickler jurisdictions, witnesses may be called before the clerk of the court to respond to these points. Some liberal states accept "self-proving wills," permitting witnesses to sign the affidavits at the same time they witness the will. If the witnesses are all dead, the will is not invalidated; it's simply accepted on the strength of its attestation clause alone.

If the will appears to be in order—all interested parties having been notified and there being no objections—the will should be admitted routinely to probate. The executor then signs an oath to faithfully carry out his duties and receives his "letters testamentary"—the authority to carry out Grandpa's will and wishes.

The will that makes one family member smile may make three others miserable, which is why will contests (I know that sounds like something network TV covers on the *Wide World of Sports*, but it's the correct legal term) brought by disinherited or disgruntled heirs are rare but not unknown events. Such proceedings are so technical that no one should file an objection without an attorney's help. By the same token, if you're acting *pro se* and objections are filed, there's no time like the present to pick up the phone and call in an attorney.

The Third Step:
If There Is No Will—Appointing An Administrator

If no will can be found, or if the executor named is dead or mentally or physically incapacitated, an application for "letters of administration" should be made by the next closest relative. If there was a will but no executor, the authority is called "letters of administration with the will annexed," and assets are distributed according to the laws of intestacy of the particular state. These laws vary in detail, but generally provide for the surviving spouse and children to share the estate—either one-half to the wife and one-half to the children, or one-third for the wife and the balance for the children. In some states, each heir receives an equal share. If there is neither wife nor child, the estate is divided among parents, brothers, sisters, and their children.

The petition for an administrator is similar to that for having the will admitted to probate, requiring much the same kind of "who's who" information. Again, all heirs entitled to share in the estate are entitled to notice. In a close-knit family, there would probably be quick agreement on a family member (or more than one) to serve as administrator or co-administrators. In all cases, the administrator must post a bond. This may be waived if there are neither infants as heirs nor estate creditors to be suitably protected.

The Fourth Step:
Marshaling the Assets

It's the executor's (or administrator's) duty to muster all the decedent's assets, pay all his debts owed and taxes due and distribute what's left among the heirs. If Grandpa Jones believed in staying liquid, all his assets are in bankbooks, and this chore is as easy as H.F.C.

It wasn't quite that simple, however, in a case I vividly remember. I had been retained to represent a woman who claimed she was the common-law wife and now widow of a man who had left no will, but had left behind the keys to three safe deposit boxes. Together with the public administrator of the City of New York, who had applied to be appointed administrator, we toured the three banks and had what proved to be a rather interesting day. In every box, we found stacks of greenbacks—well over $100,000 in each. Of course, federal, state and city governments all pounced on the money for taxes. But when they'd bitten off as much as they could legally chew, there was still a sizable inheritance remaining for the widow and her daughter. Later, she confided the source of the money. Her husband had been one of Manhattan's top "numbers" racketeers.

Cash-only inheritances are rare. Grandpa Jones is more likely to have owned a car, had an interest in a business, owned stocks and bonds, furniture, jewelry, and other you-can't-take-it-with-you valuables. If the estate goes to one person, all of this will be turned over intact, with nothing more radical occurring than a formal name change on stock certificates and bank accounts. But where several heirs inherit, valuables cannot so easily and equally be divided. A will may authorize the executor to divide the estate "in kind," in which case he can decide (after having an appraiser value each item) who gets what. Without such power, or in the absence of a court order or agreement among the heirs, the executor has only one recourse: to reduce all of the assets to cash and divide that among the heirs.

To put temptation behind him, all monies received by the executor must be deposited in a bank account opened in the name of the estate. As a fiduciary (someone trusted to handle funds or property for another), he is naturally forbidden to commingle the estate's assets with his personal funds. Of course, all bank accounts and stocks and bonds are in the name of Charles Jones. In order to transfer them to the estate, the bank or stock transfer agent will require a death certificate (obtained from the local health department), a copy of your grant of authority (letters testamentary or letters of administration) and, if the state has an inheritance or succession tax, a release or waiver of any tax claims—available as soon as the state has determined that its own financial stake has been properly protected.

The necessary tax waiver or consent can be obtained from the state department of taxation. Usually all that's required is to fill in a form listing the estate's assets and liabilities (more work for the

128

accountant if high finance is not your strongest suit) and an estimate of taxes due. Upon payment of the estimated tax, the waiver will be issued. In some states, if a bank account shows a balance of less than $2,000, the waiver requirement will itself be waived.

All assets that are not to be distributed in kind should be sold. As a fiduciary, your duty to the heirs is to get as much as possible for these items. If you want to avoid future problems, lawsuits, or just family recriminations ("We should have gotten more for that old silver—he practically gave it away"), it may be a good idea to have everything formally appraised.

The unpleasantness that can happen was demonstrated vividly recently when the children of the internationally famous artist Mark Rothko sued the three executors of their father's estate. The children charged and successfully proved that the executors disposed of the estate's 798 paintings at a value far below their actual worth, a flagrant breach of their fiduciary trust, since two of the three stood to benefit from this sale personally. The court dismissed the executors and awarded the children damages in excess of $9,000,000, later reduced by the return of some of the paintings to under $4,000,000.

All assets should be carefully inventoried, since the fiduciary eventually will have to account for every last possession. The executor usually has the power to sell real estate, but if there is no will or if there are infants involved (in legalese, even 17 years is an infant), a court order may be required. The appropriate court in your area can tell you its requirements and procedures.

Life insurance is usually payable to a named beneficiary. It's an asset of the estate only if it's payable to "the estate." The insurance broker or agent who was so helpful in selling Grandpa the policies should be equally gracious in assisting you to collect on them, providing you with necessary forms and helping you to complete them correctly. A copy of the death certificate is an absolute necessity, but unless there's a question as to the cause of death or who is entitled to the proceeds, insurance is usually paid with admirable speed and efficiency.

Proceeds of all life insurance policies owned by the deceased are included in the estate for purposes of computing federal estate taxes. Substantial savings are possible if, as estate planners often suggest, some or all policies are "owned" by the beneficiary—something any insurance agent can cheerfully explain in delicious detail.

THE FIFTH STEP:
PAYING DEBTS AND EXPENSES

Most states require newspaper publication of a notice to creditors announcing both the death and the time limits within which creditors may file claims. When and where the notice is to be published depends upon a particular state's statutes. A look at the legal notices in your local newspaper will help you write the prescribed copy. It's then the executor's job to pay any bills outstanding at the time of death—rent, utilities, doctor bills, etc.—plus several new ones: funeral expenses, administrative costs (filing fees, etc.) and the executor's commission. That last could be a substantial sum, depending on the amount of work or responsibility involved, and what the court will allow. It is usually paid when the estate is "wound up." If there are infant heirs, the court must approve the commission before it is paid. If you are both executor and heir, it's worth considering that if you take the commission, it will be taxed as earned income on your own tax return, whereas if you simply take it as part of your inheritance, you get the money tax free.

The decedent's earnings for the year until date of death must often be calculated—another job for the accountant—and all bills should be paid from the estate's checking account to assure an accurate and unimpeachable record.

THE SIXTH STEP:
PAYING TAXES

For large estates, computation of taxes may be the most difficult aspect of the fiduciary's job, which is why so many attorneys, myself included, turn it over to a C.P.A. (certified public accountant). I advise you to go and do likewise. The tax burden on small estates was substantially eased by the Tax Reform Act of 1976, while some of the tax-saving practices available to the wealthy ("loopholes" is the more familiar term) were restricted. Under the old law, a net estate of $60,000 (after deducting debts, funeral and administrative expenses) was exempt. In addition, a spouse was entitled to a deduction of up to one-half of the estate, assuming she received that much.

The new law provides for a gradually increasing tax credit that grants an equivalent exemption of $120,667 in 1977, up to $175,625 in 1981 and thereafter. In addition, the spouse's marital deduction is increased to $250,000 or one-half the estate, whichever is greater. This means that in 1977 a wife can inherit more than $370,000 from her husband without paying any federal estate taxes. This amount increases until 1981, when it will exceed $425,000.

State inheritance taxes vary from none at all to relatively substantial. Your accountant knows for sure. Consult him. *Limitation warning:* Federal estate taxes must be filed within nine months of death. Late filing draws penalties and interest charges.

THE SEVENTH STEP:
WINDING UP OR DISTRIBUTING THE ESTATE

All assets are inventoried, taxes are paid, and now it's time to distribute what's left. If it all goes to the widow, there's nothing to it. Just write a check and deposit it in her personal bank account. With the help of a broker, stocks and bonds can be transferred from the name of the estate to her individual name without any problems. She's probably already in possession of such physical assets as the home and its contents.

But the widow entitled to at least half an estate in many states may receive only a pittance for reasons her husband may have taken to the grave with him. In such a case, the widow should fall back on her "right of election," which means that no matter what the will says, she (or the husband if the situation is reversed) is entitled to the percentage which state law says she would have received as a spouse if there were no will. Filing for right of election should be done immediately after a will is probated. If there are any questions of fact, the court will decide them.

If there are infant heirs, their funds cannot be turned over to them directly but must be held subject to the direction and further orders of the court until the infants reach majority. If money is needed for a child's support during infancy, permission of the court will be required—unless the will grants the executor, as most sensibly do, broad powers to spend assets without court approval.

I recommend that my client executors or administrators obtain a receipt and release from each heir at the time any money or property is turned over. It's the best possible protection against future claims.

T 472—Release and Receipt to Executors, Administrators.
Individual or Corporation. 9-76

JULIUS BLUMBERG, INC., LAW BLANK PUBLISHERS
80 EXCHANGE PL. AT BROADWAY, N. Y. C. 10004

𝕶𝖓𝖔𝖜 𝖆𝖑𝖑 𝕸𝖊𝖓 𝖇𝖞 𝖙𝖍𝖊𝖘𝖊 𝕻𝖗𝖊𝖘𝖊𝖓𝖙𝖘,

THAT

of

hereby acknowledge(s) the receipt of the sum of

($) dollars

from

as executor(s) or administrator(s) of the estate of
        deceased
being in full payment and satisfaction for   *interest in the estate of said deceased, and in con-*
sideration of such payment I hereby, for myself and my heirs, executors and administrators, remise, release and
forever discharge the said executor(s) or administrator(s) and his heirs, executors and administrators, of and
from all claims and demands which I or my heirs, executors and administrators now have or hereafter may have
against said executor(s) or administrator(s) by reason of any acts or matters done or omitted to be done by
said executor(s) or administrator(s) in connection with said estate.

     If more than one person executes the within instrument, then words used in the singular shall be con-
sidered to include the plural, and wherever herein any particular gender is used, it shall be inclusive of the
masculine, feminine and neuter gender, where the text so requires.

Signed, sealed and delivered in the presence of

                               (L.S.)

                               (L.S.)

STATE OF NEW YORK, COUNTY OF   ss:
On the   day of   19 , before me
personally came

to me known to be the individual   described in and who executed
the foregoing instrument, and acknowledged that   executed
the same.

STATE OF NEW YORK, COUNTY OF   ss:
On the   day of   19 , before me
personally came
to me known, who, being by me duly sworn, did depose and say
that   he resides at No.

that   he is the   ;
of
the corporation described in and which executed the foregoing instrument; that   he knows the seal of said corporation; that the
seal affixed to said instrument is such corporate seal; that it was so
affixed by order of the board of directors of said corporation, and
that   he signed h   name thereto by like order.

For most estates, a formal court-approved accounting is not required. It becomes necessary where infants are heirs—to make certain they're not paid off in penny candy—or where adult beneficiaries have reason to be skeptical about the executor's conduct and insist upon a formal accounting before they'll sign a receipt and release. An informal accounting is no more than a statement setting forth all assets received, including principal and income, all debts and expenses paid, and the balance available for distribution.

The court-required formal accounting sets forth all this information in minute detail and may require appraisals to substantiate valuations. The court procedure is required, too, when there is some question about the size of the fiduciary's commissions or the attorney's fees. Often the court adjusts these downward in a final accounting proceeding. Of course, if you've gone *pro se* all the way, there'll be no attorney's fees to pay.

The probate process can easily take three to six months to accomplish. The details can be time-consuming, but when it's all over, there's the good feeling that comes from knowing that you've helped someone—often someone you loved very much—carry out his or her wishes in the only act we can perform from beyond the grave.

If you've done your job well, things will, in the long run, go as well as they did for the son of a man who feared that predatory associates would steal his substance before his beloved heir returned from his studies in another land. After much thought, he bequeathed his entire estate to a monastery, specifying that when his son returned, the monks must give him "whatever they should choose."

The monks, yielding to temptation, behaved less than righteously, keeping the old man's fortune for their order—after all, the roof needed fixing, a new bell to call them to vespers was a capital idea, and it wouldn't hurt to put some money by for emergencies—and drove the son off with a pittance. Wisely, he headed for the office of his father's lawyer, who welcomed him and proceeded to challenge the monks in court. His argument: the will specified that the son was to inherit that portion of the estate which the fathers should choose. "It is clear," he said, "what they have chosen by what they have retained for themselves. Let them give my client the share they have chosen, and he will be content." The court, impressed with the wisdom of the deceased, promptly ordered the estate returned to the son.

CHAPTER 9

Divorce I: Should I Do It Myself?

Being your own divorce lawyer isn't for everyone. For people who get lost in the potted palms at cocktail parties, or whose minds turn to cream of wheat under pressure, an attorney is as essential as a skydiver's parachute. To handle your own divorce, you have to be moderately intelligent, reasonably articulate, and very determined. And everything may not go as smooth as chocolate mousse, even for the brave in heart.

Consider the case of Stanley Gornish, a clean-cut young fund raiser for a Manhattan community service organization, who is intelligent, articulate *and* determined.

"I tried to keep my hands from shaking," says Stanley, describing his day in court as his own divorce lawyer. "I kept telling myself that I would do fine, that I'd handle myself well up there. That fell apart when I heard my name called and, straightening my tie, strode confidently toward the witness box. At the same moment, another man rose a few seats from me. When it turned out to be his name the clerk had called, not mine, I wanted to dig a hole under the bench and crawl inside."

Stanley worried all through his do-it-yourself divorce that, without benefit of counsel, something would come up that he couldn't handle. But nothing major did. And the comparative ease with which he won his divorce—and tens of thousands of lawyerless American men and women are winning theirs—would have astounded a nineteenth-century Englishman, for whom divorce required a special act of Parliament, or even twentieth-century Americans, who only a few short years ago had to scheme and conspire to "put asunder" the bonds of their matrimony.

Just such a divorce case was tried before a judge I know some twenty years ago, with adultery—at that time just about the only acceptable ground in New York and several other states—the wealthy husband-plaintiff's complaint. To make his case, the husband hired a gigolo to: 1) date his estranged wife; 2) slip a Mickey Finn into her drink; and 3) take the groggy woman to a motel and disrobe her. At his signal, a photographer entered and shot a series of staged X-rated bedroom scenes.

The frame-up might have worked if the wife's attorney hadn't asked some simple questions: "Doesn't it seem odd that my client didn't dive under the sheets or hurl a lamp at the photographer? Isn't it strange that she posed so passively and co-operatively for a series of sordid photographs that she must have known would destroy her marriage and her reputation? Isn't it surprising that she appears neither shocked, angered nor alarmed in any of these pictures but only numb?"

Persuaded that the wife looked glassy-eyed because she had in fact been drugged, the jury found against her husband.

Of such desperate schemes—often successful, sometimes backfiring like a Model T Ford—were divorces made only a few decades ago. Of course, if both parties agreed, there were other options: expensive "quickie" divorces in Nevada, Florida, and Mexico, for example. Mexican divorces were a matter of only a day, while in Florida and Nevada one merely established residence by renting a room, hanging a dress in the closet, then went home to wait out the 60- or 90-day completion of the legal fiction of residency requirement. They're still around. The Santo Domingo Special flies daily to the Dominican Republic for the one-day de luxe divorce. (I get letters regularly from a Dominican attorney who cheerfully arranges uncontested divorces for $400 in advance—which is, of course, on top of the referring attorney's fee. He's packaged things so neatly that his representative meets clients at the local airport and escorts them to the luxurious Hotel El Embajador, where they are offered a special discount.)

Marriage in the United States has always been easy. Pass a blood test, pay the $2.00, and find yourself a Marrying Sam. Divorce American style has been more like driving through a brick wall. More recently, however, it has become so common and socially acceptable that even the word *divorce* has been laundered. Legal papers in some states now read: "In the Matter of the Dissolution of the Marriage of . . ."

Like it or not, divorce has become a modern convenience as available as a self-cleaning oven, and if you know what steps to take, considerably less expensive.

The First Step:
Attempting Reconciliation

If there is one ironclad rule I urge on divorce clients, it's: "Don't make any irreversible decision until the dust has settled." The emotional storms that precede and follow a separation put common sense to flight. A woman may say (and I've heard this more than once), "Just get me out of this marriage. I hate him. I don't want anything from him." Six months later, she's two months behind on the mortgage and getting unfriendly phone calls from the bank, the car is about to be repossessed, baby-sitters, lunches, and a new working wardrobe are making her new job almost a nonprofit affair, and she realizes what a terrible mistake she has made—too late.

Divorce is not magic. After the final decree has been in hand for a while, all too many ex-spouses are shocked to discover that they are still miserable.

So the first step in a do-it-yourself divorce should be an all-out attempt at do-it-yourself reconciliation. One technique used successfully by marriage counselors is the trade-off list. Each partner lists his or her grievances. Then they sit down and negotiate. "You love your tennis racket more than you love me. I never see you except to wash your sweaty socks." "You're running wild with your charge accounts. You don't even have room in your closet for what you buy." "OK, I'll cut my spending in half if you'll cut your tennis time in half."

If things have gone too far for that, then invest in a couple of exploratory sessions with a marriage counselor. In the long run, it could be a lot cheaper than a divorce. Divorce without first attempting a reconciliation with a marriage counselor isn't much smarter than amputating a leg because of a bunion. I remember a furious husband who came into my office insisting, "There's no way this marriage can be saved." Two weeks later he was back with his wife. "Look, forget about the divorce—send me a bill for what you've done."

Certainly, when a couple have tried to reconcile—tried a marriage counselor, given their best efforts, but are unable to make it work—I don't think they should be forced to live together as husband and wife. But the lawyer's first obligation should be to make peace, not money. The real world often doesn't work that way, and

137

in fact, unintentionally and otherwise, my colleagues sometimes heighten conflict between spouses, making rapprochement or even a settlement agreement more rather than less difficult to achieve.

I remember a man who got into the hands of the kind of attorney the legal profession guardedly refers to as a "divorce bomber." The couple had been having differences for years; the wife finally demanded a separation. Again and again, the husband, who really loved his wife, begged her to reconcile. But in her head she was already on the freedom train. Finally he retained a divorce lawyer, and then his attitude grew teeth. The attorney advised him to stop sending her the mortgage payments and food money. He counseled him to take her car right out of the driveway, leaving her without wheels in the suburbs—a strategy aimed, as he put it, "at making her beg for a settlement on her hands and knees." At one point, earlier on, the wife had, in fact, had second thoughts and wanted to reconcile. But the atmosphere became so toxic that soon each spouse cheerfully hated the other, and an angry, recriminatory, and largely preventable divorce eventually took place.

It is, of course, to the attorney's financial advantage for the parties to divorce. But it's only fair to point out that I know many attorneys who go all the way to save a marriage if at all possible, and there are, I'm sure, many more like them. Picture, though, the scene in two opposing attorneys' offices. In order to reconstruct the situation that led to the present unpleasant impasse, I must ask my client for answers to questions that will inevitably resurrect the long series of acrimonious squabbles that put the marriage on the rocks in the first place. In another office, the other spouse is reliving the same pain, annoyance, pettiness, and hurt of almost forgotten events. Is it any wonder that by the time they've spilled their guts—and the legal document has been typed, signed, sworn, and served—that the flames of anger are crackling so high that reconciliation is well nigh impossible?

When New York State first liberalized its divorce laws, a provision was written in for a Reconciliation Bureau, with the requirement that the couple and their attorneys appear before a Conciliator before the divorce could be placed on the calendar. A nice idea quickly became a *pro forma* ritual. "Is there any possibility of a reconciliation between the parties?" "None whatsoever." "Case called for March 12th at 9:30 A.M."

Reconciliation attempts are, of course, not always for the right reasons. I remember a mother who asked to speak to one of my partners alone, after she and her daughter came to our office to initiate divorce proceedings against the daughter's husband. He had beaten her brutally on several occasions, but the mother told my partner, "We must do all we can to save the marriage." Why? As an anniversary gift, she had just finished spending $10,000 for furniture and wall-to-wall carpeting in her daughter's new apartment. Clearly, what she wanted to save was her "investment." He came as close to throwing her out of the office as legal etiquette permits, and I was proud of him. We never did get the case, but I learned later from the friend who referred the wife to us that the marriage limped along for another six months—until the husband beat her so savagely that she called the police to get him out of the house.

That woman has got to be better off single. But reconciliation should be explored thoroughly, even though "starting with a clean slate" and "getting it over with" are the things separated couples say they're most anxious to achieve. The fact is that divorce is not the clean break impatient husbands and wives take it to be. It's not the sinking of the ship. It's more like the oil spill that follows, and the cleanup goes on indefinitely.

THE SECOND STEP:
IF RECONCILIATION FAILS

If you've concluded that there's no turning back, the do-it-yourself road map to divorce starts with a question: "Is this the right road for me?"

Cost may well be a deciding factor. Divorce is most expensive for the middle class. The rich can afford it. (My firm's fee to a millionaire client several years ago was $18,000, partly because of the extensive negotiations needed to resolve questions of property settlement and support, partly because of the tax advice involved.) The poor—though often forced into long, unhappy delays because of under-staffing and under-budgeting problems of poverty law groups—can get it almost free. (At the Legal Aid Society of New York, in my first job out of law school, we handled divorces for as little as $30.) Thrown upon their own resources—usually stretched membrane-thin—and unable to put divorce on a BankAmericard (though some law firms, including mine, now accept it), the middle class has been stuck with legal fees which are the last straw, breaking many a plaintiff's back.

I recently negotiated a separation agreement for a husband. He had to pay my fee ($1,500), his wife's attorney's fee ($1,500), and another $750 to the other lawyer to guide the uncontested divorce through the court. Since he earns $35,000 a year, the one-time cost didn't wipe him out. But, though he knew he was paying for my professional expertise, that could have hardly softened the blow when he realized that I had probably spent no more than a dozen hours on the phone and in negotiations on his behalf.

The $350 uncontested divorce is still common in many areas, but the generally high cost makes do-it-yourself extremely attractive. A friend told me of a wife who came out of a separation badly. Their big home had a second mortgage on it, and she lost it. She hadn't had a penny from her husband in a year. But, when primed for her final appearance in court, she spoke to her attorney, he said flatly, "I get the last $500 before I go into court Monday, or we postpone." She was forced to borrow the money from her parents.

It's no wonder then that do-it-yourself separation and divorce kits selling for $75 to $125, using the form appropriate to the jurisdiction in which they're sold, have become so popular in the past year in a half-dozen states. In California, a recent study identified 12 percent of all divorces in the state as a product of do-it-yourself. And in New York, New Jersey, and several other states a company called Divorce Yourself, founded and staffed by nonlawyers, has opened a score of franchised offices and successfully defended itself in the courts against a state bar association charge of practicing law without a license. The bar sees a grim vision of self-help merchants of divorces, wills and bankruptcies, like H. & R. Block income tax storefronts on every corner, offering bread-and-butter legal services at cutthroat prices, and fears that the throats being cut will be those of attorneys. Divorce kits—complete with worksheets and follow-the-numbers instructions in layman's language—are said to be not much harder to follow than kits for making model airplanes. But state bar associations are not amused.

The childless couple are prime candidates for do-it-yourself divorce. Although it is possible to go that route when one or more children are involved, I can't advise it with any enthusiasm. It may make sense if no extensive property or estate is involved, again usually the case with young marrieds. If there are children involved, I believe the parties should be represented by attorneys to ensure that the children get what they are entitled to under the facts of the case and the law, at least until a separation agreement is signed. But let's say that two people, with or without children, have arrived at a separation agreement, have decided that there will be no alimony, and have divided their property, furniture, bank accounts, stocks, and so on. When the only thing left is to prepare the papers and to appear in court, there is no reason why they can't do-it-themselves—if they are intelligent, patient, and have a sense of humor and perspective.

If you don't use an attorney, there is a modest risk that in the future, if one party feels shafted, he or she may appeal to the court to set aside the original agreement because representation by counsel was absent. A court might conceivably be more liberal in setting aside the original settlement under such circumstances. This is, in fact, why separation agreements often include a notation that both parties were represented by independent counsel.

The man or woman of means has much to lose and clearly requires skilled counsel to handle settlement negotiations. But any husband and wife who can't agree on alimony or child support are in the kind of adversary position that demands cool-headed counsel to step in and advise them on breaking the impasse. If a divorce is contested, it's too emotional—and often too complicated—for the layperson to handle without professional help. Such a case may end in trial, and without a lawyer you may end up in trouble up to your eyeballs.

THE THIRD STEP:
EXPLORE GROUNDS AND PROCEDURES

You're a lot better off than the man who separated from his wife in 1951, but had to keep her under a detective's surveillance for five long expensive years to establish convincing grounds for divorce. His wife steadfastly testified that the coffee man whose truck was parked downstairs for one to three hours every morning on schooldays—and on weekend afternoons when the kids were off at the movies—was "just a friend of the family." But the court adjudged the coffee man's conduct too friendly and awarded the husband his divorce on the grounds of adultery.

We're spared that kind of dehumanizing ordeal these days by the widening use of "no-fault" grounds and the fact that the starch is rapidly soaking out of divorce proceedings. It doesn't take an Isaiah to prophesy that there will even be broader liberalization of grounds, residence requirements, and procedures in the years ahead.

Louisiana and Washington have already totally eliminated residency requirements. Other states have residency requirements varying from 60 days to two years. Half the states currently need to be assured of only three things: that the marriage is unsatisfactory, that there is no expectation that it will improve, and that both parties wish to terminate the arrangement. In nineteen additional states, such no-fault grounds are not recognized, but divorces are granted on evidence that the couple has been living apart for a specified period of time, usually six months to two years. In those states, finalizing the divorce may take longer than in no-fault states, but the procedures may be simpler. As of July 1976, in only three states—Illinois, Pennsylvania, and South Dakota—is it necessary to prove fault on the part of the defendant. Even where fault must be shown, if the proposed divorce is uncontested, the procedure is still easy, and an uncontested divorce can usually be obtained without the old embarrassment for either party of "pointing the finger of guilt."

In Texas, you plead irreconcilable differences, serve a summons and complaint on your spouse, and after 60 days you go back to court and are granted your divorce. In New York and most other states, you can get a divorce faster than the normally required one-year cooling-off separation period by alleging such grounds as cruel and inhuman treatment. But that route may be difficult, splotched with the acne of anger, embarrassment, and sometimes the fear of physical violence.

How do you discover the residency requirements and what grounds are acceptable in your state? If you have a friend who is a lawyer or even a legal secretary, that simplifies matters. The nearest Legal Aid Society can surely tell you that much, whether you fit their low-income financial parameters or not. And where there's a courthouse, there is a law library—usually with a librarian or clerk to staff it and answer reasonable questions; as a taxpayer, you should be entitled to the courtesy of its use. Even your local public library will probably have books on divorce law. Since the do-it-yourself road is increasingly being traveled, you're hardly likely to be the first person ever to ask your questions.

It's best that you should ferret out the answers you need, because they differ from one state to another—in grounds for divorce, residency requirements, and special conciliation attempts, among other things. Despite the fact that divorce is a national problem, there is, convenient though it might be, no national divorce law.

CHAPTER 10

Divorce II: The Separation

As a truce separates warring nations, so legal separation parts warring spouses. And as international law demands the signing of a detailed, point-by-point armistice, so family law favors the preparation of a separation agreement.

That may not be the jolliest possible analogy, but as any lawyer who handles divorces will testify, it's reasonably apt. About the only missing elements in some "breaking" homes are tank battles and aerial dogfights. Such conflicts frequently lead to an informal separation, the kind we used to see in old movies, when she went home in tears to mother, or he packed up and moved to the club.

Life is, unfortunately, not a Late Late Show movie, with a guaranteed "they-lived-happily-ever-after" ending. So if the informal separation continues for some time, and absence only makes the heart grow angrier, then the stage is set for the first statutory move toward divorce—not just living apart, but "living apart pursuant to a separation agreement."

If the spouses come to actual blows or if furious scenes occur that could do lasting psychological harm to the children, and an agreement cannot be reached, then a third category of separation may be called for. Either party could seek a separation "pursuant to a court order."

Many separations are amicable. That was the case with Stanley Gornish, whom we mentioned early in the previous chapter and whose detailed story we'll tell to illustrate the do-it-yourself divorce process in the next chapter. Stanley and his wife had wisely seen a marriage counselor before they separated, and that helped to vent the pressure cooker of anger that almost inevitably builds up steam in a rupturing marriage. "As a result," explains Stanley, "we had good communications and genuinely cared for each other. We wanted to separate, but wanted to maintain a civil relationship afterward. In fact, that's one reason we decided to handle the divorce ourselves. We felt that if we went to two separate attorneys—one for each, as many bar associations require—an adversary relationship might have been created where none existed. We thought, why not make an agreement and work it out ourselves?"

And, amicably, so they did. "There was," continues Stanley, "nothing complicated in our legal relationship. We had no extensive property or estate, no children to worry about. The only thing we argued over was the cat. We both wanted it. So I said, OK, give me the cat and you can have the next two choices. So she took the color TV set and some furniture, and I got the cat."

A separation agreement, whether worked out at no cost in a sensible give-and-take atmosphere, or hammered out in bitter negotiations with the help of hired guns—adversary attorneys—outlines the obligations and duties of both parties. It divides property, provides for child custody and visitation rights, and reaches agreement on alimony and support payments. If, because of religious beliefs, the parties do not want a divorce, the separation agreement simply formalizes the terms of their understanding. In an occasional case, it may even be the instrument of reconciliation.

When a separated couple actually begins to live the blueprint for tomorrow—when recognition dawns on both sides that two really can live a lot cheaper than one, when he is drowning in a sea of unpaid bills and she has repaired her pantyhose so many times that there's more clear nail polish in them than nylon yarn, when it's clear that there's as much loneliness as lust out there in the world of the swinging singles, when John realizes that Mary's annoying little habits aren't worth trading for Sally's or Irene's, when, in short, the Great Leap into Reality breaks a leg—some couples do get back together again.

In states where separation for a prescribed time period is one of the grounds for divorce, the signing and filing of a separation agreement with the court officially establishes the beginning of the required period.

THE FIRST STEP:
NEGOTIATING THE SEPARATION AGREEMENT

You'll get advice from all quarters. When it's moderate and calm, consider it with respect. When it's intemperate and impassioned ("Don't let that sonavabitch off easy!" "After what she did to you, don't let her have a red cent!" "Take out a Swiss bank account—that'll fix the bitch!''), politely listen and politely ignore it.

Be reasonable. Compromise. Don't try to cripple the other party. I've seen too many wives who, trying to wring every possible present and future dollar out of their estranged husbands, won the short-term victory on paper. They lost it when the embittered husband felt justified in resisting, reneging, or even running away to escape what he considered an unjust separation settlement. One doctor client of mine did just that, closing his flourishing Long Island practice to relocate with his new wife in Texas, where men are men, and alimony is tougher to collect than a rattlesnake in a Dixie cup.

How can you reach that elusive "amicable agreement"? Well, let's consider the major things you have to agree amicably upon, and how the courts generally act in ordering a separation agreement if the parties fail to agree.

THE SECOND STEP:
CONSIDER WHAT THE JUDGE MAY DECIDE

About children: Until recently, our courts generally granted custody of the children to the wife, unless she was shown to be incapable of caring for them. The husband was given liberal visitation rights, unless the wife offered overriding evidence that he should be barred from seeing them—because of chronic alcoholism or a serious and continuing criminal record, for example.

But the Women's Movement has turned the kitchen tables, and today more and more children—nearly one million by 1974, and the numbers are climbing sharply—live with the male parent.

About the home: If there are children, whichever parent gains custody usually retains custody of the home as well, with the provision that when it is sold, the proceeds are to be shared. There is often a proviso that when the children reach majority, the house *must* be sold.

Alimony and support: This is determined by the wife's needs and the husband's ability to pay. If the wife is self-supporting, or wealthy, she may not only not receive alimony, but even be required to pay it—as in *Chetham* v. *Chetham*, when a wealthy Long Island socialite, who had cut off her husband's alimony, was ordered to resume her $125 weekly payments to him and to pay him arrears for the past 21 months. If the wife is neither wealthy nor

145

self-supporting, the court usually grants alimony. But where alimony used to be until remarriage or death of either party, some courts now lean toward awarding alimony for a limited period only, within which time the wife is expected to become self-supporting.

In determining the amount of alimony a husband should pay, the court considers his present earnings and future earning potential. It's hard to predict how much alimony and support a court will grant in a contested action. What the spouse earns, his assets and hers, the social status of the parties and the standard of living to which they've become accustomed, the amount of child support and the wife's independent earnings will all be weighed on the court's subjective scales of justice in determining the amount of alimony. With so many factors to consider, it's not surprising that decisions fluctuate wildly between 20 and 50 percent of the husband's income.

If separation and divorce are based upon the wife's misconduct, she may forfeit alimony. In a recent case, the husband and wife charged one another with "cruel and inhuman treatment." Neither denied the allegations—a mistake on her part—and a dual divorce was granted. The court awarded the wife $100 weekly alimony. But on appeal the husband won a reversal of the alimony award, with the court declaring that since the wife had not denied committing acts sufficient to warrant a divorce, she was not entitled to alimony.

Third Step:
Agreeing To Disagree Agreeably

The course of true love seldom runs smooth, but it's even bumpier riding in the opposite direction. The husband and wife who can't stand the sight of one another, who snarl rather than speak, may as well let the court arbitrarily impose a separation decree. But if relations are no worse than cool and strained, with no attorneys to complicate matters in the process of proving their worth, attempting to reach agreement on your own is certainly worth trying. That may require more good will on the part of the spouses than frequently exists. But success with only moderate trauma is possible, even when ill will predominates, so long as both parties recognize that the decent burial of their marriage justifies their temporary co-operation.

146

A meeting on pleasant neutral territory might provide the right ambience—over dinner at a good restaurant, for example, with a bottle of wine to warm the cockles of your angry heart. Bring a peace offering: a tie, flowers, a box of candy. A trusted mutual friend—someone who's managed to maintain warm relations with both of you despite the break—might be a valuable arbiter to invite along. If you'd prefer to meet at the old homestead or apartment, which may feel more comfortable, do it when the kids are already in bed, so there'll be no distractions. I'd put it second-best to the restaurant, though. First, "home" may be haunted by too many ghosts of old arguments. Second, in a public place, you're both more likely to control tempers and restrain voices.

Come prepared. Each bring a list of proposals—the more realistic and reasonable the better—carefully thought out and perhaps entered on a pad by your bedside at night over a period of a week or so. Don't try to solve all the differences in one session. Be prepared to meet again, two or three more times if need be. And start with the little things, those least likely to be disputed. A quick failure may poison the negotiations: a few small successes will catalyze them.

Division of personal property can be surprisingly tricky sometimes, and, incidentally, this is one area that I've found judges want no part of. I've seen situations that started off as if agreement would be easy to reach, degenerate into a shouting match over who gets the bird cage. A former law partner of mine shrewdly bridged such a gap when, after the prickly problems of alimony and support had been fairly easily resolved, negotiations broke down over who should own which books on their paperback library shelves. The attorney took a list of the disputed titles, adjourned the meeting, and came on like Santa Claus next day with a big sack full of duplicate paperbacks. Rather than have negotiations end in an impasse and take the matter to court, my partner had simply sent his secretary out shopping.

A sensible way to avoid disagreement even before that sticking point was devised by the couple who sat down to what they called a "silent auction." After easily dividing up personal property coveted by only one spouse, they proceeded to write down bids on items that both wanted. The high bidder took the item, the low bidder took credit for the cash the other had bid. In the end, only a few dollars passed hands, but everyone went away happy.

THE FOURTH STEP:
UNCLE SAM LOOKING OVER YOUR SHOULDER

There aren't many happy moments in the months leading to a divorce, but one that usually lights up the husband's face is the information that, in one respect at least, paying alimony may be cheaper than living with his wife. The reason: Alimony is completely tax-deductible—a kind of business loss, I suppose, in the government's topsy-turvy view. So, where the $5,000 it might have cost him to keep his wife in the style to which she was accustomed would have been pure expense during the marriage, if he is in a 30 percent bracket, the government will, in effect, contribute $1,500 toward her alimony.

Of course, the I.R.S. will recapture some of that by taxing it as income to the estranged wife, and the theory behind the original deduction is really that it avoids double taxation. Since money paid in child support is *not* deductible, some attorneys recommend that the husband pay as much as he can of what he and his wife agree on in alimony, and as little as possible in child support. The problem with this is that when the kids reach majority, his child support will end, but if his wife doesn't remarry, he will still be paying her the same old high alimony. If she does remarry—terminating alimony—the kids could be hurt, if she is not getting enough to support them.

From the wife's point of view, if the children are young and she expects to hear wedding bells again in the near future, she should aim for more child support and less alimony. If the children are older and she has no plans for remarriage, it may be to her advantage to seek more alimony and less child support. One point to remember: The parent paying more than one-half of a child's support is entitled to a tax exemption.

An arrangement that makes a lot of sense would seem to be a flexible one, shaped so that when alimony falls to zero, child support rises.

THE FIFTH STEP:
PREPARING THE SEPARATION AGREEMENT

This is a matter often handled by the attorney's secretary or a specially trained paralegal assistant—simply typing up a fresh copy of a form separation agreement. No one agreement covers all situations, but forms with more variations than a Haydn quartet are available in your local law library. Your use of the photocopying machine will correspond to an attorney's direction to his paralegal to "Use articles 1 to 4 and 7 to 9, and fill in these names and dates at the top." If it's a large prosperous office, utilizing the latest time-and-motion-saving techniques, he or she won't even type it; rather they'll punch instructions into the big IBM automatic typewriter, and stand back while the robot prepares the separation agreement.

The sample agreement that follows may make your trip to the library unnecessary. This particular couple has two young children, and they've agreed upon division of property, alimony, and support, as well as the wife's continued residence in their jointly owned home until remarriage or the children's coming of age. When she vacates, the house will be sold and the proceeds divided equally between them. If the couple were childless, the agreement would be virtually identical, except that clauses 6 and 8, referring to the children, would be omitted:

Form No. 11
SAMPLE SEPARATION AGREEMENT

AGREEMENT made February 15, 1977, between JOHN DOE, hereinafter referred to as Husband, and MARY DOE, hereinafter referred to as Wife.

WHEREAS the parties were married on June 11, 1967, and there has been issue of their marriage, to wit, JANE DOE, born on December 6, 1969, and DAVID DOE, born March 1, 1972

WHEREAS in consequence of disputes and unhappy differences the parties have separated, and are now and for some time past have been living apart from each other, and since their separation have agreed to live separately and apart during the rest of their lives and

WHEREAS the parties desire to settle their mutual rights and duties, including the settlement of their property rights, the custody, support, and education of their children, the support and maintenance of the Wife, and other rights and obligations growing out of the marriage relation:

It is therefore agreed:

1. *Separation and no interference.* It shall be lawful for each party at all times hereafter to live separate and apart from the other

party at such places as he or she may from time to time choose or deem fit. Each party shall be free from interference, authority, and control, direct or indirect, by the other, as fully as if he or she were single and unmarried. Neither shall molest the other, or compel or endeavor to compel the other to cohabit or dwell with him or her.

2. *Indemnity for debts.* Each party represents and warrants to the other that they have not incurred any debts or made any contracts and will not incur any such debts or make any such contracts for which the other or their estate may be liable.

[This means that one spouse has not gone out and bought a new living room suite on their joint Bank Americard, which will come due for the other to pay after the signing of the agreement.]

3. *Mutual release.* Subject to the provisions of this agreement, the parties mutually release each other from any and all claims, rights, and demands, in law or in equity, which either party ever had or now has against the other, except any or all causes of action for divorce.

[This means that neither party will make a claim against the other for anything other than a violation of the agreement. This does not, however, prohibit the spouse with custody of the children from later petitioning for increased child support, since children are wards of the court.]

4. *Division of personal property.* The parties have divided between them, to their mutual satisfaction, the personal effects, household furniture and furnishings, and all other articles of personal property which have heretofore been used by them in common, and neither party will make any claim to any such items which are now in the possession or under the control of the other.

[Sometimes the agreement attaches schedules or lists of personal property, designating the items that go to each spouse. An easy way to do this is to provide one schedule—the husband's, for example—and say that all other property in the house belongs to the wife.]

5. *Real Property.* The parties presently own, as tenants by the entirety, the marital abode commonly known as
(address)

150

The Wife is hereby given the right of exclusive use and occupancy thereof until the earliest happening of one of the following events:

(i) her election to vacate; (ii) her remarriage; (iii) the emancipation of the children of the parties.

During the period of such occupancy by the Wife, the Wife will pay all carrying charges, taxes, and insurance thereon and, in addition, will make all reasonable repairs thereto.

Upon the termination of the Wife's occupancy of the abode, the parties shall together cooperate in their joint efforts to effect a sale of the marital abode upon the best available terms. In the event that they are unable to agree with respect to a minimum gross sales price (or upset price) therefor, they shall be bound by the appraisal of a realtor designated for such purpose by the President of the Local Real Estate Board, whose fee shall be equally shared by the parties. The net proceeds from the sale shall be equally divided between Husband and Wife.

[This is, of course, only one of many methods of handling jointly owned real property. I've seen cases where the property is sold immediately and proceeds divided, and others where one spouse gives—or sells—his or her interest to the other. I was involved in one case in which the husband kept their mansion and purchased a new house for his wife.]

6. *Custody of the children.* The Wife shall have the custody of the children who shall reside with the Wife, subject to the provisions of this paragraph. During holiday and vacation periods the children may visit the Husband at such times and for such periods of time as the Wife and the Husband shall mutually agree upon, but in any event the Husband shall, at his option, have the custody of the children as follows: (a) for one weekend, consisting of Saturday and Sunday, in each calendar month; (b) during the summer school holidays for a continuous period of one month; and (c) during each of the Christmas and Easter school holidays for a period of five days. The Husband shall exercise his option by giving the Wife at least seven days' notice in advance of his intention to do so. The Husband's partial custody shall be optional with him, and his failure to exercise such option on any occasion, or for whatever reason, shall not be construed as a waiver of his rights of partial custody as herein provided. Notwithstanding the foregoing, either party shall have the right to visit the children at any reasonable time.

All questions pertaining to the education, health, summer activities, and welfare of the children, shall be decided by the Husband and Wife jointly, and each shall consult with the other as often as it may be necessary regarding all such matters. Neither shall do anything which may estrange the children from the other or hamper the natural development of the love for both parties. In the event of a child's illness, the first party to learn of such illness will notify the other immediately. Each of the parties shall keep the other informed at all times of the whereabouts of the children, and neither party shall take them beyond the boundaries of the United States without the written consent of the other party.

[There is nothing sacred about this particular set of child custody terms. Though fairly typical, they are all negotiable.]

7. *Support of Wife.* The Husband shall pay to the Wife, for her support and maintenance, the sum of $5,000 a year, in equal monthly installments, the first installment to be paid on the date of the execution of this agreement. The liability of the Husband for the payments set forth in this paragraph shall cease upon the happening of whichever of the following events shall first occur: (a) the death of the Husband; (b) the remarriage of the Wife; (c) the death of the Wife.

8. *Support, maintenance, and education of the children.* The Husband shall pay to the Wife, for the support and maintenance of each child, the sum of $2,500 a year, in equal monthly installments, the first installment to be paid on the date of the execution of this agreement. The Husband shall also pay all charges reasonably and necessarily incurred on behalf of the children for medical and dental treatments, and for hospitalization, nursing, and surgical expenses. These payments shall be made directly by the Husband or upon the presentation to him of bills approved by the Wife. The Husband shall also pay expenses incurred for the college education of the children, such expenses to include only tuition fees, cost of necessary books, laboratory fees, and student assessments. The liability of the Husband for all the payments set forth in this paragraph shall cease upon the happening of whichever of the following events shall first occur: (a) the death of the Husband; (b) the death of the Wife; (c) as each child attains the age of 21 years; or (d) the marriage of the child.

[The father who cares about his children may also want to provide life insurance to make sure they are taken care of in the event of his unexpected death. I always try to add an insurance clause on life and hospitalization.]

9. *Waivers of claims against estates.* Each party hereby waives and relinquishes any and all rights he or she may now have or hereafter acquire, under the present or future laws of any jurisdiction, to share in the property or the estate of the other as a result of the marital relationship.

[If this clause is omitted, even a separated spouse may have the right to claim a share of the other's estate upon death.]

10. *Subsequent divorce.* In the event that a final decree of divorce shall be entered in any action between the parties, either in this State or in any other jurisdiction, this agreement shall be offered to the court for its approval, and if acceptable to the court shall be incorporated by reference in the decree that may be granted therein. Notwithstanding such incorporation, this agreement shall not be merged in the decree, but shall survive the same and shall be binding and conclusive on the parties for all time, both parties intending to be legally bound thereby.

11. *Additional instruments.* Each of the parties shall from time to time, at the request of the other, execute, acknowledge, and deliver to the other party any and all further instruments that may be reasonably required to give full force and effect to the provisions of this agreement.

[Example: the transfer of an automobile ownership, an insurance policy, or title to the house when sold.]

12. *Entire agreement.* This is the agreement between the parties, and any amendment must be in writing and signed by the parties.

13. *Situs.* This agreement shall be construed and governed in accordance with the laws of the State of_____.

14. *Partial invalidity.* If any provision of this agreement is held to be invalid or unenforceable, all other provisions shall nevertheless continue in full force and effect.

15. *Address of parties.* Each party shall at all times keep the other informed of his or her place of residence and shall promptly notify the other of any change, giving the address of the new place of residence.

16. *Binding effect.* Except as otherwise stated herein, all the provisions of this agreement shall be binding upon the respective heirs, next of kin, executors, and administrators of the parties.

IN WITNESS WHEREOF, the parties have signed, sealed, and acknowledged this agreement in four counterparts, each of which shall constitute an original.

—————————————(L.S.)

John Doe

—————————————(L.S.)

Mary Doe

STATE OF——)
COUNTY OF——) ss.:

On the — day of —,197– before me personally appeared JOHN DOE, to me known and known to me to be the individual who executed the foregoing.

_____

Notary Public

STATE OF ——)
COUNTY OF ——)ss.:

On the — day of —,197– before me personally appeared MARY DOE, to me known and known to me to be the individual who executed the foregoing.

_____

Notary Public

THE SIXTH STEP:
GOING YOUR OWN WAY

Once the agreement is signed—in the presence of a notary public, if you plan to file it with the court—you are legally separated and free to go your own way. As stated in the agreement, "Each party shall be free from interference, authority, and control, direct or indirect, by the other, as fully as if he or she were single and unmarried." This means just what it says. You can go where you want, do what you want, sleep with whomever you want. Your love life will have no substantive effect on the separation agreement, the alimony, or the up-and-coming divorce. However, it could prove embarrassing.

The signing of a separation agreement does not abrogate your marriage vows, and so committing adultery could give a vindictive spouse additional grounds for divorce. There have been cases where courts have refused to award alimony to an adulterous wife in the divorce decree, even if the act occurred after the signing of a separation agreement with a "free from interference" clause in it. Even if this unlikely event should occur, the wife is not out in the cold. She is still free to sue for the alimony specified in her separation agreement, which is a binding contract.

THE SEVENTH STEP:
DON'T FORGET TO FILE!

Important reminder: If you intend to use the separation agreement as grounds for divorce, in many states it's required that you file or record a signed duplicate—not a photocopy—with the local county clerk or appropriate court. (A preliminary phone call or two should save you a bureaucratic runaround.) Filing or recording the agreement for a small fee formally establishes the beginning of the required statutory pre-divorce period. And, if the worst comes to the best, and you and your spouse should happily reconcile, it's never too late to withdraw it.

CHAPTER 11

Divorce III: The End of the Line

You're legally separated, and there's only one thing on your mind: for better or for worse, getting your divorce over and done with. If you plan to use the separation agreement as grounds for divorce, you'll have to wait until the state-prescribed time period has passed. If you're going to use another ground—cruel and inhuman treatment, incompatibility, or a "no-fault" ground such as personality conflict or irremedial breakdown of marriage—there is no need to wait to file for your divorce.

THE FIRST STEP:
SUMMONS AND COMPLAINT

The process goes best if the days of wine and roses have not turned completely to vinegar and thorns—when if there is no longer love, at least there is residual fondness or respect. That was the case with Stanley Gornish and wife. And that's one reason their do-it-yourself-divorce went so smoothly.

We left Stanley in court, nervously waiting to be called before the judge. Now let's backtrack, so you can see how he got there, on a route that differs slightly from state to state (and sometimes minutely in jurisdictions within a state) but is essentially the one you'll need if, indeed, you'd like to follow Stanley's progress toward self-help divorce.

Picking his way through the legal paperwork jungle—learning which form to use and how to fill it out—was Stanley's first problem, as it will be yours.

In many states there are form books at the courthouse, sometimes called Forms of Pleading, which should be available for you to examine upon request. These books fully outline the contents of all required court papers. Make notes. Better yet, try to have them photostated. Any printed forms you need should be available from the local legal stationer, who is usually conveniently located near the courthouse. Terms may differ. In some states, the word "defendant" may read "respondent." "Complaint" may read "Petition." As long as you are polite, a court clerk is likely to be equally so in serving as your friendly neighborhood interpreter.

If you decide to go the divorce kit route, bear in mind that some are better than others. The instruction portfolio put out by Divorce Yourself, has, according to its designers, been experience-modified and simplified several times. It should be reasonably easy to follow.

Stanley had done some reading on divorce procedures and had talked briefly to a lawyer acquaintance. He knew that the way to officially get the action under way was to serve a summons and complaint on his wife. He purchased the summons form from a legal stationer and, with the help of a book on divorce in New York State, typed the complaint. He knew he had the option of having the papers served by a professional process server for a $15 to $50 fee or by a friend who would ask nothing at all. Recalls Stanley: "The required third party I chose was someone we both knew who could identify my wife. For purely legal reasons, I stapled her photograph to the summons, so that later, in court, I could support my claim that the proper person had been served. I waited on the corner while he served her, and they went into a bank to get the affidavit of service notarized and to have her acceptance witnessed. Then we all sat down together and enjoyed a pleasant lunch.

"While we waited for the waiter, I explained that she had 30 days to answer, after which I could ask that the matter be placed on the calendar for the actual divorce hearing. Since she didn't plan to contest the action, there was no need for her either to answer or to appear in court, and, in fact, she did neither."

The summons that Stanley served upon his wife was a printed form that may vary moderately from jurisdiction to jurisdiction, but looks very much like this sample. (Note that where an attorney's name is called for, the hypothetical plaintiff in this case, Mary Doe, has written the Latin phrase *pro se*, which means she is appearing "for herself.")

The Complaint served against John Doe with the Summons might look like the sample below in an action based on separation. In this case, Mrs. Doe has two children, legally described as "issue" in the ninth paragraph. Almost the same complaint would ap-

158

ply—omitting only that paragraph and the italicized lines in the final paragraph—if the family Doe happened to be childless. Similar complaints—for abandonment and cruelty—may be found at the end of this chapter.

Form No. 12

T 158—Summons with notice: action for a divorce 7-73.

COPYRIGHT 1973 BY JULIUS BLUMBERG, INC., LAW BLANK PUBLISHERS
80 EXCHANGE PL. AT BROADWAY, N.Y.C. 10004

Supreme Court of the State of New York
County of NEW YORK

MARY DOE

Plaintiff

against

JOHN DOE

Defendant

Index No.
Plaintiff designates
NEW YORK
County as the place of trial
The basis of the venue is
PLAINTIFF'S RESIDENCE
Summons with Notice
Plaintiff resides at
305 CENTRAL PARK W.
County of NEW YORK

ACTION FOR A DIVORCE

To the above named Defendant
    You are hereby summoned *to serve a notice of appearance, on the Plaintiff's Attorney(s) within 20 days after the service of this summons, exclusive of the day of service (or within 30 days after the service is complete if this summons is not personally delivered to you within the State of New York); and in case of your failure to appear, judgment will be taken against you by default for the relief demanded in the notice set forth below.*

Dated, MAY 1, 1978

MARY DOE, PRO SE
~~Attorney(s) for Plaintiff~~
Office and Post Office Address
305 CENTRAL PARK W.
NEW YORK, NY

NOTICE: *The object of this action is to obtain a judgment of divorce dissolving the marriage between the parties*

The relief sought is,
    A judgment of absolute divorce in favor of the plaintiff dissolving forever the bonds of matrimony between the parties in this action

159

SAMPLE COMPLAINT

SUPREME COURT OF THE STATE OF NEW YORK
COUNTY OF NEW YORK
——————————————————— x

MARY DOE,   COMPLAINT
                                                        Index No.—

                    Plaintiff,

                    against

JOHN DOE,

                    Defendant.

——————————————————— x

The plaintiff above named, complaining of the defendant respectfully alleges:

FIRST: Plaintiff, MARY DOE, married the defendant JOHN DOE, in the County, City and State of New York, on June 11, 1967.

SECOND: The plaintiff, MARY DOE, has been a resident of the State of New York, for a continuous period of at least one (1) year immediately preceding the commencement of the above entitled action, to wit: from on or about January 1, 1965, to date.

THIRD: The cause of action herein complained of occurred in the State of New York.

FOURTH: On February 15, 1976, the plaintiff and the defendant entered into an agreement of separation, a copy of which is annexed hereto and made a part hereof.

FIFTH: That said written agreement of separation was subscribed to and acknowledged by the parties hereto in the form required to entitle a deed to be recorded.

SIXTH: The aforesaid written agreement of separation dated February 15, 1976, was filed in the Office of the Clerk of the County where plaintiff resides, to wit: New York County, prior to the commencement of this action, to wit: on February 16, 1976.

SEVENTH: The plaintiff and the defendant have lived separate and

160

apart pursuant to said written agreement of separation for a period exceeding one (1) year after the execution of the aforesaid agreement, to wit: from February 1, 1976, to the present time.

EIGHTH: During the period of said separation, the plaintiff has at all times duly performed all of the terms and conditions of said written agreement of separation.

NINTH: There are two (2) issue of the marriage of the parties herein, to wit: JANE DOE, born on December 6, 1970, and DAVID DOE, born March 1, 1972.

[If there are no children, this paragraph would simply read: "There are no issue of the marriage."]

WHEREFORE, plaintiff prays for judgment against the defendant of absolute divorce, that the bonds of matrimony between the plaintiff and the defendant be forever dissolved, *that the custody of the aforesaid minor children of the plaintiff and defendant be awarded to plaintiff*, that defendant be directed to provide support for the plaintiff *and the minor children*, and that the plaintiff have such other and further relief as to this Court may seem just and proper together with the costs of this action.

> Mary Doe, Plaintiff Pro Se
> *(P.O. Address)*
> *(Telephone Number)*
>
> (Verification should be added—see page 342 for form.)

If the divorce is uncontested, it's possible to eliminate the middleman, in this case, the sheriff or process server who would ordinarily serve the papers, and to save time, trouble, and money by having the respondent "appear" in the action by signing a form (sometimes called an Entry of Appearance) similar to the following:

(title of action)

————————x

Notice of Appearance

I hereby waive formal service of summons and enter my appearance the same as though I had been regularly served with process. Notices, trial docket notations, and all other papers filed herein should be served upon me by U.S. Mail at ——————————
(address)

————————   ————————————————
(date)   (signature)

Every divorce case is assigned a number for purposes of orderly court record-keeping. It may be called an index number, a file number, a docket number, even a case number in different jurisdictions. Sometime early in the divorce process, you'll have to pay a small fee—from $3 to $25—to have a number assigned. Depending on the rules of your local court, this may be required before or after the summons is served—at which time the court clerk will stamp your papers with the number. You'll want to be sure the correct number appears on all your documents from then on, right down to the final divorce decree.

THE SECOND STEP:
GETTING ON THE COURT CALENDAR

Do-it-yourself divorce is a visit to a strange city, and it is easy to get lost—even lawyers do. Stanley got conflicting advice from attorney friends on which forms he needed. At Blumberg's, a Manhattan firm specializing in the printing of legal forms, clerical cooperation was less than enthusiastic after he answered the question "Are you an attorney?" in the negative.

"In retrospect," says Stanley, "it might have been smarter to say yes, but that I was a new law school graduate and could use a little guidance. As soon as I said no, that was it—it was clear this particular salesman wasn't going to volunteer anything. He did, of course, sell me the form I asked for—a Note of Issue, needed in New York City to put a case on the calendar. And a legal secretary friend helped me fill it out. She knew which blocks to fill in and which to cross out, a matter that was a few minutes' work for her, but over which I would have puzzled a lot longer. I then mailed it to the court with a $50 fee, only to get a phone call a week or so later saying that I would have to appear in person because they could not accept a check from a non-lawyer.

"I got the call at noon on the Friday before Labor Day weekend, and I spent the rest of the day scurrying from clerk to clerk and window to window trying to get things sorted out. Finally, I found a man who could return my check, and after bucking long lines of people, waiting to cash their paychecks at the bank for the long holiday weekend, I managed to return just in time to pay my money down at the right court window. It was quite a hassle and, with the issue still in doubt, not very much fun at the time.

"In general, the clerks were very helpful. They apparently didn't feel it was proper to give me legal advice, but if I asked a specific question, or filled out the form wrong, they set me straight. In the end, the Note of Issue was filed, and subsequently served its purpose, which was to assign me a date on the court calendar for a divorce proceeding."

THE THIRD STEP:
THE DIVORCE HEARING

Six weeks later, Stanley Gornish got his day in court. But: "I had the feeling that if I were a lawyer with a prestigious firm instead of a civilian, I might have gotten an earlier date." On the other hand, prestigious firms are expensive *and* busy, and with such a firm Stanley might, in fact, have had to wait even longer. His lawyer's schedule could have been even more backlogged than the court's.

On the specified morning, Stanley appeared in court with his heart pounding like a tomtom at a rain dance. (Stanley is unlikely to believe me but I can assure him—from personal experience—that he was no more nervous than a new law school grad on his first half-dozen days in court.) "I got lucky on the way in," he recalls. "The man next to me looked like a lawyer, so I asked him if there was anything I had to do while waiting to be called. He told me that I wouldn't be called at all if I didn't take a form from the pile near the entrance, fill it out, and give it to the clerk of the court. Even that form which should have been so simple, was difficult for me to handle. The language of legal forms seems to wander like the Great

163

Wall of China. It seems designed to keep out outsiders, to perpetuate a legal mystique. There almost seems to be a guild at work there, making sure that no one but a trained lawyer can break the code—as though the bar has constructed language barriers to keep the territory to itself."

Finally, Stanley's climactic moment came. "I got up there when the clerk called me," says Stanley, "but the moment I sat down, my brain shut off, and the hand holding my documents began to tremble. I had hoped that my acting as my own attorney would make the judge more sympathetic. But his first words were about as reassuring as a firing squad. He said that he would *not* be able to help me, and that if I intended to be my own lawyer, I had better know what I was doing. He warned me brusquely that if I wasted the court's time, I should retain a lawyer and start over.

"Now, totally paralyzed, I sat there waiting for him to ask the first question. He simply stared at me.

" 'Oh,' I said lamely, 'I guess you want me to start.' But as soon as I began, he interrupted. I had forgotten to formally state my name and my reason for being in court—which is the start of the plaintiff's required statement of fact. At that point, I might have been ready to take him up on his suggestion and find myself a real lawyer. But, fortunately, I'd already witnessed a half-dozen divorce cases that morning, all represented by counsel. Almost every lawyer had stumbled on one thing or another, and the judge had corrected them, telling them that they had omitted something or were improperly leading the witness. Now it was my turn to be embarrassed, but I didn't feel he was singling me out for special harassment.

"And one good thing had come out of the awful day before Labor Day weekend. At the clerk's window, I had discovered a giveaway procedure sheet listing the dozen or so key questions a lawyer should ask his client. I had studied them carefully and modified them into a narrative. For example, where the attorney was to ask, 'Are you the plaintiff in this action?' I simply stated, 'I am the plaintiff in this action'—and so on down the line."

In retrospect, Stanley didn't feel the judge's heart was really of stainless steel. "Maybe he didn't want to *appear* helpful," he says, "but if I made a mistake, he told me to go back. If he had really wanted to be nasty, he could have waited until I went through the whole thing and then denied my divorce. He did pick me up when I stumbled."

If Stanley had followed this outline, he might have had an easier time of it.

My name is————.

I am the Plaintiff in this action.

I live at————, City of————,

State of————.

I have lived in this state continuously for at least one year immediately prior to commencement of this action.

The Defendant is my————(Husband) (Wife).

I was married to the Defendant on the—day of—,19—, in the City of——, State of——.

My marriage to the Defendant has not been terminated by any action or proceeding in this or any court in the United States or any foreign country.

The Defendant and I have been separated pursuant to a separation agreement dated——, which agreement was filed with the County Clerk on——.

My (Husband) (Wife) is not connected with any active branch of the Military Service.

The final paragraph was added some years ago, at a time when wives were divorcing overseas GI husbands who were unable to appear to defend themselves.

Concluded Stanley: "When I finished my presentation, I looked up and waited for the judge to say something. Again, he just stared down at me. Finally, he demanded crisply, 'Well, what are you sitting there for?' I said, 'Is that it?' When he answered, 'Yes, that's it,' I practically soared out of my seat and out of the courtroom."

THE FOURTH STEP:
FINDINGS OF FACT AND CONCLUSIONS OF LAW

The next step for Stanley was to prepare and submit what is called Findings of Fact and Conclusions of Law, on a preprinted form he had already obtained at the legal stationer's. He brought it to the court clerk, who checked it for accuracy, and later submitted it to the judge for signature. The following is a sample of findings, conclusions, and judgment in an action based upon separation.

At a Special Term, Part V, of the Supreme Court of the State of New York, held in and for the County of New York at the Courthouse at 60 Centre Street, New York, New York, on the 9th day of June, 1978.

PRESENT:

HON. MARBERRY V. MADISON, Justice.

x————————————

MARY DOE,

                                                    FINDINGS
                                                AND JUDGMENT

                              Plaintiff,

                                                Index No.—

            against

JOHN DOE,

                          Defendant.

x————————————

The plaintiff having brought this action for a judgment of absolute divorce by reason of the plaintiff and defendant having lived separate and apart pursuant to a written agreement for a period of one or more years, and the Summons bearing the notation "Action for a Divorce" having been duly served upon the defendant personally within this state and the defendant not having appeared within the time prescribed therefore by statute, and it appearing from testimony given in open court that the defendant is not in the military service of the United States, and the plaintiff having applied to the court at a Special Term thereof for judgment for the relief demanded in the complaint and the matter having been set down for trial on the 9th day of June, 1978, and the plaintiff having on that day appeared before me and presented written and oral proof of service and in support of the essential allegations of the complaint, and such proof having been heard and considered by me,

I DECIDE AND FIND AS FOLLOWS:

FINDINGS OF FACT

First: The plaintiff and the defendant were both over the age of 18 when this action was commenced.

Second: That at the time of the commencement of this action

and for a continuous period of at least one year immediately preceding such commencement plaintiff resided in this state and the cause of action occurred in this state.

Third: That plaintiff and defendant were married on the 11th day of June, 1969, in the City, County and State of New York.

Fourth: That there are two children born of this marriage, whose names and dates of birth are as follows: Jane Doe, born December 6, 1970 and David Doe, born March 1, 1972.

Fifth: (a) That the plaintiff and the defendant entered into a written agreement of separation which they subscribed and acknowledged on the 15th day of February, 1977 in the form required to entitle a deed to be recorded, and,

(b) That the agreement was filed in the Office of the Clerk of the County of New York, wherein plaintiff resides on the 16th day of February, 1977, and

(c) That the parties have lived separate and apart for a period of one or more years after the execution of said agreement, and

(d) That the plaintiff has substantially performed all of the terms and conditions of such agreement.

CONCLUSIONS OF LAW

First: That jurisdiction as required by Section 230 of the Domestic Relations Law has been obtained.

Second: The plaintiff is entitled to judgment of divorce and granting the incidental relief awarded herein.

JUDGMENT

NOW, on the motion of Mary Doe, appearing *pro se*, it is

ADJUDGED AND DECREED that the marriage between Mary Doe, plaintiff, and John Doe, defendant, is dissolved on the ground that the plaintiff and defendant have lived separate and apart pursuant to a written agreement for a period of one or more years, and it is further

ADJUDGED AND DECREED that plaintiff is awarded custody of the infant issue of the marriage, to wit:

Jane Doe, born December 6, 1970, and

David Doe, born March 1, 1972, and it is further

167

ORDERED, ADJUDGED AND DECREED that defendant may have visitation with the minor children of the marriage during holiday and vacation periods, at such time and for such periods of time as the plaintiff and defendant mutually agree upon, but in any event defendant shall, at his option, have custody of the children as follows:

(a) For one weekend consisting of Saturday and Sunday in each calendar month;

(b) During the summer and school holidays for a continuous period of one month;

(c) During each of the Christmas and Easter school holidays, for a period of five days.

The defendant shall exercise his option of visitation by giving the plaintiff at least seven (7) days' notice in advance of defendant's intention to do so. The defendant's partial custody and visitation shall be optional at his discretion and his failure to exercise such option on any occasion or for whatever reason shall not be construed as a waiver of his rights or partial custody as herein provided. Notwithstanding the foregoing either party shall have the right to visit the children at any reasonable time, and it is further

ORDERED, ADJUDGED AND DECREED that the separation agreement entered into between the parties on the 15th day of February, 1977, a copy of which is on file with the court, shall survive and not be merged in this judgment, and the court retains jurisdiction of the matter, concurrently with the Family Court, for the purpose specifically enforcing such of the provisions of that agreement as are capable of specific enforcement or, to the extent permitted by law, of making such further decree with respect to alimony, support, custody, or visitation as it finds appropriate under the circumstances existing at the time application for that purpose is made to it, or both, and it is further

ORDERED, ADJUDGED AND DECREED that plaintiff is authorized to resume her maiden name, to wit: Mary Jones.

_____
Justice of the Supreme Court

Stanley's do-it-yourself judicial adventure had its happy ending a week later, when a notice from the clerk informed him that his divorce had been granted. Only a few odds and ends now remained, like returning to the court clerk for two certified copies of the divorce: one to send to his now ex-wife, the other to keep with his important papers. A helpful lawyer on line behind Stanley told him which papers he needed to send her (the decree) and which he didn't (the Findings of Fact and Conclusions), thereby saving him the $3 per page cost of each certified photocopy.

A week later Stanley met the former Mrs. Gornish for dinner. They toasted their new independence with a nostalgic bottle of champagne.

* * *

When the lump on your head finally goes down, the divorce may feel great: "I felt reborn after my divorce!" is the way I've heard many ex-husbands and wives put it.

Then, too, the marriage glue often holds better the second time around, possibly because expectations are lower and maturity is greater, possibly because enough trauma is enough and remarried spouses bend over backward to avoid the kind of head-to-head battles that broke up their earlier marriages. Of course, this isn't always so. At the moment, I'm doing a fourth divorce for one much-glued spouse.

The First Judicial District of New York recently initiated a "no show" divorce procedure that has some matrimonial lawyers so exercised that they've talked of filing a class action to challenge it. All the parties have to do in uncontested matrimonial actions is to submit papers by mail. No one—including lawyers—need appear. The rule change is aimed at ending the waste of time by attorneys, clients, and judges, easing calendar congestion on cases with predictable conclusions, and freeing judges and referees from "routine ritualistic hearings."

Some matrimonial lawyers are irked because part of the fee they charge for handling the action is for their appearance in court. Recently, when I appeared in Matrimonial Court for a client, for a calendar call of contested divorce actions, I noticed that one law firm represented either husband or wife in approximately 20 percent of the three pages of listed cases. The clients were not required to appear on that date, but I wouldn't be surprised if each was told—quite accurately—that their attorney appeared for them. All this contributes to "building the fee." Lawyers have denied that this is a concern, insisting that they fear "rubber stamp divorces" and "divorce mills." But a law journal quoted one startled attorney as saying, "A matrimonial client just asked what she needed me for." That hurts.

Although few courts have gone to the extreme of eliminating appearances entirely, many approach it. It's customary for the attorney to ask the plaintiff a series of questions: date of marriage, residence, acts committed, etc. But when my partner appeared for a woman in an uncontested divorce recently, the judge cut him short as soon as he began, with, "Just ask her if the allegations in the complaint are true." As soon as she answered yes, the divorce was granted.

In Carson City, Nevada, Judge Keith Hayes recently went further. He lined up fifteen persons seeking divorce, along with their lawyers and witnesses, asked a few general questions, and then awarded the first known multiple divorce. Said the judge, "Every divorce is a cause of regret, but when a divorce comes into my court on an uncontested basis, there is no chance at that point to reconcile the couple, so I have no reservations in pushing it through as quickly as possible." Since 90 percent of divorces today are uncontested, traffic in Judge Hayes's courtroom may soon require a traffic light.

Not surprisingly, the organized bar is less than happy with the trend to do-it-yourself divorce. But many attorneys are seriously concerned—and not only selfishly—that, as one bar association puts it in its informational leaflet on divorce:

> . . . the skill and experience of the attorneys for the husband and wife are uniquely valuable in reaching an agreement which will be fair, just, and reasonable to both parties and their children . . . In all marriage problems, substantial and long-lasting rights and duties of the spouses are usually involved . . . The emotional tensions that are a part of an unhappy marriage make it difficult, if not impossible, for the average couple to deal coolly or objectively with a divorce or separation. The lawyer, equipped with a broad background in

170

counseling and negotiation, as well as a specialized knowledge of the law, can help a client be fully aware of his or her rights and obligations in this complex field of law . . . the services of a skilled attorney are absolutely essential . . .

They're fighting the good fight. But consider classified ads like these run in California newspapers: "DIVORCE . . . WE TYPE AND FILE THE FORMS—24-HOUR SERVICE."
Or, "DIVORCE . . . YOU CAN LEGALLY DO YOUR OWN! WE HAVE PROFESSIONAL PROGRAMS DESIGNED TO SAVE YOU TIME AND MONEY . . . YOUR HOME OR OUR OFFICE. LET US DO THE WALKING. DIVORCE SIMPLIFIED."
In the long run, divorce lawyers may be fighting a losing battle. In uncomplicated divorce, at least, our clients appear increasingly ready to divorce us.

Form No. 16

FORM OF COMPLAINT FOR DIVORCE ON GROUNDS OF CRUEL AND INHUMAN TREATMENT

SUPREME COURT OF THE STATE OF NEW YORK
COUNTY OF NEW YORK
————————————————————x

MARY DOE,

Plaintiff,

against   Index No.

JOHN DOE,

Defendant.

————————————————x

Plaintiff, complaining of the defendant alleges as follows:

1. That plaintiff was married to the defendant in the County of —— City of —— , State of —— on —— .

171

2. The plaintiff was, and still is a resident of the State of —— at the time of the commencement of the above entitled action.

3. The plaintiff has been a resident of the State of —— for a continuous period of one (1) year immediately preceding the commencement of the above entitled action to wit: from on or about the — day of —— 19— to date.

4. The defendant ——— , has treated the plaintiff ——— , in a cruel and inhuman manner such that the conduct of the defendant so endangers the physical and mental well being of the plaintiff, as to render it unsafe and improper for the plaintiff to cohabit with the defendant and the defendant has repeatedly committed the following cruel and inhuman acts upon the plaintiff:

The defendant continuously maligned the plaintiff before the children and her friends; the defendant openly and wantonly dated a woman known to both parties, and upon information and belief has committed numerous acts of adultery with said individual.

5. The plaintiff and defendant have — children of their marriage. Namely ——— , who is — years of age and —— , who is — years of age.

WHEREFORE, plaintiff demands a judgment of absolute divorce against the defendant, that the bonds of matrimony between plaintiff and defendant be forever dissolved, and that plaintiff have such other and further relief as to the Court may seem just and proper, together with the costs and disbursements of this action.

> Yours, etc.
> *(Name)*
> *Pro Se*
> *(P.O. Address)*
> *(Telephone Number)*

FORM OF COMPLAINT FOR DIVORCE ON GROUNDS OF ABANDONMENT

SUPREME COURT OF THE STATE OF NEW YORK
COUNTY OF NEW YORK

——————————————————— x

MARY DOE,

                   Plaintiff,   Index No.

    against

JOHN DOE,

                   Defendant.

——————————————————— x

Plaintiff, complaining of the defendant, respectfully alleges:

1. Plaintiff —— , married the defendant —— in the City of —— , State of —— , on the — day of —— 19— .

2. The plaintiff was and still is a resident of the State of —— at the time of commencement of the above entitled action.

3. The plaintiff and the defendant had been residents of the State of New York for a continued period of five years immediately preceding the commencement of the above entitled action, and the plaintiff has been a resident of the County of —— for a continuous period of at least one (1) year immediately preceding the commencement of the above entitled action.

4. That there are two children of the said marriage, to wit: —— born on —— , and —— born on —— , both of whom are now in the custody of the plaintiff.

5. That heretofore on or about —— (date) the defendant abandoned the plaintiff and the children herein with intent not to return and without any cause or justification and without the plaintiff's consent and has continuously absented himself and abandoned them since the said date.

WHEREFORE, plaintiff demands judgment against the defendant forever; that the custody of the aforesaid minor children of the plaintiff and the defendant be awarded to the plaintiff, and that the plaintiff have such other and further relief as to this Court may seem just and proper together with the costs and disbursements of this action.

Yours, etc.
(Name)
Pro Se
(P.O. Address)
(Telephone Number)

CHAPTER 12

Buying (or Selling) a House

Centuries ago it was said that title to "an acre of land could not pass without almost an acre of parchment."

So it seemed to me, when I went to my first house closing. It's unheard of for two attorneys to show up for a $35,000 closing, but there were two of us there—myself and my equally young, equally inexperienced partner, Irv Gutin. Two of us went because I think we were both afraid to go alone.

Irv got the drop on me. "I'll check the deed," he said slyly. "You figure the adjustments."

I huddled over the figures without the faintest idea of what I was doing. After an inordinately long time, I slid them discreetly across the table to the elderly attorney representing the title company. Sympathetically—for he had been fresh out of law school once himself—he "double-checked" them for me.

When you've finished this chapter, you will know more about buying and selling a house than either Irv or I did. In law school, we learned what kind of deeds there are, and the meaning of encumbrances. None of our professors, their feet planted firmly in academic clouds, ever told us what to do at real estate closings. Twenty-two years and hundreds of houses later, here, then, are the practical down-on-earth steps to take in buying or selling your house.

Unless your name is Rockefeller or du Pont, buying a home is likely to be the biggest investment of your life. You want it to be the wisest, too. So if you're going to be your own lawyer—which can save you a bundle—you've got to know what you're doing. Even if you'd rather not attempt to do-it-yourself, it's a good idea to know what your lawyer is doing.

Choosing your home is not something your attorney normally gets involved in—unless you happen to be married to one. The lawyer enters after you've made up your mind that it's the location you want (good commuting, good schools, friendly neighbors, reasonable taxes) at a price you can handle.

The advice that follows applies most commonly to the purchase of a private house, but the steps for buying or selling a condominium are almost the same. The purchase of a cooperative apartment involves buying stock in the corporation and getting an apartment lease, but even there some of the same steps apply.

THE FIRST STEP:
DEALING WITH A REAL ESTATE BROKER

If you're Mr. (or Mrs.) Lucky, you'll find your house—or your buyer—without a broker's help, and save yourself a pretty penny in commissions. These run from as low as 4 or 5 percent to as high as 10 or 12 percent, depending on local custom, and will either come off the price you get in selling, or add to the cost of the home you buy. But if a FOR SALE sign on the lawn, a classified ad, and word-of-neighbor's-mouth fail to get the job done, impatience and anxiety are likely to set in, and, reluctantly, you'll probably pick up the phone and dial for help.

That's not all bad. A broker can save you months of frustrating matchmaking. If you're selling, brokers advertise for you and screen out people who are "just looking" or can't afford your home. Brokers are constantly in the marketplace, know what other houses on your block have sold for, and can help you set a realistic price for yours. They can suggest ways to make your home more marketable, pointing out flaws your fond eyes may rationalize away; they may recommend that you put in an inexpensive but striking flowerbed, or stain a weatherworn house for $1,000 and increase its value by $3,000. If you're buying, they can steer you to those homes most resembling your specifications. And they can fill you in on the area, on schools, commuting, and shopping.

A cautionary grain-of-salt note: The courts recognize overselling or "puffing" by a real estate salesperson (as with other salespeople) as being acceptable within limits. So when a broker tells you that the schools in the district are the best in the country, that the house is a fantastic buy, or that the trip into town is less than half an hour, double-check! Visit the schools, talk to principals, ask the neighbors. Judge the value of the house by comparing the price with others you've seen in the same area. Clock the commute yourself—during rush hour. While the seller or broker is pitching the house, bear in mind the story related by the late U.S. Supreme Court Justice John M. Harlan in illustrating the difference between disinterested and self-serving testimony.

Mr. Justice Harlan told of a home-hunting couple who, at a suburban train station, asked a boy how to get to a new development they'd seen advertised in the Sunday real estate section.

"Turn down that street," volunteered the lad. "It's about a twenty-minute walk."

"Impossible," exclaimed the prospective buyer. "The advertisement says it's a five-minute walk from the station."

Replied the boy, sagely, "You can believe whoever you want, but I ain't trying to sell you no house."

In dealing with a broker—who is—there are legal points you'll need to keep in mind, most of them relating to the brokerage contract.

The "exclusive." "We always insist on an exclusive," the broker may tell you. If he, by reputation, is the hottest broker in town, by all means go along with his demand. Knowing they have no competition, he and his salesmen are more likely to work their fingers down to the knuckles dialing prospects. But, when you fill in the expiration date, limit the exclusive to as short a time as possible, 30, 60, and certainly not more than 90 days. That will put the pressure on the office to produce in a hurry. If they haven't made a sale by then, it's time to widen your horizons by switching to multiple listing.

A "private sale" clause. Now it's your turn to protect yourself. What do you do if, after you've been listed with a broker, your sister-in-law calls and sends you a house-hunting friend, who falls madly in love with your place? Do you tear out your hair, but pay the broker an unearned $4,000 commission anyway? Not if you've written this quite reasonable fail-safe clause into your contract: "In the event that the owner sells the house privately to someone not introduced by the broker, then no commission shall be paid."

Nevertheless, both buyer and seller have a responsibility to a broker who has successfully brought them together. Occasionally people try to sidestep this responsibility.

A broker may bring a customer who pretends disinterest but, returning later, offers the seller an immediate deal, adding, "Let's not tell the broker, and we can split the commission you save." Or the broker brings a customer and shows the house while the owner is out. The customer returns later, pretends there is no broker, and makes a deal at a saving of several thousand dollars.

The astute broker keeps track of sales in his area and learns the names of buyers when houses change hands. He will rightfully sue for his commission—and win it, too. In the first case, his little conspiracy will cost the seller dear: both a lowered price and the broker's commission. In the second case, though himself victimized by a dishonest buyer, the seller is bled just as badly, *unless* protected by still another clause.

Unscrupulous brokers do exist. A client of mine recently encountered one when he decided to move his plant to New Jersey. After several weeks' search one of his employees turned up an interesting possibility—in an industrial park belonging to, let's say, J. Jones, Inc. Shortly thereafter, my client got a call from a real estate broker who suggested several properties including the J. Jones site. "I'll look at the others," said my client, "but not at Jones. I know the place, and I've already got a good contact there without you."

The realtor drove him to the other places, then said casually, "You know, we're quite close to the Jones place. Why don't we look it over?"

"Hey," said my client, "if you're planning to take me there so you can claim a commission, stop the car now—I want to get off." Protesting his disinterest, the broker nevertheless contrived to pass the site, and brazenly pointed it out, praising it warmly. The following day, my client received a letter that said, in effect: "It was a pleasure to show you the Jones property today. It would be a fine site for you. In fact, I have discussed your interest with Mr. Jones."

My client was upset. "What can you do about this leech?" he asked. My answer was a letter to the broker with a copy to Mr. Jones, declaring firmly that he was not the broker in this transaction, and that if he did not immediately send me a letter acknowledging that fact, I would file a complaint with the state licensing authorities.

The cross-fire can get pretty heavy in a war between brokers, and an indemnification clause makes a fine shield. There was, for example, a woman I represented whose home had been on the market for nine months. The first month, Broker A brought Mrs. Brown to see the house. The maid let them in. She quickly walked through, but at $150,000 said it wasn't for her. Six months later,

Broker B brought her back, and spent considerable time selling its finer points. (The owner had painted and decorated throughout and cut $15,000 off the price.)

Mrs. Brown reconsidered—and purchased. Broker A's fine-tuned antennae immediately picked up the news, and she angrily insisted that the fat commission was rightfully hers. Before I allowed my client to sign a contract to sell the house, I insisted that Broker B agree in writing to defend and indemnify any claim that might be lodged by the walk-through broker. Broker A never pressed her bluff. But even without knowing that, I could go forward with the sale without fear. My client couldn't go into the red. She had her indemnification clause down in black and white.

The commissionectomy. Don't think that a local custom of a 5 percent commission was proclaimed from Mt. Sinai. Many stalemated deals have been saved by an agreement to trim the broker's commission to bridge the gap between asking price and offer. If you find yourself close, but not close enough, the magic words—in an aside loud enough for him to hear—are sometimes these: "Now, if the broker would only cut his commission, we'd have a deal . . ."

Paying the commission. In theory, a broker earns his commission when he brings someone "ready, willing, and able" to buy for the price and at the terms offered by the seller. But what if, after he's introduced such a person, you change your mind or get a better offer? You could find yourself legally obligated to pay the commission, deal or no deal. There has been so much litigation over this point that brokerage agreements commonly contain a clause providing that "commissions will be payable only when and if title actually passes." Make sure it's in yours.

The Second Step:
Selecting a House (for buyers)

Selecting a house is not a visibly legal matter, but there are many invisible legal strings attached. The key questions you should ask as a buyer before you give a deposit include:

The price: Is the asking price close to what you want to spend? Remember that you'll need several thousand dollars in reserve to cover inspection, adjustment, and closing costs. Consider, too, whether or not you can afford the down payment, how easily you can handle the monthly mortgage payment (wishing won't make it so), increasingly costly homeowner's insurance, ever-climbing property taxes and utilities, and miscellaneous maintenance (higher in an older house). If all that hasn't discouraged you, you have the heart of a lion and should be ready to confront the next string of questions.

Exactly what is included in the price? (Lighting fixtures, "built-ins," appliances, etc.?) What will be removed? I had one nickel-nursing client who almost killed the sale of her house when, the night before the closing, she pettily removed her pet lucite towel rods from the master bathroom. The buyer's falcon-eyed morning tour caught the confiscation, and it took all the high-viscosity oil two attorneys could pour on the suddenly troubled waters to keep the stormy argument that followed from sinking the $65,000 deal over a set of $9.95 towel rods.

Are there tenants in the house at present? What kind of lease do they have? What rent do they pay? Can they be asked to leave? When?

When will the property be available for you to take possession?

What kind of zoning is the property set in and surrounded by? Make sure it's residential, with no downzoning ordinance in prospect, or you could wake up one morning to find a gas station or a plastics factory rising next door. Are there easements, restrictions, or covenants that might in any way interfere with your use of the property? (Does a neighbor have an easement through the backyard so you can't fence it in?) Answers to these questions may come from the deed recorded at the county clerk's office, rather than from the seller. Friendly public officials or a helpful real estate agent can help you get them.

Are there adequate public services —police, fire, sanitation, and so on? It's also helpful to know if there are plans to improve some of these, which might lead to an unexpected $2,000 sewer assessment in the near future. (Sometimes this may be paid out over a period of years, but it still hurts.)

Is there an existing mortgage? What is the amount? How much is the interest? How much longer will it run? Is it assumable: can you take it over, instead of getting a new one?

Is any part of the property owned by a neighbor? In one such case the neighbors were old friends and unconcerned about a driveway overlap. But when the family with the infringing driveway tried to sell the house, the potential buyer discovered the discrepancy, and refused to go through with the deal unless he could either purchase the piece of land the driveway was built on, or received a written easement, or right-of-way. He got what he wanted, thus guaranteeing that no matter how badly relations deteriorated with his new neighbor, a spite fence could never be built barring him from his own garage.

THE THIRD STEP:
GOOD FAITH MONEY—THE BINDER

If you're the seller: The binder is like the fraternity pin college men used to affix to a co-ed's sweater in the romantic 40s and 50s. It fell short of official engagement but did signify a certain interest in eventual ownership. You'll want a deposit from the potential buyer who wants you to "hold" the house, until a real estate contract can be prepared and signed. But even if you pocket a cash binder—be it $50 or $250—you don't have a deal until that contract is formally signed, since the law sensibly requires all real estate transactions to be in writing. So you should ask him to sign a binder—an offer to buy, also known as a deposit receipt. Pending a contract, this temporary document should specify a limited period of time during which you agree to take your house off the market, preparatory to going to contract.

I don't advise more than several days, because if the buyer is serious, that's all he'll need. If the contract isn't signed by then, back goes your home on the market. Unless otherwise noted in the binder, the buyer technically forfeits the deposit. In effect, that's your compensation for time lost in disposing of your home. Yet in practice, although this is a very gray area, binder money is often refunded, however grudgingly.

If you're the buyer. Unless you're very sure this is the house for you, you'd be better off not signing anything. Your best approach is to hand over a deposit (as small a sum as the seller will accept), ask for a receipt, and do your best to keep your signature in your fountain pen, If the seller insists on a written binder, keep it as simple as possible. And be sure to get a copy of it—as you should of anything you sign. Prudence and wisdom dictate that you make every effort to insert a clause that assures you "a refund of deposit if a formal contract to purchase the property is not entered into."

THE FOURTH STEP:
INSPECTING YOUR NEW HOME (for buyers)

Now—before you go to contract, not after you move in—is the time to learn if that house is as good as it is good-looking. If for any reason you go to contract before the house is professionally inspected, be sure to include a clause that makes the offer to buy contingent upon a clean report. Something like: "Buyer has ten days within which to have the house inspected. If the buyer is not satisfied with the inspection report, he shall have the right to cancel the contract and have his down payment returned."

If serious flaws show up, but you're so in love with the house that you see no evil, at least use what you've discovered to negotiate a better price. A purchaser did just that to a client of mine recently, during negotiations for a loft building. The parties had previously agreed on a figure of $340,000, but after an examination and discussion of the contract, the buyer smugly drew an engineer's report from his briefcase.

The report stated that a new roof would be needed in a short time, that many window frames were rotted and should be replaced, and that several other major items were in less than satisfactory condition. After passing the report around the table, the buyer advised us that estimates he'd received indicated that repairs would cost at least $10,000. And—final hammer blow—unless the price was reduced by this amount, he would not go through with the transaction. My client was anxious to sell. He feared it might be many months before he found a new buyer and in the interim he would have to make the repairs himself. He concurred, and he forthwith offered to reduce the price by $5,000, thereby splitting the cost of the needed repairs.

You can use an inspector's report in the same way on a property of any price. Whether the house is old or new, defects not visible to the inexperienced eye may be present. In a recently built house, corners may have been cut to reduce the builder's costs. In a sturdy old house, deterioration of heating or plumbing systems may have set in. Not long ago, I had a client about to go to contract when an inspector found serious termite damage in the basement. I insisted that without beam repairs, termite extermination, and a one-year guarantee, the deal was off. Rather than spend the money, the owner gave up the sale—but may well have gone on to sell his home to someone less careful.

182

Care is needed. The mind boggles at the deceptions practiced by otherwise perfectly charming people to unload a home with a closetful of structural skeletons. They'll pile an old mattress and a dozen bags of junk against an inside garage wall to camouflage a massive crack created by a teenager parking on a full tank of beer. They'll install a false basement floor—and claim it's for acoustical purposes for a son who plays his electric guitar there—to hide the original floor beneath that's been ruined by water that comes in every time it rains. An experienced inspector will see through such shams, and a wise seller will blush briefly, then contritely offer to trim his price to compensate.

Most buyers, happy with a house in other ways, will go this route rather than walk away from a house entirely. They can then choose to live with the problem or to make repairs—as do families who buy homes with controversial aluminum wiring branded hazardous by some fire departments. For about $300, they simply "pigtail" the sockets.

Home inspectors are usually listed in the Yellow Pages under "building inspection services." Or you might prefer someone recommended by a friend, especially someone in the building trades. Not all inspectors are equally reliable, so get references if you can. Remember that a recommendation from the real estate broker, with several thousand dollars in commissions at stake, may not be the height of wisdom. I know one homeowner who retained as inspector his broker's candidate, only to find after he moved in that the roof of his $60,000 home was so mushy it was unlikely to survive the year. There is a suit now pending against that particular inspector for malpractice. I know. I filed it.

Inspection costs vary and may range from $50 to $200 or more. Some inspectors base their fee on an eight-room house, adding charges for extra rooms or for inspecting "extras" like central air conditioning or a swimming pool. Others base their fees on the price of the house. If you want to go along on the tour, the inspector may charge an extra consultation fee. It may be worth it. With you looking over his shoulders, you know he's going to do a thorough job.

THE FIFTH STEP:
GOING TO CONTRACT

You like the house. Your spouse likes the house. The home in-

183

spector likes the house. And the seller likes the snap-crackle-pop of your money. Now you can "go to contract." This agreement ranges from very simple in some areas (Virginia) to complicated in others (New York City with its special tax assessment clauses). Contracts are customarily prepared by the seller's attorney. But in some communities the real estate broker handles the matter, using a printed form—say that of the local Shady Valley Realty Association. If you're going to do without benefit of attorney, you can pick up a real property sales contract from a title company or legal stationer. That standard form looks alarmingly final, but it's only a framework. Clauses may be deleted, added, or altered to meet the needs and protect the interests of either party.

Whether you have an attorney or not, it makes sense to read the contract carefully to be sure that the points we're about to discuss are stated to your satisfaction in black and white. No matter how charming he may be, what the seller, real estate agent, or builder promises orally is only written on the wind. So a couple relocating in Florida painfully discovered. The builder's agent assured them the house would be ready in four months. They trustingly sold their Connecticut home and, a few weeks before delivery date, moved to Florida with their two children. They had planned on a pleasant two-week stay in her parents' little two-bedroom condominium apartment. That stretched into three uncomfortable months. When, having discovered that the lot they'd purchased was as innocent of activity as a desert island, they complained to the builder, they were told: "Read your contract—it gives us up to two years to build your house." So, to their dismay, it did. What it should have had was a penalty clause, about which more later. But this contract was so blatantly one-sided that threat of suit by a lawyer they promptly retained was sufficient to persuade the builder that they were not about to lie down and play sidewalk. Convinced that he could not walk all over them, he put his crew to work and the house was delivered only four months late. *Moral:* Never read a contract with your eyes closed.

When you do read it, your open eyes should be sure that these points are included in the contract:

Names and addresses of seller and buyer. (I've never seen a contract where this was forgotten, but there's always a first time.)

A description of the property involved, including dimensions and location (block, lot number, map number, if any, etc.). There should be no doubt about which property you are buying. If it's a development or resale house, be sure the address ("also known as 12 Cheerful Way") is included. If it's an empty lot, check the development or town map to be certain you have the right property. A proper survey (see page 192) will remove the last vestige of doubt.

Price. Money matters should be detailed in full: total price of the property; amount of the down payment or deposit, and whether it is to be held in escrow; details about the mortgage, if any, and whether an old mortgage will be assumed or a new one sought; and when and how the money will be paid. When representing a buyer, I always insist that the down payment be held in escrow until closing. This makes it easier for the buyer to get his money back if the transaction falls through.

Escrow funds are usually held by the attorney for the seller—or by the real estate broker—in a special account segregated from the escrow agent's personal funds. Since attorneys or brokers who violate escrow agreements usually lose their licenses, you can feel confident that the money is safe as IBM stock. If you're supercautious, and the seller's attorney looks like Peter Lorre, you may be able to arrange for a bank to hold the money in escrow. A method that will earn, not cost you money, is to open a joint savings account with the attorney representing the other side, so that money may only be withdrawn with both signatures.

Down payments are not paltry sums, and it's a good idea to keep them on a leash even after you pay one out. Escrow is that leash. Example: A lawyer for the seller called to say, "Our clients have agreed that *your* client's $9,000 down payment will be turned over to *my* client so he can use it as a down payment on a home in Arizona." Sometimes the lawyer must be tougher than his client. "No," I said, "not until we get our mortgage commitment and a satisfactory title report."

The following week, my client thought he'd retained a genius. When the report came through, it showed $15,000 in federal tax liens and judgments. If the deal had fallen through, my man would have had a tough time getting his money back. It would have been just another judgment.

If the contract is contingent upon getting a mortgage, it should state that the buyer will make every effort to obtain a mortgage or be penalized. An appropriate clause to handle this might be: "If the buyer is unable within (30) (60) days from this date to obtain a mortgage for $00,000 payable over 00 years with interest at no

185

more than 0 percent, after making a diligent and good faith application to a lending institution, this contract shall be declared null and void and the buyer shall be entitled to return of his down payment."

This implies that if he does not work at getting the loan (possibly because he's discovered something he likes better), he'll either have to go through with the deal or forfeit his down payment. If the time limit passes without the buyer notifying the seller that his mortgage application has been rejected, the buyer remains bound by the contract.

Of course, there's no need to fool around with obtaining a new mortgage if you can take over the old one—in which case you can buy the house "subject to the existing mortgage." Because of the fluctuation of interest rates in recent years, banks have added a clause stating that the mortgage cannot be assigned without their prior consent. There's big money to be saved if you can win that consent and hold on to a low interest mortgage. You will also save by avoiding mortgage recording taxes, title insurance policy cost, bank attorney fees, and the like.

Personal property and "extras." You fell in love with that dining room chandelier the minute you set eyes on it. You naturally assumed that when you bought the house, the chandelier was part of the bargain. Not so. Not if it wasn't specifically mentioned in the contract. The same applies to removable appliances (refrigerator, washing machine, etc.), carpeting, drapes, window blinds, and fireplace andirons. If you're buying from a builder's model, be sure that the Spanish bathroom tile, the super-recovery name-brand water heater, and the cherrywood kitchen cabinets in the model house are specified in the contract. If they're not, the builder may substitute "builders' standard" materials or brands, often considerably less than the best.

Condition of house. The real estate broker assures you that the leaky roof will be fixed by the seller, and the unsightly shed removed from the backyard. Don't count on it—unless you get it in writing. If you're selling, you can avoid arguments and misunderstandings, even litigation later, if you put this clause into the contract: "The buyer has examined the property, knows its condition, and is not relying upon any representations by the seller, broker, or others, and the house, with the exception of express warranties contained in this contract, is being purchased as is." The "express warranties" that the buyer will want, protecting him against un-

186

seen defects, can be covered in an added clause such as this: "The seller represents that the heating, plumbing, and electrical systems are in good working order, and will be in good working order at the time of closing." The buyer should request a similar clause for any appliances included in the sale, as well as a guarantee that "the roof is in good repair and does not leak." These warranties usually expire once the deed is delivered, so it's a good idea to make sure everything works the day before the closing. The contract should state, too—if the form contract does not already do so—that the house will be delivered "vacant and broom-clean" on the closing date.

The deed. At the closing of every real estate transaction comes the moment both parties have been waiting for: the dramatic culmination when the deed is delivered and received. There are basically three main types of deeds, with the one surrendered determined by the contract and what is customary in the area.

For the purchaser, the most desirable is the "Full Covenant and Warranty Deed"—where the seller represents that he owns the property, has the right to convey, guarantees absolute, clear title to the property, and agrees to forever defend if a claim is ever made attacking title. This type of deed is common in some areas but, with the increase in the use of title insurance, is used less frequently in others.

The "Bargain and Sale Deed With Covenants Against Grantors Acts" is routinely used in New York City and many other areas. This deed passes absolute title and warrants that the seller has not done anything to adversely affect that title (indiscriminately granting easements, for example, or building a structure that violates zoning regulations). This deed, plus title insurance from a reputable company, should be enough to satisfy even the most neurotic purchaser.

The "Quitclaim Deed" is the least desirable of the three. It properly and legally transfers any rights the seller may have in the property, but makes no representations as to his title or what he did while he owned the land. All the seller does is "quit any claim" he may have. Again, if a title insurance company is willing to insure title, not to worry. This type of deed is commonly used to correct defects in title, when one spouse conveys property to another or if someone gives property as a gift. Why should your Uncle Tom, who is, out of the goodness of his heart, giving his favorite nephew two acres in the country—and his cabin thereon—guarantee that he is giving you more than he owns? An ex-partner of mine almost backed out of buying a house several years ago when the attorney for the seller stated that he would get no more than a quitclaim deed. Then, realizing that if the title company was willing to issue a policy, he had nothing to fear, he bought it—and later sold it without any problems.

Armageddon clause. Catastrophes happen. People downstream of earthen dams find that out. So do people who smoke in bed. So what happens if you sign a contract to buy a house, and two days before the closing it burns down or is washed away? Is it his house or yours, his hard luck or yours? To avoid litigation, insert a rarely needed but sometimes supremely important clause: "The seller assumes all liability for fire or other damage prior to closing."

Broker clause. This one is for everyone's protection. It's in most contracts because realtors have made sure that it is: "The parties agree that (name) is the broker who brought about this sale, and the seller agrees to pay any commission earned thereby."

It's equally important when no broker is involved in the deal to take note of that in the contract: "The buyer represents that no broker was involved in this transaction, and if a claim for commission should be asserted by a broker, the buyer agrees to indemnify the seller and hold him harmless for any commission that he may become obligated to pay."

"Time is of the essence." Filling in a time, date, and place of closing (usually in the office of the lending institution or of the seller's attorney) is essential in the contract. But though the date looks rigidly official, it is only considered to be "on or about" that date. Either side can ask for a reasonable postponement, reasonable usually being considered two weeks to 60 days.

If, however, either party *must* have the closing on a particular date—you're leaving for South America the next day—then the magic words to insert in the contract are "time is of the essence." With that added, September 1 means September 1, not October 15. For further reinforcement, a penalty can be written in against the delaying party.

I recently handled a contract that was particularly harsh because time was critical to the buyer. We wrote in a clause that for each month's delay the purchase price would be reduced by $1,000— and you can be sure the seller didn't let any grass grow under his moving van.

188

If it's a new home you're buying, the way to make sure that yours is the first one the builder constructs on the block is to have him back up his sincerity with a clause to match. It should state that he'll pay your storage and motel costs if the house isn't finished by the time (specified in the contract) that you've moved out of your apartment or closed on the sale of your old home.

"Subject to" clauses. Most form contracts provide that the premises are sold subject to zoning regulations, encroachments, covenants, restrictions, and easements of record. If you are the seller, you'll want these clauses left intact. If you are the buyer, you'll want to add: "providing the same do not render title unmarketable."

Assessments. The seller should/be willing to pay all assessments—for sewers, roads, etc.—up to the date of closing. If the seller knows a high assessment for new sewer installations is about to be imposed, he may reasonably argue that the purchaser will be the one to benefit and should be the one to pay.

Apportionment. The contract should include a clause saying that: "taxes, water charges, rents, if any, interest on mortgages, premiums on insurance policies being transferred, and fuel will be apportioned at closing."

Title company approval and insurance clause. Though it is implied that the seller possesses and will deliver a marketable title, the buyer needs an escape clause if this should prove not to be so. This is it: "The seller shall give and the purchaser shall accept a title such as any reputable title company [you can name a specific firm] will approve and insure."

The survey clause. Since surveys are made after going to contract, the contract should hinge upon whether or not the survey confirms the seller's representations.

A clause in the standard sales contract usually states that it is "subject to any state of facts that an accurate survey may show." This means that without even seeing the survey, you agree to accept what it shows. I always add, "providing same does not render title unmarketable." The seller is trying to say this is the house we're selling you—five feet more or less shouldn't make any difference. The buyer is saying, "I agree with you. But I'll be the final judge of whether it's important or not. If the five feet includes a driveway for the next-door-neighbor's house (or a fence), either you clear up the problem or the deal is off."

THE SEVENTH STEP:
THE TITLE SEARCH

In an eighteenth-century farce by Joseph Fielding, an attorney asks, "What would you do without lawyers? Who'd know his property?" Two centuries later, he might have added: "And what would lawyers do without title companies and abstractors?"

In this age of subspecialization—from hematologists in hospitals to designated hitters on the baseball diamond—abstract and title companies more and more relieve attorneys of the chore of searching title and the responsibility of guaranteeing it.

When you buy a house, how do you know the person who's selling it to you really owns it? OK, he's signed the deed and handed over the keys. But do you know for sure there are no liens against the house you've bought or overdue taxes that you'd be responsible for, and no restrictions that would prevent you from building that swimming pool you contemplate? What an insecure world we'd live in if it weren't for the protection of title search, survey, and title insurance, which establish that all's right with your new world.

Can you save a few hundred dollars by doing the title search yourself? Certainly, but title searching is like riding a Brahma bull. Not too many people can do it the first time without getting hurt. And to err is expensive when your life savings—and borrowings—are at stake.

The person who searches the records at the county clerk's office may be a title or abstract company representative or employee, who in effect then guarantees his work. His company sells the buyer an insurance policy that protects the new owner in perpetuity against any defect in title that the searcher may have failed to discover. In many rural communities, the purchaser's attorney examines the title, and if it appears clear will certify and guarantee it, sometimes backing that up with a special blanket insurance policy he holds, or simply with his or her professional word.

The best reason for you not to do your own search is this: Even professionals mess up. You won't read about it in the newspapers, but title insurance companies are regularly called upon to clear up defects in title resulting from human error—their own—such as failure to note a judgment entered against the previous owner prior to closing. To avoid publicity and the cost of litigation, they readily—and quietly—pay for their mistakes.

190

If your finger walks through the Yellow Pages under "Title Insurance" or "Abstracts" to no avail, then our old familiar friend, the clerk at the county courthouse, where deeds are registered, can tell you who does title searches in your community. But chances are you'll find a name like American (or Lawyers', or Security, or Precise) Title Company in the phone book.

The search could cost from $50 to $200, and insurance could add several hundred dollars more. When an attorney does the search, the cost is generally included in his fee. In theory, chain of title should be searched all the way back to the Indians, but in fact, if the same company handled 145 Lincoln St. five years ago, all it would do is bring its files up to date. If another title company handled it, the title man might do it from scratch, but more likely would exercise his professional courtesy muscles asking the first firm to photocopy its file and pass it along for his update. With a minimum of effort and a maximum fee, title company work has always been profitable, indeed. But of late the natives have been restless in some areas of the country, and if Indian Power ever becomes more than a slogan, and lawsuits for return of tribal lands by Maine, Massachusetts, New York, and other tribes succeed, some title insurance companies could lose their scalps.

I have a client in New York City who owns property that's been in his family for more than one hundred years. When he wanted to sell his land, the buyer's title search turned up a defect in the original grant, dating back to the first Dutch settlements. He's learned that he doesn't actually own a key piece of the property he'd planned to sell, and will have to buy it from Peter Stuyvesant's legal lineal administrative descendants: the government of New York City.

A title report and search may turn up such benign things as a covenant by a community association not to display for sale signs on the property. Or it may discover somewhat less innocent covenants like one in the deed of a Long Island home on which I represented the buyer, forbidding its sale to anyone not of the Caucasian race. Since such restrictions have since become violations of law, naturally we omitted it from the new deed.

The search will unveil any judgments against the previous owner that are now liens against the property—such encumbrances as a mechanic's or contractor's lien. It will tell you what the taxes on the property are and whether or not they are paid—a double check on what the seller has told you.

For each parcel, there's a record in a book that tells you where deeds, mortgages, easements, and restrictions are recorded for that particular parcel—in another book, or even on microfilm. The older notations, including complete word-for-word deeds, are in longhand, entered by the local scribe before typewriters and photocopiers gave the quill back to the goose. A title report officially describes the property, sometimes referring to a filed map, and noting a particular section, lot, block, or parcel of land—filed, for example, in "the land records of Fauquier County, Virginia in Deed Book 302 at page 132."

The bride is not always perfect, but the many possible defects—easements, encroachments, covenants, zoning restrictions among them—do not always make title unmarketable. Though it's not what is known as a perfectly "clean title," the title company will insure it, simply listing these defects as exceptions to their coverage.

THE EIGHTH STEP:
THE SURVEY

Just as you want to know that the house is in good shape, so you want to know that the shape of the land is what you've been led to believe it is. Many older houses and parcels may have no survey, but only stakes (often overgrown and difficult to locate) driven in at the corners (or no stakes at all). The property may be described in "metes and bounds," may refer to "the big oak tree" or "the large boulder." On a property that I recently purchased for a new office, a father had deeded a piece of his land to his daughter for a dowry, and simply paced it off. When our surveyor walked it, he couldn't make ends meet; the measurements were off by six feet. Without a survey, this faulty description might not have been corrected. The sky wouldn't have fallen, but 50 years from now, someone—perhaps my grandson—might have had unnecessary problems.

The surveyor's product is the survey, a drawing of the property setting forth its dimensions and boundaries in relation to surrounding property, and noting and accurately locating all structures, driveways, paths, major trees, improvements such as swimming pools, and other significant property landmarks.

If no survey exists or is available—the owners have searched bureau drawers and safe deposit box in vain—a survey should be ordered from a licensed surveyor, either straight from the Yellow Pages or perhaps on recommendation by the title company.

If a survey exists, you should walk the property with it in hand, to make sure there have been no structural changes or obvious encroachment, either by the owner against neighbors or vice versa. If changes have occurred, it's a good idea to contact the original surveyor—assuming it wasn't George Washington—for an updating. He should have all his old records on file, and should charge you less than someone else will for a start-from-scratch survey. The bank will insist—and you should, too—that he certify his work.

Now that you've got a title report and survey, it doesn't hurt to review them with the title company rep. When he understands that you're handling the transaction yourself, he'll appreciate your need to understand any defects that his title search may have revealed. And he ought to be able to explain them in layman's language.

Once it's clear to you, make sure that its full import is clear to the seller by forwarding a copy of your report to him (if he's representing himself) or to his attorney. This gives him the exact description your title company wants entered in the deed. It provides him with any questions or objections to title that he must clear up before closing—which is about to take place.

THE NINTH STEP:
FINANCING YOUR FIND

The simplest way to purchase your new property is with cash. Unfortunately, few of us can do this. I once attended a closing where the buyer drew out the largest wad of $100 bills anyone at the table had ever seen outside of a bank vault, to pay for his purchase. Unless you strike it rich in a state lottery, you're much more likely to rely upon a mortgage to finance most of the cost of your house.

The long-term mortgage we know (though hardly love) today is a relatively new innovation. Until Franklin Roosevelt's reforms of the 30s, Little Nell and her ailing dad were frequently evicted by black-mustachioed villains in cape and derby, because mortgages were short-term—five or six years, during which only interest was paid and after which the entire principal became due, or it was: "Marry me, or out into the howling blizzard with you!"

Today there are two basic ways in which you can obtain a home mortgage: (1) take over the present owner's mortgage; (2) apply for a new mortgage. There are advantages and disadvantages to each.

Taking over an existing mortgage. If the house you've chosen has an existing mortgage, and you have enough cash (over and above that mortgage), you can save money in several areas. The old mortgage may have a low interest rate. Furthermore, you will not have to pay the lending institution for initiating and recording the mortgage, and for legal and other fees.

The biggest savings of all, however, may be in the way your monthly mortgage payments are applied by the bank toward interest and principal. During the early years, almost all of each payment goes to interest. If you take over a 30-year mortgage at, say, the 10-year mark, you'll find it has aged gracefully, indeed, and a much greater share is being applied toward amortizing (or reducing) your mortgage.

Of course, it may not be that easy. More and more mortgages these days contain clauses—designed to protect banks in a rising interest market—that either prohibit transfer of the mortgage without the bank's written consent, or simply state that the mortgage "will be due and payable upon sale of the house." If current interest rates are no higher than that in the existing mortgage, and your credit checks out, bankers will generally smile benevolently and grant their consent.

Obtaining a new mortgage. If you can't come up with the money, your real estate broker won't get his commission. So brokers usually have mortgage applications in their office desk drawers and not only can't wait to help you fill them out, but will even run them down to the bank for you.

The telephone is your second best mortgage connection. Call your own bank first. Savings, savings and loan associations, commercial banks, mortgage companies, and life insurance companies all write mortgages, with the best terms usually available from the first two. Your home purchase contract requires you to move with all due speed and to apply in good faith. If you're unable to get your mortgage commitment within the 30 to 60 days allowed, you get your deposit back—but only if you've made a good faith effort (completely, truthfully, and within a reasonable time) to get the mortgage.

What's on the bank loan committee's mind as it considers your application? Their first concern is to be sure that, if you fail to meet your mortgage payments the property will bring enough under the auction hammer to cover what you've borrowed plus their expenses. So even before meeting, they have the property appraised. Depending on bank policy and your personal credit, the mortgage

194

approved will be 50 to 95 percent of the appraised value, though on government-backed GI and FHA loans it could rise to 100 percent.

They consider, too, your ability to meet those inexorable monthly payments. Their credit department checks salary and longevity with your employer, and other credit references you've offered. They call your bank to verify your claimed balance, and they check court records in counties where you live or have lived, to establish that you've left no trail of unpaid debts.

For your part, you have the right to remain silent, but this is the time to make some important inquiries of your own. Is the interest rate competitive with other lending institutions? Is there a penalty for early prepayment? (Ironically, banks penalize you 1 to 3 percent or more if you want to pay off the mortgage before it's due.) How many years will the mortgage run? (The longer the term they are willing to offer—15, 25, even 35 years, the smaller the monthly payment. But the longer the period, the greater the total interest paid. If the house is an old one, they may not wish to offer a long-term mortgage.)

Some more questions: What's the grace period before a penalty will be payable? How much will the lateness charge be? If you sell the house, can the buyer assume your mortgage? (This is an attractive feature, but increasingly rare.) Does the bank require you to pay escrow—one-twelfth of the real estate tax and one-twelfth of insurance each month? Does it pay you interest on this escrow? At what interest rate? (Some states now require that interest be paid. The higher the rate your bank pays, of course, the better. But don't blow that $20 or $30 on a night on the town. Better save it for next year's increased taxes.)

THE TENTH STEP:
PREPARING FOR CLOSING

The contract is signed, the mortgage approved, and the movers have been hired. Then the phone rings: "I'm terribly sorry, but something's come up and we're not going to be able to go through with the transaction."

This doesn't happen very often, but when it does, the injured party can sue for "specific performance"—an action in equity in which the court compels the defendant to either take or deliver title, as the case may be. The blow can fall harder than that. Damages may be awarded, too—not just for hotel expenses and commuting costs, but for storage and inconvenience as well.

Sometimes the wronged party has a heart. Recently, a woman came to me in mortal fear that she was about to be nailed to the wall of a house she'd wanted to buy. She had had a love affair with a married, though separated, man. After six crowded months in her one-bedroom apartment, they decided to buy a house in their joint names. They pooled their resources and split a $4,500 down payment. But shortly thereafter, her lover split, too. He decided to return to his wife and children, and left her holding the contract on a $45,000 home she could in no way afford alone.

The seller could have stonewalled and legally had every right to keep the down payment and possibly sue for more. But when the seller's attorney heard my client's tale of woe, he sympathetically offered to see what he could do. A few days later, he called to tell me that his good-hearted client had agreed to return the down payment—less $1,000 "to cover legal fees and inconvenience." I saw to it that my client, the innocent victim, received her entire $2,250 contribution, with the unfaithful lover getting the balance.

The fates having, happily, been kinder to you, however, let's get on with the final preparations for closing.

Setting the date. Several weeks before the closing date set in the contract, check with the other party to make certain that date is still firm. (Unless time is of the essence, each side is entitled to a reasonable adjournment.) Clear the date with your bank to be sure its attorney will be available. Advise the title company representative and any other interested parties.

Search and survey. Make sure that the title search and survey have been completed and that the seller (or his attorney) has received a copy. If there were objections, have they been cleared up?

The deed. The seller's attorney usually prepares and brings the deed to the closing. Double-checking it, to be sure the deed matches the reported description, is only common sense.

Adjustments. Compute all adjustments in advance. If possible, have your figures checked by someone who knows closing customs and his numbers, possibly your accountant. To save time and avoid conflicting figures on the big day, phone the other party's attorney a day or so before to be sure your numbers match his.

Your closing statement worksheet should look something like this:

CREDITS TO SELLER:

Purchase Price	$50,000.00
Adjustments: Real estate taxes ($950.00 per year, prepaid by seller for next 6 months)	425.00
Fuel oil in tank (600 gls. at 50 cents gl.)	300.00
Fire insurance (4 months remaining of prepaid policy—premium $144 per year)	48.00
Prepaid interest on mortgage (for last 15 days of month)	62.00
TOTAL CREDITS TO SELLER	$50,835.00

CREDITS TO PURCHASER:

Down payment	$5,000.00
Assumption of mortgage	28,550.00
Water and sewer ($21 due next month for 3- month period)	14.00
TOTAL CREDITS TO PURCHASER	$33,564.00
BALANCE DUE SELLER AT CLOSING	$17,271.00

Some explanations: Taxes are the most common adjustment. Real estate taxes may include village, town, county, state, and school. Since they are often payable at different times of the year, separate adjustments for each may be necessary. In my community, taxes are paid in advance for the next twelve months; with school taxes due in September; town, county, and state in January; and village taxes in June.

So someone who buys a house on August 1, will owe the seller one month's school tax, five month's town, county, and state, and nine month's village tax—provided, of course, that he's been a good citizen and paid his taxes. In some areas, taxes are paid partly in advance and partly for a past period. For example, an annual tax due June 1 may cover January 1 through December 31. If Riley buys Ricci's home and the closing takes place on April 15, Ricci will owe Riley the taxes that Riley will pay on June 1 for the final 3 1/2 months that Ricci occupied the house. This adjustment will appear as a credit to Riley on the closing statement.

Prepaid insurance premiums work on the same principle, as do water and sewer charges. But if the old mortgage is being assumed, interest is apportioned on the basis of figures furnished to both parties by the bank. Some banks require monthly interest to be paid in advance, while with others the mortgage payment covers the previous month's interest. If closing takes place on April 15 and Ricci has paid in advance, he'll be entitled to a half-month's interest credit. If, on the other hand, interest is paid at the end of the month, then Riley, who's going to pay for the entire month (but will have lived there for only half a month) is entitled to a half-month's credit. Any questions?

Oil should be apportioned by obtaining a measurement of what's on hand from the fuel company. No adjustments are necessary for gas or electric homes, since the utility company will read the meter on closing day, closing the seller's account and opening one for the buyer. No need to count sunbeams if the house is solar-heated. They're still free.

Final inspection. The contract allows the buyer to pay a final visit to check warrantied plumbing, heating, and appliances to be sure they are in good working order. If the furnace wheezes its last two days later, that's the buyer's tough luck—except when you're buying a new house from a builder, whose warranties usually extend for at least a year.

Other financial surprises. If you're buying, be prepared for a cornucopia of assorted closing costs. If the bank requires escrow for taxes and insurance, you may be hit with a sizable outlay. This depends, of course, on the time of year. If, for example, taxes are paid in January and you close in July, you'll be asked to pay at least six month's escrow in advance so the bank will have the money needed when due.

Other closing costs include title insurance and search, the bank's (and your own) legal fees, transfer and mortgage taxes, documentary stamps, and the fees for recording the mortgage and deed. To avoid future shock, get all of this information in advance.

Arrange for the needed money in advance, too. The $17,271 due the seller should be by certified or bank teller/cashier's checks. In practice, to leave margin for minor error, I always advise my clients that these checks should total several hundred dollars less—$17,000 in this case. This is because the lower figure permits last-minute-problem flexibility, and once a check is certified at the bank, it's inflexible. By long custom, purchasers accept a personal check for the small balance—holding their breath till it clears. It's a good idea to make any certified or bank checks payable to yourself, and then endorse them over at the closing. Then, if the deal falls through, you may merely redeposit them in your account. If you've had them made out to Sam Seller, it could be a hassle.

All other closing costs can be paid by personal check. Just be sure you have enough money in your account.

THE FINAL STEP: TAKING TITLE

If you've done all your homework, the closing should be as easy as falling off a skateboard. As an attorney, I normally prepare a closing agenda only for a complicated transaction. It's second nature to me now, several hundred closings after my "opening closing" as an uncertain, uneasy young lawyer. But I heartily commend such a closing checklist to you. Now let's walk through a typical closing together.

A. *List the cast of characters.* List and identify everyone who'll be at the closing: the buyer, seller, attorneys, bank representative, title company rep, broker. (This is not just an exercise. Later the list will serve as a valuable record, in the event that questions or problems come up months or years from now.)

B. *Dispose of objections.* The title report, generally delivered several weeks earlier, identifies any "objections" the title company may have turned up—for example, a break in the chain of title (the discovery that 25 years ago, someone failed to get a spouse's signature on the deed). Other common objections include unpaid mortgage, unsatisfied judgments, and unpaid taxes or other liens.

Ordinarily many of these objections are cleared up by the seller in advance of closing. He's paid those unpaid taxes, obtained that missing signature, satisfied those judgments. But sometimes the seller doesn't have the money to pay off a judgment. It may even be the reason he's selling the property. And only rarely does he have the money to pay off the old mortgage.

So what happens? Recently I attended a closing in which I represented neither buyer nor seller. I was there for a client who had a $7,000 judgment against the seller. When checks changed hands, by prearrangement a certified check to my client, carved right out of the purchase price, went to me in return for a written satisfaction of the lien that removed the major obstacle to the transaction.

At another closing, the seller's old mortgage, held by a bank in an adjoining state, had to be satisfied. A certified check for some $27,000 was given to the title company representative (plus two days' extra interest), to be delivered to the bank in exchange for their document discharging the mortgage.

Some objections remain in limbo beyond the closing. Example: You're seated at the bank's long walnut conference table. Last week, you called the seller and told him the title report had turned up a $400 mechanic's lien. "Have them check it again," he insisted. "I paid that months ago." But a double-check revealed that the records showed the lien was still open. The title company then lists that lien as an exception to its insurance, unless it is either satisfied at the closing (the seller shows him the satisfaction of lien papers which he's forgotten to file with the county clerk) or $400 plus interest is placed in escrow with the title company.

It's customary for the title company rep to make a last-minute call to the county clerk's office—where someone is standing by on the hot line at all times—to be sure no last-minute liens have been slapped on the property of the parties. If there are, and you don't find out about them, you've bought them, too. (That, by the way, is another reason for that title insurance policy you're buying. If their man missed it, it's their bill, not yours.)

C. *Balance the books.* In the tenth step, you computed the adjustments, and reviewed them on the phone with "the other side." Now re-review them face to face, to make sure there have been no changes and you both come up with the same bottom line. You came with a pocketful of certified checks. Now you've got to write a personal check for the small balance and get ready to hand them all over. But first, since the bank checks won't come back to you, now's a good time to photocopy them for your records. While you're at it, throw the personal checks on the photocopy machine, too.

D. *Clear up the additional costs.* If you've done your homework, you know exactly what they're going to be. When you received a "we are pleased to inform you" letter from the bank, committing themselves to entrust you with their depositors' money, they thoughtfully reminded you of their additional charges—their attorney's fees and other charges (appraisal fee, credit check, etc.), costs for recording the mortgage, and additional originating fees or "points," if any (a one-time charge of some banks, which suspicious minds might say fattens their piece of the action without violating usury laws).

The letter from the bank may have some other interesting news for you—that you are required to deposit an escrow with them for the payment of property taxes and, possibly, insurance. This means that each mortgage payment will have an add-on of one-twelfth of the estimated annual taxes and insurance premium. Let's assume you close in April and taxes will be payable the following June. Since you will only have made two mortgage payments by then, where will the money necessary to pay the remaining ten months' taxes come from? Your pocket, of course. At the closing, the bank will require you to advance the additional escrow needed to insure that government may continue to function and that default will not take place.

Among other goodies for the buyer will be a bill from the title company for search, insurance, and the cost of recording the deed and the mortgage. Documentary stamps (or transfer tax) for the deed will be required, too, but the seller pays for these. He also pays the legal and recording fees involved in satisfying his old mortgage.

If there is a broker involved, he'll sit quietly in the corner, a small smile of anticipation curling the corners of his mouth, until he sees checks start to change hands. Then smile will change to grin and he'll step forward to receive his long-awaited due.

E. *Sign, seal, and deliver.* Now it's final paper-shuffling time, but examining them carefully comes first.

•*The deed.* Prepared by the seller or his attorney, this should be examined to make sure that all names are correct and that the description fits the property. This document (starting with "This indenture . . .") is signed by the seller, and his signature acknowledged by a notary public (often the title man, sometimes the bank representative or an attorney). If the purchaser is taking over the mortgage, he, too, may be required to sign the deed.

Technically, the deed is now ready for delivery to the purchaser.

Actually, it is shuffled past him to his lawyer or the title company rep who will record it.

•*The mortgage obligation.* If you're assuming the seller's mortgage, he should give you a photocopy—or his own copy—for your records. If it's a brand-new mortgage, there will be a sheaf of additional papers for the buyer to examine and sign. If you're representing yourself, request copies of these papers a few days early so that you can study their often arcane and bewildering language at leisure. These are usually preprinted forms the bank's lawyers developed years ago and modify periodically. It's usually take-it-or-leave-it boilerplate with little room for negotiating maneuvers, but there are some things you should check. Verify the numbers—the interest rate quoted, the amount of the mortgage, so you're not borrowing $10,000 more than you need because of a clerical error, the monthly payment, and such things as the prepayment clause. If any points are unclear, this is no time to be shy. Ask the bank's representative to explain them to your satisfaction.

One of the things you may ask him to explain is why he's asking you to sign both a mortgage and a note, or bond. He should know. But just in case he's been doing it by rote, let me explain. The note is evidence of your debt and promise to repay. It contains all the terms—principal amount, interest, and time of repayment. The mortgage is security for the note—giving the bank your property as collateral, and the right to sell it if you fail to meet your payments.

After the mortgage and the note are signed, the originals are delivered to the lender. The mortgage is signed by both borrower and lender. The note is signed by the borrower-buyer. The mortgage (though not the note) is then recorded at the county clerk's office. Recording gives notice to the world that the property has a new owner and he owes a lot of money on it.

•*Other documents.* Some will be signed, some exchanged. If you're selling the house and have any unexpired warranties or service contracts (on the roof, appliances, heating or cooling systems) or instruction booklets, it's customary—and nice—to turn them over to the new owner. (If you're the buyer, you may want to require this in the contract.)

Any woman involved, particularly if she's a seller (or buyer, if she's a mortgagor) will be given special attention—an extra sworn statement that she has not been known by any other name (maiden, or prior marriage, for example) in the past ten years. This is assurance that there are no liens against the property in another name.

202

•*Delivery of the keys.* The balance of the purchase price can now be delivered to the seller, in exchange for the properly executed deed to the premises. This is a scene right out of the Geneva peace talks: everyone sitting around a long document-strewn table. On the seller's side: the signed deed awaits delivery. On the buyer's side: a pile of checks for the purchase price balance and incidentals. The buyer sits hunched over the table, a checkbook in front of him, filling in one check after another. Every time he thinks he's finished, someone says, "One more for . . ."

Finally the ordeal is over. Buyers and sellers shake hands warmly—if they're ethnic Mediterraneans, they embrace and kiss—and wish one another good luck in their new homes. It's all over but the recording.

•*Recording the documents.* Resisting the impulse to drive to the new home for a first exultant look as lord and lady of all you survey, take a short detour to the office of the county clerk—or arrange for the title man to do it for you—to record your deed. Every locale has a recording method, often a map dividing the county into section, lot, and block numbers, but sometimes by town, city, or village. Take special pains to be sure that the instrument you are filing has the proper information on it by double-checking it with the filed locality map.

If the clerk makes a mistake and indexes it incorrectly (right information but wrong location), the office is liable for any damages. But if the information on the document is wrong, you'll have no recourse for any damages you suffer.

The recording of an instrument—such as a deed or a mortgage— is "constructive notice" to the world of whatever is in that instrument. So failure to record, or inaccurate recording, leaves the door open for quite serious future problems. Make sure it's shut.

Now you can go home and tremble as you watch the moving men bounce your barrel of antique china onto the driveway.

203

CHAPTER 13

Unequal Warfare: *Landlord* v. *Tenant*

My late Uncle Nate often reminisced fondly about the Good Old Days, but not if the days under discussion were the early 1930s. Along with tens of millions of other Americans, he was out of work then—in his case, "only two years." But one thing Uncle Nate did enjoy recalling—besides two-for-a-penny rolls and milk at 10¢ a quart—was the tenant's market in housing.

"Half the apartments were vacant at that time," he overstated cheerfully. "Landlords gave you three to six months' concession on two-year leases, just to get their hands on one month's hard-cash security deposit. We would sign a lease, stay the three months, then arrange a new three months' concession somewhere else and move out. In those days, families moved so often that sometimes after school children would get mixed up and go home to last month's apartment house."

Today, for 90 million U.S. tenants, it's a somewhat different story. About the only concession a tenant can get out of a landlord these days is ten minutes to read the lease. Then, it's often, "Take it or leave it!" We have not regressed quite far enough in time so that the landlord, as in common-law days of yore, is the undisputed Lord of the Land once more. But in most situations—barring the terraced penthouse apartments of the very rich, where the long-term tenant can do a certain amount of dictating, or the bombed-out rat-ridden tenements of the urban poor, which many landlords have abandoned entirely—the landlord-tenant relationship today is unequal warfare, indeed. It's elephant gun against peashooter. It's the U.S.S.R. against Luxembourg.

THE FIRST STEP:
WHAT KIND OF LEASE DO YOU HAVE?

THE ORAL LEASE

Oral leases are surprisingly common, and not only in rooming houses. Legally, an oral lease ("How much is this room?" "$50 a week." "OK, I'll take it") cannot run more than a year, but it can be renewed. The "tenancy at will" situation which it creates can be terminated by either party, upon notice equal to the term of the original agreement.* Thus, if you're renting by the week, you can't just up and leave on the last day. If you don't give your landlord a week's notice, you could be legally liable for another week's rent. The razor has twin blades, however. Even if someone else offers him double your rent, the landlord can't throw you out without giving you a week's notice.

For long-term apartment rental, oral leases can be unwise and formidable to enforce. I learned that many years ago from the case of Alice Kelly, a sweet little lady in her seventies, who lived alone (if we don't count her dozen cats) in her old three-story frame house until the money ran out. The corner druggist—let's call him Godfrey Goodheart—who'd been filling her prescriptions and giving her arthritis advice for years, generously volunteered to take the aging house off her hands. He offered to pay all future taxes and upkeep costs for her. Alice, he said, could just sit pretty, rent-free for the remainder of her earthly tenancy.

It sounded like a good deal to Alice, who had neither a head for business, nor relatives to turn to for advice. She trustingly deeded the building over to him. Goodheart, ever the shrewd businessman, proceeded to rent out the top and bottom floors, leaving the parlor floor to Alice. She was happy, but the new tenants, bombarding their landlord with complaints about Alice's thundering herd of cats, were not. Goodheart, who had come to enjoy the pleasures of collecting rent, conveniently forgot that Alice had ever owned the building at all. The fact that he had carefully avoided committing himself to her on paper certainly helped. At first, Goodheart simply asked Alice to get rid of her cats. Then, incensed at her insensitivity to the wishes of his paying tenants, he served her with an eviction notice, on the grounds that her menagerie was a nuisance to the other tenants.

In tears, with no money and nowhere to go, Alice came to the Legal Aid Society, where I was then employed as a new law school graduate for salary-plus-experience. After a brief trial, the eviction proceeding was dismissed. But shortly thereafter, a building inspector mysteriously learned that three families were living in a house zoned for two, and issued a violation. Of course, the family

---

*In Louisiana, the month-to-month lease requires only ten days' notice.

that had to go, Goodheart decreed, was Alice and her cats. Happily, the courts decreed otherwise. The case was argued in four courts—from Municipal Court all the way up to the state Court of Appeals, and it took some 300 hours of legal talent and time—mine at Legal Aid, plus that of two excellent volunteer attorneys: Helen Buttenweiser and Stephen Weise. In the end, we won our action to reform the deed to give Alice her life tenancy—which she and her cats enjoy to this day. I know. I got a Christmas card from her not long ago.

THE WRITTEN LEASE

A document prepared for the rental of real property by one or both of the parties to it is called simply a "written lease." In my opinion, the simpler the better. The first legal agreement between myself and the young attorney who later became my partner was a simple written lease—a brief letter we both signed, setting forth the terms of his rental of a room in my law office. Any such agreement should describe the property unmistakably. Generally, street, building, and apartment or room number will suffice, but it doesn't hurt to specify rights to common areas like balconies, laundry rooms, or backyards. The "term," or length, of the lease and the amount of rent should also be spelled out, and—no matter how much goodwill exists, at the euphoric moment of signing—you'll save recriminations later if you're specific about who's responsible for repairs, painting, and the like.

But such an informal contractual soufflé is light-years away from the typical apartment hunter's experience. When you've found an apartment you like at a rental you can almost afford, the landlord or real estate agent slaps an imposing document on the table—4 inches thick and as many as 3,500 words of small type, of which the only parts the agent calls to your attention are the opening line (reassuringly phrased "Standard Form of Apartment Lease—Approved by the Shady Valley Real Estate Board") and the closing line (reading "Tenant's signature"). You are faced with what is known as a printed formal lease—also known as a *fait accompli*—and whoever printed it, sponsored it, or approved it, you can rest assured that they get along very well indeed with landlords. The standard lease has, in fact, been described by one disgruntled tenant as "the cruelest instrument devised by man since the invention of the bear trap."

The standard lease comes in all shapes, sizes, and forms. But the fact that it's printed and formal doesn't mean that it's etched in bronze and inviolable, though that is surely what your renting agent would like you to believe. If you take the time to read and evaluate the lease—something that may immediately brand you as a troublemaker—you'll find some pretty outrageous advantages are awarded to the landlord. If you have any bargaining clout at all, you may be able to have some of the more offensive clauses stricken or altered. Whatever you do, don't sign in a hurry and regret for the next two years.

THE SECOND STEP:
EXERCISE YOUR CLOUT—HOWEVER LIMITED

If you're moving from Fifth Avenue to Sutton Place, and deciding between several $1,200-a-month luxury apartments, or if you're a physician moving into an as yet only half-rented suburban professional building, you have much muscle. If you know there are a number of vacancies, call the landlord's bluff when he tries his "hurry up and sign before someone else grabs it" gambit.

On the other hand, if you're a college student trying to rent a Boston studio apartment in a building with a waiting list, you may well have to either take it on the landlord's terms or renew your weary search. With luck, you may find that some of the lease clauses that remind you of your "Feudal Society" course are illegal in your area, and because they violate "public policy" could conceivably be held invalid in court if it later comes to a crunch. But don't count on it. Legislation must be very specific and deliberate to circumvent explicit contract clauses, and under the traditional *caveat lessee* ("let the tenant beware"), it's easy to sign away legal and even constitutional rights—such things as trial by jury.

THE THIRD STEP:
READ THE SMALL PRINT

Now let's look at a standard lease's most important clauses through a lawyer's eyes to find out what you're getting into, and what you can sometimes get out of. Most of this form lease happens to be the New York Real Estate Board version—with clauses shuffled around for purposes of exposition and explanation—but if you've seen one standard real estate board lease, you've pretty

208

much seen them all. When you're finished, you might want to look at the back of this chapter at the proposed model lease put together by interested parties in our nation's capital. You'll find some refreshing and encouraging differences. And, any clauses you can adroitly persuade your landlord to insert will put you that much ahead of the game.

THE PREMISES, TERM, AND RENT

WITNESSETH: That Landlord hereby leases to Tenant and Tenant hereby hires from Landlord, the apartment known as Apartment —— on the —— floor, in the building known as —— in the County of ——, State of ——, for the term of (or until such term shall sooner cease and expire, as hereinafter provided), to commence on the —— day of ——, nineteen hundred and —— and to end on the day of ——, nineteen hundred and ——, both dates inclusive, at a rental of $——, which Tenant agrees to pay in lawful money of the United States, which shall be legal tender in payment of all debts and dues, public and private, at the time of payment, in equal monthly installments in advance on the first day of each month during said term, at the office of Landlord or such other place as Landlord may designate, without any set-off or deduction whatsoever, except that Tenant shall pay the first monthly installment on the execution hereof.

The amount of rent is negotiable, but in most places, current supply (tight) and demand (great) make successful bargaining difficult. If you should encounter a surprisingly low rent, the surprise when your lease is up may be even greater. It could be a tactic called "lowballing," sometimes used in areas with apartment surpluses, as was the case when my Aunt Augusta moved into a lovely beachfront apartment in a modern new building in South Florida at a $300 monthly rental, considerably lower than anything comparable in the area. The surprise came when her two-year lease was up—a $65 monthly increment that was enough to give the landlord a plump 20 percent increase, but still low enough so that it was cheaper for her to stay than to move.

Landlords are twice-blessed by rent raises. They increase profits. And because of a formula used by realtors in selling apartment houses, they increase their equity and the building's value as well. An apartment house is sold at a multiple of its rent roll (the combined annual rent of all its apartments), with different multiples in different areas. A modern building in an excellent neighborhood might go for eight times its rent roll, which is to say that a building taking in $300,000 a year in rents would sell for roughly $2.4 million. In middle-class areas, depending upon its condition, a building might sell for only four to six times its rent roll. A rundown house in a blighted urban area might go for only double its rent roll—which means that, in many cases, the new landlord becomes a slumlord. His game plan is to collect rent for two or three years, while evading real estate taxes, and providing little or no heat or repairs, after which he abandons the property, walking away with a neat profit.

So it's not just the $65 a month my aunt's landlord was after. Nor was it even the $780 a year that represented. It was the fact that the increase multiplied by eight (it was a brand-new building) had, just on that one apartment alone, increased the value of his building by $6,240. Is it any wonder that landlords play the rent hike game so hard?

Even the renting agent's arithmetic can get you in trouble. Several years ago, I had a case that ended in court because of the former owner's error in preparing the lease. The rental agreed upon was $185 a month. For a three-year lease, that would amount to $6,600. When the landlord computed the total rent, he multiplied mistakenly—though innocently—by four years, and the lease provided for "a total rental of $8,880, payable in equal monthly installments." While the original landlord owned the building, he collected the agreed $185, but the next landlord had a pocket calculator. He quickly discovered that $8,880 divided by 36 months equaled $244.44 and demanded the difference. Two years of rent receipts clearly established the original intent, but at the cost of legal fees, lost time, indignation, and inconvenience.

Similarly, the term in years should correspond with the specified beginning and ending dates. On more than one occasion, I've seen leases providing for a term of years that did not correspond with the dates. I recently saw a lease that provided for a term of five years, commencing November 1, 1975, and ending October 31, 1979. When '79 comes along, will the tenant have another year or will he have to "renegotiate or vacate?" The intent of the parties will govern, but it may prove expensive to establish.

OCCUPANCY

The demised premises and any part thereof shall be occupied only by Tenant and the members of the immediate family of Tenant, and as a strictly private dwelling apartment and for no other purpose.

If a cousin from Oregon—or a girlfriend from across town—moves in with you bag and baggage, don't expect the landlord to applaud and put an extra name on the mailbox. He might, but then again he could start eviction proceedings because you've violated your lease. If, however, your landlord goes beyond threatening—possibly in an effort to raise your rent—he may or may not succeed. A New York City judge ruled against the landlord who tried to use the "immediate family" clause to evict an unmarried couple from a rent-controlled apartment, declaring that "she certainly is [immediate family] in the eyes of today's world."

Less liberal interpretations are certainly possible, but most courts will not frivolously put people out on the sidewalk. They evict only for "substantial violations" of the lease—three families packed like anchovies in a two-bedroom apartment, for instance. Still, if you plan to have someone move in later, it's a good idea to get the landlord's written permission up front.

Don't think that your pets (dogs, cats, monkeys, or snakes) will be accepted as members of your immediate family either—not by a landlord who has a clause barring them in the lease or its "rules and regulations" section. If you plan to keep a pet, it's a good idea to let the landlord know and get his permission in writing—or you could find yourself and/or your pets starring in an eviction proceeding.

ASSIGNMENT, MORTGAGE, ETC.

Tenant, and Tenant's heirs, distributees, executors, administrators, legal representatives, successors and assigns, shall not assign, mortgage or encumber this agreement, nor underlet, or use or permit the demised premises or any part thereof to be used by others, without the prior written consent of Landlord in each instance.

This means you can't assign your apartment lease to someone else—sublet, underlet, or rent out the entire flat, or one or more rooms in it—without the landlord's prior written consent. "Assignment" is a marathon sublet—turning over the entire premises to the end of your lease.

Getting permission may not be easy after you sign. But a reasonable landlord will let you add to this clause something like, "permission to assign or sublet will not be unreasonably withheld," or "will not be withheld if suitable substitute is found" (meaning someone roughly equivalent or superior in socioeconomic standing, credit rating, etc.). In some pro-consumer states, limitations on the landlord's power to reject subtenants have been legislated. In general—in Louisiana, for example—if nothing is stipulated in the lease, you have the right to sublet.

If clearing the ground for assigning or subletting is difficult, the formal process itself is simple enough: The tenant and subtenant sign an agreement to the effect that the subject premises are assigned or sublet, and tenant transfers to subtenant all (assignment) or a part (subletting) of the rights and responsibilities set forth in the original lease, of which it is wise to attach a copy.

SECURITY

Tenant has this day deposited with Landlord the sum of $ as security for the full and faithful performance by Tenant of all the terms, covenants, and conditions of this lease upon Tenant's part to be performed, which said sum shall be returned to Tenant after the time fixed as the expiration of the term herein, provided Tenant has fully and faithfully carried out all of said terms, covenants, and conditions on Tenant's part to be performed.

Leave the premises in reasonably good condition, and your landlord is obligated to return your security deposit. But this is an obligation that some landlords find excruciatingly painful, so much so that I have known landlords whose brazen policy it is to keep security deposits on any pretext they can dream up. Some won't even bother to declare their reasons. ("Dear Sir: I am keeping your security deposit out of pure greed and avarice" might not sound too good anyway.) They will simply ignore your letters until you run out of stamps. Others will claim that the building has changed hands, and the previous owner failed to turn over his tenants' deposits. (Don't buy that Golden Gate Bridge—even if true, it's his fault and problem, not yours.)

Some landlords will blandly inform you that the deposit was used to repair damage you inflicted on the premises. But you can build a fortress against that tactic by having a clause added to your lease before signing that no reasonable landlord could refuse—requiring the landlord to send you, within ten days of your moving out, either your deposit or his itemized reasons for not returning it.

Even with this precaution, you may have to take your landlord to court.

Most states require the landlord to keep security in a separate bank account, and some insist the account be interest-bearing. If this isn't so in your state, you may be able to negotiate it into the lease. Even if it is the case, it doesn't hurt to write it in to jog your landlord's memory. This isn't penny wisdom. Six percent a year for three years on $800 yields a handsome $150 bonus to help pay the movers. And after all—though your landlord may seem to have forgotten that when it's time to return it—it's your money!

Californians report that landlords have introduced what tenants consider a new rip-off—a "cleaning security fee" of $50 or $60, which is ostensibly to be used to clean the apartment for the next tenant, if the old tenant fails to do the job. In some instances, such cleaning is badly needed—but $25 would easily do the job, and many landlords stubbornly retain the fee even when flats are left broom-clean. The solution: a reliable witness and a visit to Small Claims Court.

ALTERATIONS

Tenant shall make no alterations, decorations, additions, or improvements in or to demised premises without Landlord's prior written consent, and then only by contractors or merchants approved by Landlord. All such work shall be done at such time and in such manner as Landlord may from time to time designate. All alterations, additions, or improvements upon demised premises, made by either party, including all paneling, decorations, partitions, railings, mezzanine floors, galleries, and the like, shall, unless Landlord elect otherwise (which election shall be made by giving a notice pursuant to the provisions of Article 25 not less than 3 days prior to the expiration or other termination of this lease or any renewal or extension thereof), become the property of Landlord, and shall remain upon, and be surrendered with said premises, as a part thereof, at the end of the term hereof.

The tenant who wants to improve the apartment to make his stay more enjoyable should first make sure that the landlord shares his idea of the good. Otherwise, the landlord may legally remove the improvement at the tenant's expense. If you paint, don't flirt with dark colors, unless you don't mind being stuck with a painting bill. Landlords prefer pastels because it takes only one coat to cover them for the next tenant. They'll bill you for the second coat.

If you know ahead of time what alterations you'd like to make—painting, wallpapering, partitions—try to get the landlord's permission in the lease before signing. He's more likely to grant it when he's (however mildly) anxious for your signature. But don't forget that "all alterations . . . become the property of the Landlord." He can keep your cherrywood paneling—unless you've arranged otherwise in writing beforehand, or can remove it without damaging the walls. Having improved his building at your expense, he can raise the rent for the next tenant.

NO REPRESENTATIONS BY LANDLORD

Landlord or Landlord's agents have made no representations or promises with respect to the said building, the land upon which it is erected or demised premises except as herein expressly set forth and no rights, easements, or licenses are acquired by Tenant by implication or otherwise except as expressly set forth in the provisions of this lease. The taking possession of the demised premises shall be conclusive evidence, as against Tenant, that Tenant accepts same "as is" and that said premises and the building of which the same form a part were in good and satisfactory condition at the time such possession was so taken.

This clause makes clear the true value of the renting agent's brisk assurances that the landlord will repaint, fix the exposed wiring, and put in a new toilet before you move in. If you don't have it in writing, you don't have it. But it isn't easy to get a landlord to acknowledge in writing any responsibility for repairs in the lease. It's very much to his advantage to stick to the standard form, where the hot potato of responsibility is passed on to the tenant. Watch out for that "as is" phrase. Inspect the premises carefully—do toilets flush, bedroom doors close snugly, refrigerators cool, air conditioning, range, and oven work? If they don't and you fail to have that fact noted in your lease (again, don't take the renting agent's promise), the repair costs could be on you.

REPAIRS

Tenant shall take good care of demised premises and fixtures therein and, subject to provisions of Article 4 hereof shall make, as and when needed, as a result of misuse or neglect by Tenant, all repairs in and about demised premises necessary to preserve them in good order and condition, which repairs shall in quality and class be equal to the original work. Except as provided in Article 11 hereof, there shall be no allowance to Tenant for a diminution of rental value, and no liability on the part of Landlord by reason of inconvenience, or annoyance arising from the making of any repairs, alterations, additions, or improvements in or to any portion of the building or demised premises, or in or to fixtures, appurtenances, or equipment, and no liability upon Landlord for failure to make any repairs, alterations, additions, or improvements in or to any portion of the building or demised premises, or in or to fixtures, appurtenances, or equipment.

The net result of this dense prose is that the tenant is responsible for everything, the Landlord for next-to-nothing. To guard against costly charges of "misuse or neglect," the tenant must leave the apartment the way he found it—give or take a few smudges on the walls, cracks in the plaster, or a loose knob on the kitchen cabinet. (Even if the lease does not relieve the tenant of responsibility for "normal wear and tear," it is implied by law.)

SERVICES

As long as Tenant is not in default under any of the provisions of this lease, Landlord convenants to furnish, insofar as the existing facilities provide, the following services: (a) Elevator service; (b) Hot and cold water in reasonable quantities at all times; (c) Heat at reasonable hours during the cold seasons of the year. Interruption or curtailment of any such services shall not constitute a constructive or partial eviction nor, unless caused by the gross negligence of Landlord, entitle Tenant to any compensation or abatement of rent. Mechanical refrigeration equipment, if provided, is for the accommodation of Tenant, and Landlord shall not be responsible for any failure of refrigeration or for leakage or damage caused by or as the result of such mechanical refrigeration or failure thereof for any reason whatsoever. If electric current be supplied by Landlord, Tenant covenants and agrees to purchase the same from Landlord or Landlord's designated agent at the rates charged to residential consumers by any electric corporation subject to the jurisdiction of the Public Service Commission and serving the part of the city where the building is located; bills therefor shall be rendered at such times as Landlord may elect and the amount, as computed from a meter installed by Landlord, or Landlord's agent, shall be deemed to be and be paid as additional rental. Landlord may discontinue such service upon thirty (30) days' notice to Tenant without being liable therefor or in any way affecting the liability of Tenant hereunder. In the event that Landlord gives such notice, Landlord shall permit Tenant to receive such service from any other person or corporation and shall permit

215

Landlord's wires and conduits to be used for such purpose. Tenant shall make no alteration or additions to the electric equipment and/or appliances without the prior written consent of Landlord in each instance. It is expressly understood and agreed that any covenants on Landlord's part to furnish any service pursuant to any of the terms or provisions of this lease, or to perform any act or thing for the benefit of Tenant shall not be deemed breached if Landlord is unable to perform the same by virtue of a strike or labor trouble or any other cause whatsoever beyond Landlord's control. If any tax be imposed upon Landlord's receipts from the sale or resale of electrical energy or gas or telephone service to Tenant by any Municipal, State, or Federal agency, Tenant covenants and agrees that, where permitted by law, Tenant's pro-rata share of such taxes shall be passed on to and included in the bill of and paid by Tenant to Landlord.

Are you beginning to feel that you're getting a raw deal? You are. And perhaps nowhere in the lease more than in the clauses on Repairs and Services is it clear why the standard lease has been called "the last stronghold of feudalism." But, of course, the lease and its supporting common law hark back to the days when the lord of the manor permitted you to work his land and live in a cottage thereon, in return for a lordly portion of your produce. The landlord's only obligation then was to give you possession, and to leave you to quietly enjoy and reasonably use his property. He didn't have to deliver the premises in livable condition. He didn't have to make repairs. He didn't have to do anything but collect rent.

Modern landlords go their medieval antecedents one better by providing elevator service, heat, electricity, and running water—if all goes well. If it doesn't, the lease, echoing common law, warns that you can't complain, unless it's the result of the landlord's "gross negligence." But you do have a legal ace-in-the-hole. If there is one clause to cherish in the standard lease, one that points the way—to court, if necessary, as we'll see later—to a solution to problems that may arise later, it's this one.

QUIET ENJOYMENT

Landlord covenants and agrees with Tenant that upon Tenant paying said rent, and performing all the covenants and conditions aforesaid, on Tenant's part to be observed and performed, Tenant shall and may peaceably and quietly have, hold, and enjoy the premises hereby demised, for the term aforesaid, subject, however, to the terms of the lease and of the ground leases, underlying leases, and mortgages herein before mentioned.

Keep it in mind when you sign the lease. It could be your salvation later. This clause is the tenant's best friend.

THE FOURTH STEP:
BE SURE THE LANDLORD SIGNS THE LEASE

Additions or alterations, if any, that you artfully manage to negotiate should be typed in and initialed by both parties. It takes two to make a contract. The lease isn't binding until the signatures of both parties adorn it. I've heard of less than scrupulous landlords who, when leases signed by new tenants are sent to them by the agent for signature, conveniently "forget" to return a signed copy* to the tenant. They put off with sundry excuses any tenant smart enough to suspect he's being had. The naive renter thinks he's bound by the lease, while the crafty landlord knows he's free to consider him an eminently dumpable "tenant at will."

THE FIFTH STEP:
PROBLEMS WITH THE LANDLORD

For centuries until modern times, the courts separated the tenant's obligation to pay rent from the landlord's responsibility to provide services. This meant that even if the landlord failed to live up to the lease, the tenant could not retaliate by withholding rent payments. Many leases still buttress this ethically questionable principle.

But consumerism has begun to make its mark even in the archaic world of landlord-tenant relations. Courts and legislatures have begun to recognize that a landlord lets not just a piece of real estate, but a package of goods and services as well. State courts in Wisconsin, New Jersey, and New York have held that a lease is a contract. And a U.S. Court of Appeals has declared that "by signing the lease, the landlord has undertaken a continuing obligation to the tenant to maintain the premises in accordance with all applicable law." Thus, the provisions of local housing codes are being read into the lease as an "implied warranty of habitability." As one judge recently put it: "The rule . . . that separated the landlords' right to rent from their duty to provide services as required by law has been thoroughly sapped of vitality."

The position of the tenant in relation to the landlord still remains, in most jurisdictions, a weak one. But there are a growing number of routes you can follow if you feel that a landlord has not lived up to his obligations or your reasonable expectations. Depending

---

*Because it is signed by both parties, the legal term is actually not "copy," but "duplicate original."

217

upon the landlord, state and local statutes, and the circumstances, you may meet frustration and failure, or you may successfully redress your grievances. The more knowledgeable you are and the more persistent, the better your chances of success. The most common forms of recourse for the unhappy tenant are:

CALLING THE BOARD OF HEALTH

The lease you've signed probably attempts to relieve the landlord of his responsibility for maintaining sanitary premises. Many even include a clause that says "landlord or landlord's agents shall not be liable for the presence of bugs, vermin, or insects, if any, in the premises, nor shall their presence affect this lease." But housing and sanitary codes recognize the responsibility of landlords to meet certain standards. So, if despite frequent protests, the toilet continues to back up, the exterminator hasn't rung your bell, or the temperature hasn't edged over 50° F. throughout December, call your local board of health, or housing or building authority. In some areas, an inspector will arrive within hours—in others, heavily backlogged, it may take weeks—to write a "violation," ordering owner to make necessary repairs within, say, 30–60 days or face criminal proceedings.

You will feel vengeance is yours, until, as the days go by, you realize that your landlord intends to ignore the order. Technically, he may have committed a misdemeanor and could be prosecuted. But in many crowded courts, the case flow makes molasses seem a quick-flowing torrent. And when your case finally does come up, it may very well be dismissed. Our harried criminal courts have bigger fish to try. Even when convictions are won, imprisonment is extremely rare, and the average fine imposed in New York City, for example, decreased from about $25 in 1960 to well under $15 in 1968, about enough to make the payment seem more like a license than a penalty. To deal with this tendency of criminal courts to try and get housing cases out of the way as quickly as possible, some major cities (Baltimore, Chicago, and Atlanta, among others) have established special housing courts, making it the business of a group of judges to become sensitive to and deal consistently and effectively with housing violations.

TAKING THE LANDLORD TO CIVIL COURT

If the criminal courts won't get the hot water running, how about the civil courts? In New York City, a tenant sued his landlord for

218

the money he'd spent repainting his apartment after the landlord failed to comply with the housing authority's order to do so. The court found for the landlord, holding that a landlord's statutory duty to the municipality "does not create a contractual duty to the tenant which the latter could enforce."

A LAW SUIT AFTER INJURY OR PROPERTY DAMAGE HAS OCCURRED

The courts won't ordinarily allow an individual tenant to repair a ceiling to prevent plaster from hitting her, and then collect costs from the landlord. But many will allow her to recover damages after she's hit by falling plaster. Some courts have recently held that such a suit to recover damages for the landlord's wrongful act is the tenant's proper avenue of redress for housing violations.

The key in such situations is whether or not the landlord has been guilty of gross negligence in the events that led up to the damage or injury. Most leases clearly spell out the landlord's lack of liability for the loss of "property by theft or otherwise . . . for any injury or damage to persons or property resulting from falling plaster, steam, electricity, water, rain, or snow which may leak from any part of said building or from the pipes, appliances, or plumbing works . . . unless caused by or due to the negligence of landlord, landlord's agents, servants, or employees . . ."

How do you prove a landlord's negligence? First of all, if you've given your landlord sufficient and repeated notice of the need for a repair for which he is responsible, preferably by registered mail with a carbon copy for your files, and his failure to perform results in injury or damage, he is negligent. So if a corroded pipe you've asked him to fix finally ruptures and ruins your carpet, you have a good case.

So long as it is reasonably foreseeable, the landlord may even be negligent where the cause of a damage or injury results from the action of a third party. The tenant of a fifth-floor apartment repeatedly asked her landlord to repair a broken window opening onto the fire escape. When an intruder put his hand through the broken pane, unlocked the window, entered, and raped her, she recovered $10,000 from the landlord. In a similar case, Howard Johnson's recently paid singer Connie Francis well over $1 million for the motel's negligence in failing to provide adequate safeguards for the easily opened sliding glass doors of her room.

WITHHOLDING RENT

In a battle with the landlord, one quick way to get results—or, at least, capture his attention—is to withhold your rent. Such a tactic may occasionally motivate a landlord to take care of needed repairs, provide absent services, even pay for damages. Much more often, however, the immediate results will be considerably less salutary.

When a tenant stops paying rent, the landlord has several options. He can wait until the lease is up and sue for all the back rent; he can sue for each month's rent as it comes due; or he can bring action to evict you and sue for the rent you owe. The first alternative is too risky, and the second too costly, so landlords understandably tend to choose the third.

The courts have provided a quick, easy, inexpensive, and relatively fair way for the landlord to evict the tenant and legally recapture his property. This is known as "summary proceedings." The grounds on which these proceedings can be instituted vary from state to state, but generally include nonpayment of rent, breach of a major lease provision, and staying on after the term of the lease has ended. (If he doesn't want to evict you, the landlord has a good shot at legally requiring a holdover tenant to stay for another rental term of equal length.)

Depending on the grounds and the state, the landlord may or may not have to warn you before starting proceedings. He begins by serving a legal document called—again, depending upon the state—a warrant, a precept, a summons, or a notice. In different jurisdictions, this document may be served in a variety of ways: personally; by posting on the tenant's door; or by a combination of posting and mailing, known as "nail and mail." (The name is a bit outdated, cellophane tape having replaced the nail.)

A colorfully unethical method known as "sewer service" is all too common. The process server provides a fraudulent affidavit to the effect that the tenant has been legally served, but the tenant knows nothing about it until the sheriff shows up with a court order to evict.

A strategy we used at Legal Aid neatly counters such gutter tactics as sewer service. The first move is to bring a motion in court to vacate the judgment on grounds of nonservice. Because requirements differ from jurisdiction to jurisdiction, it might be best to phone or visit the court clerk to find out what form your motion papers should take.

Once this paper has been filed, the burden is now on the landlord

220

to prove the summons was properly served. A hearing is held at which the process server must testify, recounting to the best of his recollection the circumstances of the service. At Legal Aid, I used to invite someone other than my client to sit with me at the counsel table during the hearing, while my client sat unobtrusively in the front row. Invariably, the server would mistakenly point to the person beside me. Invariably, my motion to vacate would be granted. Bring several people with you—a friend, a cousin—and stay quietly in the background early in the proceedings, while one of them forcefully insists that the process server identify the person in the courtroom on whom he served the summons. With luck, he'll point to one of them, instead of at you.

In most states, the summons is paired with another document called a petition (or affidavit, or complaint), specifying the grounds for the proceedings and the relief sought. The landlord can ask for possession of the property and a money judgment for rent due. In some states, a separate "action for rent" is required.

The moment the process server hands you the "eviction notice" will be a traumatic one. But take comfort: It's also the moment that allows you to go to court to file your counterclaim. If the counterclaim relates directly to the landlord's claim for rent, such as his failure to provide essential service, the judge will hear them together. If he upholds your claim, you will be able to offset your damages against the rent owed. If your counterclaim is only indirectly related—say, personal injury from falling plaster—it is possible that the claims will be severed and yours heard at a later date, with the judge ordering you to pay the rent in the meantime. If you have a case against the landlord, follow the procedures suggested in the Sixth Step: Going To Court (see p. 226).

An occasional landlord will not bother with the legal proceedings involved in an eviction. In common law, the aggrieved property owner has always had the right to perform a "self-help" eviction—though since 1381, the law has thoughtfully insisted that the means be peaceful. Indications in the lease to the contrary, force or the threat of force are illegal. Also illegal, though often effectively used, is the procedure aptly named "lockout," in which the landlord enters the property with a passkey when the tenant is out, removes her property, and changes the lock.

BREAKING THE LEASE

If you'd rather not wait for the ceiling to fall in or frostbite to set in, you may just want to pack up and move out, lease notwithstanding. *Don't*—at least, not until you've collected strong evidence (diaries, witnesses willing to testify to conditions, complaint letters to the landlord, etc.) showing that it was your only prudent course. The lease usually protects the landlord against your unscheduled departure, no matter how great his guilt.

As the *Remedies of Landlord* clause indicates:

In case of any such default, re-entry, expiration, and/or dispossess by summary proceedings or otherwise, (a) the rent shall become due thereupon and be paid up to the time of such re-entry, dispossess, and/or expiration, together with such expenses as Landlord may incur for legal expenses, attorneys' fees, brokerage, and/or putting the demised premises in good order, or for preparing the same for rental; (b) Landlord may re-let the premises or any part or parts thereof, either in the name of Landlord or otherwise, for a term or terms which may at Landlord's option be less than or exceed the period which would otherwise have constituted the balance of the term of this lease and may grant concessions or free rent; and/or (c) Tenant or the legal representatives of Tenant shall also pay Landlord as liquidated damages for the failure of Tenant to observe and perform said Tenant's covenants herein contained, any deficiency between the rent hereby reserved and/or covenanted to be paid and the net amount, if any, of the rents collected on account of the lease or leases of the demised premises for each month of the period which would otherwise have constituted the balance of the term of this lease. In computing such liquidated damages there shall be added to the said deficiency such expenses as Landlord may incur in connection with re-letting, such as legal expenses, attorneys' fees, brokerage, and for keeping the demised premises in good order or for preparing the same for re-letting. Any such liquidated damages shall be paid in monthly installments by Tenant on the rent day specified in this lease and any suit brought to collect the amount of the deficiency for any month shall not prejudice in any way the rights of Landlord to collect the deficiency for any subsequent month by a similar proceedings. Landlord at Landlord's option may make such alteration and/or decorations in the demised premises as Landlord in Landlord's sole judgment considers advisable and necessary for the purpose of re-letting the demised premises; and the making of such alterations and/or decorations shall not operate or be construed to release Tenant from liability hereunder as aforesaid. Landlord shall in no event be liable in any way whatsoever for failure to re-let the demised premises, or in the event that the demised premises are re-let for failure to collect the rent thereof under such re-letting. In the event of a breach or threatened breach by Tenant of any of the covenants or provisions hereof, Landlord shall have the right of injunction and the right to invoke any remedy allowed at law or in equity as if re-entry, summary proceedings, and other remedies were not herein provided for. Mention in this lease of any particular remedy shall not preclude Landlord from any other remedy, in law or in equity. Tenant hereby expressly waives any and all rights of redemption granted by or under any present or future laws in the event of Tenant being evicted or dispossessed for any cause, or in the event of Landlord obtaining possession of demised premises, by reason of the violation by Tenant of any of the covenants of this lease or otherwise.

For many, the traditional method of choice for breaking a lease has been to pull a Houdini—disappear and leave no forwarding address. But this presumes that one has expertise in the fast getaway, expects no important mail, and doesn't mind kissing a security deposit goodbye. Furthermore, the tenant who leaves a trail can expect to be sued for breach of the lease. In most states the tenant in such a case is liable for the costs of reletting the apartment (repainting, advertising, and rental agent's commission), and any rent the landlord loses until the apartment or house is rerented or sold, or until the lease expires.

The penalty is often well-deserved in the cases of good landlords (there are many) and bad tenants (of whom there are not a few). That was the case with the couple who signed a two-year lease and moved into a furnished home owned by a widow who depended upon the $550 monthly rental for income. After six months, the tenants moved out without paying the current month's rent, saying only, "Go ahead and sue!" When the widow did just that, the tenant counterclaimed that he had put in $3,000 worth of improvements. He was, however, unable to produce a single documenting bill in court, and his claim that he'd paid a housepainter $100 a day for twelve days was so patently absurd that the judge wondered aloud, "Did he paint every house on the block?" At one point, when the defendant felt things were going against him, he rose in court to declaim dramatically: "Your Honor, until now, my pride did not permit me to reveal this, but I have been unemployed ever since I moved into that house." This confession—which was neither relevant nor true—was undermined considerably by the later admission that he owned and drove a new Cadillac Seville. The widow subsequently was awarded judgment for ten months' rent, from the time of default until she sold the house.

CONSTRUCTIVE EVICTION

You're liable for rent and other costs if you move out of an apartment you've rented, but common law protects you from that

223

rent liability when you're evicted illegally. This principle has been extended to include cases tantamount to eviction, called "constructive eviction." If the landlord's harassment or interference, or his failure to provide you with essential services, deprives you of the use of the premises and is so serious and permanent that you're forced to move out, the courts view this *as if* you were evicted. This may be used as a defense should the landlord sue.

Exactly what constitutes constructive eviction is difficult to define. For example, under the lease the landlord and his agents are permitted to enter "during reasonable hours." They may do this for a number of reasons, including inspection of any pipes that happen to run through the premises, and showing the apartment to prospective tenants (usually starting seven months before your lease is up). But when the landlord or superintendent abuse this right and consistently enter the apartment to snoop or harass (again, keep a diary as evidence), this could be construed as a violation of your right to quiet enjoyment of the premises, allowing you to move out.

Serious harassment by violence-prone neighbors that the landlord refuses to do anything about, no heat, a gas leak, a collapsed section of ceiling, or patched-up pipes that finally burst and cut off the water supply are even more likely to be considered constructive eviction—or, at least, valid defenses for not paying rent.

PROTECTING YOUR SECURITY

The final indignity inflicted by the unscrupulous landlord is the confiscation of the tenant's security deposit when the lease is up and the tenant moves out. Such withholding is sometimes justified, but often borders on pure avarice.

Several years ago, a long-time client of mine had wallpaper hung and carpeting laid when he moved into an apartment, and carefully removed both when he moved out. When he asked for the routine refund of his $800 security deposit—two months' rent—his landlord's reply was a bill for $900, and the claim that he'd had to scrape and repaint the walls and pick up the tackless carpet stripping. The suit and counterclaim were settled before trial, and my client recovered $600. But since my firm got half of that, he would have done better if, in Small Claims Court or negotiating with his landlord, he'd toughed out a split-the-difference $450 settlement.

You can fare well in Small Claims Court without a lawyer if you can present convincing evidence: photos of the apartment, for example. Or the testimony of a reliable witness (a friend will do), who carefully inspects the premises at your request, checking to see that sinks and plumbing are functional, that walls and floor are unscarred, and that all is "broom clean" when you vacate.

Many tenants, believing that legal fees often exceed recoveries, allow unscrupulous landlords to get away with trumped-up "repair" charges that permit them to pocket security deposits. To discourage this kind of conduct, Pennsylvania courts award double damages to tenants whose security has been unjustly withheld. New Jersey inflicts a criminal penalty on the avaricious landlord—$200 or 30 days. Of course, tenants can represent themselves and avoid legal fees in Small Claims Courts, where security deposit cases are commonly heard.

The best way to keep a landlord you have reason to distrust from holding on to your deposit is not to let him have it, which you can do indirectly by withholding your final month's rent. Technically, you can't use the security to pay the last installment (although with a "hungry" landlord, I have occasionally negotiated such a provision into a lease). If, after you move out, your landlord sues for the rent, you can promptly counterclaim for the security deposit; so chances are he won't bother.

The danger here is a landlord who is fast on your feet. Some clients of mine, planning a move from their apartment into a home they'd just bought, were warned by several tenant friends that the landlord would hold on to their security as the mountain climber grips his rope. When they decided not to pay their last month's rent, the landlord had them served with eviction papers by the 5th of the month, and had them in court by the 15th. The judge quite properly set aside the question of the security deposit, and they had to pay the rent or get out immediately. Since they couldn't take possession of the house until the end of the month, they made the obvious choice. My friend observed sadly on leaving the courtroom, "I'll probably never get my security back."

Some people, as shifty as the landlord, stall by mailing an empty envelope or unsigned check as the last month's rent, then exclaim when called, "How silly of me!" But every landlord has heard that song before. He could have you in court before you have time to write another check.

BANDING TOGETHER WITH OTHER TENANTS

Some of the remedies we've discussed will get you out of your lease, or help you collect damages after the fact. Rarely will they be likely to get your landlord to do any major repairs on your building, fix boilers, or keep your rent from rising with every tide where there is no rent control. To deal with problems of this order, and with particularly flint-hearted landlords in general, tenants may have to organize. Increasingly, rent strikes and rent escrow (where rent is withheld and retained by the court as a communal fund for significant repairs) have been effective.

In Southern California, where tenant unions are blossoming like avocado groves, tenants in one 22-apartment building organized a rent strike. After three days, the landlord agreed to meet with them. He showed them figures purporting to prove that inflation and increased costs made a $9,000 annual increase essential to his survival. With his figures on the table, the tenants' committee was able to send members to the utilities and the tax department, where they discovered that, in fact, the landlord's costs would be closer to $4,000. Faced with that information, he capitulated and cut his projected increase by more than half. The individual tenant is rarely a match for the landlord, but in tenant union there is strength.

THE SIXTH STEP:
GOING TO COURT IN A LANDLORD-TENANT DISPUTE

Even if you live in a relatively enlightened jurisdiction, it's possible that—in other than a consumer-oriented Small Claims or Housing Court—you'll come before a judge whose sympathies may seem largely with the landlord (whether because landlords contribute more heavily to political campaigns, or because the judge is a property owner). The poor may have an especially hard time of it. Many of them find that, as one tenant dweller put it, "Court's just a step you take on the way to being evicted." The state provides lawyers for those who can't afford them when in criminal court they're in danger of losing their liberty, but not when they're in danger of losing their homes. The Legal Aid Society, however, often rides to the rescue.

Obstacles notwithstanding, the informed tenant can do well in court if she builds her case with care. First, complain to the local health or housing department to get an inspector to visit and cite the dwelling for whatever violations of community sanitary or safety codes have been troubling you. Even if it's irrefutably clear to you that the landlord has reneged on services promised in the lease, such as providing adequate heat in the winter, an official substantiating nudge from the authorities helps the judge make the leap of imagination it takes to believe the tenant.

226

Second, if you've spent the rent money you've withheld on repairs, keep itemized bills and receipts to show in court. If you've kept the money in a special account until repairs are made by the landlord, have a bank deposit slip or money order showing the exact amount. If you've simply frittered away the rent money, you'll get little sympathy from the court.

Third, be prepared with additional hard evidence (witnesses to your harassment, discomfort, or injury) or soft evidence (a diary to reinforce your memory: "December 21: No heat. Temperature range in apt: 35–47. Mary has a cold. Jimmy seems to be getting pneumonia.")

Fourth, find out which judge is scheduled to sit on your case and inquire about his attitude toward tenants from a Legal Aid lawyer or a tenant association officer, or even sit in on a session. If the judge seems to be strongly pro-landlord, call in sick and have your case rescheduled. It's an extreme—but sometimes prudent—tactic.

If you are taken to court by your landlord, a response in writing, giving your defense or counterclaim, should be filed, which means going to the clerk of that court in person—generally within three days.

If you don't answer, you automatically lose the case. In a recent year in New Jersey, three out of four summary proceedings against tenants—many of which could surely have been defended successfully—went uncontested.

You may find that you can contest not only your landlord's record of living up to the lease, but also some of its more outrageous provisions. Some of these clauses have been invalidated by the courts on the grounds that they constitute "unconscionable contracts of adhesion"—conditions the tenant agreed to only because a necessity of life was being offered, "Take it or leave it," by someone holding all the cards in the landlord-tenant game. That neat invalidation feat was accomplished in a recent New York case, in which the judge found that a special clause the landlord had written into his leases requiring a tenant to pay him $100 in attorney's fees "upon either party's commencing a suit" was both unconscionable and illegal.

The clause waiving the right of trial by jury is valid unless prohibited by state law—which it generally is not. Landlords usually want no part of jury trials, not only because they take too much time, but because urban juries consist mostly of their natural enemies: tenants. They feel they have a better chance if they draw a conservative judge. Because of the waiver-of-jury-trial clause, and because a trial would cost the state far more than the small sums generally involved, the landlord almost always gets his wish. A random statistic: Of more than 8,000 contested landlord-tenant cases in New Jersey in a recent year, only three were tried by juries.

In a growing number of states, the long-standing doctrine—that the tenant's duty to pay rent and the landlord's duty to provide services are totally unrelated responsibilities—no longer stands.

The tenant may successfully argue in court that the obligation to pay rent should be suspended until the landlord fulfills his obligation to keep the premises in livable condition. Usually, the practical outcome is a rent abatement—you pay the landlord the back rent minus, say, 20 percent, and keep paying 20 percent less until satisfactory repairs are made. Or if you used rent money to make repairs yourself, that amount may be deducted from the rent you owe, according to the "repair and deduct" principle pioneered by the New Jersey Supreme Court. In some states (New York, Massachusetts, Pennsylvania), rent abatement is statutory; in others, rent-and-repair statutes are on the books, but their usefulness is limited by the unrealistically low maximum deduction ($50–$100, or one month's rent), and by harsh lease provisions waiving the tenant's rights.

Suppose, despite a noble attempt in court, you lose. The bad news is that a lease clause requiring you to pay the landlord's "reasonable" attorney's fees will be upheld in most states. But now the good news: in some states, that provision is interpreted to mean that if the landlord loses, he must pay the tenant's attorney's fees. If the case was for nonpayment of rent, you will, of course, be expected to pay up. In most states you can avoid eviction by paying the overdue rent in court, or at any time up until the actual eviction order is served. Your payment automatically dismisses the case against you.

Sometimes the judgment itself will include a conditional "stay of execution," allowing a period of several days for you to redeem yourself by paying rent and costs. When that time is up, the landlord can get a warrant of eviction, but the sheriff may then have to give you three days to pack and depart before he moves in to move you out. Some leases waive your right of redemption after the judgment, a stipulation the courts in your state may or may not uphold and one you should try to eliminate from your lease before signing.

The Final Step:
Moving Out

We've talked at length about eviction, because it's the ultimate and most intricate legal agony in a landlord-tenant relationship. But though landlords have been known to press for the eviction of entire buildings full of tenants, most people, probably including you, will never be placed in that awkward and humiliating position.

You may not love your landlord, and that may be mutual. He may not treat you royally. He may perform grudgingly. But chances are, there'll be no major conflicts. If there are, the nice thing about a free society like ours is that you can always move when your lease is up.

Proposed Model Rental Agreement

This monthly agreement is made duplicate original this—day of ——,19—by and between——hereinafter called landlord and ——hereinafter called tenant.

The landlord rents to the tenant premises known as——in the District of Columbia, by the month commencing on the—day of each month.

The landlord and tenant hereby agree as follows:

1. The landlord covenants and warrants that at the time of the signing of this agreement or at the time of delivery of possession the premises are in compliance with the Housing Regulations of the District of Columbia, in a clean, safe and sanitary condition, in repair and free from rodents and vermin, as well in compliance with all other applicable laws and regulations of the District of Columbia relating to health and safety.

2. The landlord covenants and agrees to maintain said premises in such condition for the duration of this agreement and in accordance therewith; provided, however, that the creation other than through normal wear and tear, of unclean, unsafe, and unsanitary or rodent or vermin infested conditions by the negligence of the tenant shall be the responsibility of the tenant and not the landlord to correct.

3. It is further agreed that if the landlord breaches any of the covenants or warranties herein regarding the condition and maintenance of these premises after the tenancy has commenced, and the tenant gives notice of the need for repairs, restoration of said premises or replacement of certain parts thereon, and reasonable time passes without the repair, restoration, or replacement having been made by the landlord, the stipulated rent payable by the tenant for these premises shall be reduced by 50% until said repairs, restoration, or replacement have been made. "Reasonable time" means reasonable in the circumstances but in no event shall be longer than the maximum Allotted Time allowed for similar repairs under the Housing Division Procedural Manual of the District of Columbia Department of Licenses and Inspection. Full rent shall begin to be due on the day repairs, restoration, or replacements are completed; and only 50% of the stipulated rent shall be due for the interval between the expiration of time for the repairs to have been completed and the time when they are actually completed. At the option of the tenant, the landlord shall either credit the amount of the reduction under this paragraph toward the succeeding month's rent, or shall refund said amount in cash to the tenant within two weeks of the date of completion of repairs, restoration or replacement.

4. The tenant shall not waive any rights or remedies under this agreement or under the laws of the District of Columbia by taking possession of the premises when one or more conditions of the premises violate the warranties and covenants of this agreement.

5. The landlord agrees specifically among his other warranties to the following: To maintain in operable condition a water heating facility; plumbing facilities; kitchen sink and heating facility; to furnish sufficient heat to maintain a minimum of 68 degrees F. between the hours of 6:30 A.M. and 11:00 P.M. whenever temperatures fall below this level regardless of the time of year; to furnish hot water of at least 120 degrees F. continuously to kitchen and bathroom sink and bathtub in amounts sufficient for normal demands; to furnish water, gas and electricity for airconditioning when these or any of them are supplied as part of the consideration for the payment of rent; to maintain in operable condition the refrigerator and cooking stove when furnished by the landlord; to maintain the roof in good repair; to maintain interior wall surfaces free of moisture, loose or peeling paint or paper, or cracked plaster, unless the need for repairs or correction results from the misuse or abuse by the tenant or his invitees of the facilities. The landlord agrees to complete repairs for which he is responsible in accordance with Paragraph 3 of this contract. The landlord further agrees to provide at the outset of the lease one complete set of screens for all windows and outer doors.

6. The tenant covenants that all statements made by him in his applications for the renting of these premises are true; that the actual occupants will be————; that he will not use any portion of the premises in which there is a furnace, water heater, or gas meter for sleeping purposes, nor permit them to be used by his invitees. The tenant further agrees to conserve the heat and to avoid waste of hot water. The tenant agrees to keep the premises under his control in a clean, safe and sanitary condition including but not limited to floors and floor coverings, and other walking surfaces. The tenant further agrees to keep walls, ceilings, windows, and doorways clean and free of any unsanitary matter. The tenant agrees to keep plumbing fixtures in a clean and sanitary condition and agrees to use care in the proper use and operation of the plumbing facilities. The tenant agrees to use the premises for residential purposes only. It is understood by the parties that not more than—persons may lawfully reside on these premises.

7. The landlord recognizes his continuing obligation to maintain this property. The landlord agreed that he or his duly appointed agent will inspect the premises subject of this agreement at least twice yearly during daylight hours or by special appointment, to note conditions and to arrange for the immediate correction of those con-

231

ditions which fall within the landlord's responsibility in accordance with this agreement. The tenant hereby agrees to permit the inspection of these premises twice yearly and as well when emergency requires, and to arrange and pay for the immediate correction of those conditions which have been caused by his negligence or that of his invitees. The tenant further agrees to notify the landlord of conditions which require correction.

8.   In the event the landlord requires a security deposit or any additional monies to be paid by the tenant as a condition to the completing of this agreement the landlord agrees to hold such monies in a separate interest bearing bank account and to pay any accumulated interest for the period for which the monies are held as security and not used for the purpose of defraying unpaid rent or paying for repairs which were the duty of the tenant to make in accordance with his agreement. The landlord further agrees that he will not use such security deposit or additional rent money for any other purpose.

The landlord agrees without demand to refund to the tenant within fifteen days of the expiration of this tenancy the security deposit and any additional deposits, and any accumulated interest thereon, paid by the tenant as a condition of his tenancy and in addition to the stipulated rent, or within such fifteen-day period to notify the tenant, by personal service or certified mailing to the tenant's last known address, of his intention to withhold and apply such monies toward defraying the cost of repair which under the terms of this agreement should have been made by the tenant. Failure to give the tenant such timely notice shall be a bar to the landlord's right to withhold and apply these funds in whole or in part. Within 30 days after the landlord has properly notified the tenant of his intention to withhold such monies he shall give the tenant an itemized and signed statement of the use to which such monies were applied, including names, addresses and fees of the persons making repairs, and he shall refund the balance. Failure to submit such an itemized accounting within the time allowed will render the landlord liable for the entire sum withheld. The landlord is authorized to incur reasonable costs in effecting repairs. In the event the landlord himself effects such repairs he shall within 30 days from the giving of notice of intention to withhold provide an itemized statement of the cost of material and the reasonable value of his services.

9.   The tenant hereby waives notice to quit in the event he fails to pay rent within five days after the due date. In the event the landlord seeks to recover possession for any breach of this contract, he agrees prior to the filing of any legal action to notify the tenant by either certified mail or personal service of his intention to commence suit in the District of Columbia Court of General Sessions; provided,

however, that, provisions of the law to the contrary notwithstanding failure by the landlord to so notify the tenant, if timely pleaded by the tenant, shall constitute a complete defense to the suit for possession.

10. The landlord hereby waives notice to quit from the date he receives notice from the tenant, under paragraph three (3) of this agreement, of the need for repairs or restoration of the premises or replacement of certain parts thereon. Under any other circumstances both the landlord and the tenant agree to give each other written notice to quit in accordance with this agreement when either of them shall wish to bring this agreement to an end. Said notice to quit when given by the landlord shall be accompanied by a statement of reasons therefor and shall be given thirty (30) days in advance and at such time as to expire on the day—the tenancy commenced to run. Not less than fifteen (15) days notice shall be given by the tenant and such notice may be given at any time. If such notice is given and the tenant vacates these premises in accordance with such notice, the tenant shall be liable for rent or for use and occupancy for the period during which the notice runs, but not for longer. Where the period during which the tenant's notice to quit runs will expire in a new monthly rental period the tenant at the usual time shall pay an amount equal to the number of days for which the notice thereafter runs multiplied by 1/30 of the agreed monthly rental figure.

Where the tenant's notice expires and the tenant vacates in advance of the expiration of rental period for which the tenant has already paid rent in full, the landlord shall refund an amount equal to the number of days between the expiration date of the monthly rental period, including the latter day but not the former, multiplied by 1/30 of the monthly rental figure.

11. The landlord and the tenant hereby agree that the conditions and agreements contained herein are binding on, and may be legally enforced by the parties hereto, their heirs, executors, administrators, successors and assigns respectively. Feminine and neuter nouns shall be substituted for the masculine form and the plurals shall be substituted for the singular number in any place herein in which the context may require such substitution.

12. At the execution of this agreement the tenant shall pay the sum of——dollars for the first month's rent in advance beginning—the day of——19—, and shall be given a separate rental receipt for such payment.

13. The landlord agrees to provide receipts in writing for all money paid as rent by the tenant and to state on each receipt the amount received, the date the money is received by him and the period for which the money pays the rent on these premises. In the event

the landlord fails to provide receipts in accordance with this agreement, and a dispute over rent arises, the landlord shall be obligated to refer to and to pay the cost of an accountant for an accounting.

14. The landlord agrees to accept rental money without regard to any other obligation owed by the tenant to the landlord and to seek separate legal remedies for other debts which may accrue to the landlord from the tenant. Where a landlord's refusal of cash payments for rent requires the tenant to purchase a money order or other cash equivalent, any service charge or other expense incurred in securing said money order or other cash equivalent may be deducted, along with any postage, from succeeding rental payments.

15. The tenant agrees to return all keys to the landlord at the time of the termination of this agreement and, except for changes due to normal wear and tear, to return the premises in the same condition as when he received them.

16. In the event these premises become uninhabitable as a result of fire, flood, civil disorder or other cause beyond the control of either the landlord or the tenant the obligation to pay rent shall cease immediately and the tenant agrees to vacate said premises within a reasonable time.

In testimony whereof, the landlord and the tenant have signed this agreement this—day of——19—. The tenant herewith acknowledges receipt of the duplicate copy of this agreement.

_____   _____
Tenant   Landlord

CHAPTER 14

Going into Business

We live in the Land of Opportunity. Consider Jean Gordon, a thoroughly bored housewife, resolved to find something to constructively occupy her time (and augment her family's income) now that her children were all in school. Her enthusiastic dinner guests were always telling her, "Jean, if you ran a restaurant I'd be there every night for dinner," and one day she decided to test that out.

Jean got some excellent advice (and took it, too) from one dinner guest, an accountant who suggested that she visit the nearest field office of the Small Business Administration, which turns out more booklets than the U.N. does Middle East resolutions.

They're darned good booklets, and it's darned good advice, even if it's free. If you're going into business, you'd be wise to do as Jean did—acquire and study all the appropriate S.B.A. booklets you can get your hands on*, as well as library books on starting a business, and any relating directly to the venture you're planning. Why unnecessarily repeat the mistakes of others? You'll have plenty of opportunities to make your own.

THE FIRST STEP:
A CHECKLIST FOR GOING INTO BUSINESS

This is S.B.A. booklet no. 71, and we're reprinting it almost in its entirety. Not to take up space, but because it's well-done and thought-provoking. It's especially nice to see our federal government do something well besides collect taxes.

In quizzing herself, would-be restaurateur Jean found that her score was high in most areas but less than satisfactory in planning and follow-through. Happily, a friend, Adrienne, who was good at both, but weary of organizing P.T.A. fund-raisers, had recently

---

*Address: Small Business Administration, Washington, D.C.

sma|71

Small Marketers Aids
U.S. Small Business Administration

Checklist
for Going
into Business

Thinking of starting a business?
Ask yourself these questions.

You want to own and manage your own business. It's a good idea—provided you know what it takes and have what it takes.

Starting a business is risky at best. But your chances of making it go will be better if you understand the problems you'll meet and work out as many of them as you can before you start.

Here are some questions to help you think through what you need to know and do. Check each question if the answer is YES. Where the answer is NO, you have some work to do.

BEFORE YOU START

How about YOU?

Are you the kind of person who can get a business started and make it go? (Before you answer this question, use the worksheet on pages 4 and 5.)   ____

Think about *why* you want to own your own business. Do you want to badly enough to keep you working long hours without knowing how much money you'll end up with?   ____

Have you worked in a business like the one you want to start?   ____

Have you worked for someone else as a foreman or manager?   ____

Have you had any business training in school?   ____

Have you saved any money?   ____

How about the money?

Do you know how much money you will need to get your business started? (Use worksheets 2 and 3 on pages 6 and 12 to figure this out.)   ____

Have you counted up how much money of your own you can put into the business?   ____

Do you know how much credit you can get from your suppliers—the people you will buy from?   ____

Do you know where you can borrow the rest of the money you need to start your business?   ____

Have you figured out what net income per year you expect to get from the business? Count your salary and your profit on the money you put into the business.   ____

Can you live on less than this so that you can use some of it to help your business grow?   ____

Have you talked to a banker about your plans?   ____

2

237

How about a partner

If you need a partner with money or know-how that you don't have, do you know someone who will fit—someone you can get along with? ____

Do you know the good and bad points about going it alone, having a partner, and incorporating your business? ____

Have you talked to a lawyer about it? ____

How about your customers?

Do most businesses in your community seem to be doing well? ____

Have you tried to find out whether stores like the one you want to open are doing well in your community and in the rest of the country? ____

Do you know what kind of people will want to buy what you plan to sell? ____

Do people like that live in the area where you want to open your store? ____

Do they need a store like yours? ____

If not, have you thought about opening a different kind of store or going to another neighborhood? ____

(More questions on page 8)

3

WORKSHEET NO. 1

Under each question, check the answer that says what you feel or comes closest to it. Be honest with yourself.

Are you a self-starter?

☐ I do things on my own. Nobody has to tell me to get going.

☐ If someone gets me started, I keep going all right.

☐ Easy does it. I don't put myself out until I have to.

How do you feel about other people?

☐ I like people. I can get along with just about anybody.

☐ I have plenty of friends—I don't need anyone else.

☐ Most people irritate me.

Can you lead others?

☐ I can get most people to go along when I start something.

☐ I can give the orders if someone tells me what we should do.

☐ I let someone else get things moving. Then I go along if I feel like it.

Can you take responsibility?

☐ I like to take charge of things and see them through.

☐ I'll take over if I have to, but I'd rather let someone else be responsible.

☐ There's always some eager beaver around wanting to show how smart he is. I say let him.

How good an organizer are you?

☐ I like to have a plan before I start. I'm usually the one to get things lined up when the group wants to do something.

☐ I do all right unless things get too confused. Then I quit.

☐ You get all set and then something comes along and presents too many problems. So I just take things as they come.

How good a worker are you?

☐ I can keep going as long as I need to. I don't mind working hard for something I want.

☐ I'll work hard for a while, but when I've had enough, that's it.

☐ I can't see that hard work gets you anywhere.

4

239

Can you make decisions?

☐ I can make up my mind in a hurry if I have to. It usually turns out O.K., too.

☐ I can if I have plenty of time. If I have to make up my mind fast, I think later I should have decided the other way.

☐ I don't like to be the one who has to decide things.

Can people trust what you say?

☐ You bet they can. I don't say things I don't mean.

☐ I try to be on the level most of the time, but sometimes I just say what's easiest.

☐ Why bother if the other fellow doesn't know the difference?

Can you stick with it?

☐ If I make up my mind to do something, I don't let *anything* stop me.

☐ I usually finish what I start—if it goes well.

☐ If it doesn't go right away, I quit. Why beat your brains out?

How good is your health?

☐ I *never* run down!

☐ I have enough energy for most things I want to do.

☐ I run out of energy sooner than most of my friends seem to.

Now count the checks you made.

How many checks are there beside the *first* answer to each question?   ____

How many checks are there beside the *second* answer to each question?   ____

How many checks are there beside the *third* answer to each question?   ____

If most of your checks are beside the first answers, you probably have what it takes to run a business. If not, you're likely to have more trouble than you can handle by yourself. Better find a partner who is strong on the points you're weak on. If many checks are beside the third answer, not even a good partner will be able to shore you up.

Now go back and answer the first question on page 2.

5

WORKSHEET NO. 2

ESTIMATED MONTHLY EXPENSES

Item	Your estimate of monthly expenses based on sales of $_____ per year	Your estimate of how much cash you need to start your business (See column 3.)	What to put in column 2 (These figures are typical for one kind of business. you will have to decide how many months to allow for in your business.)
	Column 1	Column 2	Column 3
Salary of owner-manager	$	$	2 times column 1
All other salaries and wages			3 times column 1
Rent			3 times column 1
Advertising			3 times column 1
Delivery expense			3 times column 1
Supplies			3 times column 1
Telephone and telegraph			3 times column 1
Other utilities			3 times column 1
Insurance			Payment required by insurance company
Taxes, including Social Security			4 times column 1
Interest			3 times column 1
Maintenance			3 times column 1

241

Legal and other professional fees		3 times column 1
Miscellaneous		3 times column 1
STARTING COSTS YOU ONLY HAVE TO PAY ONCE		Leave column 2 blank
Fixtures and equipment		Fill in worksheet 3 on page 12 and put the total here
Decorating and remodeling		Talk it over with a contractor
Installation of fixtures and equipment		Talk to suppliers from who you buy these
Starting inventory		Suppliers will probably help you estimate this
Deposits with public utilities		Find out from utilities companies
Legal and other professional fees		Lawyer, accountant, and so on
Licenses and permits		Find out from city offices what you have to have
Advertising and promotion for opening		Estimate what you'll use
Accounts receivable		What you need to buy more stock until credit customers pay
Cash		For unexpected expenses or losses, special purchases, etc.
Other		Make a separate list and enter total
TOTAL ESTIMATED CASH YOU NEED TO START WITH	$	Add up all the numbers in column 2

GETTING STARTED

Your building

Have you found a good building for your store? ____

Will you have enough room when your business gets bigger? ____

Can you fix the building the way you want it without spending too much money? ____

Can people get to it easily from parking spaces, bus stops, or their homes? ____

Have you had a lawyer check the lease and zoning? ____

Equipment and supplies

Do you know just what equipment and supplies you need and how much they will cost? (Worksheet 3 and the lists you made for it should show this.) ____

Can you save some money by buying secondhand equipment? ____

Your merchandise

Have you decided what things you will sell? ____

Do you know how much or how many of each you will buy to open your store with? ____

Have you found suppliers who will sell you what you need at a good price? ____

Have you compared the prices and credit terms of different suppliers? ____

Your records

Have you planned a system of records that will keep track of your income and expenses, what you owe other people, and what other people owe you? ____

Have you worked out a way to keep track of your inventory so that you will always have enough on hand for your customers but not more than you can sell? ____

Have you figured out how to keep your payroll records and take care of tax reports and payments? ____

8

243

Do you know what financial statements you should prepare? ____

Do you know how to use these financial statements? ____

Do you know an accountant who will help you with your records and financial statements? ____

Your store and the law

Do you know what licenses and permits you need? ____

Do you know what business laws you have to obey? ____

Do you know a lawyer you can go to for advice and for help with legal papers? ____

Protecting your store

Have you made plans for protecting your store against thefts of all kinds—shoplifting, robbery, burglary, employee stealing? ____

Have you talked with an insurance agent about what kinds of insurance you need? ____

Buying a business someone else has started

Have you made a list of what you like and don't like about buying a business someone else has started? ____

Are you sure you know the real reason why the owner wants to sell his business? ____

Have you compared the cost of buying the business with the cost of starting a new business? ____

Is the stock up to date and in good condition? ____

Is the building in good condition? ____

Will the owner of the building transfer the lease to you? ____

Have you talked with other businessmen in the area to see what they think of the business? ____

Have you talked with the company's suppliers? ____

Have you talked with a lawyer about it? ____

9

MAKING IT GO

Advertising

Have you decided how you will advertise? (Newspapers—posters—handbills—radio—by mail?) ——

Do you know where to get help with your ads? ——

Have you watched what other stores do to get people to buy? ——

The prices you charge

Do you know how to figure what you should charge for each item you sell? ——

Do you know what other stores like yours charge? ——

Buying

Do you have a plan for finding out what your customers want? ——

Will your plan for keeping track of your inventory tell you when it is time to order more and how much to order? ——

Do you plan to buy most of your stock from a few suppliers rather than a little from many, so that those you buy from will want to help you succeed? ——

Selling

Have you decided whether you will have salesclerks or self-service? ——

Do you know how to get customers to buy? ——

Have you thought about why you like to buy from some salesmen while others turn you off? ——

Your employees

If you need to hire someone to help you, do you know where to look? ——

Do you know what kind of person you need? ——

Do you know how much to pay? ——

Do you have a plan for training your employees? ——

10

245

Credit for your customers

Have you decided whether to let your customers buy on credit? ___

Do you know the good and bad points about joining a credit-card plan? ___

Can you tell a deadbeat from a good credit customer? ___

A FEW EXTRA QUESTIONS

Have you figured out whether you could make more money working for someone else? ___

Does your family go along with your plan to start a business of your own? ___

Do you know where to find out about new ideas and new products? ___

Do you have a work plan for yourself and your employees? ___

Have you gone to the nearest Small Business Administration office for help with your plans? ___

If you have answered all these questions carefully, you've done some hard work and serious thinking. That's good. But you have probably found some things you still need to know more about or do something about.

Do all you can for yourself, but don't hesitate to ask for help from people who can tell you what you need to know. Remember, running a business takes guts! You've got to be able to decide what you need and then go after it.

Good luck!

11

U.S. GOVERNMENT PRINTING OFFICE : 1977—O—247-716

WORKSHEET NO. 3

LIST OF FURNITURE, FIXTURES, AND EQUIPMENT

Leave out or add items to suit your business. Use separate sheets to list exactly what you need for each of the items below.	If you plan to pay cash in full, enter the full amount below and in the last column.	If you are going to pay by installments, fill out the columns below. Enter in the last column your downpayment plus at least one installment.			Estimate of the cash you need for furniture, fixtures, and equipment
		Price	Downpayment	Amount of each installment	
Counters	$	$	$	$	$
Storage shelves, cabinets					
Display stands, shelves, tables					
Cash register					
Safe					
Window display fixtures					
Special lighting					
Outside sign					
Delivery equipment if needed					
TOTAL FURNITURE, FIXTURES, AND EQUIPMENT (Enter this figure also in worksheet 2 under "Starting Costs You Only Have To Pay Once," page 7.)					$

Copies of this Aid are available free from field offices and Washington headquarters of the Small Business Administration. Aids may be condensed or reproduced. They may not be altered to imply approval by SBA of any private organization, product, or service. If material is reused, credit to SBA will be appreciated. Use of funds for printing this publication approved by the Office of Management and Budget. March 20, 1975.

247

started to think about raising funds for herself. She and Jean decided to join forces and to open something they thought the community conspicuously lacked: a small, trendy health-food restaurant.

THE SECOND STEP:
SHOULD YOU INCORPORATE?

In the next few weeks, the partners spent many hours reading and researching, and discussing and debating hotly over herbal tea and toasted soya nuts at each other's kitchen tables. They thought out and listed their needs, set priorities, dreamed big dreams about franchising and a chain from N.Y. to L.A., and, oh yes, agreed on a name for their first restaurant: The Good Earth. They found they had a great many choices to make—first among them what legal structure would be most practical for their business.

They learned that a small business can take three basic forms: a sole proprietorship (inappropriate in their case), a partnership (a distinct possibility), or a corporation (not to be ruled out).

That last may be owned by one person (like the local dry cleaners), or by tens of thousands (like A.T.&T.). Sole proprietors and partners are mere mortals, but a corporation is, to quote Chief Justice John Marshall, an "artificial being, invisible, and intangible" that exists "only in the eyes of the law, and with the blessing of the state."

Many clients who come to me for help in starting a business like the sound of incorporation. "Inc." or "Ltd." after a company name has a certain solidity to it, the feeling of oak-tabled boardrooms, of prestige, power, and respectability, which some feel are well worth the extra costs and added taxes. But there are more important factors to consider.

Start-up costs. Unless you light your cigarettes with $10 bills, this is a not unimportant factor. The sole proprietorship and the partnership are cheapest and easiest to set up. The corporation is most complex *in* form, most complex *to* form, and, luxury model that it is, involves annual maintenance costs—about which more later. But if you form a small corporation yourself, the costs aren't all that heavy.

Personal liability. If your business is not incorporated, you (and any partners) will be personally liable for everything—the rent, the cost of merchandise purchased, and (unless this is covered by liability insurance, as it should be) the claim of the woman who chips

248

a tooth on a stone in the whole-wheat cherry pie. Of course, if you're going into a service business, your personal liability is likely to be much lower than if you're stocking a hardware store with an inventory of nuts, bolts, chainsaws, and corkscrews.

With a corporation, your liability is theoretically limited to the amount of your investment. Lease obligations, money-due suppliers, and that file cabinet drawer full of unpaid invoices are the responsibility of that "artificial being" created by the state.

There is a Catch-22, however. In my experience, landlords, suppliers—in fact, almost anyone dealing with a small new corporation with a less than Rockefellerian opening capital—cautiously insist on personal guarantees from the owners: the individuals' written pledge to pay the debts of the otherwise invulnerable and unresponsive corporate entity. This doesn't always happen, of course. Some companies are so anxious to make the sale that they're careless about checking credit. But it's more than likely that before suppliers ship Jean and Adrienne $1,000 worth of sunflower seeds, vegetarian steaklets, and wheat germ, they will exact their signatures on personal guarantees to pay if the corporation does not. That, of course, negates one of the chief benefits of incorporating. General Electric and The Good Earth may both be corporations, but the former will be treated with considerably more respect by readers of Dun & Bradstreet than the latter.

Your partner's keeper. The actions of one partner are binding upon all other partners. If Smith rashly decides to buy the Empire State Building on behalf of the company, and puts down a $1,000 deposit, Jones, too, may be held liable for the multimillion-dollar balance. Appallingly, not only the partnership's assets but the partners' personal resources (homes, bank accounts, automobiles) will be placed in jeopardy. If, on the other hand, the building is purchased in the name of a corporation, their loss is limited to their investment in the corporation.

You've picked a partner prudently when you pick a prudent partner. If Jean buys a mink coat on the installment plan and defaults, it may not be Adrienne's problem, but she may be indirectly damaged. When the sheriff arrives at the restaurant to auction off Jean's half interest and decides the stove is a good place to start, Adrienne is in big trouble. A partnership works on the principle that if one partner drills a hole in the boat, even if it's under her own seat, the whole boat sinks. On the other hand, if it's a corporation, Jean's stock may be sold, but the restaurant remains afloat.

Death of a partner. An unincorporated business automatically dies upon the death of any partner, but a corporation has a life of its own. It can, in fact, be immortal. Philo Remington and James Henry Rand are long gone, but their corporation, Remington-Rand, Inc., lives on. To prevent dissolution of their business at an inconvenient time, or through forced sale, partners in an unincorporated business should decide whether or not—and in what way—to carry on the business after one of them dies, and write that decision into the partnership agreement.

Running the show. When sole proprietors or partners want to buy a building, they can act without fear of contradiction. When the president of a corporation wants to buy a building, corporate counsel advises, "We'll need to call a meeting of the board of directors." Directors' meetings are required not only for all major decisions, but for some that sound minor, like opening a bank account. A formal resolution is introduced. A vote is taken. The minutes duly record that a quorum, due notice, and all formalities have been met, and the officers are hereby authorized to take all necessary measures to acquire the property.

But running a small, closely held corporation, happily, is a lot less complicated. Although stockholders and directors may be required to meet at least once a year—as compared to monthly or even bimonthly meetings of the biggies—they may, in fact meet only on paper. In practice, a set of minutes is typed at fiscal year's end to reflect reelection of officers and directors, and to retroactively "ratify and approve" their actions. More—a lot more—about this in the Sixth Step.

The money tree. Every business needs one, for capital to get started and for operating funds that may be needed from time to time if the business is to survive and thrive. So when deciding which of the three legal structures to assume, consider its ability to attract needed money. In a single proprietorship, the owner may raise the requisite funds by borrowing, by purchasing on credit, or, with a silent prayer, by investing whatever remains of his savings. Since he is personally liable for all debts of his company, banks and suppliers will look carefully at his personal financial situation before extending credit. Consequently, the funding available to him will always be limited by his own circumstances.

In theory, two partners should be able to raise—and earn—twice as much money. But in practice, it doesn't always work that way.

The business case history of a Lower East Side entrepreneur

250

may be instructive in this connection. Proudly recounting his success story to a fellow Ft. Lauderdale condominium owner as they sunbathed at poolside, he recalled, "I started with one ramshackle old pushcart, and then I expanded to two. Pretty soon I had three. I took in a partner and we went to six pushcarts, then nine, and pretty soon we had twenty." Interrupted his acquaintance, "So that's how you made your fortune?" "Oh, no," replied the tycoon, "my uncle died and left me a million dollars."

Small start-up corporations are often in no better position to attract capital than unincorporated companies. All three forms may acquire additional funds by borrowing money and pledging assets. The chief advantage of the corporation over the others in raising capital lies in its unique ability to sell shares of stock, which in making your fortune is a far more reliable method than waiting for a rich uncle to die and leave you his.

Even the smallest corporation with a big idea can use this device to get swiftly off the ground. One quick example: About ten years ago, three engineers asked me to incorporate a company to manufacture a computer part that was in short supply and great demand. Their sales and profit projections were so impressive that they sold me, too, and I decided to take stock in the company in lieu of a fee.

They sold $50,000 worth of shares among friends and relatives in a matter of weeks, and crawled slowly into production. They had just about reached the break-even point a year later, and we were all euphorically looking forward to big dividends the following year, when the next-generation computer came along. In one grim, grinding moment, the company's product became obsolete. Nine years later the corporation is still limping along as a machine shop. But the dreams of glory—and profits—have faded, and though I still hold the stock, it's clear that I would have been better off taking my legal fees in dollars.

Still, that ability to sell stock is an important one for the infant corporation, even if shares have to be peddled among first cousins and maiden aunts, instead of sold with dignity through the stock market.

Because naive maiden aunts have eaten a lot of pie-in-the-sky, every state has its own set of rules on how shares may or may not be sold. In selling interstate, the rule of thumb used to be if you sold to fewer than 35 shareholders, you were not required to register the stock with the U.S. Securities and Exchange Commission (S.E.C.) Now the rules have been tightened so that even with groups so small that registration is not required, you must fully disclose to your investors everything there is to know about the venture. As a result, some of the "offering" memoranda I've seen are as detailed as an S.E.C. prospectus.

The tax burden. The only thing certain in business is tension and taxes. All (for-profit) businesses pay taxes—property, occupancy, and real estate, for example—but only corporations pay income tax. That sounds like an argument against incorporating, but, as you'll see, it may not be.

A sole proprietor doesn't escape income taxes. He is required to attach a "Schedule C" to his individual tax return, reporting his business profit or loss for the year, which is then figured in with his other income to compute his personal income tax.

A partnership files something called an Information Return, setting forth its income, expenses, and profit or loss for the year. Since this form confides each partner's share to Uncle Sam, that amount must be reported on their individual tax returns.

A corporation files an annual income tax return with federal and state governments and sometimes even with the city. Since a corporation is a separate entity, it pays taxes on its profit, in addition to the taxes paid by its shareholders on their salaries and dividends. Let's assume Jean and Adrienne get lucky and earn a profit of $20,000 the first year in their new business. If they are unincorporated, each must pay taxes on $10,000. If they decide to draw only $5,000 each, leaving the balance to buy new kitchen equipment and refurbish the dining room, each must still pay taxes on $10,000. Somebody must pay on that income, even if it's buried in the business.

If, however, they incorporate, they need only pay individual income taxes on their $5,000 salaries. The other $10,000 will be taxed to the corporation—in some cases, depending on family income, at rates that result in a tax saving. This is a highly sophisticated area, however, and an accountant should help you decide which way to go.

Your accountant may also advise you to become a sub-chapter "S" corporation. This will give you all the benefits of the corporate structure, but for tax purposes you'll be treated as a partnership. He'll undoubtedly have some words of wisdom for you, too, on the cost of our increasingly swollen Social Security contributions—slightly higher in the corporate form.

Fringe benefits. Uncle Sam generously allows corporations to contribute to pension, profit-sharing, and medical plans and to pay some life insurance premiums out of the company's pocket with pre-tax dollars. If you don't incorporate, you must pay for these benefits out of your own pocket in post-tax dollars—unless you arrange for a Keogh retirement plan (which allows a contribution of 15 percent of annual income to a maximum of $7,500) or an I.R.A. (Individual Retirement Account, allowing annual squirreling of up to $1,500). This is another area to discuss with your accountant.

THE THIRD STEP:
NAMING YOUR BABY

It's harder to name a business than a child. It doesn't matter how many kids named Mark, Cathy, or Jon there are on the block. But if Jean and Adrienne name their restaurant "Howard Johnson's"—even if that's Adrienne's husband's name—they'll be hit with a lawsuit in about the time it takes to fry an order of clams.

The law, quite fairly, won't permit you to trade on someone else's success. If it did, there'd be a counterfeit Colonel Sanders on every corner, and a two-bit Tiffany's in every town. No matter what name you choose, it's important to "clear" it first, to be sure, for example, that you won't legally be forced to remove that traffic-stopping neon sign you just invested $2,500 in. The extent of the search you make may depend upon your anticipated investment in the name—in advertising, elegant menus, trademark design, and the like—and your dreams of expansion.

Most states have enacted a Fictitious Name Law for unincorporated businesses, requiring the filing of identifying information (name of business, address, names and address of owners) in the county where the business does business, unless the owners happen to be operating under their own names. The law's purpose is to protect the public, so that if Jean and Adrienne carelessly blend ground glass into their Good Earth vegetable soup, the hapless diner knows whom to sue. The first place to search to make sure that someone hasn't beaten you to the name is the county clerk's office. However, the fact that it's not registered there doesn't mean you have a green light; you may find a stop sign further on.

Someone who attaches importance to a business name may protect it by registering it under state or federal trademark laws. For nineteen out of twenty clients, I don't bother to check out state or federal trade name duplications. Common sense will tell you if that's necessary. You know that naming your motel the Holiday Inn is asking for legal trouble, but you may get away—as a motel I once drove past in California appeared to have done—with the name Holiday Out. The imitation of a trade name or trademark is the most common form of unfair competition, and there are hundreds of cases (*Hilton* v. *Hilton; American Radio Stores* v. *American Radio and Television Stores; American Heritage Life Insurance* v. *Heritage Life Insurance; Ed Sullivan* v. *Ed Sullivan Radio & TV*) where injunctions against use of the name and damages were sought and often granted.

If the name you have in mind isn't well-known or registered, it still may duplicate that of another corporation in your state, and you may want to check it out. If you plan to incorporate, you *must* check, since the name will only be accepted by the state division of corporations if it does not conflict with any other. Before I prepare any papers, I usually mail in four or five alternate names (enclosing the necessary $10 New York State fee), with the request that the first "open" one be reserved.

Sometimes none are open. A client in the communications business submitted more than 150 names before one was approved, and that was a weary last resort: his own initials. It's best to choose an uncommon concocted name, as two clients of mine did. One had a son named Wayne, the other Ralph. They named their company "Rayne" because they felt that somehow "Walph" lacked the dignity they sought.

The principle at stake isn't simply two businesses using the same name, but the confusion that may result. One way to avoid confusion with The Good Earth Sand & Gravel Corp. would be for our heroines to name their business The Good Earth Restaurant Corp. Another way would be geographic—to call it The Good Earth Restaurant of Cook County, Inc. The restaurant could safely feature the name The Good Earth on a large sign, with a small line on the window adding "Owned and Operated by . . ."

If you're concerned about someone stealing your good name, the thing to do is register it under trademark laws in the states where you plan to do business, and with the federal government. Even that may not be enough, as two leading U.S. car rental agencies discovered when they decided to do business in Australia, and found that an enterprising Aussie had shrewdly registered both their names. Reportedly, they were forced to pay him handsomely for the right to use their own trademark.

Because trademark registration is a specialized field, I always refer clients to a patent and trademark specialist. I don't suggest that you do it yourself.

THE FOURTH STEP:
FILING THE CERTIFICATE OF DOING BUSINESS

Earlier, I referred briefly to the Fictitious Name Laws. Now let's comply with them. Forms may vary from state to state, but essentially a Certificate of Doing Business under a Fictitious Name will require the same information as the two New York forms below—one for sole proprietors, the other for partners. In some states, a corporation, too, may be required to file such a certificate, if it is operating, as many do, under a fictitious name—for example, Standard Oil operating, as it used to do, under the name Esso.

This certificate, like so many other forms you've encountered in this book, must be filed in the office of the county clerk—in this case in each county in which the company has a place of business. The fee? Modest. In most states, you may have to prominently display a copy of the certificate on your premises, and your bank will probably want a certified copy before it will let you open a business checking account. (See pages 256 and 257 for forms.)

THE FIFTH STEP:
INCORPORATION

If, after weighing the pros and cons, Jean and Adrienne opt for incorporation, this is what they'll have to do:

Prepare a certificate of incorporation. Your name has already been chosen and reserved. The certificate (or charter, or articles of incorporation) that this name will adorn may vary from state to state. Some certificates—depending on state laws and the needs of the company—are only a single page, others many. The charter of a widely held public corporation may be longer because it includes provisions (such as several classes of stock and the rights of each) not required by the kind of small closely held corporation we're discussing here.

Depending on custom in the area, your certificate may be pre-printed, or wholly typed. But this depends upon the preparer, too. Although New York accepts a printed form, I rarely see one used. This is not because it has any less validity than one that has been

X 201—Certificate of Conducting Business under an Assumed Name
For Individual

JULIUS BLUMBERG, INC., LAW BLANK PUBLISHERS
80 EXCHANGE PL. AT BROADWAY, N. Y. C. 10004

𝔅usiness Certificate

I HEREBY CERTIFY *that I am conducting or transacting business under the name or designation*

of

at

City or Town of   *County of*   *State of New York.*

*My full name is**
and I reside at

I FURTHER CERTIFY *that I am the successor in interest to*

the person or persons heretofore using such name or names to carry on or conduct or transact business.

IN WITNESS WHEREOF, *I have this*   *day of*   *19*   *, made*
and signed this certificate.

....

* Print or type name.
* If under 18 years of age, state "I am................years of age".

STATE OF NEW YORK
COUNTY OF   } *ss.:*

On this   *day of*   *19*   *, before me personally appeared*

to me known and known to me to be the individual   *described in and who executed the foregoing*
certificate, and   *he*   *thereupon*   *duly acknowledged to me that*   *he*   *executed the same.*

256

X 74—Certificate of Conducting Business as Partners.
Individual — Corporation.

COPYRIGHT 1973 BY JULIUS BLUMBERG, INC., LAW BLANK PUBLISHERS
80 EXCHANGE PL. AT BROADWAY, N. Y. C. 10004

Business Certificate for Partners

The undersigned do hereby certify that they are conducting or transacting business as members of a partnership under the name or designation of

at

in the County of   , State of New York, and do further certify that the full names of all the persons conducting or transacting such partnership including the full names of all the partners with the residence address of each such person, and the age of any who may be infants, are as follows:

NAME Specify which are infants and state ages.   RESIDENCE

....

....

....

....

....

....

WE DO FURTHER CERTIFY that we are the successors in interest to

the person or persons heretofore using such name or names to carry on or conduct or transact business.

In Witness Whereof, We have this   day of   19   made and signed this certificate.

....

....

....

....

....

....

State of New York, County of   ss.:   INDIVIDUAL ACKNOWLEDGMENT

On this   day of   19   , before me personally appeared

to me known and known to me to be the individual   described in, and who executed the foregoing certificate, and   he   thereupon   duly acknowledged to me that   he   executed the same.

257

professionally typed and given that customized look, which may simply be the product of a preprogrammed automated typewriter in the attorney's office. It could also be because giving the client something that looks as though, "Holy smoke—all he did was fill in a form!" could sow seeds of discontent about the size of the legal fee.

Small trade secret: There are firms in various parts of the country which, for a fee, form corporations for overburdened or underskilled attorneys: Prentice-Hall, Commerce Clearing House, and the Corporation Trust Co. among them. At one time or another, I've dealt with all three—for the first reason, not the second, I hasten to add. But they firmly limit their services to the legal profession. There is at least one service, however, that deals primarily with the public: The Company Corporation of Wilmington, Delaware, founded by Ted Nichols, author of *How to Form Your Own Corporation Without a Lawyer for Under $50.* If you follow every step in his book and do it all yourself, the job can be done for that price—but economy, not first class.

Nichols' book ($10) is cleverly designed with perforated pages, so that you can tear out and fill in the required certificate of incorporation, minutes, and bylaws. The "under $50" promise presupposes that you will do all the work yourself—file the certificate and arrange for a friend or relative in Delaware to act as your registered representative without charge. It means doing without printed stock certificates, a corporate seal, and a loose-leaf book for corporate records, all of which Nichols (or a legal stationer) will be glad to sell you for $25 to $30 more. Then, for an additional fee, The Company Corporation will file your certificate and act as your required local rep ($25 for the first year).

It's my personal belief, however, that there's no overriding advantage for the Mom-and-Pop business to incorporate in Delaware. The savings won there are quickly lost when such a corporation has to register in its home state—the one in which the business is to be conducted—as a foreign corporation. Not only must an additional filing fee be paid, but corporate name clearance must be repeated. There's no savings in state taxes either.

But let's suppose you'd rather do it yourself, in your home state. I can't supply different forms each state requires, but I can tell you what information is required by just about all. To get the exact form you need, you'll have to do a little legwork—first, to a legal stationer's, and second, if he doesn't carry certificate of incorporation forms, to your nearest law library where you can photocopy

258

the one you need out of a corporation form book. Another way to copy the form (and check to see that you're doing it right) is to pay a visit to your county courthouse. If you're lucky, your state requires that in addition to the copy filed at the state capital, duplicate corporate charters must be filed in the clerk's office of the county where the company's main office is located. (In my state, a duplicate is automatically sent to the county from the capital.)

What information is usually needed for a certificate of incorporation? Nothing that an intelligent twelfth-grader couldn't handle:

Corporate name. ———

Address. Of the corporation or—if its home is in another state—of its registered representative: someone who is, for example, authorized to accept a summons if you are sued for any reason. You may also have to designate the secretary of state as your agent to accept service. He will then mail the summons to your designee. It's not an imposition. It's his job.

Purpose clause. This sometimes states simply, "to engage in any lawful act or activity for which corporations may be organized under the general Corporation Laws of this state." On the other hand, it may run four or five single-spaced pages, enumerating every activity the corporation intends to engage in now or in the future. If it does, it should also include a general clause, like the one mentioned earlier in this paragraph.

Capital structure. This is a declaration of the number and classes of shares the corporation is authorized to issue. This gets pretty complicated if you're forming a General Motors, but what it comes down to in starting a small, closely held corporation is issuing the maximum number that can be authorized for the minimum filing fee. In New York, this happens to be 200 shares at no par (stated) value. Your state may have a different minimum formula.

The directors. Elected by the stockholders to run the company, they, in turn, elect its officers. Most states require a minimum of three directors, but some tolerantly add that, "if there are less than three shareholders, the number of directors may be equal to the number of shareholders." Your state may or may not require you to list the names and addresses of your directors on the certificate of incorporation.

Signing the certificate (the dummy incorporator). I've been "dummy" for hundreds of corporations. This is a custom of convenience, permitted—partly so papers don't have to be mailed back and forth unnecessarily—in many, if not all, states. At the first stockholders' meeting, the dummy conveniently resigns; the

259

real parties in interest stand up and promptly elect the powers that will be. Their names will not appear on the certificate, and so their participation in the corporation is concealed from prying eyes by one layer of paper. (It is, however, easily ripped away by subpoena when necessary.)

You have the same choice. You can be your own incorporator, or use your brother-in-law—or anyone 18 years of age or older—as your dummy.

These forms—for New York and Delaware—point out the similarities as well as the differences between the requirements of two states. They may be helpful to you, but they should not be copied verbatim as your situation may be different. Delaware's form here is short, New York's a bit longer, but they could just as easily have been reversed. (See pages 261 and 263 for forms.)

Filing the Certificate. Each state designates a place—usually the office of the secretary of state—where certificates are to be filed by mail or, if you're compulsive, hand-delivered. Bureaucracies being what they are, papers sometimes sit around for a while. Here lawyers have an advantage over you. We have services that file incorporation papers, do searches (to save time in checking to see if a name a client wants to use is already taken), and check the status of a corporation (Is it current in its taxes?). But, alas, they exclude those who have not crossed the bar. Never mind. By doing it through the mail, you'll lose a little time, but save yourself some money.

Your certificate of incorporation must, of course, travel with the required filing and recording fees, plus any taxes your state may demand. You'll have to check out the exact costs with the secretary of state's office, which will probably remind you that it accepts only certified checks from laypersons. (An attorney's check will be accepted uncertified. With good reason—if it bounces, he can be disbarred.) Forward your certificate of incorporation and fees, which may run from $50 to three or four times that much, with a letter requesting an official receipt as soon as filing has been completed.

If the certificate of incorporation is properly filled out and contains all the required information, if nothing in it violates the law and your name does not infringe on one already in use, the state will issue your charter—which may be an elaborate document suitable for framing or a simple computer-print receipt suitable only for filing.

Either way, you're official.

CERTIFICATE OF INCORPORATION

HIGH RIDGE DRY CLEANERS, INC.

Under Section 402 of the Business Corporation Law.

The undersigned, for the purpose of forming a corporation pursuant to Section 402 of the Business Corporation Law of the State of New York, does hereby certify and set forth:

FIRST: The name of the corporation is HIGH RIDGE DRY CLEANERS, INC.

SECOND: The purposes for which the corporation is formed, are:

To erect, construct, establish, purchase, lease, and otherwise acquire, and to hold, use, equip, outfit, supply, service, maintain, operate, sell, and otherwise dispose of laundries, dry cleaning establishments, coin operated laundromats, tailor shops, drive-in laundries and dry cleaning establishments, cleaning concessions, linen supply and cleaning, renovating, repairing, dyeing and disinfecting of clothing, cloths and fabrics of all kinds by washing, steaming, bleaching, starching, ironing, dry cleaning, or otherwise; and to engage in all activities, render all services and to buy, sell, use, handle, and deal in all plants, fixtures, machinery, apparatus, equipment, delivery trucks, materials, and supplies of all kinds incidental or related thereto or of use therein.

To manufacture, buy and sell, import and export, and generally deal in machinery, equipment and supplies for tailors, laundries, dry cleaning establishments, including sewing machines, pressing machines, irons, pressing boards, trimmings, buttons, buckles, linings shears, coat fronts, and all other things used or usable by tailors, laundry, and dry cleaning establishment operators. To conduct, operate, and maintain refrigerated storage for furs and other garments.

To acquire by purchase, subscription underwriting or otherwise, and to own, hold for investment, or otherwise, and to use, sell, assign, transfer, mortgage, pledge, exchange, or otherwise dispose of real and personal property of every sort and description and wheresoever situated, including shares of stock, bonds, debentures, notes, scrip, securities, evidences of indebtedness, contracts, or obligations of any corporation or association, whether domestic or foreign, or of any firm or individual or of the United States or any state, territory or dependency of the United States or any foreign country, or any municipality or local authority within or without the United States, and also to issue in exchange therefor, stocks, bonds, or other securities or evidences of indebtedness of this corporation, and, while the owner or holder of any such property, to receive, collect, and dispose of the interest, dividends and income on or from such property and to possess and exercise in respect thereto all of the rights, powers, and privileges of ownership, including all voting powers thereon.

To construct, build, purchase, lease or otherwise acquire, equip, hold, own, improve, develop, manage, maintain, control, operate, lease, mortgage, create liens upon, sell, convey or otherwise dispose of and turn to account, any and all plants, machinery, works, implements and things or property, real and personal, of every kind and description, incidental to, connected with, or suitable, necessary or convenient for any of the purposes enumerated herein, including all or any part or parts of the properties, assets, business, and good will of any persons, firms, associations, or corporations.

The powers, rights, and privileges provided in this certificate are not to be deemed to be in limitation of similar, other or additional powers, rights, and privileges granted or permitted to a corporation by the Business Corporation Law, it being intended that this corporation shall have all the rights, powers, and privileges granted or permitted to a corporation by such statute.

THIRD: The office of the corporation is to be located in the City of Yonkers, County of Westchester, State of New York.

FOURTH: The aggregate number of shares which the corporation shall have the authority to issue is Two Hundred (200), all of which shall be without par value.

FIFTH: The Secretary of State is designated as agent of the corporation upon whom process against it may be served. The post office address to which the Secretary of State shall mail a copy of any process against the corporation served upon him is:

Walter L. Kantrowitz, Esq.
277 Old Nyack Turnpike
Spring Valley, New York 10977

SIXTH: The fiscal year of this corporation shall terminate on September 30.

IN WITNESS WHEREOF, this certificate has been subscribed to this 7th day of October, 1977 by the undersigned, who affirms that the statements made herein are true under the penalties of perjury.

_____
(Signature of Incorporator)

262

CERTIFICATE OF INCORPORATION
of

A CLOSE CORPORATION

FIRST. The name of this Corporation is _____

SECOND. Its registered office in the State of Delaware is to be located at _____

County of _____ The registered agent in charge thereof is _____

THIRD. The nature of the business and, the objects and purposes proposed to be transacted, promoted and carried on, are to engage in any lawful act or activity for which corporations may be organized under the General Corporation Law of Delaware.

FOURTH. The amount of total authorized capital stock of the corporation is divided into _____ shares of _____

FIFTH. The name and mailing address of the incorporator is as follows:

SIXTH. The powers of the incorporator are to terminate upon filing of the certificate of incorporation, and the name and mailing addresses of the persons who are to serve as managing stockholder(s) until their successors are elected are as follows:

Name and address of managing stockholder(s)

SEVENTH. All of the corporations issued stock, exclusive of treasury shares, shall be held of record by not more than thirty (30) persons.

EIGHTH. All of the issued stock of all classes shall be subject to the following restriction on transfer permitted by Section 202 of the General Corporation Law.

Each stockholder shall offer to the Corporation or to other stockholders of the corporation a thirty (30) day "first refusal" option to purchase his stock should he elect to sell his stock.

NINTH. The corporation shall make no offering of any of its stock of any class which would constitute a "public offering" within the meaning of the United States Securities Act of 1933, as it may be amended from time to time.

I, THE UNDERSIGNED, for the purpose of forming a corporation under the laws of the State of Delaware do make, file and record this certificate, and do certify that the facts herein stated are true; and I have accordingly hereunto set my hand.

DATED AT: ⸺

_____
(Signature of Incorporator)

The only records an unincorporated business is required to keep are those for bookkeeping and accounting, tracking income and outgo for the benefit of owners and tax collectors. A corporation must do better. It must have bylaws, minute books, stock record books, and a corporate seal—the latter probably a hangover from the days when it took an Act of Parliament to form a corporation.

But in many states, it's all so easy now. Everything's preprinted in that $25 to $30 kit we talked about earlier, which you can order from your legal stationer. The kit you should ask for is one in which the required meetings have already taken place on paper, and all you have to do is fill in the name, date, and place. It includes, too, a set of all-purpose, preprinted, commonly used bylaws that will guide the operations of your corporation forever, even if you never look at them again. Then there is the pocket corporate seal. (If, with the help of the enclosed instruction sheet, you are able to put it together, you will probably be unable to take it apart.) In some states, it is simply a relic, never used. In others, it is a necessity for opening up a bank account or entering into a contract. Well, not an absolute necessity. More than once, I've taken a half-dollar, a quarter, or even a bottle cap, drawn a circle, and filled in the corporate name, to serve in lieu of the corporate seal.

The kit contains everything but the men's room sink. There are meticulous step-by-step, page-by-page instructions for completing minutes and bylaws. There are even instructions on how to prepare the notice for next year's annual meeting and suggestions for completing its minutes.

In actual practice, a small corporation's meeting may verge on the Theatre of the Absurd. It takes place—between the roller and platen of a typewriter—on a sheet of paper, as the secretary fills in the blanks. The sole stockholder designates himself temporary chairman and secretary of the first meeting. He then nominates himself—and seconds his nomination—as sole director. He is then elected by acclamation. He approves the bylaws unanimously, selects a bank, and designates who shall be sole signator: himself. He adjourns that meeting (without dissent) and calls the first meeting of the board of directors to order—where he nominates and seconds his name as president, vice-president, secretary, and treasurer. He then unanimously elects himself to hold office until the next annual meeting, and, if that is his desire, votes himself a salary and a medical reimbursement and pension plan.

Everyone knows the meeting never took place. But that fictitious being, the corporation, sometimes acts in mysterious ways. And it's an ego trip second only to being dictator of a banana republic.

Your store-bought corporate kit usually includes 20 stock certificates imprinted with the corporate name—evidence, when issued, of ownership of the business. Stock should, of course, be issued to each owner in proportion to his or her interest in the business. Not all the authorized shares need be issued, and probably should not be. If Jean and Adrienne's corporation is authorized to issue 200 shares, they may elect to take 10 shares each as their 50-50 participation, leaving 180 shares unissued.

Then, as the business grows and requires more capital, they may decide to bring in fresh money by selling 10 more shares to their ambitious waitress Alice. It doesn't matter how many shares are issued, as long as they are issued in proportion to ownership. In this case, of course, ownership will have been diluted, so that hard-pressed Jean and Adrienne now only own one-third of the business each.

Issuing the stock is no legal big deal. It's a matter of simply typing—or even writing—the owner's name on the certificate, filling in the number of shares he owns, applying the corporate seal (by now you've figured out how it works), and having two officers sign it. A notation of ownership is made on the certificate stub that remains in the stock records book, and Alice is now a shareholder of record.

THE SEVENTH STEP:
GETTING LICENSES AND PERMITS

Not every business needs a license, but as government and consumers put eager fingers in more and more pies, the trend is toward increased licensing.

There are three basic license types. Almost anyone can get the first kind—for a restaurant or a place of public congregation, such as a cinema—by complying with health rules and building and safety codes, and then applying and paying a fee.

The second license category—for a liquor store, a restaurant liquor license, even a grocery selling beer—demands proof of good moral character and/or financial responsibility. To keep shady

265

characters out of the liquor business (a hangover from post-Prohibition days), state licensing boards want to know the source of every dollar of your capital. If you've borrowed the money, they even investigate the lender.

The third type is a "skill" license, and its categories vary from state to state. Plumbers, electricians, TV and auto repairmen, barbers and hair stylists, pilots, teachers, doctors, lawyers, psychological counselors, accountants, and real estate brokers all may be required to pass a test in order to get their license.

For certain businesses, a permit from the department of health (a restaurant) or of education (nursery school) is likely to be needed. These are issued after inspection, usually just prior to opening of a business—if and when everything is in order. If you are building or doing major renovations or extensions, you will need a building permit and, when the work is completed, a certificate of occupancy.

If there's a sales tax in your community, city, or state, your accountant should advise you on requirements for obtaining what is sometimes called a "resale number." This allows merchants to buy merchandise they are going to resell without paying a sales tax, and authorizes them to collect the tax at the point of sale.

Money collected as sales—or withholding—taxes should be put away religiously in a separate "trust fund" account. Too many small businesses get into bad trouble borrowing from Uncle Sam to pay Paul. Corporate officers can't hide behind the corporate shield. They will be held personally responsible for these funds if the company fails to pay them. One of my clients is currently paying Uncle Sam and the State of New York over $20,000 for withholding taxes that, in a sense, he used to finance his troubled business. The corporation eventually went "belly up," but the actual amount of the "trust funds" became his personal responsibility.

THE EIGHTH STEP:
THE PARTNERSHIP AGREEMENT

The number of things that can go sour between partners is only exceeded by the number of stories told about partners. Example: Two partners meet with their lawyer to frame a partnership agreement, something which, though not legally required, is always a good idea in today's complex business world. When the lawyer suggests a clause in the agreement to cover the eventuality of fire

266

or bankruptcy, one of the partners exclaims, "Great idea—but in each case, make sure the profits are divided equally!"

There is really no need for specific references to fire or bankruptcy in a partnership agreement, but an agreement may be necessary someday to put out a fire between the partners. Here's what it should contain: 1) the name of the partnership; 2) the term of the partnership (for a specific period—say, five or ten years, or "until terminated by the partners"; 3) the location of the business; 4) the capital investment of each partner (usually money, but sometimes property or services); 5) each partner's draw and how profits and—heaven forbid!—losses are to be divided; 6) the time each proposes to devote to the business (full time for one, occasional consulting for the other, etc.); and 7) where the bank account will be maintained, and who has the right to sign checks (singly or jointly).

Those are the "musts," but there are "optionals" as well: 1) restriction on a partner's right to devote time to other business (you don't want him out selling insurance when he should be waiting on tables); 2) resignation of a partner (providing for notice, and option of the remaining partner to purchase his interest, or to liquidate and dissolve the partnership—to prevent Big Al from walking in and saying, "I just bought out Charlie—I'm your new partner"); 3) disability of a partner (how long is he entitled to continue drawing his full "salary," and at what point, if any, does the remaining partner get the option to buy out the disabled partner?); 4) death of a partner (a partner's son or widow may or may not be able and willing to step in, and the remaining partner may or may not want them, so the partners' desires should be spelled out; under the law, death of a partner terminates the partnership, unless the agreement provides otherwise); and 5) arbitration or other means of settling disputes (this comparatively inexpensive and speedy procedure must be in the contract or your only remedy is the courts).

Often the first thing two people ask when they come to my office to start a partnership, is, "But do we really need an agreement? We've been best friends since childhood, and never disagree on anything." I tell them that may be so, but the only business I've ever seen where everyone agrees to everything is the sole proprietorship. The agreement is never necessary so long as things are going well and everybody is content. All business agreements are prepared for that unpleasant moment when things go wrong. In the best of all possible worlds, all business will be handled with the ten-finger contract: a handshake.

A typical troublesome situation arises when one partner contributes the skill or sweat, and the other the bankroll. Let's say Tom Talent does all the work with a $100-a-week draw and an agreement to split any profits beyond that with his partner Monte Moneybags. When the business suddenly begins clearing $1,000 a week, human nature takes its course, and Thomas begins to brood, "I'm working my buns off, and all he does is come around once a week and collect." A partnership agreement will not only remind him who put up the money to make him rich in the first place but—if he's really all that dissatisfied—spell out how to go about dissolving the partnership. I've divided the partnership agreement that follows so that you can stop after the "musts" and add any of the "optionals" you feel fit your needs.

Form No. 22
PARTNERSHIP AGREEMENT

Agreement made on July 1, 1978, between Jean Gordon and Adrienne Johnson, both of Chicago, Illinois.

("Must" Clauses)

1. *NAME AND BUSINESS.* The parties hereby form a partnership under the name of The Good Earth Restaurant, to conduct a restaurant business.

2. *TERM.* The partnership shall begin on July 1, 1978, and shall continue until terminated as herein provided.

3. *LOCATION.* The principal office of the business shall be in Chicago, Illinois.

4. *CAPITAL.* The capital of the partnership shall be a sum of $10,000.00; and each party shall contribute, simultaneously with the execution of this agreement, the sum of $5,000.00 in cash. Either party's contribution to the capital of the partnership shall bear interest in her favor.

5. *DRAWINGS.* Each partner shall be entitled to draw $100 a week from the funds of the partnership. The net profits of the partnership shall be divided equally between the partners and the net losses shall be borne equally by them.

6. *MANAGEMENT, DUTIES, AND RESTRICTIONS.* The partners shall have equal rights in the management of the partnership

business, and each partner shall devote his entire time to the conduct of the business. Neither partner shall, without the written consent of the other, make, execute, deliver, endorse, or guarantee any commercial paper, nor agree to answer for, or indemnify against, any acts, debt, default, or miscarriage of any person, partnership (other than of this partnership), association, or corporation.

7. *BANKING AND BOOKS.* All funds of the partnership shall be deposited in its name in such checking account or accounts as shall be designated by the partners. All withdrawals therefrom are to be made upon checks signed jointly by both partners. The partnership books shall be maintained at the principal office of the partnership and each partner shall at all times have access thereto.

8. *VOLUNTARY TERMINATION.* The partnership may be dissolved at any time by agreement of the partners, in which event the partner shall proceed with reasonable promptness to liquidate the business of the partnership. The partnership name shall be sold with the other assets of the business. The assets of the partnership shall be used to discharge the debts of the partnership and all monies and other assets of the partnership then remaining shall be divided between the parties share and share alike.

("Optionals")

9. *RETIREMENT OR RESIGNATION.* Either partner shall have the right to retire from the partnership at the end of any year. Written notice of intention shall be served upon the other partner at least 3 months before the end of the year. The retirement of either partner shall have no effect upon the continuance of the partnership business. The remaining partner shall have the right either to purchase the retiring partner's interest or to terminate and liquidate the business. If the remaining partner elects to purchase the interest of the retiring partner, she shall serve notice in writing of such election upon the retiring partner within 2 months after receipt of her notice of intention to retire.

A. If the remaining partner elects to purchase the interest of the retiring partner, the purchase price and method of payment shall be the same as stated in paragraph 11A with reference to the purchase of a decedent's interest in the partnership.

B. If the remaining partner does not elect to purchase the interest of the retiring partner, the partner shall proceed with reasonable promptness to liquidate the business. Procedure as to liquidation and distribution of the assets of the partnership shall be the same as stated in the paragraph with reference to voluntary termination.

10. *DISABILITY*. In the event any of the partners shall become so disabled from disease, injury, or otherwise, that she is unable to perform her duties and such disability continues for more than — weeks, the draw to which the disabled partner shall be entitled shall be as follows:

A. For a period of — weeks commencing with the date of disability, the disabled partner shall receive a draw equal to that of the remaining partner, provided, however, that in the event the disabled party shall receive any amount from any disability insurance policy maintained by the partnership then the draw shall be reduced by the amount received under said disability insurance.

B. If the disability shall continue for more than — weeks, the disabled partner shall be entitled to receive a sum equal to one-half (½) of the draw of the other partner. The obligations to pay this reduced amount shall continue for an additional — weeks from the expiration of the original — weeks called for in paragraph 10A.

C. If such disability continues for more than — weeks, the remaining partner, at her option, shall have the right to purchase the interest of the disabled partner or to terminate and liquidate the partnership business. If the remaining partner elects to purchase the interest of the retiring partner, she shall serve notice in writing of such election upon the retiring partner at any time of the expiration of — weeks.

If the remaining partner elects to purchase the interest of the retiring partner, the purchase price and method of payment shall be the same as stated in paragraph 11A, referring to the purchase of a decedent's interest in the partnership.

If the remaining partner does not elect to purchase the interest of the retiring partner, the partner shall proceed with reasonable promptness to liquidate the business. Procedure as to liquidation and distribution of the assets of the partnership shall be the same as stated in paragraph 8, referring to voluntary termination.

11. *DEATH*. Upon the death of either partner, the surviving partner shall have the right either to purchase the interest of the decedent or to terminate and liquidate the partnership business. If the surviving

partner elects to purchase the decedent's interest, she shall serve notice in writing of such election, within 3 months after the death of the decedent, upon the executor or administrator of the decedent, or, if no legal representative has been appointed, upon any one of the known legal heirs of the decedent at the last known address of such heir.

A. If the surviving partner elects to purchase the interest of the decedent in the partnership, the purchase price shall be equal to the decedent's capital account, as at the date of her death, plus the decedent's income account, as at the end of the calendar month in which her death occurred. No allowance shall be made for goodwill, trade name, patents, or other intangible assets, except as those assets have been reflected on the partnership books prior to the decedent's death. The survivor shall be entitled to use the trade name of the partnership. The purchase price shall be paid without interest in semiannual installments beginning 6 months after the end of the calendar month in which the decedent's death occurred.

B. If the surviving partner does not elect to purchase the interest of the decedent in the partnership, she shall proceed with reasonable promptness to liquidate the business of the partnership. The surviving partner and the estate of the deceased partner shall share equally in the profits and losses of the business during the period of liquidation, except that the decedent's estate shall not be liable for losses in excess of the decedent's interest in the partnership at the time of her death. No compensation shall be paid to the surviving partner for her services in liquidation. Except as here and otherwise stated, the procedure as to liquidation and distribution of the assets of the partnership business shall be the same as stated with reference to voluntary termination.

12. *ARBITRATION.* Any controversy or claim arising out of or relating to this contract or the breach thereof, shall be settled by arbitration in accordance with the rules of the American Arbitration Association, and judgment upon the award rendered may be entered in any court having jurisdiction thereof.

Witness whereof the parties have signed this agreement.

_____
Jean Gordon

_____
Adrienne Johnson

271

One thing a partnership agreement can't cover—but that should definitely be taken into consideration when choosing a partner—is business ethics. Your partner's should strongly resemble yours. I can't, however, say that I'm in agreement with the definition advanced by the partner when asked by his son to explain business ethics: "A customer," he replied, "pays me with a new twenty-dollar bill. As she walks out, I notice there is another twenty stuck to it. Now, here's where business ethics come in: Should I tell my partner?"*

THE NINTH STEP:
THE STOCKHOLDERS' AGREEMENT

Ninety-nine times out of 100, a stockholders' agreement is filed and forgotten. It is about as useful in running a corporation as a used styrofoam cup on a secretary's coffee break. But that one time in 100, you may be very glad it's there. So if you choose to go the corporate—rather than partnership—route, and there are two or more stockholders, it makes sense to draw up the human relations insurance policy known as the stockholders' agreement.

Although corporate bylaws ostensibly guide business operations, that all-purpose security blanket doesn't cover everything. That "artificial being," the corporation, should itself be a party to the stockholders' agreement (you'll see how that's done in the introduction to the sample agreement at the end of this step) and here are the agreement's essentials: 1) how much capital each stockholder will contribute to the business; 2) an assurance that each stockholder will vote for the other as a director and for the officer's position it's been agreed he will hold (only, of course, as long as he remains a stockholder); 3) the salary each will receive, and an understanding that increases will be at the same time and in the same proportion; 4) restriction on the sale of holdings (they must be offered to the corporation and other stockholders before they can be sold to outsiders); 5) death and disability provisions (as in the partnership agreement); 6) a detailed formula for valuation of stock upon sale (this may be a fixed sum, or one determined by agreement, by net worth, by appraisal, or by some formula based upon prior profits—like 2½ times last year's net earnings—but advisedly

*Confession: I tell this story not because it advances your knowledge of how to form a partnership, but to liven up this chapter. Business law can be pretty dreary stuff.

in consultation with your accountant); and 7) an arbitration clause (as in the partnership agreement).

The form that follows is one I've used as my "Model T" basic agreement for a number of clients, with modifications as needed.

Form No. 23

AGREEMENT, made July 1, 1978, by and among JEAN GORDON, ADRIENNE JOHNSON, both of Chicago, Illinois, and THE GOOD EARTH RESTAURANT, INC., a domestic corporation having its principal office in Chicago, Illinois (hereinafter called the "Corporation").

WITNESSETH:

WHEREAS, the parties hereto are the sole shareholders of the Corporation; and

WHEREAS, the parties hereto wish to make certain agreements relating to and affecting the Corporation, and their respective rights, interests, and obligations in and to the Corporation, and as to the capital shares of the Corporation, and further wish to impose certain restrictions upon the transfer of the capital shares of the Corporation, and to provide for the purchase by the Corporation of a decedent's interest in the Corporation, and finally, to provide the funds necessary to carry out such purchase;

NOW, THEREFORE, in consideration of the mutual covenants herein contained, the parties hereto agree as follows:

1. A. The Corporation shall have an authorized capital of two hundred (200) shares, all of which shall be without par value.

B. In consideration of the payment of $5,000.00 paid by JEAN GORDON and $5,000.00 paid by ADRIENNE JOHNSON the corporation shall issue 10 shares of its stock to each, which shares shall represent all of the corporation's issued and outstanding shares.

2. The Board of Directors of the corporation shall consist of two (2) members and the parties covenant and agree to vote for JEAN GORDON and ADRIENNE JOHNSON, so long as they are shareholders and are not disqualified to serve as directors under the laws of the State of Illinois.

3. The officers of the corporation shall be as follows:

President & Treasurer: JEAN GORDON

Vice-President & Secretary: ADRIENNE JOHNSON

273

4. That so long as the parties are shareholders of the Corporation, they shall be employed by the Corporation and shall manage its business subject to and in accordance with the policies of the Board of Directors. They shall be paid equal salaries and such salaries may be increased, provided that the salary of one shall not be increased unless the salary of the other shall be increased by an equal amount. Said salary is conditioned upon devotion of full time to the business and neither of the parties shall engage in any other business without the consent of the other.

5. The parties agree that all matters of policy, including but not limited to, the determination of employees' salaries, shall be decided by a majority vote of all of the shareholders.

6. No party shall sell, assign, convey, pledge, hypothecate, mortgage, or otherwise encumber or transfer any of the shares of the Corporation except as herein provided:

A. In the event that any shareholder should desire to dispose of any of her shares in the Corporation during the lifetime, she shall first offer to sell all of her shares to the corporation. The offer shall be made in writing and the price shall be its book value, to be determined as hereinafter provided. The Corporation shall within sixty (60) days after receipt of such written notice, notify the offerer and the other shareholder, in writing, of its acceptance or its rejection of such offer.

B. In the event that the Corporation fails to accept such offer within the time specified, such shares shall then be offered, in writing, to the other shareholder of the Corporation, at the book value, thereof.

C. The individual party shall, within thirty (30) days after receipt of such written offer, notify the other party to this Agreement, in writing, of her election to purchase or not to purchase the shares so offered to her.

D. In the event the Corporation and the other shareholder refuses to accept the offer, then and in that event the offering shareholder may offer the shares to outside parties. In the event an outside party shall agree to purchase the shares, but the price which he is to pay shall be less than the price at which the shares were offered to the Corporation and the other shareholder, then the offering shareholder must reoffer the shares to the Corporation and then to the other shareholder at the same price which he has received an offer of from the outside party. The Corporation shall have fifteen (15) days from the receipt of said written offer to either accept or reject this

274

subsequent offering. If the Corporations reject the offer, the other shareholder shall have ten (10) additional days to either accept or reject the subsequent offer.

E. In the event the shares are sold to an outside party, then they must be sold subject to all of the restrictions contained in this Agreement.

7. Upon the death of any shareholder, the Corporation shall purchase, and the estate of the decedent shall sell, all of the decedent's shares now owned or hereafter acquired. The purchase price for such shares shall be computed in accordance with the provisions hereinafter made.

8. The book value or net worth of all the shares of the corporation sold pursuant to this Agreement shall be determined annually as follows:

The two (2) officers of the Corporation are hereby appointed Attorneys-in-Fact for all parties to this Agreement to serve as long as both survive, and upon the death of any one of them, the then surviving one together with the accountant then servicing the Corporation shall serve as such Attorneys-in-Fact, to compute and determine the net worth or book value of the Corporations, and to thereupon set forth in writing signed by all of them:

A. The amount of the net worth or book value of both corporations, taking into consideration not only all the tangible assets of the Corporations but all intangible assets, as well as including goodwill;

B. A statement that this determination of the net worth or book value of both Corporations is made for the purpose of this Agreement and that all of said Attorneys-in-Fact concur therein;

C. The date as of which this determination is made and signed by said Attorneys-in-Fact.

9. In the event of the death of any of the parties hereto, the value of the outstanding capital shares of the Corporation, for the purpose of this Agreement, shall be its book value as determined pursuant to paragraph 8 above, providing said determination had been made within twelve (12) months prior to the death of the shareholder. In the event a determination has not been made within twelve (12) months prior to the death of the shareholder, then the book value shall be determined by the surviving Attorney-in-Fact together with the accountant, and such determination shall be binding upon all the parties to this Agreement.

10. A. In the event shares are purchased by the Corporation or individual shareholder pursuant to this Agreement, 25% of the purchase price shall be paid at the time of closing and the balance in 24 consecutive monthly payments beginning one month after the closing date. The unpaid balance shall be evidenced by a series of negotiable promissory notes made by the purchaser to the order of the offerer and shall bear interest at 6% per annum.

B. If notes are delivered as part of the purchase price, the shares of the selling shareholder shall be held in escrow by the attorney for the Corporation until the last note is paid. In addition until the last note is paid, the Corporation and the individual shareholder are prohibited from (a) selling or disposing of the assets of the Corporation out of the normal course of business, (b) liquidating or dissolving the Corporation, (c) increasing officers' salaries, or (d) doing any act out of the normal course of business which would jeopardize payment of the notes due.

C. This Agreement shall be binding upon the Corporation and the shareholders, their heirs, legal representative, successors, and assigns.

11. In the event any of the parties shall become so disabled from disease, injury, or otherwise, that she is unable to perform her duties as an officer and employee of the Corporations, and such disability continues for more than — weeks, the salary or draw to which the disabled party shall be entitled shall be as follows:

A. For a period of — weeks commencing with the date of disability, the disabled party shall receive a draw or salary equal to that of the remaining party, provided, however, that in the event the disabled party shall receive any amount from any disability policy maintained by the Corporations, then the amount payable by the Corporation to the disabled party shall be reduced by the amount received under said disability insurance.

B. If the disability shall continue for more than — weeks, the disabled party shall be entitled to receive and the Corporation shall be obligated to pay a sum equal to one-half (½) of the salary or draw being paid to the other party hereto. The obligations of the Corporation to pay this reduced amount shall continue for an additional — weeks, from the expiration of the original — weeks.

C. If such disability continues for more than — weeks, the Corporation, at its option, shall have the right to purchase the interest and shares of the disabled party, at its book value as defined un-

276

der this Agreement. In the event that the Corporation fails to purchase the interest or shares of the disabled partner within thirty (30) days after the expiration of the — week period, then the other shareholder of the Corporation may purchase the interest or shares of the disabled party, at the book value.

D. Notice of this election by the Corporation or by the other shareholder shall be served upon the disabled party in writing in accordance with paragraph 18 of this Agreement.

12. The shareholders agree to endorse the certificate or certificates of shares held by them as follows:

"The transfer or encumbrance of this certificate is subject to the terms and provisions of a shareholders' agreement dated July 1, 1978, and can only be transferred upon proof of compliance therewith; a copy of said agreement is on file at the office of the Corporation."

13. This Agreement may be altered, amended, or terminated only by a written instrument signed by both Corporation and all of the shareholders.

14. This Agreement shall terminate on the occurrence of any of the following events:

A. Bankruptcy, receivership or dissolution of the Corporation;

B. Death of all of the shareholders simultaneously or within a period of thirty (30) days.

15. This Agreement shall be subject to and governed by the laws of the State of Illinois, irrespective of the fact that one or more parties now is or may become a resident of a different state.

16. Should any provision of this Agreement be void or invalid, the remaining provisions shall nevertheless be binding and shall remain in full force and effect to the same extent as though such void or invalid provision had been deleted from or had not been included in this Agreement.

17. Should any of the terms and provisions of the Certificate of Incorporation or the bylaws of either Corporation conflict with the terms and provisions of this Agreement, this Agreement shall be controlling and shall take precedence.

18. Any notice sent to any party to this Agreement shall be deemed sufficient if sent by such party by certified mail, or served at

277

the address listed above for such party, or at the last address listed for such party in the stock record books of the Corporations.

WITNESS WHEREOF, the parties have hereunto set their hands and seals the day and year first above written.

_____

JEAN GORDON

_____

ADRIENNE JOHNSON

The Good Earth Restaurant, Inc.

By: _____

Jean Gordon, President

DETERMINATION OF NET WORTH PURSUANT TO PARAGRAPH 8

The undersigned, JEAN GORDON and ADRIENNE JOHNSON, having computed and determined the net worth of The Good Earth Restaurant, Inc. as Attorneys-in-Fact, pursuant to paragraph 8 of the Agreement dated July 1, 1978, between said Corporation and the shareholders, do hereby state:

a) That the amount of the net worth of said Corporations, taking into consideration not only all the tangible assets of the Corporations but all intangible assets, as well as including goodwill, is determined by the undersigned to be ten thousand ($10,000.00) Dollars;

b) The foregoing determination of the net worth or book value of the Corporations is made for the purpose of said Agreement and all of the undersigned concur therein;

c) This determination is made and is signed by all of the undersigned as said Attorneys-in-Fact as of July 1, 1978.

_____ L.S.
Jean Gordon

_____ L.S.
Adrienne Johnson

278

THE TENTH STEP:
BUY-OUT INSURANCE

I always suggest to clients going into business—particularly where there are partners or more than one stockholder—that they consider purchasing life insurance. Let's assume that your agreement provides that upon the death of a principal the corporation or survivors are to buy out the deceased's interest.

All very well, but if the purchase price is based upon the value of the business, paying out half the worth may kill it too. One alternative would be an agreement calling for long-term payout. That may work, but not quite so well if he was a working partner who must be replaced with a hired hand. In a small business, the combination of the additional salary and the payout may be too hard to handle.

Insurance can be used not only to fund the purchase of the deceased's interest, but also as added financial support for the business during the period of adjustment after the death of a valuable contributor. Your insurance company representative will be happy to provide you with applicable *pro forma* paragraphs that the company's legal department has worked out, to be incorporated into the partnership or stockholders' agreement. (Boy, will he be happy!)

THE ELEVENTH STEP:
KEEPING THE CORPORATION ALIVE

Earning a profit is the best way to do this, but a few formalities must be followed, too. A corporation must file an annual franchise tax return, and, in some states, a form annually redesignating your official representative or naming a new one. Failure to act on these responsibilities may result in the state's revoking your corporate charter in what is dramatically known as "dissolution by proclamation."

This isn't just a term in the law books. Recently, in a transaction in which one of my clients was buying the assets of another corporation, I routinely checked the seller's status with the secretary of state's office. I learned that several years earlier the corporation had been dissolved by proclamation for failure to pay its franchise taxes. Before we went through with the deal—which might have made my client liable for back franchise taxes and penalties—I made sure that the corporation cleared up its obligations and was formally reinstated.

Keeping your minutes book up to date, by recording directors' and stockholders' meetings, may not be mandatory to keep your corporate charter. But the minutes legally substantiate that actions of the officers were with the approval of the directors and stock-holders—which then gives all concerned the broadest possible protection of the corporate umbrella. Directors and officers may be personally liable for their actions when they exceed their authority. Minutes establish that authority.

The Final Step:
Death of a Business

"I can't understand," the fire marshal said sarcastically to the businessman, as they stood on the sidewalk across the street from the blazing furniture store, "why so many businesses end by fire." Replied the entrepreneur slyly, "How do you start a flood?"

As any arson squad member will tell you, an increasing number of businesses are victims of premeditated murder. But most terminate less abruptly. You sold the assets at a handsome profit. You've made so much money you've decided to retire and enjoy. On the other hand, the reason may well be financial. Or domestic. Jean and Adrienne's husbands may be weary of filling in as waiters and cashiers when the help phones in sick.

In a partnership, any partner can call for dissolution of the business—by conflict in the courts, if not by consensus. Upon dissolution, all partnership debts and liabilities must be settled before the partners may take anything for themselves. By agreement, the remaining assets can be sold and converted into cash or distributed in kind ("You take the tables and chairs. I'll take the cash register").

If, back in those exciting early days, you filed a Certificate of Doing Business as Partners Under a Fictitious Name, it's now time to notify the county clerk that you're doing business no more. It's easy enough—all you do is file the form on page 281.

A corporation is made of sturdier stuff. In most states, the only way to dissolve it is by a two-thirds vote of stockholders (a voluntary dissolution), or, kicking and screaming, by order of the court directing involuntary dissolution.

The voluntary route requires a stockholders' meeting, or the written consent of the necessary number. A Certificate of Dissolu-

T 341—Certificate of Discontinuance,
Business Conducted Under Assumed Name
For Individual,

JULIUS BLUMBERG, INC., LAW BLANK PUBLISHERS
80 EXCHANGE PL. AT BROADWAY, N.Y.C. 10004

Certificate of Discontinuance of Business

I, HEREBY CERTIFY that I have conducted or transacted business under the name or designation of

at   in the

County of   State of New York and that a certificate of conducting business

under an assumed name was filed in the office of the County Clerk, County of

State of New York, on the   day of   19   under index

number   and that the last amended certificate was filed on the   day of

                              19   in the office of the said County Clerk under index number

                              ; and I hereby further certify that the filing of a certificate in said County is no

longer required for the reason that the said business was discontinued on the

day of   19   or the conditions under which the business is conducted

have changed so that the filing of a certificate in said County is no longer required for the reason that

I therefore desire to file this certificate of discontinuance.

In Witness Whereof, I have this   day of   19   , made
and signed this certificate.

....

State of New York,
County of   } ss.:

On this   day of   , 19   , before me personally appeared

to me known and known to me to be the individual   described in, and who executed the foregoing

certificate, and   he   thereupon   duly acknowledged to me that   he   executed the same.

tion (right out of a form book) must be filed with the secretary of state declaring that the requisite number of stockholders have voted for it. In some states, proof of payment of franchise tax up to dissolution date may be required.

The attorney-general may bring about involuntary dissolution for a number of reasons, including failure to pay taxes, abuse of authority, or fraudulently obtaining articles of incorporation—like the "temple of meditation" that registered in New York State as a not-for-profit religious corporation, but was later discovered to be a massage parlor.

A stockholder, too, may exercise muscle in bringing down the corporation, if he can establish that the directors or shareholders are helplessly deadlocked in the company's management, or that corporate assets are being misapplied or wasted. This is a complicated procedure, however, and it's likely to take legal reinforcements: a real live lawyer.

There are other ways to go out of business—and you'll meet them in the next chapter. It is, we hope, a chapter you'll never need to use.

CHAPTER 15

Bankruptcy: Is There a Life After Debt?

Early Roman law blithely permitted a man's creditors to recoup a debt by selling his family into slavery. If the sum realized at the auction block failed to square accounts, the creditors could then liquidate the man's remaining assets in a grisly dismemberment that awarded each creditor a piece of his body, with the largest share to the principal creditor.

In seventeenth-century France, a bankrupt debtor was often sentenced to lengthy confinement on bread and water—a fate possibly worse than dismemberment for many Frenchmen. For heavily-in-debt American families today, the options, though still unpleasant, are considerably less painful.

Take the Gardners, for example. Reared in an easy credit, pay-after-you-go society, they had no training in family finance, none of the guidance of earlier generations schooled in the virtues of thrift by Horatio Alger and McGuffey's *Reader*. When they married, the Gardners bought everything on credit: furniture, TV, auto, washing machine. With their monthly installment obligations so high, there was little left for cash purchases. So they opened charge accounts and used them for clothing, household items, dinners out. Their monthly bills soon outdistanced their salaries. But their situation wasn't hopeless. As the thoughtful reader who knows how to read chapter titles has undoubtedly already anticipated, there was a way for them to escape the punishing cycle of plastic-card poverty into which they had rashly charged.

The Millers were good money managers. Older and more experienced, they never let bills pile up. They'd even banked money for their children's education. That fund, however, thanks to ever-spiraling school costs, had evaporated by the time their first child finished college. Then Ron suffered a heart attack and required bypass surgery. Hospital expenses, as is so often the case in catastrophic illness, far exceeded health insurance coverage. Income dwindled, and there appeared no way out of the deepening hole.

Then there was Tom Tycoon. He had always dreamed of his own business, but just when he decided to make his move, economic conditions soured. His young company failed to thrive, and Tycoon found himself unable to repay the money he'd borrowed to finance his venture, while drawing barely enough money out of the business to support his family. But even the subsequent failure of the firm, discouraging as it was, didn't mean total unsalvageable disaster for the Tycoons.

Such financial crises are becoming more and more common in the United States, and not necessarily because more Americans are spendthrifts today than were those of earlier generations. Many honest hardworking people have been pushed to, and through, the limits of their financial resources by inflation and a tightening job market. In an emergency—illness, job loss, business reversal—they have no cash to cushion the blow.

For some, skilled in the art of using other people's money, owing huge sums is a comfortable way of life—as it was for the businessman who left in his will the name of six bankers he wanted as pallbearers, "because," he wrote archly, "they've carried me all my life, and they might as well finish the job." Getting into financial trouble is not, however, necessarily an indication of weakness, carelessness, wickedness, or foolishness. It happens to the best of people, often because of circumstances beyond their control. It is not something to celebrate, but neither is it something to be ashamed of.

Anyone who senses the approach of serious financial troubles should not wait until the economic lightning strikes to face and assess the situation. The earlier the analysis, the better the chance of problem resolving without irreparable damage to your credit rating and psyche.

The warning signs are usually clear. It's increasingly difficult to pay all bills each month; you put off more and more for "next week's paycheck." All cash reserves are depleted, and easily convertible assets like stocks are sold off. Parents and relatives are tapped for loans. Nasty letters and phone calls escalate into summonses. If you're lucky, you're spared the ultimate embarrassment that occurred to a businessman client of mine, who invited his accountant, his attorney (me), and the vice-president of his bank to lunch at an expensive restaurant to try to arrange the urgently needed extension of a large loan his firm had taken.

Things were going well. The banker seemed impressed with his business acumen and his glowing sketch of the firm's prospects. And then the check came. My client handed the waiter his American Express card. Several long minutes later, the waiter returned. "Excuse me, sir," he said discreetly, "there's a phone call for you in the rear." The call was *about*, not *for* him. The cashier had routinely called American Express to check his credit, and had been instructed to confiscate my client's card, which was well beyond its credit line and on which no payments had been made in several months. Fortunately, he had a healthy Diners Club card. The bank loan extension went through, and my client thanked the Lord and that discreet waiter. "If he'd said anything at the table," he confided later, meaningfully slashing his forefinger across his throat, "I'd have been deader than the trout I ate for lunch."

Wait as long as my client did to face the facts, and even with the best of waiters and intentions, there may be no way to satisfy your creditors and still buy groceries. A very few people seem to thrive on that kind of stress—like eighteenth-century British statesman Charles Fox, whose father remarked that he was astonished that his 25-year-old son could sleep at night in view of the enormous gambling debts he owed. Replied the suave Sir Charles: "Sir, your astonishment should rather be at how my creditors can sleep."

If you find yourself, like Fox, encircled by sleepless creditors, but unlike him, worried and weary, what can you do?

THE FIRST STEP:
ASSESS YOUR FINANCIAL SITUATION

To do this, you've got to throw away your rose-colored glasses and carefully list *all* your assets (everything of value you own or have coming to you) and all your liabilities (everything you owe). Subtract total liabilities from total assets. If liabilities exceed assets, you're insolvent. (The accounting term "insolvency" is frequently a transitional stage before the onset of "bankruptcy," a legal term.) Austerity is in order, and you should immediately consider taking one of the alternatives listed further on in this chapter to straighten out your financial affairs.

Even if you find assets are greater than liabilities, your financial situation may warrant some action. The penalties—including marriages that break up or require counseling—for not facing up to these problems are many, so the earlier you confront them the better. When Selig "Pop" Grossinger, founder of the famous Catskill

Mountain resort that bears his name, was a small farmer, new to the community of Ferndale, New York, he realized that he was not going to be able to meet the first payment on a bank loan. A week before the note was due, he went into the bank to explain his difficulty. Said the banker, "I like your honesty, Mr. Grossinger, and the fact that you were man enough to face the situation squarely and early. I'm going to extend your note." Pop Grossinger's direct approach still works with creditors today. They'll extend themselves—and credit—a lot more readily to someone who puts his best foot and a visible sense of responsibility forward. A week before the problem, not two weeks after it.

Failure to act, frantic vacation-taking escapism, stalling tactics, and delaying actions will only spur an annoyed or impatient creditor to take action against you. Such actions—beyond the routine 12 to 24 percent annual interest on "easy credit" and finance company charges that bleed many families of thousands of dollars a year because they "can't afford" to pay their debts in full—include:

Repossession of items bought on the installment plan. The merchant who has sold you an auto, TV, furniture, or anything with a resale value is in a strong legal position if you fall behind on payments. You've breached your contract, and he can repossess—drive, haul, or tow it away. There's nothing subtle about the way it's done. No papers need be served. You go downstairs one morning, and find your driveway or parking space empty. Flustered, you phone the police. "Excuse me for asking, sir," they say, "but are you current with the bank on your payments?" It's a fair question. My office overlooks a bank parking lot. There are always a few cars parked there with license plates removed and auction notices forlornly pasted on their windows.

At this stage, all is not necessarily lost. After repossession, most states give you a short period—say, ten days—in which to pay what you owe plus the seller or chattel mortgage-holder's collection expenses, and allow you to redeem your property. If you don't claim it—and many people don't realize they can, or are too upset to act—the property is sold. The creditor takes what is due, plus expenses, and gives you the balance, if any.

Foreclosing a chattel or other mortgage. If you've borrowed money, pledging your home or other chattel (personal property) as security or collateral, and you can't make the payments, creditors have the right to, and probably will, foreclose. That means they, too, can take possession of the property, sell it, take their share of the proceeds (what you owe), and give you the balance. The bad news usually is that, somehow, the amount of money realized is just enough to pay your debt. Sometimes, it's not even enough, in which case you're still obligated to pay the balance.

Collecting on a lien. The owner of a warehouse where your furniture is stored, the mechanic who overhauls your transmission, the shop where you left your drapes for dry cleaning automatically have liens (from the Latin, meaning a tie or band) on your property and can hold it until your bills are paid. If that doesn't happen within a reasonable time, they can sell your property at public auction to settle up. Those "Abandoned Property Warehouse Sale" ads you see in the newspapers are frequently for property abandoned involuntarily, because the owner couldn't pay the storage charges.

A lawsuit. The "lawyer's letter," familiar to those often late in paying their bills, can become more than a threat if the bill in question is not quickly paid. To "make an example of him," some firms will press a suit for an insignificant sum, even though legal costs may far exceed the recovery. Early in my law practice, a messenger service put me on a monthly retainer—which considerably cut their costs—to sue to collect chronically delinquent accounts. Even if only $5 or $10 was at stake, if the debtor was still in business, they wanted me to sue "as a matter of principle" and as a punitive measure, since the very filing of a suit could affect the delinquent's credit rating.

Others will only press a case when the sum involved is over a particular limit—say, $200. As the debtor, however, you ordinarily have no way of knowing a particular company's legal boiling point. The initial lawyer's letter is not a legal action, simply a preview of coming destruction, a warning or threat claiming what is due. If the letter goes unanswered or the claim unpaid, a summons is almost sure to follow. That usually gives you 10 to 30 days to respond, depending upon the court. If you neither pay within that time nor file an answer and defense (which may require a visit to the clerk of the court, who can guide you), a default judgment will be entered against you.

While you're entangled in a lawsuit—or, as we lawyers are fond of saying, "even prior thereto"—the next net may drop: the "attachment" of your property by your creditor, in effect freezing your assets (a home, a bank account, a car) until the case is concluded. Because this could mean that your assets might be tied up by an unjust claim, such attachment is not casually granted by the judge, but is ordinarily allowed only if the creditor can show that you live outside the state, are concealing assets, or are about to skip town.

A client of mine had been owed more than $6,000 by one of his customers for more than a year. One afternoon, the umpteenth statement he'd sent returned with a postal notation that Mr. Nopay had moved to Florida. My client tracked him, then sent the runaway a registered letter, to which Mr. Nopay responded blandly that he was selling his home and business, and would pay his debt as soon as possible. Not good enough. When my client spotted an ad in the newspaper advertising what he recognized as Nopay's house for sale, he asked me what, if anything, he could do. Armed with photocopies of the certified letter and Nopay's response, the classified house ad, and a sheaf of unpaid invoices, I went to court. Upon posting a surety bond to ensure that my claim was not frivolous, I was able to get an order of attachment on all Nopay's property in the state, which the sheriff, at my request, then employed to attach his house. When Nopay found a buyer shortly thereafter, he had no choice but to pay every penny, including interest and expenses. Now that it was clearly in his best interests, he did so forthwith. If he hadn't once the judgment was entered, there would still have been other legal steps we could have taken to collect, including garnisheeing salary (not possible in this case) or executing on his property. (See chapter 6, Collecting Judgment.)

THE SECOND STEP: DETERMINING YOUR ALTERNATIVES

The person in serious debt has a great many options—all painful, but some less painful than others—with the last resort straight bankruptcy. We'll run down the options briefly, then spell out the steps in each.

WAGE EARNERS PLAN (CHAPTER XIII)

The "chapters" referred to are sections in the Federal Bankruptcy Act of 1898, modified in 1938, and now again in the throes of Congressional reshaping and trade-offs. That process will produce a bill for our times, worlds away from the Panic of '98 that inspired the original bill, and the 1930s Depression that led to its remodeling—and, among other provisions, it's expected to make the Wage Earner Plan more attractive to debtors.

Chapter XIII is designed for individuals whose major income is from wages, salaries, or commissions, and who earn enough to pay their debts over a period of up to three years. XIII gives you a chance to get out of debt without the stigma of bankruptcy. (Details, p. 296.) All your creditors are compelled to go along with this stretchout if more than 50 percent—in number and in dollars—agree to it. (If you have ten creditors, more than five must agree; if you owe $8,000, those agreeing must account for more than $4,000 of your debt. So if you persuaded your chief creditor, the man to whom you owe $4,500, you'd still need the consent of five others, even if you only owed them $5 apiece.) Presently, Chapter XIII won't work for the person who can't possibly pay up within three years, and the Wage Earner Plan requires paying 100 percent on the dollar, something those electing the rockier path of bankruptcy rarely do. The proposed legislation would permit a longer payback period and settlement for less than a dollar on the dollar.

THE INFORMAL ARRANGEMENT (AGREEMENT OR COMPOSITION).

Called informal because it's worked out without involving the courts, this option for either individuals or small businesses may allow you to arrange with creditors to postpone or extend payments over a period of time. (Details on page 293.) This has the advantage of removing the weight of debt, while restructuring your financial lifestyle, as a supervised diet restructures your eating style, and may prevent your getting into trouble again in the future. But you need cooperative creditors. If one or more doesn't agree to the arrangement and sues you for collection, you may be unable to keep up with the obligations you've agreed to with the others. In some areas, for a fee, specialists called credit counselors will assist in putting together this kind of financial plan.

FORMAL ARRANGEMENT UNDER CHAPTER XI

This is largely for businessmen and—though this is an equal right few will be eager to share—businesswomen, too. It's similar to the Informal Arrangement but is entered into and arranged under the formal protection of Bankruptcy Court, a federal court found in every jurisdiction, with generally uniform rules and procedures. The arrangement allows the debtor to continue in business if he can work out a plan for debt payment acceptable to his creditors. Plans ordinarily vary from 10 cents on the dollar to 100 percent stretched out in time. As with the Wage Earners Plan, you need the consent of more than half your creditor constituency in number and dollars.

The person or firm filing under this option is called "the debtor" rather than "the bankrupt," so theoretically Chapter XI doesn't carry the stigma of bankruptcy. But in the real world, people often use the two words interchangeably, if incorrectly. ("Poor guy went Chapter XI—yep, totally bankrupt!") Chapter XI demands a tremendous amount of paperwork, and the best efforts of an expert. It's definitely not a do-it-yourself process. I've done my share of bankruptcy work, but when I see Chapter XI as the best solution to financial woes and worries, I cheerfully defer and refer the client to an attorney who is a full-time bankruptcy specialist.

ASSIGNMENT FOR THE BENEFIT OF CREDITORS

It's possible in many states for someone to turn over all his assets to a trustee (known as an assignee) and, in effect, walk away from the whole sad dissolution of his business. The assignee arranges for an auction, converts any remaining assets into cash, and then—usually at a fee of 5 percent for himself and another 5 percent for his lawyer—it's his job to distribute the proceeds to each creditor in proportion to amounts owed.

Sometimes there are no proceeds for anyone but "preferred creditors," such as employees who have not been paid or the government which has not received sales or withholding taxes. These, held "in trust" by the employer and supposedly put aside, are often, in desperation, spent to keep the company afloat.

CORPORATE REORGANIZATION—CHAPTER X

This provision of bankruptcy law allows corporations that are basically sound but experiencing temporary financial difficulties to reorganize under court direction and stretch out debt payments, instead of dissolving in bankruptcy. It is often used so that creditors will realize more than they would if a company were liquidated. This complex procedure is about as unlikely for do-it-yourselfers as piloting a Boeing 747.

THE DRIBBLE METHOD

This one isn't described in standard business texts. Its father is desperation and its mother a telephone that never stops ringing.

Many people manage to keep the ship afloat for years with a swiss cheese hull, patching the holes in their fragile financial barque with small sums, doled out to those creditors most vociferous in threatening to scuttle them.

One eloquent client of mine kept his corporation going for two years in this way, in order to avoid bankruptcy. Whenever a check came in, he dribbled token payments to those creditors pressing him the hardest, and (to protect his home) those who had his personal written notes or guarantees. Another client, after dribbling for several years, hit paydirt when one of his new products caught on. He was able to pay off everyone in full and successfully continue his business.

Package Warning: Dribbling may cause such disturbing side effects as insomnia, ulcers, and impotence, plus, of course, the constant tension (to some rare birds this is challenge and excitement) of wondering where the next dollar will come from, and which creditor will be first to padlock the office door. It's the hardest way out, but may be the most rewarding if delaying tactics permit repairs. It doesn't "do" anyone out of anything, and leaves one with ragged nerves but a clear conscience.

BANKRUPTCY

In this proceeding—which is reminiscent of the early Roman dismembering of the debtor—all assets are distributed to creditors, except those specifically protected and exempted by law (see p. 307). Any balance is legally forgiven, except debts exempted and nondischargeable by law. If the debtor is a corporation, it is eviscerated and its bones buried. The individual debtor, however, is freed of the obligation of paying most debts and, once feelings of relief replace those of depression, is able to make a fresh start with a relatively clean slate.

THE THIRD STEP:
CAN YOU BE YOUR OWN BANKRUPTCY LAWYER?

The answer to that is a cautious yes—with caveats. If you're a homeowner, or you or your spouse own any other major property, which could be lost if bankruptcy is not handled skillfully, an experienced lawyer might be a wise investment. But the individual declaring ordinary bankruptcy, or the individual or small businessperson going into Informal Arrangement, should be able to cope by following the step-by-step procedure outlined in this chapter, if you can fill out necessary forms and can find time for the legwork that may be required for an Informal Agreement.

Those who stumble on the forms might consider purchasing a good do-it-yourself bankruptcy kit with line-by-line explanations from a reliable company. Such kits are becoming increasingly available in many areas and cost $50 to $75, as opposed to the less than $5 for legal stationery store forms alone. Check out the kit seller with the local Better Business Bureau first, to see if there are any complaints in his file. And ask for random references, three or four people you can call who've bought kits in the past year, so you can get their reactions and results.

Don't try doing a Chapter XI (Formal Arrangement) yourself—too complicated. And remember that the expenses of a business bankruptcy—in an uncomplicated case, from $300 to $1,500—come out of the assets of the business. It probably pays to play it safe and retain a lawyer, even though the ordinary bankruptcy of a small business isn't all that difficult if you're good at asking and answering questions. In any case, before deciding, read on. Even if your final decision is to hire a lawyer, you'll be that much better prepared, knowing what to expect each step of the way.

An experienced attorney who's been there before can be a valuable buffer in individual bankruptcy, handling the depressing details, filling out the forms, and giving you assurances that you'll get all the asset exemptions to which you're entitled, so you don't go naked into the world. Where an individual's assets are being cut up, the attorney's cost comes, in effect, out of the proceeds due to the creditors rather than out of the debtor's empty pockets. This is why the courts monitor attorney's fees closely and, when they appear inflated, ask that a refund be returned to the assets pool.

The courts are accustomed to *pro se* bankruptcies, sometimes even in the matter of small corporations. As U.S. District Court Judge Jack B. Weinstein said recently: "No doubt the rule [requiring attorneys to appear for corporations] protects the court from proceedings awkwardly drafted and motions inarticulately presented . . . [But] . . . a person's day in court is more important than the convenience of the court . . . [Laymen's mistakes are] a manageable nuisance."

292

The Alternatives Spelled Out In Detail

THE INFORMAL ARRANGEMENT

Creditors these days are an unimaginative lot, who for the most part follow the well-marked form-letter highway, starting friendly, progressing to icy, and motoring predictably on to indignant. One almost longs for the good old days when the discerning creditor confronted an uncooperative merchant with a reputation for putting off payment of bills until his creditors died of old age or exasperation, and insisted: "I'd like my money—now." Replied the businessman blandly: "I'm sorry, but I don't have it." Said the ingenious creditor: "Pay me now, or I'll tell all your other creditors that you paid me in full."

Rather than wait for your creditors to gang up on you, it's sensible to show good faith by meeting them at least halfway. One measure halfway to bankruptcy, but meriting your creditors' praise rather than their censure, is the Informal Arrangement. It's best to move to it, however, before the financial picture becomes thoroughly bleak, before lawyers' letters pile up higher than junk mail, and dunning phone calls become more frequent than false alarms at a firehouse.

The basic idea is to talk to each creditor and attempt to either reduce your obligations or stretch the terms over a period of time so that you'll be able to meet them in full. You'll find creditors sometimes more than happy to work out terms tailored to your budget, since—though it may take longer to get their money—there's a greater likelihood of their ultimately being paid. Experience has taught them that if they push you into that yawning chasm called bankruptcy, their hopes of ever seeing penny one topple over the brink with you.

The Informal Arrangement is relatively easy to accomplish without benefit of counsel, with steps as follows:

Step A: *Prepare a budget*

First, prepare a monthly budget for yourself. Include all your rent or mortgage payments, fuel and utility bills, food costs, insurance payments, clothing and transportation expenses, and all the other expenditures of day-to-day survival. Include everything except your overdue bills, and add a cushion for inflation.

Now total these monthly expenses and subtract them from your net monthly income: take-home pay after deductions of taxes, Social Security, union dues, pension payments, medical insurance, and the like. What's left is the amount of money you can channel into paying overdue bills, if—and you and your spouse must psychologically accept this or the plan will fail—you're willing to live frugally for as long as the arrangement requires to erase your debts.

Step B: *List past due obligations*

Now make a second list of all your past due bills, outstanding loans due monthly, and other indebtedness not listed in your monthly budget.

Step C: *Determine if you can pay these debts*

If the amount of money left over in Step A is enough for you to pay the debts listed in Step B over a reasonable period— say, two or three years—this alternative is viable. You can determine that this way: Divide monthly surplus into total debt, and you'll know how many months it will take to pay it off. This approach will only work, of course, if you don't incur fresh debt. This may mean a radical change in lifestyle—stifling impulse buying and impromptu "Let's eat out tonight!" decisions not provided for in the budget, checking books out of the library instead of buying them, free TV instead of front row center.

One thing to recognize when you try for an informal agreement is that, should you fail to meet payments because of business reverses or unexpected medical or other expenses, you can still opt for bankruptcy.

Step D: *Prepare the necessary papers*

Draw up a neatly typed copy of your budget (Step A) and debts (Step B) and an outline of the payment plan you propose. Make a photocopy for each creditor. The proposed settlement agreement should look something like this:

Form No. 25
SETTLEMENT AGREEMENT

This Agreement is made in the City of   , State of   , between   residing at   (the "Debtor") and such of the creditors of the Debtor who shall become parties hereto (the "Creditors").

The Debtor acknowledges that he has incurred the debts as set forth on the Schedule attached hereto and that he is unable to pay the said debts in full at this time.

The Debtor proposes, subject to the approval of his creditors, to pay the amount due to each of his Creditors as follows:

294

A. One-twenty-fourth [or whatever other arrangement you propose] of the amount due to each Creditor participating in this Agreement on the first day of   , 197   and a like sum on the first day of each month until the entire debt is paid in full.

(OR)

B. Fifty percent [or whatever other percentage you decide upon] for each and every dollar of debts, to be paid in three equal installments, three months, six months and nine months from and after   (date)   , without interest, which payment shall be in full satisfaction and discharge of the claim of each Creditor participating in this Agreement.

That each Creditor participating in this Plan agrees as follows:

1. That upon the signing of this Agreement and for as long as the Debtor shall not be in default in making any of the payments provided for herein, no further action shall be taken by the Creditor to enforce its claim.

2. That upon the delivery of the final payment called for herein, such delivery shall operate as a complete release and discharge of the creditor's claim and demand against the Debtor, and thereupon the Creditor shall surrender to the Debtor any and all notes, or other evidences of indebtedness, that it may hold against the Debtor.

Dated: 197

_____

Debtor

_____

Signature of Debtor

AGREED TO:

(Name and Address of Creditor)

(Amount of Debt)/ $

Step E: *Contact your creditors*

If your creditors are relatively few in number and located in your immediate area, it may be advantageous to visit each of them by appointment, with repayment plan in hand. You might say, "Look, several of my creditors have agreed to this. If you go along, I'm confident that I can handle paying off everyone." If that doesn't win them—and your sincerity and straightforwardness should—you might try one curtain line: "If you don't accept this plan, I may be forced into bankruptcy—and that won't do anyone any good." They'll know what that means—ten cents on the dollar.

If you can't manage personal visits, send a letter to each creditor outlining your plan. With a large corporate creditor—GMAC, Sears Roebuck, American Express—it's a good idea to make a phone call or two first. Call the credit department and ask to speak to whoever is authorized to OK such arrangements. Discuss your plan, if possible get tentative oral approval, and take the name of the person to whom your plan should be mailed for official written approval. The very fact that you make this kind of effort instead of burying your head in a pile of bills should help to win your creditors' confidence, show them your intentions are honorable, and persuade them that you deserve a chance.

Your goal should be 100 percent creditor agreement—and, if necessary and possible, to persuade them to reduce your debt by 20 to 50 percent to help you over the hump.

Another method, which saves a lot of footwork, is to invite all your creditors to a meeting and explain your proposal to them en masse. This takes unlimited courage—something like a lion tamer shampooing with beef gravy before stepping into a cage of hungry carnivores. And there's a possible disadvantage: The creditors get to know one another and may decide to hold a meeting of their own, ganging up to mug you with a counter-proposal less advantageous to you than your own.

In any case, if one or more creditors elects to bring a court action against you to collect the amount due at a rate faster than proposed by your plan, you may be unable to fulfill the other obligations you've undertaken. In that case, you may be forced to seek the uneasy sanctuary of the bankruptcy courts.

WAGE EARNERS PLAN—CHAPTER XIII OF THE NATIONAL BANKRUPTCY LAW

When Ron Miller (mentioned earlier in this chapter) recovered from bypass surgery, he was welcomed back to his job, but found himself with a hill of bills. Miller was well-positioned to pay off his debts over a long period of time. Unfortunately, his creditors were restless. When he approached them, though most were cooperative, several—possibly worried by his heart surgery instead of reassured by it—refused to grant him extensions. Miller's back was by no means against the firewall. He was an ideal candidate for Chapter XIII of the bankruptcy act: The Wage Earner Plan, requiring agreement from only 50 percent of his creditors. Since Wage Earner is carried out under court auspices, steps are, not surprisingly, a bit more complicated than the Informal Agreement it resembles.

Step A. *Preparations*

Follow steps A, B, and C of the Informal Agreement. If your "surplus" is sufficient to support your family and still pay off your creditors in the next 36 months, you're on the right track.

Step B. *Obtain the necessary papers*

Chapter XIII forms are inexpensively available at stationery stores handling legal forms. If you can't locate such a store, a bankruptcy court clerk can certainly direct you to a source.

Step C: *Complete the papers*

Fill in the forms on pages 298–305. (All legal forms in this chapter are through the courtesy of Julius Blumberg, Inc.)

Step D: *File your petition*

Once completed, the forms must be filed with the bankruptcy clerk of the jurisdiction in which you live. You can locate it by calling the local U.S. District Court and asking where to bring the papers. Ask, too, the least busy hour, so there's a chance of getting the most possible help. A $50 fee is ordinarily paid at this time. But paying it in installments is possible, and the procedure for doing this is detailed on page 307 in Ordinary Bankruptcy.

Step E: *Notice to creditors*

The next move is the court clerk's. He'll send notices to all your creditors advising them that you've filed a Chapter XIII petition, and giving them the date of the first hearing. You'll find that the order issued by the judge for this meeting acts as a legal headache powder. His words ("the filing of the petition . . . operates as a stay of the commencement or continuation of any action against the debtor . . . ") will effectively end the harassments you've so long endured.

Step F: *The hearing*

The best way to prepare for this (or any) hearing is to visit the particular court in session. You'll be much more comfortable when it's your turn, if you've seen others survive the ordeal before you. (In addition, read chapter 5, Trying Your Case.) A few quick words of advice: Refer to the judge as "your Honor," and try not to tense up. Bankruptcy judges range from punitive to positively permissive, but most are on the sympathetic end of the spectrum. Recently, while waiting for my client's case to be called at a bankruptcy

Form No. 26

DISTRICT OF

In re

BANKRUPTCY NO.

ORIGINAL PETITION
UNDER
CHAPTER XIII

Debtor, Soc. Sec. No.
[Include here all names used by bankrupt within last 6 years.]

1. Petitioner's post-office address is

2. Petitioner has his *principal place of employment — residence — domicile* within this district.

3. No bankruptcy case initiated on a petition by or against petitioner is now pending.

4. Petitioner is qualified to file this petition and is entitled to the benefits of Chapter XIII of the Bankruptcy Act

5. Petitioner is *insolvent — unable to pay his debts as they mature.*

6. *A copy of petitioner's proposed plan is attached.*

7. *Petitioner intends to file a plan pursuant to Chapter XIII of the Act.*

Wherefore petitioner prays for relief under Chapter XIII of the Act.

Signed: ....
Attorney for Petitioner

Address: ....

....

....
Petitioner
[*Petitioner signs if not represented by attorney*]

STATE OF   County of   ss.

I,   the petitioner named in the foregoing petition, do
hereby swear that the statements contained therein are true according to the best of my knowledge, information, and belief.

....
Petitioner

Subscribed and sworn to before me on

....

....
Official Character

OF 13-1: Original Petition Under Chapter XIII   © 1973 BY JULIUS BLUMBERG, INC., 80 EXCHANGE PL., N.Y.C. 10004

Instructions: cross out inapplicable italicized words.

In re

BANKRUPTCY NO.

Debtor, Soc. Sec. No.
[Include here all names used by bankrupt within last 6 years.]

CHAPTER XIII
STATEMENT

[Each question should be answered or the failure to answer explained. If the answer is "None," this should be stated. If additional space is needed for the answer to any question, a separate sheet, properly identified and made a part hereof, should be used and attached.

The term, "original petition," as used in the following questions, shall mean the original petition filed under Rule 13-103 or, if the petition is filed under Rule 13-104 in a pending bankruptcy case, shall mean the bankruptcy petition by or against you which originated the pending bankruptcy case.

This form must be completed in full whether a single or a joint petition is filed. When information is requested for "each" or "either spouse filing a petition" it should be supplied for both when a joint petition is filed.]

1. **Name and residence**

   (*a*) Give full name: Husband

                     Wife

   (*b*) Where does   (1) Mailing address: Husband
       each spouse   **Wife**
       filing a
       petition   (2) City or town: Husband
       now   **Wife**
       reside?   (3) Telephone number: Husband
                                 Wife

   (*c*) What does each spouse filing a petition consider his or her residence, if different from that listed in (*b*) above?

       Husband

       Wife

2. **Occupation and income**

   (*a*) Give present occupation of each spouse filing a petition. (If more than one, list all for each spouse filing a petition.)

       Husband

       Wife

   (*b*) What is the name, address, and telephone number of present employer (or employers) of each spouse filing a petition? (Include also any identifying badge or card number with employer.)

       Husband

       Wife

   (*c*) How long has each spouse filing a petition been employed by present employer?

       Husband

       Wife

   (*d*) If either spouse filing a petition has not been employed by present employer for a period of 1 year, state the name of prior employer(s) and nature of employment during that period.

       Husband

       Wife

   (*e*) Has either spouse filing a petition operated a business, in partnership or otherwise, during the past 3 years? (If so, give the particulars, including names, dates, and places.)

       Husband

       Wife

(*f*) Answer the following questions for each spouse whether single or joint petition is filed unless spouses are separated and a single petition is filed:

(1) Is your current pay period: *Husband*   *Wife*

    (a) Weekly

    (b) Semi-monthly

    (c) Monthly

    (d) Other (specify)

(2) What are your gross wages, or commission per pay period?   Husband $........................   Wife $........................

(3) What are your payroll deductions per pay period for: *Husband*   *Wife*

    (a) Payroll taxes (including social security) $........................ $........................

    (b) Insurance   ....

    (c) Credit union   ....

    (d) Union dues   ....

    (e) Other (specify)   ....

(4) What is your take-home pay per pay period?   Husband $........................   Wife $........................

(5) Is your employment subject to seasonal or other change?   Husband ....   Wife ....

(6) What was the amount of your gross income for the last calendar year?   Husband $........................   Wife $........................

(7) Has either of you made any wage assignments or allotments? (If so, indicate which spouse's wage assigned or allotted, the name and address of the person to whom assigned or allotted, and the amount owing, if any, to such person. If allotment or assignment is to a creditor, his claim should also be listed in Item 11a.)

3. Dependents

(To be answered for each spouse whether single or joint petition is filed unless spouses are separated and a single petition is filed.)

(*a*) Does either of you pay [*or* receive] alimony, maintenance, or support?   If so, how much per month?

For whose support? (Give name, age, and relationship to you.)

Husband

Wife

(*b*) List all other dependents, other than present spouse, not listed in (*a*) above. (Give name, age, and relationship to you.)

Husband

Wife

4. Budget

    (*a*) Give estimated average future monthly income for each spouse whether single or joint petition is filed unless spouses are separated and a single petition is filed.

        (1) Husband's monthly take-home pay .... $.....................................

        (2) Wife's monthly take-home pay ....

        (3) Other monthly income (specify) .... _____

                                                          Total $.....................................

    (*b*) Give estimated average future monthly expenses of family (not including debts to be paid under plan), consisting of:

        (1) Rent or home mortgage payment (include lot rental for trailer).. $.....................................

        (2) Utilities (Electricity $.................... Heat $.................... Water $.................... Telephone $....................) ....

        (3) Food.. ....

        (4) Clothing ....

        (5) Laundry and cleaning ....

        (6) Newspapers, periodicals, and books (including school books)... ....

        (7) Medical and drug expenses ....

        (8) Insurance (not deducted from wages) : (a) Auto $........................ (b) Other $.................. ....

        (9) Transportation (not including auto payments to be paid under plan) ....

       (10) Recreation ....

       (11) Club and union dues (not deducted from wages) ....

       (12) Taxes (not deducted from wages) ....

       (13) Alimony, maintenance, or support payments ....

       (14) Other payments for support of dependents not living at home.. ....

       (15) Other (specify) : ....

                                                            ....

                                                            ....

                                                            ....

                                                            Total $.....................................

    (*c*) Excess of estim. future monthly income (last line of Item 4(a) above) over estim. future exp. (last line of Item 4(b) above) ...... $.....................................

    (*d*) Total amount to be paid each month under plan .... $.....................................

5. Payment of attorney

    (*a*) How much have you agreed to pay or what property have you agreed to transfer to your attorney in connection with this case?

    (*b*) How much have you paid or what have you transferred to him?

6. Tax refunds

    (To be answered for each spouse whether single or joint petition is filed unless spouses are separated and a single petition is filed.)

    To what tax refunds (income or other), if any, is either of you, or may either of you be, entitled? (Give particulars, including information as to any refunds payable jointly to you or any other person. All such refunds should also be listed in Item 13(b).)

7. Bank accounts and safe deposit boxes

    (To be answered for each spouse whether single or joint petition is filed unless spouses are separated and a single petition is filed.)

    (*a*) Does either of you currently have any bank or savings and loan accounts, checking or savings? (If so, give name and address of bank, nature of account, current balance, and name and address of every other person authorized to make withdrawals from the account. Such accounts should also be listed in Item 13(b).)

7. **Bank accounts and safe deposit boxes (continued)**

(b) Does either of you currently keep any safe deposit boxes or other depositories? (If so, give name and address of bank or other depository, name and address of every other person who has a right of access thereto, and a brief description of the contents thereof, which should also be listed in Item 13(b).)

8. **Prior Bankruptcy**

What proceedings under the Bankruptcy Act have previously been brought by or against either spouse filing a petition? (State the location of the bankruptcy court, the nature and number of each proceeding, the date when it was filed, and whether a discharge was granted or refused, the proceeding was dismissed, or a composition, arrangement, or plan was confirmed.)

9. **Foreclosures, executions, and attachments**

(To be answered for each spouse whether single or joint petition is filed unless spouses are separated and a single petition is filed.)

(a) Is any of the property of either of you, including real estate, involved in a foreclosure proceeding, in or out of court? (If so, identify the property and the person foreclosing.)

(b) Has any property or income of either of you been attached, garnished, or seized under any legal or equitable process within the 4 months immediately preceding the filing of the original petition herein? (If so, describe the property seized, or person garnished, and at whose suit.)

10. **Repossessions and returns**

(To be answered for each spouse whether single or joint petition is filed unless spouses are separated and a single petition is filed.)

Has any property of either of you been returned to, repossessed, or seized by the seller or by any other party, including a landlord, during the 4 months immediately preceding the filing of the original petition herein? (If so, give particulars, including the name and address of the party getting the property and its description and value.)

11. **Debts** (To be answered for each spouse whether single or joint petition is filed.)

(a) *Secured Debts.*—List all debts which are or may be secured by real or personal property. (Indicate in sixth column, if debt payable in stallments, the amount of each installment, the installment period (monthly, weekly, or other) and number of installments in arrears, if any. Indicate in last column whether husband or wife solely liable, or whether you are jointly liable.)

Creditor's name and address (if unknown, so state); zip codes recommended	Consideration or basis for debt	Amount claimed by creditor	If disputed, amount admitted by debtor	Description of collateral (include year and make of automobile)	Installment amount, period, and number of installments in arrears	Husband or wife solely liable, or jointly liable

OF 13-5: Chapter XIII Statement: page 4   © 1975 BY JULIUS BLUMBERG, INC., 80 EXCHANGE PL., N.Y.C. 10004

11. Debts (continued)

(b) *Unsecured Debts.*—List all other debts, liquidated and unliquidated, including taxes, attorneys' fees and tort claims.

Creditor's name and address (if unknown, so state); zip codes recommended	Consideration or basis for debt	Amount claimed by creditor	If disputed, amount admitted by debtor	Husband or wife solely liable, or jointly liable

12. Codebtors (To be answered for each spouse whether single or joint petition is filed.)

(a) Are any other persons liable, as cosigners or in any other manner, on any of the debts of either of you or are either of you so liable on the debts of others? (If so, give particulars, indicating which spouse liable and including names of creditors, nature of debt, names and addresses of co-debtors, and their relationship, if any, to you.)

(b) If so, have such codebtors made any payments on such debts? (Give name of each codebtor and amount paid by him.)

(c) Have either of you made any payments on such debts? (If so, specify total amount paid to each creditor, whether paid by husband or wife, and name of codebtor.)

13. Property (To be answered for each spouse whether single or joint petition is filed.)

(a) *Real Property.*—List all real property owned by either of you at date of filing of original petition herein. (Indicate in last column whether owned solely by husband or wife, or jointly.)

Description and location of property	Name of any co-owner other than spouse	Present market value (without deduction for mortgage or other security interest)	Amount of mortgage or other security interest on this property	Name of mortgagee or other secured creditor	Value claimed exempt, if any	Owned solely by husband or wife, or jointly

13. Property (continued)

(b) *Personal Property.*—List all other property owned by either of you at date of filing of original petition herein.

Description	Location of property if not at debtor's residence	Name of any co-owner other than spouse	Present market value (without deduction for mortgage or other security interest).	Amount of mortgage or other security interest on this property	Name of mortgagee or other secured creditor	Value claimed exempt, if any	Owned solely by husband or wife, or jointly
Autos (give year and make):							
Household goods:							
Personal effects:							
Other (specify):							

STATE OF　　　　　　　　　　　*County of*　　　　　　　　　　*ss:*

I,　　　　　　　　　　　　　　　　　　do hereby swear that I have read the answers contained in the foregoing statement, consisting of　　　　　sheets, and that they are true and complete to the best of my knowledge, information, and belief.

Subscribed and sworn to before me on

....
　　　　　　　　　　　　　　　　　　　　　　　　　　　Husband

....

....
　　　　　　　　　　　　official character

I,　　　　　　　　　　　　　　　　　　do hereby swear that I have read the answers contained in the foregoing statement, consisting of　　　　　sheets, and that they are true and complete to the best of my knowledge, information, and belief

Subscribed and sworn to before me on

....
　　　　　　　　　　　　　　　　　　　　　　　　　　　Wife

....

....
　　　　　　　　　　　　official character

Attorney for Debtor(s):

　　Name:

　　　　Address:

OF 13-5:　Chapter XIII Statement: page 6 　　　　　　　© 1973 BY JULIUS BLUMBERG, INC., 80 EXCHANGE PL., N.Y.C. 10004

In re

BANKRUPTCY NO.

Debtor, Soc. Sec. No.
[Include here all names used by bankrupt within last 6 years.]

CHAPTER XIII
PLAN

1. The future earnings of the debtor are submitted to the supervision and control of the court and the *debtor — debtor's employer* shall pay to the trustee the sum of **$**   *weekly — semi-monthly — monthly.*

2. From the payments so received, the trustee shall make disbursements as follows:

(*a*) The priority payments required by Rule 13-309(a).

(*b*) After the above payments, dividends to secured creditors whose claims are duly proved and allowed as follows:

(*c*) *Subsequent to — pro rata with* dividends to secured creditors, dividends to unsecured creditors whose claims are duly proved and allowed as follows:

3. The following executory contracts of the debtor are rejected:

4. Title to the debtor's property shall revest in the debtor *on confirmation of a plan — upon dismissal of the case after confirmation pursuant to Rule 13-215 — upon closing of the case pursuant to Bankruptcy Rule 514.*

Dated:

....
Debtor

Acceptances may be mailed to

....

....
Post Office Address

OF 13-6: Chapter XIII Plan   © 1973 BY JULIUS BLUMBERG, INC., 80 EXCHANGE PL., N.Y.C. 10004

Instructions: cross out inapplicable italicized words.

court, I watched about a dozen hearings on petitions under Chapter XIII. Roughly half the petitioners were represented by attorneys, the others represented themselves. The judge was among the most sympathetic human beings I've ever seen. In each case, he carefully reviewed the situation with the individual concerned. It was obvious that his only objective was to be helpful. If he found a particular plan impractical, he carefully explained the law to the parties and suggested that they amend the petition rather than attempt the impossible.

Basically, the hearing is simple. The judge questions you on your ability to make payments sufficient to clear up your debts within three years, a period which may be modified by the proposed new law. Questioning relates to your income as well as your day-to-day living expenses and, of course, is based on the figures in the schedule you filed with the court. If a surplus after payment of your daily expenses seems likely, and the judge believes it will be sufficient to satisfy all your debts in the allotted period, he'll appoint a trustee. You'll be directed to make periodic payments to the trustee, who— for 5 percent of the money he collects and pays out—will then see to it that the agreed-upon payments are made to each creditor. He's bonded to be sure that he does.

If, on the other hand, the judge decides that your plan is unrealistic, his last words may be, "I strongly recommend that you file for Ordinary Bankruptcy."

Step G: *Acceptance by your creditors*

In order to begin a successful Wage Earner Plan, at least 50 percent of your creditors (number *and* dollars—remember?) must agree. The court having sent each creditor notice of your filing and of the first meeting of creditors, it is now up to each to file a proof of claim and acceptance or rejection of the plan. (If they fail to file proof of claim, your debt to them is automatically erased.) At this stage, it's your job to contact those creditors you feel will be most receptive, and urge them to file acceptances. Once the required number have filed acceptance, the court will issue an order confirming the plan, after which the rest is up to you.

Step H: *Meeting the obligation*

Let's say you've agreed to pay $200 monthly to the trustee. If you meet the obligation until all your debts have been paid, the court will then issue an order called Discharge of Debtor. This is Chapter XIII's happy ending. If you don't live up to your pledges, the ending will be less than happy—Ordinary Bankruptcy.

The Bible provided relief for debtors by ordering that debts be forgiven every seventh year. Modern U.S. law, too, offers the opportunity for the financially troubled to be released from the obligation to pay their debts, but not more than once every six years. The mechanism, known as a Petition in Bankruptcy, in effect, acknowledges that "to err is human, to forgive divine, and to go bankrupt a common occurrence." All too common. In fiscal 1976, some 247,000 Americans, roughly the entire population of the State of Wyoming, took this way out of debt.

Bankruptcy doesn't mean one will necessarily end up a penniless resident of Skid Row. Many bankrupts emerge phoenixlike from the ashes, with enough resources to start life over again fairly comfortably. Some—like the Florida builder whose recent $800 million bankruptcy was among the largest in U.S. history—through canny manipulation come out with major businesses intact, cash on hand, and sufficient assets to begin rebuilding.

Today, more than a century after the last debtors' prison closed its doors, bankruptcy carries no criminal implications. You forfeit no civil rights; no government criminal agency is involved. Initially, bankruptcy feels like an impending death in the family. But financial surgery is performed instead, and when the operation is over, the patient not only lives, but feels as though an elephant has been removed from his back. He no longer needs to duck creditors, hide when the doorbell rings, change telephone numbers, or live in fear that tomorrow his salary will be garnisheed or his property attached.

Critics of the bankruptcy concept—and there are many—feel it borders on fraud for someone to avoid paying just debts. Some individuals, many college graduates defaulting on student loans, and some less than ethical businessmen have certainly abused the privilege, like the shady merchant who conferring with his accountants during preparations for his sixth bankruptcy, was irate when told that things were so bad this time that he'd be lucky to pay a nickel on the dollar. "I'll have no part of shenanigans of that sort," he declared indignantly. "I've always paid ten cents on the dollar in my bankruptcies, and, by gosh, I'll do it this time, too—even if I have to take it out of my own pocket!"

There are such people, to be sure, and I've encountered more than a few. But bankruptcy laws do relieve honest debtors unable to limp another dollar further. They save families from becoming destitute and a burden on the community. They allow a second chance to those who experience financial disaster. They give creditors a chance to recover at least some of their money.

Most bankruptcies are voluntarily brought by the insolvent debtor seeking relief. An occasional case is involuntary, brought by creditors anxious to get some return on delinquent obligations. Such an involuntary bankruptcy action may be brought by any single creditor owed $500 or more, if there are fewer than twelve creditors in all. If there are a dozen or more creditors, three people owed a total of $500 must sign the petition. But creditors can take matters in their own hands in this way only when the debtor owes $1,000 or more, and has committed "an act of bankruptcy" within four months prior to the day of filing.

Creditors may push the involuntary bankruptcy panic button when any one of these six causes for alarm occurs:

1. A fraudulent transfer of your property. (You put your car in your brother's name for no—or a ridiculously paltry—payment at a time when you know you are unable to pay your bills.)

2. A preferential transfer. (You pay your father-in-law what you borrowed from him in full, with the result that there is not enough to pay others their proportionate shares.)

3. A creditor obtains a judgment against you that you cannot satisfy.

4. You assign for the benefit of creditors.

5. A trustee is appointed to take over your property and pay your debts.

6. You admit in writing, perhaps in a letter to a creditor, that you are unable to pay your debts and that you consent to be declared a bankrupt.

In any case, you can feel the wall pressing against your back, and there's nothing for it but to file for bankruptcy.

STEP A: *Obtaining the necessary papers*

Uniform bankruptcy forms, designed to satisfy official guidelines, are available at any legal stationery store. You can purchase a bankruptcy kit from a do-it-yourself firm for up to $75, or buy a packet of blank forms for under $5 and follow the instructions outlined below. The forms are in sets, with enough copies to give you one for a worksheet, one to keep, and three to file with the court. They consist of the petition itself, assorted schedules of debts and assets, a general statement of affairs, and legal covers. The set may also include gummed labels or a master list for the court's use in notifying creditors.

STEP B: *Filling out the petition*

If the petition is voluntary, it must be filed with all the schedules and the statement of affairs. In exceptional cases—a large corporation like W.T. Grant with a small army of accountants and auditors hard at work in warehouses full of records—the court may permit the petition to be filed first and the volumes of data later. In an involuntary petition, the creditors file the initiating petition, but the debtor must submit schedules and the Statement of Affairs.

The first space to be completed is "the caption"—the spaces for name of court and other identifying information that appear at the top of the page. First, you must determine the court district in which you live; this is accomplished simply enough with a phone call to the clerk of the U.S. District Court. In small states, there may be only one district. In others, there may be many, generally broken down into southern, eastern, and other geographical areas.

This form is relatively simple and should be completed as outlined in the following sample.

Form No. 27

DISTRICT OF **(YOUR STATE)**

In re

YOUR NAME HERE

}

BANKRUPTCY NO.

Bankrupt

Include here all names used by bankrupt within last 6 years.

VOLUNTARY PETITION

1. Petitioner's post-office address is **(YOUR ADDRESS HERE)**

2. Petitioner has[1] **resided within this district for the preceding 6 months.**

3. Petitioner is qualified to file this petition and is entitled to the benefits of the Bankruptcy Act as a voluntary bankrupt.

Wherefore petitioner prays for relief as a voluntary bankrupt under the Act.

Signed: .... **(SIGN YOUR NAME HERE)**

☐ *Attorney for Petitioner*   ☐ *Petitioner*
(Petitioner signs if not represented by attorney.)

Address: **YOUR ADDRESS** ....

HERE ....

VERIFICATION

State of   County of   ss.:

INDIVIDUAL: I   the petitioner named in the foregoing petition, do hereby swear that the statements contained therein are true according to the best of my knowledge, information, and belief.

CORPORATION: I   the[2]
do hereby swear that the statements contained therein are true according to the best of my knowledge, information, and belief, and that the filing of this petition on behalf of the corporation has been authorized.

PARTNERSHIP: I **(YOUR NAME)**   *a member*
— *an authorized agent* — of the partnership named as petitioner in the foregoing petition, do hereby swear that the statements contained therein are true according to the best of my knowledge, information, and belief, and that the filing of this petition on behalf of the partnership has been authorized.

(SIGN YOUR NAME HERE)
....
Petitioner

Subscribed and sworn to before me on

(DATE)

(NOTARY PUBLIC SIGNS HERE)

NOTARY PUBLIC STAMP

OR SEAL)
....
Official Character

OF 1, 4 & 5: Petition for voluntary bankruptcy: verifications

[1] Insert appropriate allegations — resided [or has had his domicile or has had his principal place of business] within this district for the preceding 6 months [or for a longer portion of the preceding 6 months than in any other district].
[2] Insert president or other officer or an authorized agent of the corporation named as petitioner in the foregoing petition.

STEP C: *Filling out schedule A—statement of your debts*

This schedule is broken down into three subschedules: A-1 for creditors with priority, A-2 for secured creditors, and A-3 for unsecured creditors.

Now on to A-1. Priority claims—sometimes referred to as non-dischargeable debts—often include wages due your employees. (In an individual bankruptcy, this might be a maid, but when a small business or corporation goes under, its owner may be held responsible, even in an accompanying personal bankruptcy, for up to $600 owed each employee.) Any taxes that you owe also have priority. For the individual, this would include federal, state, and city income taxes (though none more than three years old), and property taxes on your home. Priority goes, too, to alimony and child support, and up to three months' rent due your landlord. If you were a stockholder and officer of a corporation, you could be held responsible for employees' withholding taxes which were not paid to the government.

Schedule A-2 requires you to list creditors who hold security. They might include the automobile company that sold you your car on installments, the bank that holds your home mortgage, and the stockbroker who advised you to buy stock on margin (which may be the cause of many of your problems), and savings bank passbook loans.

Schedule A-3 is for those unfortunate "Creditors Having Unsecured Claims Without Priority." All debts not set forth in A-1 and A-2 should fit here—among them, credit cards, unsecured bank loans, department store charges, and medical, dental, and legal (I've been hurt a time or two) bills.

Be sure to list every debt you owe, as well as debts of others that you may have guaranteed, such as the time in better days when you co-signed for your brother-in-law's new car.

Any debts you fail to list, you'll still be obligated to pay when this proceedings is over, so don't overlook any. An application to amend the schedule can be made later if you recall or discover a forgotten debt, but it involves more paperwork, appearances in court, and time that could be better devoted to your life after debt.

STEP D: *Listing all your property*

Schedule B, like A, is broken down into subsections. B-1 lists real property, B-2 personal property, B-3 other property, and B-4

UNITED STATES DISTRICT COURT FOR THE   DISTRICT OF

In re

BANKRUPTCY NO.

Bankrupt

Include here all names used by bankrupt within last 6 years.

Schedule A — STATEMENT OF ALL DEBTS OF BANKRUPT

Schedules A-1, A-2, and A-3 must include all the claims against the bankrupt or his property as of the date of the filing of the petition by or against him.

SCHEDULE A-1 — CREDITORS HAVING PRIORITY

Nature of Claim	Name of creditor and residence or place of business (if unknown, so state); zip codes recommended	Specify when claim was incurred and the consideration therefor; when claim is contingent, unliquidated, disputed, or subject to setoff, evidenced by a judgment, negotiable instrument, or other writing, or incurred as partner or joint contractor, so indicate; specify name of any partner or joint contractor on any debt	Amount of Claim	
(a) Wages and commissions owing to workmen, servants, clerks, or traveling or city salesmen on salary or commission basis, whole or part time, whether or not selling exclusively for the bankrupt, not exceeding $600 to each, earned within 3 months before filing of petition.	(List name and address of anyone to whom you owe wages) if none say so		$ NONE	
(b) Taxes owing (itemize by type of tax and taxing authority:) (1) To the United States (2) To any State (3) To any other taxing authority	Internal Revenue Service Federal Income Tax (List state and city taxes owed if any)		800	00
(c) (1) Debts owing to any person, including the United States entitled to priority by laws of United States (itemized by type) (2) Rent owing to a landlord who is entitled to priority by the laws of any State accrued within three months before filing the petition, for actual use and occupancy.	(This will include trust funds or union deductions) (Name your landlord here, if you owe any back rent)			
		Total		

OF 6: Schedule A-1

© 1973 BY JULIUS BLUMBERG, INC., 80 EXCHANGE PL., N.Y.C. 10004

312

Schedule A-2 — Creditors Holding Security

Name of creditor and residence or place of business (if unknown, so state); zip codes recommended	Description of security and date when obtained by creditor	Specify when claim was incurred and the consideration therefor; when claim is contingent, unliquidated, disputed, subject to setoff, evidenced by a judgment, negotiable instrument, or other writing, or incurred as partner or joint contractor, so indicate; specify name of any partner or joint contractor on any debt	Market value		Amount of claim without deduction of value of security	
			$		$	
Bank of St. Louis 2000 First Street St. Louis, Mo.	July 1976 1976 Chevrolet	Purchased new Auto Financed through Bank	3,000	00	2,800	00
(LIST ALL CREDITORS THAT HOLD SECURITY OF ANY KIND)						
		Total				

Schedule A-3 — Creditors Having Unsecured Claims Without Priority

Name of creditor (including last known holder of any negotiable instrument) and residence or place of business (if unknown, so state); zip codes recommended	Specify when claim was incurred and the consideration therefor; when claim is contingent, unliquidated, disputed, subject to setoff, evidenced by a judgment, negotiable instrument, or other writing, or incurred as partner or joint contractor, so indicate; specify name of any partner or joint contractor on any debt	Amount of claim	
		$	
A & B Dept. Store (address)	Merchandise purchased-August 1977	264	00
Dr. Phil Uptight (address)	Medical treatment-July to Sept. 1977	125	00
(List name and address of all creditors who are not secured or preferred, briefly describing the nature of the debt and when incurred)			
	Total		

OF 6: Schedule A-2 & A-3

© 1973 BY JULIUS BLUMBERG, INC., 80 EXCHANGE PL., N.Y.C. 10004 property claimed as exempt. In legalese, "It is important to note at this juncture that making a false statement about one's assets or property, or trying to conceal either could be grounds for the court's denying your discharge in bankruptcy." This could lead to somewhat rougher treatment, indictment and criminal prosecution.

Schedule B-1 covers real property, and you must list your house and any lots or homes you own anywhere in the world from a ski lodge at Vail to a retirement lot in Acapulco. It must be listed whether in your individual name, joint ownership with someone else, or even something in which you have a future interest (like property left in trust for your mother during her life, then, upon her death, goes to you). You must list the property's value as well. An official appraisal is unnecessary—your estimate of current market value is sufficient. Note the full value before deducting any mortgages.

Schedules B-2 and B-3 list all your personal and other property. The official form is self-explanatory. The only property that should

314

not be listed here is that which is legally exempt. To make things simpler, let's discuss Schedule B-4.

Schedule B-4 lists property that you may properly claim as untouchable. Exempt property is determined by state law rather than by the Federal Bankruptcy Act, with each state decreeing which assets a debtor is allowed to keep, generally the same ones protected from seizure after a judgment is entered against you.

Many of the laws are very old, and they sound it. In Texas, a man may keep his horse. In Ohio, "the cabin of a miner" is exempt; in Mississippi, "two head of cows and calfs, 10 head of hogs, 20 sheep and goats and all colts under three years raised in the state"; in New York, "all stoves kept for use in the debtor's dwelling house and necessary fuel therefore for sixty days; one sewing machine; the family Bible, family pictures . . . a seat or pew occupied by the debtor or the family in a place of public worship . . . all necessary food for the debtor or his family for sixty days."

Common exemptions in most states include wearing apparel, household furniture, appliances, radios, cooking utensils, wedding rings, one watch, a person's tools of the trade (an actress' mink stole might conceivably qualify), professional instruments, and, sometimes, some equity in a primary home ($20,000 in generous California). In some states, property held in trust for a debtor—where the trust has been created by another person—may also be exempt. Others allow a bankrupt to keep some cash ($2,500 in California) and some credit union or savings and loan association shares. But exempt goods not fully paid for may be repossessed by the creditor, and ordinarily exempt items used to secure loans may, in some instances, become nonexempt.

Before filing for bankruptcy, it's reasonable to focus special attention on property that can be either exempt or nonexempt depending on what you do with it. This includes:

Your Home. To safeguard your home from becoming fair game for creditors, it may be necessary in your state to file a homestead declaration with the county clerk or county recording office before filing for bankruptcy. You can only homestead one home, your legal residence. Most states place a limit on the value and area of homesteadable land and this varies considerably.

When a home is jointly owned, but only one spouse files for bankruptcy, that partner's share in the house may be sold to the highest bidder by the bankruptcy trustee, with the cash proceeds

315

going into the pot for creditors. In practice, at a meeting of creditors, the trustee usually permits the other spouse to buy the bankrupt's share for a nominal amount, often as little as several hundred dollars. This is more than a benign humanitarian conspiracy. Because of the joint ownership, the half that's up for grabs is of little or no value to anyone who buys it, until the share-holding spouse dies. Even then the speculative purchaser might well find himself part-owner with three young children who inherited their mother's share.

I remember one recent case, though, where an incensed creditor—tired of seeing debtors "get away" with this little transfer while creditors ended up with virtually nothing—bid against the wife for the bankrupt husband's share of a very expensive home. He spiritedly escalated the bidding, then let her have it. She had to raise $20,000—which went into the creditors' kitty—in order to buy her husband's share of their home.

Often, of course, the bankruptcy, too, is joint, perhaps because the wife was involved directly in her husband's business, but more often because she obediently co-signed his business loans or other obligations. Wives become involved in a bankruptcy simply by signing credit cards on which the family owes money. Even if the accounts are in her husband's name, she becomes liable merely by signing hers for gasoline, a restaurant dinner, or shoes for the kids. In such cases—where both husband and wife declare bankruptcy—the home, excepting its homestead value, is a seizable asset.

Your Life Insurance. In many states, life insurance is exempt property, so long as the bankrupt does not unwisely list his estate as beneficiary. I've observed that one of the first security measures a businessman in financial difficulties takes is to make certain his wife or children are listed as his life insurance beneficiaries. The second is to arrange a transfer of ownership of all policies to his spouse, something an insurance broker can very simply arrange.

Your Federal Benefits. Federal law exempts federal pensions, GI bonuses, and certain federal retirement plans (including Social Security) from bankruptcy seizure. Exempted, too, are properties purchased with these resources, if you can prove they were actually purchased with exempt funds. But once money from such federal sources is banked, it immediately becomes nonexempt.

Incidentally, in one instance, California courts surprisingly allowed the conversion of nonexempt funds into exempt ones, only three weeks before a man filed for bankruptcy. The debtor took out a loan from a finance company on vehicles previously owned free and clear, then put most of the proceeds into credit union shares, exempt under state law. Creditors objected, but the State Court of Appeals allowed his action to stand. Clearly, differences between states on what is and is not exempt are broad enough, so that prudence dictates that you check with your local bankruptcy court clerk or legal aid society chapter for information about exemptions specific to your needs and state.

Schedule B-4 — Property Claimed as Exempt

Type of property	Location, description, and so far as relevant to the claim of exemption, present use of property	Reference to statute creating the exemption	Value claimed exempt
LIST ALL PROPERTY THAT IS EXEMPT UNDER THE LAWS OF YOUR STATE SUCH AS WEARING APPAREL, FURNITURE, TOOLS, ETC.			$
		Total	

Now back to B-2 and B-3. Fill in all other property, following the pattern shown in the sample forms that follow.

Schedule B-2 — Personal Property

Type of Property	Description and location	Market value of bankrupt's interest without deduction for secured claims listed on schedule A-2 or exemptions claimed in schedule B-4	
a. Cash on hand		$ 50	00
b. Deposits of money with banking institutions, savings and loan associations, credit unions, public utility companies, landlords, and others	NONE	NONE	
c. Household goods, supplies, and furnishings	MISCELLANEOUS	250	00
d. Books, pictures, and other art objects; stamp, coin, and other collections	NONE	NONE	
e. Wearing apparel, jewelry, firearms, sports equipment, and other personal possessions	MISCELLANEOUS	200	00
f. Automobiles, trucks, trailers, and other vehicles	1976 Chevrolet	3,000	00
g. Boats, motors, and their accessories	NONE	NONE	
	Total	3,500	00

Type of property	Description and location	Market value of bankrupt's interest without deduction for secured claims listed on schedule A-2 or exemptions claimed in schedule B-4	
h. Livestock, poultry, and other animals	IF YOU OWN ANY OF THE ITEMS SET FORTH ON THIS SCHEDULE, SET FORTH A DESCRIPTION, ITS LOCATION, AND VALUE.	$	
i. Farming supplies and implements			
j. Office equipment, furnishings, and supplies			
k. Machinery, fixtures, equipment, and supplies (other than those listed in items j and l) used in business			
l. Inventory			
m. Tangible personal property of any other description			
n. Patents, copyrights, franchises, and other general intangibles (specify all documents and writings relating thereto)			
o. Government and corporate bonds and other negotiable and nonnegotiable instruments			
p. Other liquidated debts owing bankrupt or debtor			
q. Contingent and unliquidated claims of every nature, including counterclaims of the bankrupt or debtor (give estimated value of each)			
r. Interests in insurance policies (itemize surrender or refund values of each)			
s. Annuities			
t. Stocks and interests in incorporated and unincorporated companies (itemize separately)			
u. Interests in partnerships			
v. Equitable and future interests, life estates, and rights or powers exercisable for the benefit of the bankrupt or debtor (specify all written instruments relating thereto)			
	Total		

OF 6: Schedule B-2 (Continued)

Schedule B-3 — Property Not Otherwise Scheduled

Type of property	Description and location	Market value of bankrupt's interest without deduction for secured claims listed in schedule A-2 or exemptions claimed in schedule B-4
a. Property transferred under assignment for benefit of creditors, within 4 months prior to filing of petition (specify date of assignment, name and address of assignee, amount realized therefrom by the assignee, and disposition of proceeds so far as known to bankrupt)	THIS ONLY APPLIES IF YOU MADE AN ASSIGNMENT FOR THE BENEFIT OF CREDITORS WITHIN FOUR MONTHS OF FILING THE PETITION IN BANKRUPTCY.	$
b. Property of any kind not otherwise scheduled	LIST ANY OTHER PROPERTY HERE.	
	Total	

STEP E: *Filling out the summary of debts and property*

Take the total from each prior schedule and sub-schedule and transfer that information to the appropriate slot on this summary, as shown below. Add it up. Now, among other things, you know how much you went bankrupt for.

319

SUMMARY OF DEBTS AND PROPERTY
(From the statements of the bankrupt in Schedule A and B)

Schedule	Debts and property	Total
	DEBTS	
A—1/a	Wages having priority	
A—1/b(1)	Taxes owing United States	
A—1/b(2)	Taxes owing States	
A—1/b(3)	Taxes owing other taxing authorities	
A—1/c(1)	Debts having priority by laws of the United States	
A—1/c(2)	Rent having priority under State law	
A—2	Secured claims	
A—3	Unsecured claims without priority	
	Schedule A total	
	PROPERTY	
B—1	Real property (total value)	
B—2/a	Cash on hand	
B—2/b	Deposits	
B—2/c	Household goods	
B—2/d	Books, pictures, and collections	
B—2/e	Wearing apparel and personal possessions	
B—2/f	Automobiles and other vehicles	
B—2/g	Boats, motors, and accessories	
B—2/h	Livestock and other animals	
B—2/i	Farming supplies and implements	
B—2/j	Office equipment and supplies	
B—2/k	Machinery, equipment, and supplies used in business	
B—2/l	Inventory	
B—2/m	Other tangible personal property	
B—2/n	Patents and other general intangibles	
B—2/o	Bonds and other instruments	
B—2/p	Other liquidated debts	
B—2/q	Contingent and unliquidated claims	
B—2/r	Interests in insurance policies	
B—2/s	Annuities	
B—2/t	Interests in corporations and unincorporated companies	
B—2/u	Interests in partnerships	
B—2/v	Equitable and future interests, rights, and powers in personality	
B–3/a	Property assigned for benefit of creditors	
B–3/b	Property not otherwise scheduled	
B—4	Property claimed as exempt $	XXXXXXXXXX
	Schedule B total	

OATHS TO SCHEDULES A AND B

State of   County of   ss.:

Individual: I   do hereby swear that I have read the foregoing schedules, consisting of   sheets, and that they are a statement of all my debts and all my property in accordance with the Bankruptcy Act, to the best of my knowledge, information, and belief.

Corporation: I   the [insert president or other officer or an authorized agent] of the corporation as bankrupt in this proceeding, do hereby swear that I have read the foregoing schedules, consisting of   sheets, and that they are a statement of all the debts and all the property of the corporation in accordance with the Bankruptcy Act, to the best of my knowledge, information, and belief.

Partnership: I   a [insert member or an authorized agent] of the partnership named as bankrupt in this proceeding, do hereby swear that I have read the foregoing schedules, consisting of   sheets, and that they are a statement of all the debts and all the property of the partnership in accordance with the Bankruptcy Act, to the best of my knowledge, information, and belief.

Signed: ....

Subscribed and sworn to before me on

....

....
official character

* In the opinion of the bankrupt-debtor the net value of the non-exempt assets will not exceed $150.00.

OF 6: Summary of debts & property: oaths
© 1973 BY JULIUS BLUMBERG, INC., 80 EXCHANGE PL., N.Y.C. 10004

....
(To be signed if applicable)

* Massachusetts District requires this statement, if applicable. Other Districts may require this or similar statements.

320

STEP F: *Filling in the statement of affairs*

The forms you get from the stationery store may have two Statement of Affairs forms: one for someone engaged in business, the other for someone not so engaged. Choose the one that fits. The questions are direct and simple, and should be answered briefly and to the point. Question 4—on bank accounts and safe deposit boxes—requires you to search your memory and records for two years, and to be sure you list every one in your name or jointly held with another person. A reminder: Failure to list everything could create problems, and it is best to be completely honest. If the maxim learned at your mother's knee—or across your father's lap—wasn't enough, remember that bank and credit company computer networks know every move you've ever made on credit, right down to how much you tipped the waitress last time you took your girlfriend out to dinner.

Item 5 relates to failure to keep books and records. The court ordinarily doesn't expect salaried employees to keep detailed records of expenses and expenditures, but those earning high salaries, self-employed, or in business for themselves are expected to keep records. If a bankrupt won't or can't make records available—or they are suddenly lost, burned, stolen, "accidentally fed into a shredder," or disappear—a petition of bankruptcy may be denied.

Prior bankruptcies are the subject of Item 7. For the benefit of both debtor and creditor, individual bankruptcy can be declared only once every six years. With that over, the debtor is, in a financial sense, reborn. He has, however, a dual image. Some conservative lenders may still see him as a "deadbeat," but if he has a decent income source, others will see him as a prime candidate for more credit, since, after all, he can't default through bankruptcy for another half-dozen years. Ex-bankrupts are often stunned to find themselves solicited by department stores who, having written off old debts, cordially invite them to open new charge accounts. Credit card companies offer the same privileges that got the debtor in scalding water earlier on. It seems ironic. It's just business. A department store credit manager figures he can sell you enough in six years to make up what he lost.

Item 10 relates to "suits, executions, and attachments." When I handle a personal bankruptcy, I rarely find enough room in the space allotted for this one, and have to attach a separate schedule. Usually, by the time someone files a petition, there are more lawsuits against him than chips in a Toll House cookie.

321

In re

BANKRUPTCY NO.

Bankrupt

STATEMENT OF AFFAIRS
FOR BANKRUPT
NOT ENGAGED IN BUSINESS

Include here all names used by bankrupt within last 6 years.

Each question should be answered or the failure to answer explained. If the answer is "none," this should be stated. If additional space is needed for the answer to any question, a separate sheet, properly identified, and made a part hereof, should be used and attached.

The term "original petition," as used in the following questions, shall mean the petition filed under Bankruptcy Rule 103, 104 or 106.

1. Name and residence.

a. What is your full name and social security number?

b. Have you used, or been known by, any other names within the 6 years immediately preceding the filing of the original petition herein?
(If so, give particulars.)

c. Where do you now reside?

d. Where else have you resided during the 6 years immediately preceding the filing of the original petition herein?

2. Occupation and income.

a. What is your occupation?

b. Where are you now employed?
(Give the name and address of your employer, or the address at which you carry on your trade or profession, and the length of time you have been so employed.)

c. Have you been in a partnership with anyone, or engaged in any business during the 6 years immediately preceding the filing of the original petition herein?
(If so, give particulars, including names, dates, and places.)

d. What amount of income have you received from your trade or profession during each of the 2 calendar years immediately preceding the filing of the original petition herein?

e. What amount of income have you received from other sources during each of these 2 years?
(Give particulars, including each source, and the amount received therefrom.)

3. Tax returns and refunds.

a. Where did you file your last federal and state income tax returns for the 2 years immediately preceding the filing of the original petition herein?

b. What tax refunds (income and other) have you received during the year immediately preceding the filing of the original petition herein?

c. To what tax refunds (income or other), if any, are you, or may you be, entitled?
(Give particulars, including information as to any refund payable jointly to you and your spouse or any other person.)

4. Bank accounts and safe deposit boxes.

a. What bank accounts have you maintained alone or together with any other person, and in your own or any other name within the 2 years immediately preceding the filing of the original petition herein?
(Give the name and address of each bank, the name in which the deposit was maintained, and the name and address of every other person authorized to make withdrawals from such account.)

b. What safe deposit box or boxes or other depository or depositories have you kept or used for your securities, cash, or other valuables within the 2 years immediately preceding the filing of the original petition herein?
(Give the name and address of the bank or other depository, the name in which each box or other depository was kept, the name and address of every other person who had the right of access thereto, a brief description of the contents thereof, and, if the box has been surrendered, state when surrendered, or, if transferred, when transferred, and the name and address of the transferee.)

5. Books and records.

a. Have you kept books of account or records relating to your affairs within the 2 years immediately preceding the filing of the original petition herein?

b. In whose possession are these books or records?
(Give names and addresses.)

c. If any of these books or records are not available, explain.

d. Have any books of account or records relating to your affairs been destroyed, lost or otherwise disposed of within the 2 years immediately preceding the filing of the original petition herein?
(If so, give particulars, including date of destruction, loss, or disposition, and reason therefor.)

6. Property held for another person.

What property do you hold for any other person?
(Give name and address of each person, and describe the property, or value thereof, and all writings relating thereto.)

7. Prior bankruptcy.

What proceedings under the Bankruptcy Act have previously been brought by or against you?
(State the location of the bankruptcy court, the nature and number of each proceeding, the date when it was filed, and whether a discharge was granted or refused, the proceeding was dismissed, or a composition, arrangement, or plan was confirmed.)

322

8. Receiverships, general assignments, and other modes of liquidation.

a. Was any of your property, at the time of the filing of the original petition herein, in the hands of a receiver, trustee, or other liquidating agent?
(If so, give a brief description of the property, the name and address of the receiver, trustee, or other agent, and, if the agent was appointed in a court proceeding, the name and location of the court and the nature of the proceeding.)

b. Have you made any assignment of your property for the benefit of your creditors, or any general settlement with your creditors, within one year immediately preceding the filing of the original petition herein?
(If so, give dates, the name and address of the assignee, and a brief statement of the terms of assignment or settlement.)

9. Property in hands of third person.

Is any other person holding anything of value in which you have an interest?
(Give name and address, location and description of the property, and circumstances of the holding.)

10. Suits, executions, and attachments.

a. Were you a party to any suit pending at the time of the filing of the original petition herein?
(If so, give the name and location of the court and the title and nature of the proceeding.)

b. Were you a party to any suit terminated within the year immediately preceding the filing of the original petition herein?
(If so, give the name and location of the court, the title and nature of the proceeding, and the result.)

c. Has any of your property been attached, garnished, or seized under any legal or equitable process within the 4 months immediately preceding the filing of the original petition herein?
(If so, describe the property seized or person garnished, and at whose suit.)

11. Loans repaid.

What repayments on loans in whole or in part have you made during the year immediately preceding the filing of the original petition herein?
(Give the name and address of the lender, the amount of the loan and when received, the amounts and dates of payments and, if the lender is a relative, the relationship.)

12. Transfers of property.

a. Have you made any gifts, other than ordinary and usual presents to family members and charitable donations, during the year immediately preceding the filing of the original petition herein?
(If so, give names and addresses of donees and dates, description, and value of gifts.)

b. Have you made any other transfer, absolute or for the purpose of security, or any other disposition, of real or tangible personal property during the year immediately and preceding the filing of the original petition herein?
(Give a description of the property, the date of the transfer or disposition, to whom transferred or how disposed of, and, if the transferee is a relative, the relationship, the consideration, if any, received therefor, and the disposition of such consideration.)

13. Repossessions and returns.

Has any property been returned to, or repossessed by, the seller or by a secured party during the year immediately preceding the filing of the original petition herein?
(If so, give particulars including the name and address of the party getting the property and its description and value.)

14. Losses.

a. Have you suffered any losses from fire, theft, or gambling during the year immediately preceding or since the filing of the original petition herein?
(If so, give particulars, including dates, names, and places, and the amounts of money or value and general description of property lost.)

b. Was the loss covered in whole or part by insurance?
(If so, give particulars.)

15. Payments or transfers to attorneys.

a. Have you consulted an attorney during the year immediately preceding or since the filing of the original petition herein?
(Give date, name, and address.)

b. Have you during the year immediately preceding or since the filing of the original petition herein paid any money or transferred any property to the attorney or to any other person on his behalf?
(If so, give particulars, including amount paid or value of property transferred and date of payment or transfer.)

c. Have you, either during the year immediately preceding or since the filing of the original petition herein, agreed to pay any money or transfer any property to an attorney at law, or to any other person on his behalf?
(If so, give particulars, including amount and terms of obligation.)

State of _____ County of _____ ss.:

I, _____ do hereby swear that I have read the answers contained in the foregoing statement of affairs and that they are true and complete to the best of my knowledge, information, and belief.

Subscribed and sworn to before me on _____

_____
Bankrupt

_____
Official character

323

Items 11 and 12 relate to repaid loans and transfer of property. Loans repaid within the four months prior to filing a petition may be considered "preferential"—that is, paid to a favored creditor or even falsely to a friend or relative—and the trustee may properly attempt to recover that money and distribute it proportionately among all creditors. Similarly, property transferred within one year prior to filing may be traced and reclaimed for the common good. If such a property transfer must be made—if the money from its sale is needed for living expenses, for example—then it must be transferred for fair compensation (at going market value), with evidence like a canceled check available to prove the transfer was legitimate.

Property should not be given away within a full year before bankruptcy, unless you can prove that you were solvent at the time of the gift. Any transfer made within a year's time (and none may be made under any circumstances within four months time) in payment of a past debt must be substantiated by proof of the debt, as well as evidence that the value of the debt equaled the value of the property. Anything less discreet would be as suspect as the conduct of the customer in a bar that was being held up who, as the gunman approached his table, hurriedly handed his companion a crisp bill and said, "By the way, Charlie, here's the $20 I owe you."

STEP G: *Signing the papers*

As your own attorney, you'll be required to sign the petition schedules and statement of affairs. The first signature goes on the petition page in the place provided for "signature of attorney for petitioner," or the petitioner if acting *pro se*. That's the only autograph that doesn't have to be notarized; all other signatures must be filled in before a notary public.

On the bottom of the petition, sign the verification: a sworn statement attesting to a document's truth. Then, sign the oath to Schedules A and B, at the bottom of the summary sheet. Your final signature appears at the bottom of the statement of affairs. In certain jurisdictions, you may also have to sign a statement saying the net value of your nonexempt assets does not exceed $150—if that is a fact. This guides the court in whether or not to appoint a trustee. For such small sums, it isn't worth the trouble.

STEP H: *Wrap it up and deliver it*

You'll find a colored page in the package of forms. It's called, in the profession you've "joined," a legal back. This sheet requires the same identifying information as that on the caption. There's a space, too, for the attorney's name. Type in yours (and beneath it "in person" or "*pro se*"), as well as your address, and—if the phone company hasn't already cut it off (as is, alas, sometimes the case by this time)—your phone number. This legal back becomes the cover and will either have a line to follow or may be scored for a ¾-inch fold, under which firmly staple all your papers in place.

You're now ready to file the original and two copies (similarly "backed") of your completed petition, including, of course, the schedules and statement of affairs. If you have the $50 filing fee, you can bring these papers to the clerk of the bankruptcy part of your Federal District Court. But not every bankrupt has the filing fee, and the court has thoughtfully provided for that embarrassing eventuality. Official Form #2—Application to pay filing fees in installments—neatly solves that problem. It will expedite matters if

Form No. 28

FORM OF APPLICATION AND ORDER FOR
PAYMENT OF FILING FEES IN INSTALLMENTS:

Application To Pay Filing Fees in Installments

1. Applicant is filing herewith a voluntary petition in bankruptcy.

2. He is unable to pay the filing fees except in installments.

3. He proposes to pay such fees to the clerk of the district court upon the following terms: ———

4. He has paid no money and transferred no property to his attorney for services in connection with this case or any pending case under the Act, and he will make no payment or transfer to his attorney for such services until the filing fees are paid in full.

Wherefore applicant prays that he be permitted to pay the filing fees in installments.

Dated: ———

Signed: ———,
Applicant.
Address: ———

———

This is an official form and should be observed and used with such alterations as may be appropriate to suit the circumstances.

The application should be filed in duplicate, one copy for the clerk and one for the bankruptcy judge.

Order for Payment of Filing Fees
in Installments

The application of the bankrupt for permission to pay the filing fees in this case in installments having been heard;

It is ordered that the bankrupt pay the filing fees still owing, namely, $————, as follows: ————.

It is further ordered that all payments be made at the office of the clerk of the United States District Court located at ————, and that until the filing fees are paid in full, the bankrupt shall pay no money and shall transfer no property to his attorney, and his attorney shall accept no money or property from the bankrupt for services in connection with this case.

Dated: ————.

————,

Bankruptcy Judge

This is an official form and should be observed and used with such alterations as may be appropriate to suit the circumstances.

you file an "Order for payment of filing fees in installments" for the judge's signature at the same time.

Unless there's only one judge in your district, only the good Lord knows who will hear your case, since each is randomly assigned. In busy urban and suburban districts in which I've practiced, a kind of lottery system is used. A different judge's name is written at random on each page of a pad, which is then inverted and a new sheet ripped off for each case. Justice isn't blind. But for a moment she discreetly covers her eyes.

STEP I: THE FIRST MEETING OF CREDITORS

One is all you'll have to suffer through if there are no special problems. Within 30 days of your filing, the judge will notify all your creditors of the date, time, and place (usually his courtroom) of their first meeting. As the petitioner, you are required to be there—squadrons of butterflies in your stomach, knots in your throat, and all—to answer questions about your financial status under oath. If you took our earlier advice, you'll already have observed a few of these sessions on prior court days, and the procedure should be familiar and somewhat less stressful.

Creditors aren't required to appear, and if they're convinced your assets are all but nonexistent, they usually don't. If one creditor appears, it's often because he's skeptical, or even openly suspicious, of some aspect of your bankruptcy. Creditors will be asked by the judge to vote on a trustee, a selection in which obviously the bankrupt has no voice. If they don't select one, the judge usually appoints a trustee, who might well be the attorney for the lone creditor who appears. That's not surprising, since the trustee is charged not only with administering the bankrupt's estate and liquidating his assets, but also with ferreting out irregularities. He'll then distribute the proceeds fairly and proportionately among creditors, after, of course, taking the 5 percent commission he's earned off the top.

If more than nickels and dimes are at stake, be prepared for questions. There could be many of them—from creditors, their attorneys, the trustee, or the judge. Often the interrogation is bare minimum, and it might go something like this:

JUDGE:	Are you the petitioner here?
YOU:	Yes, your Honor.
JUDGE:	Did you prepare these papers yourself?
YOU:	Yes, your Honor.
JUDGE:	Is everything in your petition true?
YOU:	Yes, your Honor.
JUDGE:	Are you sure you've listed all your assets and all your debts?
YOU:	Yes, your Honor.
JUDGE:	What did you do with the money that you borrowed from Generous National Bank three months ago?
YOU:	I used it to pay rent and just to keep the family going, your Honor.
JUDGE:	Are there any creditors in the courtroom who want to question this bankrupt? (PAUSE) Since there are none, and it appears that this bankrupt has no assets, I'll waive the apppointment of a trustee. Make sure you pay the installments on your $50 filing fee as they come due. Step down!
YOU:	Thank you, your Honor.

If no creditors file objections to your discharge (and in this case, it seems unlikely that they will), it may be granted on the spot. In a recent "no asset" case that I handled, we filed the Petition on January 27, a notice of the First Meeting of Creditors was mailed scheduled for February 19. The notice set that same date as the last day for filing objections, either to the entire proceeding or the dischargeability of (release from) a particular debt. On February 19, after a five-minute hearing, the judge issued his order discharging the bankrupt.

If you think penicillin is a miracle drug, you should see the effect those final words of the judge have on someone who has been the resident of his own private hell from many months to several years—juggling debts like Circus Boy, mollifying suppliers, making excuses ("the check is in the mail") to creditors, trying to make a quarter do the work of a dollar.

"You pop tranquilizers like Chiclets," one client told me. "You think about suicide—and reject it. You fight with your wife and scream at your kids—and hate yourself in the morning. You've got the libido of a pickled herring. The experience leaves you scarred inside and outside. When you're worn to a frazzle, and you know it's no use any more, and you finally surrender and file your petition, all you want to do while you're waiting the thirty days until the creditors' meeting is sleep. Well, that's the way I felt. But the minute the mess was all settled, I got up full of energy and enthusiasm, and started to rebuild."

THE OTHER SIDE OF THE COIN: WHEN YOU'RE THE CREDITOR

Time passes. You've been on a lucky streak. You've rebuilt your fortune. Now you're the creditor, and in the mail one day comes the depressing news from a bankruptcy judge that someone who owes you money has filed a petition. You're sympathetic—but you want to get your share. If you think there are grounds for objecting to the bankruptcy (the debtor is hiding assets, has fraudulently transferred assets, etc.), it makes sense to see a lawyer. Acting on your hunch without seasoned guidance may get very complicated indeed. If you're not going to object, but there are assets (the notice will tell you if there are none), file a Proof of Claim immediately. Legally, of course, you have six months, unless the claim period has been shortened by the judge in his notice to you, as is often the case in "no asset" situations.

Proof of Claim forms can be obtained from that local legal stationer you've been keeping so busy. There are forms for individuals, partnerships and corporations, and the model below can be used for all three by crossing out what doesn't apply.

328

Form No. 29

T 262— Proof of Claim: Bankruptcy: Official Form 15: Power of Attorney:
Individual, Partnership or Corporation:

TYPE OR PRINT ALL NECESSARY PARTS. INCOMPLETE OR ILLEGIBLE CLAIMS MAY RESULT IN DISALLOWANCE.

(left margin, vertical:) 18, U.S.C., Sec. 152. PENALTY FOR PRESENTING FRAUDULENT CLAIMS.—Fine of not more than $5,000 or imprisonment for not more than five years or both—Title

UNITED STATES DISTRICT COURT FOR THE   DISTRICT OF

In re   )   BANKRUPTCY NO.

Include here all names used by bankrupt within last 6 years.   Bankrupt   )   PROOF OF CLAIM

1. **If claimant is an individual claiming for himself** The undersigned, who is the claimant herein, resides at *

If claimant is a partnership claiming through a member The undersigned who resides at *

is a member of   a partnership, composed of the undersigned and †

and doing business at *
and is authorized to make this proof of claim on behalf of the partnership.

If claimant is a corporation claiming through an authorized officer The undersigned, who resides at *

is the   of   , a corporation organized under the laws of
and doing business at *
and is authorized to make this proof of claim on behalf of the corporation.

If claim is made by agent The undersgined, who resides at *
is the agent of
of *   and is authorized to make this proof of claim on behalf of the claimant.

2. The bankrupt was, at the time of the filing of the petition initiating this case, and still is indebted [or liable] to the claimant, in the sum of $

3. The consideration for this debt [or ground of liability] is as follows:

4. [If the claim is founded on writing] The writing on which this claim is founded (or a duplicate thereof) is attached hereto [or cannot be attached for the reason set forth in the statement attached hereto].

5. [If appropriate] This claim is founded on an open account, which became [or will become] due on

as shown by the itemized statement attached hereto. Unless it is attached hereto or its absence is explained in an attached statement, no note or other negotiable instrument has been received for the account or any part of it.

6. No judgment has been rendered on the claim except

7. The amount of all payments on this claim has been credited and deducted for the purpose of making this proof of claim.

8. This claim is not subject to any setoff or counter-claim except

9. No security interest is held for this claim except

[If security interest in property of the debtor is claimed] The undersigned claims the security interest under the writing referred to in paragraph 4 hereof [or under a separate writing which (or a duplicate of which) is attached hereto, or under a separate writing which cannot be attached hereto for the reason set forth in the statement attached hereto]. Evidence of perfection of such security interest is also attached hereto.

10. This claim is a general unsecured claim, except to the extent that the security interest, if any, described in paragraph 9 is sufficient to satisfy the claim. [If priority is claimed, state the amount and basis thereof.]

Dated: Signed: ....   TYPE OR PRINT NAME SIGNED ....

To
of *

POWER OF ATTORNEY

The undersigned claimant hereby authorizes you, or any one of you, as attorney in fact for the undersigned and with full power of substitution, to vote on any question that may be lawfully submitted to creditors of the bankrupt in the above-entitled case; [if appropriate] to vote for a trustee of the estate of the bankrupt and for a committee of creditors; to receive dividends; and in general to perform any act not constituting the practice of law for the undersigned in all matters arising in this case.

Dated: Signed: ....

[If appropriate] By .... As ....

Address: ....

STATE OF   COUNTY OF   ss.:   **ACKNOWLEDGMENT**

INDIVIDUAL-PARTNERSHIP-CORPORATION: Acknowledged before me on

PARTNERSHIP: by   who says that he is a member of the partnership named above and is authorized to execute this power of attorney in its behalf.

CORPORATION: by   who says that he is the   of the corporation named above and is authorized to execute this power of attorney in its behalf.

....

* State post-office address.
† Name and post-office address of each partner.

     official character

Sign the form before a notary and have your signature notarized. You can bring it to the bankruptcy court yourself. If you mail it in, enclose a self-addressed return postcard, and ask that it be used to acknowledge receipt, neatly providing you with proof that you've filed. If you're not a major creditor, there's nothing more to do. Just stand back and hope for better than a dime on the dollar.

Bankruptcy can be a shattering experience. If you're lucky, only a sobering one. For sure, it changes the financial lifestyles of a lot of people. So many times I've seen a bankrupt couple embrace after leaving the courtroom, and say, "From now on it's cash all the way. If we can't afford it, we don't buy it!"

Sometimes they forget quickly. Six months later, they're back in the old fly-now-cry-later groove. But if they're smart, they change. They may never go quite so far as President Calvin Coolidge, whose frugality was legendary, but they could do worse than emulate his thrift.

Asked by a visitor "for a cigar from the box on your desk, as a souvenir for a friend who collects cigar bands," the President reportedly considered the request thoughtfully for a moment. Then, carefully removing the band from a fresh cigar and handing it to his guest, he picked up a match, lit the cigar, and proceeded to enjoy it himself.

CHAPTER 16

A Lawyer's Half-Dozen

1. "Also Known As"—Changing Your Name

●Flushed with excitement after your first N.O.W. (National Organization of Women) meeting, you return home resolved to be known henceforth and forever as Goodperson rather than your hereditary name: Goodman.

●You're about to marry, and you and your spouse agree to unite your names as well: Mr. and Mrs. Smith-Jones.

●Your Central-European name, four unpronounceable syllables, barely fits the nameplate on your doorbell, and you want to Americanize it.

●Your father the classics professor named you Beowulf, but you'd rather be known by your middle name: Percy.

No lawyer needed—all you really have to do is start using it. Inform family, friends, employer, bank, department stores, utilities, landlord. After you've used the new name for a while, it's yours by common law, unless you've changed it for illegal or fraudulent purposes like ducking debts or fleeing prosecution.

That's the unofficial route, and it's fine for many purposes. But if you want to make the alteration a matter of public record, so that you can officially change your auto license, marriage certificate, school records and be reborn—i.e., have a corrected birth certificate issued—there's only one way: through the courts. Here, though, the court has the last word. You have every right to change your name unofficially to something offensive or silly—Adolf Hitler or Gargantua Greenberg, but if the court has "a reasonable objection," it is not obliged to sanction such a change. Some courts have not, for example, endorsed the use of single names, on the grounds that it would set an undesirable precedent in a society "founded on the use of both a given name and a surname . . ."

The judge's own name may color his thinking. That may have been so in the case of a former judge surnamed Schmuck, who, veteran lawyers in the back room at Gasner's Restaurant used to say, was far from your best choice for a name-change petition.

Another judge, referring emotionally to Nazi atrocities in World War II, refused the request of a 23-year-old American to Germanize his name by prefixing it with "Von." He reinforced his refusal by pointing out that "Von" often denoted noble ancestry, and "Article I, section 9, clause 8, United States Constitution prohibits the grant of any title of nobility by the United States." An Appellate Court conceivably could decide otherwise.

Much the same rationale, however, was cited in Maurice Lee Thompson's petition to assume the name Chief Piankhi Akinbaloye. Stated the court sternly: ". . . to permit petitioner's application as proposed would be tantamount to the bestowal of an apparent title of authority . . . would tend to confuse . . . the public." So no one can stop you from assuming the name Prince Romanoff or even King Kong—but it may not be easy to find a judge willing to officiate at your coronation.

Changing the name of a minor child can be as difficult as changing a teenager's mind. Traditionally, the court will base its decision on what the judge perceives as "in the best interests of the child." Eloise Wing, having embraced the Muslim faith, petitioned the court to allow her to change her name to Zakiyyah Ashraf, and her daughter Cheryl's to Annisto Hafsah Ashraf. The judge granted the mother's application but rejected the change requested for the daughter, reasoning that "the proposed name would set the child apart and seem strange and foreign to her schoolmates and others."

Name changes for infants (the court's term in most states for anyone under eighteen) have also been denied when one parent objects. This happens most often when parents divorce, the children are in the custody of the mother, and she remarries and decides to change their name to that of her new husband "to avoid confusion." When, quite naturally, the natural father objects, the courts generally prefer the "confusion" to a name change that will undermine the relationship between a child and its natural father—unless that father has abandoned the child and neglected its support, or being associated with him might be damaging to the child in some way. (Example: The father is serving a life sentence for murder.)

But we've been citing exceptions. In practice, most name changes are routinely approved. And though the procedure may vary from state to state, it is ordinarily relatively simple with or without a lawyer. Acting *pro se* in New York, for example, you would type (or write in longhand—though that would be most unusual) a "petition for change of name," copied from a form book in a law library —like the sample that follows. It may seem odd, but it's your job to type out the court's "order changing name" as well.

No formal hearing is held. You bring all papers to the court clerk who checks them over, tells you either to wait while he brings them in to the judge or to come back next day or next week. If there's no contest—which is almost always the case—and no "reasonable objection" is in view, the judge's signature on the order you've prepared will be almost as routine as a rap of the gavel calling court to order.

When the order is signed, you should photostat it and obtain as many certified copies as you think you'll need (usually at about $1 a copy) to notify the Board of Health (birth certificate change), marriage registry bureau, Social Security Administration, your bank, etc. The clerk may remind you, "Don't forget to place the ad." He's referring to the newspaper designated by the judge in the order—an act of notification to the world required in many states. He may then smile and say, "Good day, Mr. Newname."

The deed is done. You've changed your name.

Form No. 30
Petition on application for change of name. (New York)

—— Court, County of ——

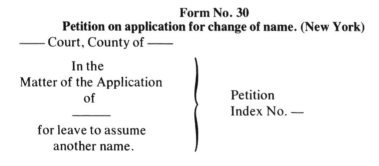

In the
Matter of the Application
of

————

for leave to assume
another name.

Petition
Index No. —

To the —— Court of the County of ——
The petition of ——— respectfully alleges that:

1. Your petitioner is upwards of the age of —— years and resides at No. — Street in the city of ——, county of ——, and state of ——, and has so resided for the period of —— months prior to the making of this application.

2. Your petitioner desires to assume another name than now held by him and the name which he proposes to assume is ———.

3. The grounds for this application for such change of name are as

follows, to wit: ——— [state grounds of application, such as difficult spelling, confusion with other person of same name, etc., in detail].

4. Your petitioner is not married and has no children.

5. Your petitioner is a citizen of the United States of America [having been duly naturalized by the —— county on the — day of —].

6. Your petitioner was born at —— on the — day of — and the name of his father is ——— and that of his mother is ———.

7. A certified transcript of your petitioner's birth certificate [a certificate of the local board of health of ——, New York, stating that no birth certificate is available for your petitioner] is annexed hereto and made a part hereof.

8. Your petitioner, under the name by which he is now known, or under any other name he has ever used, has never been convicted of a crime and has never been adjudicated a bankrupt.

9. There are no judgments or liens of record, and no actions pending, against your petitioner in any court of this state or of the United States, or of any governmental subdivision thereof, or elsewhere, whether the court is a court of record or not. There are no bankruptcy or insolvency proceedings, voluntary or involuntary, pending against your petitioner in any court whatsoever or before any officer, person, body, or board having jurisdiction thereof, and your petitioner has not at any time made an assignment for the benefit of creditors.

10. There are no claims, demands, liabilities, or obligations of any kind whatsoever on a written instrument or otherwise against your petitioner under the only name by which he has been known, which is the name sought herein to be abandoned, and your petitioner has no creditors who may be adversely affected or prejudiced in any way by the proposed change of name.

11. No previous application for this relief has been made.

WHEREFORE, your petitioner prays that an order of this court may be entered granting leave to him to assume the name of ——— in place of that of —— on a day to be specified therein not less than thirty days after the entry of such order, and for such other and further relief as may be proper.

Dated ——, 19—.

[Signature, with name printed underneath]
Petitioner

[Verification] (Form 35, Page 342)
[Annex certified transcript of birth certificate]

334

Form No. 31
Order changing name.

—— Court, —— County

In the Matter of the Application
of
——
for leave to change his [*or*, her] name to
——

} Order

Index No. —

Present: Hon. ——, Justice.

On reading and filing the petition of ——, verified ——, 19—, for leave to change the name of petitioner [*or*, of the above-named infant], and it appearing that petitioner [*or*, said infant] was born on ——, 19—, at ——, and that the certificate of petitioner's [*or*, said infant's] birth issued by —— bears No. — [*or*, and that a certificate of petitioner's (*or*, said infant's) birth is not available]; that petitioner [*or*, said infant] is not registered and not required to be registered under the provisions of the U. S. Selective Service Act [*or*, is registered under the name of —— with Local Board No. — of the U.S. Selective Service at ——]; and the court being satisfied that said petition is true and that there is no reasonable objection to the change of name proposed [*add, in case of infant:* and due notice of the presentation of the petition having been given to ——, ——, and —— (*parents and guardian)*],

Now, on motion of ——, attorney for the petitioner, it is

ORDERED that said —— be and he [*or*, she] is hereby authorized to assume the name of —— in the place and stead of ——, on the — day of ——, 19—, upon complying with the provisions of Article 6 of the Civil Rights Law, and of this order; namely, that this order be entered and the papers upon which it is being granted be filed in the office of the Clerk of this Court within ten days from the date hereof; that within twenty days from the date of the entry of this order a notice be published once in the —— [*newspaper*], published in the —— County, in substantially the form prescribed in § 63 of the Civil Rights Law: that the affidavit of publication thereof be filed in the office of the Clerk of this Court within forty days after the making of this order; that within twenty days after the entry of this order petitioner serve a copy of it [by certified mail] upon the Chairman of Local Board No. — of the U.S. Selective Service at which petitioner [*or*, said infant] is registered for selective service; and that proof of such service be filed with the Clerk of this Court within ten days after such service; and it is further

ORDERED that after such requirements are complied with, said

335

petitioner [*or*, said infant] on and after ——, 19—, shall be known as and by the name of ——, which petitioner [*or*, said infant] is hereby authorized to assume, and by no other name.

Signed this — day of ——, 19—, at ——, N. Y.

ENTER

[Signature or initials, with name
printed underneath]

In some states, this notice must be published in a newspaper designated by the Court.

Notice of Change of Name

Notice is hereby given that an order entered by the —— court, —— County, on the — day of ——, bearing Index Number —, a copy of which may be examined at the office of the clerk, located at ——, in room number —, grants me the right, effective on the — day of ——, to assume the name of ——. My present address in ——; the date of my birth is ——; my present name is ——.

* * *

2. Power of Attorney: Your Alter Ego

Your daughter the college student drove the family's second car, on its last wheels, back to school with her. Now it's months later. Transmission enfeebled by age, an immobile modern sculpture, it's been enshrined in the student parking lot with only its reverse gear operative. You agree she should advertise for a buyer.

Suddenly she gets a live one, willing to take the car "as is," but he wants it in a hurry. No time for her to send you the auto registration for your signature, and for you to rush it back. So by special delivery, you send a power of attorney allowing her to sell the car and to legally sign your name on the dotted line.

A power of attorney is a document by which you transfer to another—wife, relative, friend, business associate—the authority to perform some specific act (sign checks) or carry out a transaction (real estate, stocks and bonds, insurance, etc., or sale of a chattel like your aging car) in your name, as if you were doing it yourself. It may be a general power of attorney, designating someone to handle all your business affairs while you're on an extended

336

trip, or in the coronary care unit. Incidentally (and we hope you will recover quickly), such a power of attorney ends with the death of the individual giving it.

The power of attorney is usually a printed form available at a legal stationer's, but it's perfectly legal when typed or handwritten. For your protection, it's important that it clearly spell out the powers you are delegating and their duration.

A general power should not be given lightly—especially where large sums of money, valuable property, or negotiable securities are concerned. Like any unlimited power, it can be abused. More than once, good old Uncle Charlie in the nursing home has been persuaded to sign power of attorney over to a favorite nephew, who has proven to be a thoroughgoing scoundrel, cleaning out the vault, pocketing three dollars for himself every time he changes five, and bleeding poor Charlie like an abdominal hemorrhage.

At such a time, when there is no one you are confident can resist temptation, when, in Jimmy Durante's words, you feel "surrounded by assassins," and there is enough money to turn even saint into sinner, speak to your banker and consider setting up a bank-administered trust. As for Uncle Charlie's favorite nephew, you can deal with that blackguard by determining from your Circuit or District Court clerk the provisions of something called the Statute of Conservatorship in your state. This allows you to salvage the assets of such an aging, exploited relative, by fully informing the court in a formal petition (available at most stationers') and asking for the appointment of a conservator.

In legalese, the person giving the power is called "the principal" and the one receiving it "the agent" or "attorney in fact." These terms appear in the forms below. The first, a New York form purchased from a stationery store, permits you to cross out any powers you're *not* authorizing. The second, a commonly used all-purpose form, is generally typed, and you fill in the specific powers granted—like to "sell my 1970 Pontiac sedan, registration #123456789," or "withdraw funds from my savings account at the First Federal Savings, account #987654321."

337

Form No. 32

T 44—Statutory Short Form of General Power of Attorney. 8-67.

JULIUS BLUMBERG, INC., LAW BLANK PUBLISHERS
80 EXCHANGE PLACE AT BROADWAY, NEW YORK

NOTICE: THE POWERS GRANTED BY THIS DOCUMENT ARE BROAD AND SWEEPING. THEY ARE DEFINED IN NEW YORK GENERAL OBLIGATIONS LAW, ARTICLE 5, TITLE 15, SECTIONS 5-1502A THROUGH 5-1503, WHICH EXPRESSLY PERMITS THE USE OF ANY OTHER OR DIFFERENT FORM OF POWER OF ATTORNEY DESIRED BY THE PARTIES CONCERNED.

Know All Men by These Presents, which are intended to constitute a *GENERAL POWER OF ATTORNEY* pursuant to Article 5, Title 15 of the New York General Obligations Law:

That I

(insert name and address of the principal)

do hereby appoint

(insert name and address of the agent, or each agent, if more than one is designated)

my attorney(s)-in-fact TO ACT

(a) If more than one agent is designated and the principal wishes each agent alone to be able to exercise the power conferred, insert in this blank the word "severally". Failure to make any insertion or the insertion of the word "jointly" will require the agents to act jointly.

First: in my name, place and stead in any way which I myself could do, if I were personally present, with respect to the following matters as each of them is defined in Title 15 of Article 5 of the New York General Obligations Law to the extent that I am permitted by law to act through an agent:

[Strike out and initial in the opposite box any one or more of the subdivisions as to which the principal does NOT desire to give the agent authority. Such elimination of any one or more of subdivisions (A) to (K), inclusive, shall automatically constitute an elimination also of subdivision (L).]

To strike out any subdivision the principal must draw a line through the text of that subdivision AND write his initials in the box opposite.

(A) real estate transactions; [   ]

(B) chattel and goods transactions; [   ]

(C) bond, share and commodity transactions; [   ]

(D) banking transactions; [   ]

(E) business operating transactions; [   ]

(F) insurance transactions; [   ]

(G) estate transactions; [   ]

(H) claims and litigation; [   ]

(I) personal relationships and affairs; [   ]

(J) benefits from military service; [   ]

(K) records, reports and statements; [   ]

(L) all other matters; [   ]

[Special provisions and limitations may be included in the statutory short form power of attorney only if they conform to the requirements of section 5-1503 of the New York General Obligations Law.]

Second: with full and unqualified authority to delegate any or all of the foregoing powers to any person or persons whom my attorney(s)-in-fact shall select.

In Witness Whereof, *I have hereunto signed my name and affixed my seal this*....................

day of.., *19*........

....*(Seal)*

(Signature of Principal)

STATE OF

COUNTY OF } *ss.:*

On the   *day of*   *19*   *before me personally came*

to me known, and known to me to be the individual   described in, and who executed the foregoing instrument, and   he   acknowledged to me that   he   executed the same.

POWER OF ATTORNEY
KNOW ALL MEN BY THESE PRESENT:

I, (Your name here), residing at (your address here), hereby make, constitute, and appoint (name of person you are appointing) my true and lawful attorney in fact for and in my name, place, and stead, to (INSERT THE POWER YOU INTEND TO GIVE IN CLEAR, CONCISE, AND PRECISE LANGUAGE).

I grant and give to my attorney in fact full authority and power to do and perform any and all acts necessary or incident to the performance and execution of the powers expressly granted herein as fully to all intents and purposes as I might or could do if personally present (ADD "with full power of substitution" IF YOU INTEND YOUR ATTORNEY TO HAVE THE POWER TO APPOINT SOMEONE TO TAKE *HIS* PLACE).

In witness whereof, I have hereunto signed my name this — day of ——, 197—.

———————————
(SIGN HERE)

State of ——:

             : ss.;

County of ——:

On the — day of ——, 1978, before me personally came (YOUR NAME HERE), to me known and known to me to be the individual described in, and who executed the foregoing instrument, and (s)he acknowledged to me that (s)he executed the same.

———————————
NOTARY PUBLIC

*   *   *

3. "Sworn To Before Me": When You Need a Notary Public

As a child, I remember passing a corner drug store with an impressive sign in the window: NOTARY REPUBLIC. It looked very important and official. Many years later, I learned that my childhood impression was correct, but my reading skills (the second word was "public") left something to be desired.

340

A notary's functions, though routine, *are* official and important. Many documents are not considered legal, valid, or binding if they lack the notary's signature, stamp, or seal.

In some countries, where the notary prepares and validates many official documents, this position has become highly influential. In many states, any resident adult, free of a criminal record, may become a notary by passing a relatively simple test and taking an oath to uphold the law and carry out his functions with integrity. In some states, merely applying and posting a bond are sufficient.

When are you most likely to need a notary?

For acknowledgment of a signature. Many contracts, deeds, mortgages, and other legal documents require an "acknowledgment"—a short statement tagged on the end confirming the identity of the person who signed it, countersigned and sealed by a notary. The form of an acknowledgment may vary slightly, but if you have a document that requires corroboration, you might use this one:

Form No. 34

ACKNOWLEDGMENT

STATE OF ——:
                    ss.:
COUNTY OF ——:

On the — day of —— 19— before me personally appeared ——, known to me to be the same person who executed the foregoing instrument, and (s)he acknowledged to me that (s)he executed the same.

————————————
Notary Public
Commission expires ——

For a sworn statement. Any affidavit or other document requiring signature under oath must be signed before a notary public. This is usually done in one of two ways. If it's your own first-person statement ("I did this... I saw that... ," etc.), it can be sworn to by simply adding just below your signature: "Sworn to before me the — day of —— 19—." If it's not a first-person document you are swearing to (a complaint in a law action, a petition to change your name, or various other papers used in court proceedings), the oath is set forth in a separate verification either on the final page or one that's attached:

Form No. 35

VERIFICATION

STATE OF   )
)ss.:
COUNTY OF   )

————, being duly sworn, deposes and says that (s)he is the
——, in the above action; that (s)he has read the foregoing ——,
knows the contents thereof, and the matters and things stated therein
are true.

————————
Signature

Sworn to before me this
— day of ——,19—.

————————
Notary Public

In either case, the notary will ask you (in theory, yes, in practice,
maybe) if you swear that the contents are true. If your answer is
yes, you sign and he countersigns.

Like many lawyers, I've been a notary since I started to practice. For the same reason—client convenience—I've always asked
my secretaries to take the notary exam. Clients occasionally ask
me to notarize a signature for a relative or business associate who's
not present. It's hard to say no, but the words "before me" must
be strictly observed, under penalty of losing one's notary certification, criminal charges for false statements, or, in the case of an at-
torney-notary, possible disbarment. So I say no.

Few professional notaries own estates in Newport, but the quarters or half-dollars most notaries charge (a few may go as high as $2
or $3) do add up. I'll never know. Most lawyers—like many
banks—notarize documents free as an accommodation to clients.

* * *

4. "You're Under Arrest!": What To Do Until the Lawyer Comes

One recent chill October night, my home phone rang. It was a
friend of a friend calling from the police station. He and his wife
had been shopping at a self-service department store for a winter
wardrobe for their children. They had purchased several hundred

dollars' worth of clothing, including—proud moment—their youngest child's first pair of shoes. To try them on, the father had cut the cord fastening the booties and absently tucked the tag in his breast pocket. Rounding up his kids, and juggling the baby (still wearing the new shoes) plus an assortment of packages his wife had paid for, he'd forgotten the tag dangling conspicuously from his pocket. So the man was thunderstruck when a store guard arrested him for theft the moment he stepped out the store's front door.

You don't have to burglarize a house or stick up a gas station to get yourself arrested. A whip-sawing chain of circumstances— what WW II GIs used to call the fickle finger of fate—could bring you suddenly and conspicuously to the attention of the police, to be abruptly frisked, fingerprinted, photographed, and interrogated.

Fortunately, we live in a country that's still what all the old stem-winding Fourth of July orators used to say it was, with a constitution that shields our liberties like no other in the world. The judicial system supporting it may not always be efficient. It may not always be so effective in dampening crime as we might like. But the premise under which it works—that this free people would rather see 99 guilty men go free than one innocent man hanged—is a magnificent guardian of our rights. The constitution can't do it alone, though. There are things you should know, on the chance that the rights that need guarding may someday be your own.

This is no time to be your own lawyer. You're not involved in a Small Claims Court dispute with a shopkeeper over who's responsible for a set of badly cleaned drapes. When you're accused of a crime, the people of the State of Illinois (or Oregon or Texas)—or, if it's a federal case, the United States of America—are formidable adversaries, and should you be convicted, more than your money or property are at stake. They can take away your freedom and thoroughly mess up the rest of your life. In such a situation, the psychological pressures can be overwhelming. So I can't emphasize this too strongly: Get yourself a good lawyer!

Go Peaceably. Resistance is guaranteed to turn bad into worse. If you are stopped by a police officer, even for a traffic violation, or searched or taken into custody, no matter how bizarre it all seems, be respectful, don't argue, and restrain the impulse to snarl, "Police state!" You should ask for an explanation, of course, but losing your temper and becoming abusive only stiffens your captor's nightstick. Even a casual comment, if misunderstood and presumed "smart alec" can get you hauled off to the stationhouse.

So a distinguished professor of philosophy from a leading Eastern university learned when he stepped into the shelter of a Manhattan subway entrance one windy night to light his cigarette. "Hey, buddy," said a policeman, "no smoking in the subway!" Replied the professor mildly, "But I only ducked in out of the wind to light up."

Retorted the policeman, "What if everybody did that?"

Struck by the officer's paraphrase of the philosophical concept of the categorical imperative, the professor asked good-humoredly, "Who do you think you are—Kant?" The officer, angered by what he took to be an obscenity, instantly collared the professor and ran him in for use of abusive language and resisting arrest. Happily, the desk sergeant on duty at the stationhouse had taken a philosophy course in college. He recognized the literary reference and explained it to the embarrassed policeman, who promptly dropped the charges.

Resisting arrest is itself a crime, and a peace officer may use all necessary means including force to—in the cloudy syntax of law enforcement—"apprehend the perpetrator." If the arrest proves unlawful, you may later have a cause of action for false arrest. But it's the police officer's move now, and if he has reason to suspect you've committed—or are in the act of committing—a crime, he has not only the right but the responsibility to arrest you.

Take advantage of your rights. Miranda warnings, the most familiar ones are called, and an officer's failure to recite these constitutional rights to his prisoner can invalidate his arrest. It would, however, be an inept enforcement officer these days who would forget something so elementary, and your rights are often read directly from a card (which you may be asked to sign) informing you: 1) you have the right to remain silent; 2) any statement you make may be used against you; 3) you have a right to speak to a lawyer, and one will be assigned if you cannot afford one; 4) your lawyer may be present when you are questioned.

Make no admissions. The Geneva Convention requires a captured soldier to give no information other than name, rank, and serial number. You don't even have to give that much. Don't worry about seeming unsociable. You have the absolute constitutionally guaranteed right to say nothing at all to the arresting police officer. Nothing you say can help your case at this point anyway. A denial will by cynically ignored. An innocent remark may entrap you.

Example: the youngster caught with a small quantity of marijua-

344

na. Hoping to win innocent bystander status, he volunteered: "I was just holding that grass for my friend." In ten foolhardy words or less, he had legally and irrevocably confessed to possession of an illegal substance.

You can anticipate that shortly after reminding you of your right to remain silent, the officer will begin asking you to speak up: "Why did you steal the car? Whose grass is this? How many times have you done this before?" There is only one correct answer: "I'm sorry, but I'm not answering any questions until my attorney gets here." This will immediately dampen his interest in conversation.

Search and seizure. The Fourth Amendment of the U.S. Constitution—part of that marvelous mechanism that is our Bill of Rights—prohibits unlawful search and seizure. Before a police officer can search your home, he must first obtain a search warrant. He can't get that until he has convinced a judge that there is "probable cause" to believe that evidence of a crime will be discovered. Be it ever so humble, a man's home or apartment is his castle, and an officer without a warrant may not enter without milord's consent. Unless he has a "no-knock warrant" (to prevent a suspect from flushing away easily disposable evidence such as drugs or gambling slips), he must identify himself at the door and show you his search warrant. If you unwisely let him in without a warrant and *allow* him to search, any evidence he finds may be used against you. If he forces his way in, such evidence—no matter how damaging—will be suppressed by the court.

The law tilts slightly in favor of enforcement where search of cars, boats, or planes (or presumably mopeds) is concerned, on the theory that these "movable castles" will speedily move out of reach of the law's long arm if an officer must first locate a judge to issue a search warrant. So if the trooper who stops your car for a traffic violation has "reasonable suspicion," he can order you to open your trunk for search, *and* he can use any evidence he finds in court.

It's an old problem—*Law and Order* v. *Civil Rights*—with the balance swaying back and forth over the years. Sometimes it ends up in an unlikely equilibrium—as it did when Prohibition raiding officers swooped down on a hood they suspected of bootlegging, only to find ten cases of empty whiskey bottles. "OK, Lefty," bluffed an officer, "we caught you with the goods. Confess— where'd you get this stuff?" Replied the bootlegger virtuously:

"Geez, Lieutenant, how would I know? I never bought an empty whiskey bottle in my life."

Freedom pending trial. In all but murder and the most violent crimes, the defendant is entitled to be free while awaiting trial. In minor cases, he's usually released in his own custody, but on more serious charges the court requires the defendant to post bail. This "security deposit" to assure your return for further proceedings is ordinarily provided by a bondsman, frequently found in a storefront up, down, or across the street from the courthouse. The premium paid usually ranges from 5 to 10 percent ($1,000 bail—$50 to $100 fee), plus some sort of collateral or a guarantee from a financially responsible third party.

Some important additional rights:

•To use the phone to call a lawyer, relative, or trusted friend to let them know where you are and to enlist their aid. You are not, incidentally, limited to a single nickel phone call, as in an old Bogart movie.

•The police have the right to put you in a line-up to give a witness or victim the opportunity to identify you—or, better yet, fail to pick you out. But you, in turn, have the right to refuse to participate until your lawyer is present.

•To a "reasonably prompt" trial—by jury.

•To confront and cross-examine your accuser—with your lawyer's help—and to call witnesses in your own behalf.

•Not to be tried twice for the same crime—which would be double jeopardy.

•If released, or if tried and found not guilty, to have fingerprints, mug shots, and the police record destroyed—or to take them home as souvenirs.

•If convicted and a first offender, you may be able to win relief from the disabilities that are automatically imposed on people convicted of serious crimes: loss of right to vote, loss of licenses and permits, loss of the right to hold certain jobs. At its discretion, the court may grant a certificate of relief for any or all of these disabilities. Request it—a sympathetic judge just might grant it.

* * *

5. "But I Was Only Doing 55!": Traffic Violations

Moving violations—speeding or running a red light or a stop sign—can quickly add up to suspension of a driver's license in

346

many states these days. So it becomes more and more important not to "pay the $25 and forget it." In any case where there are extenuating circumstances or you've any doubt at all about your guilt, I recommend: Plead not guilty, and fight.

Police are only human. They make mistakes, and judges know it. They know, too, that just as in a criminal case, the People must prove guilt "beyond a reasonable doubt." If the judge has even the slightest doubt of your guilt, he should dismiss your case. It doesn't always work that way, of course. The A.A.A. has letters from members piled fender-high complaining angrily about traffic court judges who run assembly-line justice with the end product inevitable: "$25—next case." But in most jurisdictions, with a fair-minded judge, you have a 50-50 chance of winning a dismissal.

Several years ago in upstate New York, I had the uncomfortable experience of having to put my theory to the test. "I clocked you doing 65 in a 55-mile-an-hour zone," the state trooper declared, after his screaming siren had brought me to a sorrowful standstill. I disagreed. Not to him, of course. That would have been about as sensible as trying to slip him a $10 bill with my driver's license.* I pleaded "not guilty" by mail.

Weeks later, after receiving a notice of the trial date, I entered the back door of the local firehouse as instructed and asked where I could find the courtroom. "You're in it," replied a man sitting at a desk in the rear, "and I'm the justice of the peace."

"Well, your Honor," I said, "I'm Walter Kantrowitz, and I'm ready for my trial."

He looked surprised. "Didn't they call you? The trooper who gave you the ticket was transferred to a barracks upstate. He called and said he couldn't make it today, so I gave him a postponement."

Now it was my turn to look surprised. I had driven sixty miles to argue my case, only to find that there would be no trial. I explained

---

Other do's and don'ts when stopped by a trooper: Don't hand over your entire billfold or you could be accused of attempted bribery. Don't reach into glove compartment or pockets without first alerting the officer that that's where your documents are. Any sudden movement could be misinterpreted as reaching for a weapon. For the same reason, at night, turn on your interior dome light so your movements can be seen clearly. And don't assume you're being given a ticket and start to argue. It could be just a security check for a stolen car, or to tell you one of your taillights has burned out. Argue and you could wind up with a summons the officer hadn't planned to give.

that I thought this was unfair, and I requested that the case be dismissed.

"Granted," responded the J.P., and I went home with an unblemished driving record.

Don't count on being as lucky as I was—though I have known other cases of dismissals because a police officer failed to appear. If you do decide to fight a traffic violation charge, either moving or stationary, go well-prepared. If you have a witness or two who can contradict the police officer's testimony—or corroborate yours—bring them to court. Diagram a disputed intersection—dramatize it by sketching it large and clearly on posterboard—if that will make your case easier to follow. Take photos and use them as exhibits, to show the unpruned tree branch blocking the stop sign, the out-of-order parking meter, the empty pole from which vandals had wrenched off the no-parking placard, or whatever could be considered an extenuating circumstance in your case.

If you were charged with speeding—whether the police used radar equipment or clocked you on an ordinary patrol car speedometer—ask when this equipment was last checked and serviced, and ask them to prove it was properly calibrated. If you can raise "reasonable doubt" about the case against you, you've got a fighting chance to walk away a winner.

* * *

6. The Vigilante: Citizen's Arrest

Early one morning last summer, I glanced out my office window and noticed two men running down the busy road behind our law office. One was my law partner, who should have been at his desk. And he wasn't jogging casually but in hot pursuit.

Paul was on his way to make a citizen's arrest. From his window, he'd witnessed a youth attacking a woman in the parking lot below. Dashing down three flights of stairs, he'd scared him off, then pursued and collared him. I phoned the police, who arrived just as Paul returned with his quarry, who was later convicted and is now serving time.

Paul's citizen's arrest made the front page of the local newspaper. Clearly, you don't have to be Kojak to make an arrest (the citizen's is as binding as the policeman's), but there are some important caveats. For a misdemeanor—lesser crimes like petty theft—there's no question about your right to arrest someone you see

348

committing the crime. The suspect must be handed over to the police "without unnecessary delay"—meaning as soon as possible. For felonies—major crimes like burglary, arson, robbery, rape, or murder—you don't have to be an eyewitness if you are, in fact, certain that the person you arrest did commit the crime.

But there are significant differences between the citizen's and the policeman's act. A peace officer can arrest any suspect with only "reasonable cause to believe" a crime has been committed. If the suspect proves innocent, he has no legal recourse. But in the same situation, the innocent party would have an excellent case for damages—for false arrest and imprisonment—against the *citizen* who ran him in.

Citizens, like law enforcement personnel, also have the right to arrest someone who has committed a felony, meaning a serious crime such as robbery, even if they didn't see the crime committed. But there's a catch. The police officer can arrest a person on "reasonable cause to believe." If the suspect turns out to be innocent, the arrest is still lawful. But, in the same circumstances, you or I could be sued for false arrest.

Suppose you hear that someone has just snatched your good friend Vera Virtue's purse. You get into your car and cruise the neighborhood. Two blocks away you see Norman Nogood skulking hastily down a side street, with a pocketbook slung over his shoulder. Always the good citizen, you leap from your car, sprint down the street, and execute a neat flying tackle, hurling Norman to the ground. You ask a passerby to call the police while you pin him down. Alas, after Norman has been booked, fingerprinted, and mugged, it turns out that he didn't lift that pocketbook after all. It was his sister's, and he had just picked it up at the repair shop. Question: Are you in trouble? Answer: You bet. You can—and probably will—be sued by Norman Nogood for false arrest.

So if you want to play good citizen—and I'm all in favor of that—be absolutely sure you've got the guilty person before you act. In this situation, you would have been wiser to call the police to report having seen a suspicious character with a possibly snatched purse. The arrest would then be up to them.

There is, however, one time when you can pursue a criminal without being sure of his guilt. That's when a police officer identifies himself and says: "I need your help." At that moment, you become a member of the sheriff's posse of the Old West, a private citizen unofficially deputized in the best interests of law and

349

order. If you're called upon for such assistance—to help an officer subdue a prisoner, to turn over your car or pilot it in a wild chase through the streets—you not only may help, but your refusal to do so is a misdemeanor.

In general, be aware—as Confucius might have put it pithily—citizen who takes prisoner also takes chance. That's what two nonsmoking Washingtonians discovered when they found themselves in close quarters with a man who ignored both the D.C. ordinance against smoking in elevators and their polite request that he cease and desist. When he refused, they detained him until they could place a formal complaint with a nearby law officer.

The smoker was mightily nettled, and responded with a massive $800,000 suit for false arrest and malicious prosecution against his civilian captors. They counterclaimed with a volley of legal grapeshot—a modest $20,000 suit for health endangerment. The warning on that pack of cigarettes might well have read, "These cigarettes may be dangerous to your *wealth*," because at this writing, this "Winston War" has raged furiously for almost two years through Superior Court (twice) and U.S. District Court (once), with no end in sight.

And it all began with a citizen's arrest.

CHAPTER 17

Law Forms and Libraries— Now to the Nitty-Gritty

My partner Paul Goldhamer's gratifying first reaction to the early chapters of this book was, "If I'd had this when I graduated law school, it sure would have made the transition easier from theory to practice."

No such problem here—as we now come to two vital and eminently practical components of the attorney's nitty-gritty procedural world: the use of law forms and law libraries. Learning to use them adroitly—skills which, like any other, improve with practice—will speed and simplify anything you do in this book, from going to court to going into business.

Law Forms: Greasing The Wheels on Which A Lawyer's Practice Runs

When reaching a legal decision, a judge relies heavily on prior precedents. When preparing documents for a client, an attorney relies on forms that he and other lawyers have successfully used before. In your *pro se* practice, you can—and should—do the same.

When I draft a will or prepare a contract with an unusual clause—something requiring a special effort and time to research or construct—I always place a copy in a looseleaf binder. Months or years may go by before I have occasion to use that clause again. Turning to that binder has always been a handy time-saver when I do. (Of course, now that my office has a computerized word-processor for storing standard material, that looseleaf will probably only collect dust.)

But no lawyer relies on his personal files and experiences alone. We refer often to the many standard form books found in every lawyer's library—sometimes having a secretary copy a needed form word for word, sometimes using it only as a guide, as a creative dressmaker uses a pattern. Beyond convenience and time-saving, forms have a third important virtue: the security that comes from knowing there is a solid legal precedent behind every form that finds its way into a form book. Each has been tested and interpreted over the years. It's courtroom-safe. Some forms are distributed for national use—bankruptcy forms are one example. But in most cases, the safest forms (and form books) for you to use are those published with the specific legal demands of your state's courts in mind.

There are form books specifically designed to deal with every possible legal situation from Accidents to Zoning. A form book on divorce may offer eight different separation agreements, with hundreds of special clauses that may be added. There are sets of books on court proceedings that run twenty volumes of summonses, motions, pleadings and complaints for actions of slander, negligence, advertising contract, or boat charter parties. There are books that run two-thousand pages or more and weight more than a small roast beef.

You can obtain many forms free—some right from this book. Courts sometimes supply probate forms. Federal district courts provide summons forms. Real estate forms (deeds, contracts of sale, mortgages) are often given away free by title insurance companies. Most forms must be purchased at legal stationers, but pocket change is often all they cost. Many are sold in minimum sets of three—the original for submission, a carbon for your files, another available to give to your co-defendant if need be, or to an adversary on request. Having a fourth for use as a practice worksheet is a good idea, but a photocopy will do well enough for that.

Every region has its own major form printer. Local legal complexities force such specialization. On the West coast, it may be Wolcott's. In New York, it's been Julius Blumberg since 1887, and New Jersey and Connecticut are in the Blumberg empire, too—with the family slogan, originally voiced whimsically by founder Julius: "I care not who makes the laws of the country, so long as I make its law blanks." Many corner stationers have legal forms in stock, but one near the courthouse will have the biggest turnover and freshest forms—not unimportant when every year a number of forms are rendered obsolete by the legislature or judiciary. If your stationer has only a few dozen forms on a dusty shelf, beware. Press the clerk who sells them to be sure you're buying something currently in use. If, however, you happened to submit the wrong

352

form, or have filled it out incorrectly, it would be a small delay but no large tragedy. The courthouse clerk would simply point out the error and tell you to resubmit it "in good form."

Using forms requires common sense. The words in a form, though important, are not sacred. If your circumstances don't quite fit, then feel free to slightly alter a line, drop one clause, substitute another. There may be three or four different apartment house form leases. Read them and choose the one closest to your needs. If it's a walk-up apartment, cross out the paragraph about elevator maintenance. Every form has blank spaces you can use to add an appropriate clause or clauses. In forms of agreement (contracts, partnerships, leases), words or phrases may be crossed out and altered. In forms of proceedings (court documents), filling in blanks or crossing out where "not applicable" is the usual pattern.

There'll be times when you'll need help with a form. Many clerks at courthouses have sample forms filled out to show to young attorneys, paralegals and secretaries, and they should be willing to let you look them over, too. Alternatively, they should be willing to pull a file out of public records—and for a modest fee photocopy it for you—that can serve as your guide. I would be less than candid if I failed to note that some clerks are less accommodating than they should be. You'll encounter a grouch now and then who'll respond to nothing but the threat to see his superior. But most clerks are courteous and friendly, and if you admit you need help, you're almost sure to get it.

Forms are to the lawyer what patented drugs and medications are to the doctor. There's at least one to deal with every common problem. They've worked before. They'll work again. They make it unnecessary to daily reinvent a cure. So, as doctors lean on their pharmacopeia, we lawyers depend on our form-acopeia. Learning to use it well can make all the difference in the legal world—and your friendly county law library is a good place to start.

THE LAW LIBRARY:
INTIMIDATING BUT INFORMATIVE

The law student's first visit to the college law library is a humbling experience. All those books—tens of thousands of them, floor to ceiling, wall after wall of them. But the first lesson he learns is that he doesn't have to memorize it, just master it. And when in doubt, there's always a librarian there to help.

Most of the time, in performing your own *pro se* work, you won't need a law library. The preceding chapters have pretty much spelled out your needs and either provided the basic documents you'll require or told you how and where to obtain them. The local legal stationer and court clerk will be careful not to advise you so thoroughly that they can be accused of practicing law without a license, but they can give you a good deal of unofficial help when things are quiet. Try to match your visits to their "slow" time.

I'd like to think that I've taught you all you'll ever need to know about the law, but that's hardly likely. Laws vary from place to place. Laws change. It costs me $2,000 a year in supplements just to keep my personal law library up to date and add important new works. Since that is an expense you will not be anxious to incur, you'll be happy to know that county law libraries, though established for and used primarily by members of the bar, are wide open to the public. You'll ordinarily find them in the white pages of your phone book under county government office listings—sometimes under "Law," sometimes under "Libraries." The county or state pays for books and librarians, and your tax money makes its contribution, so the staff knows it's there to serve "the people," whether their names are followed by a J.D. or an L.L.B. or not. I'm confident you'll find them uniformly helpful in steering you to the reference books you need, and even—again depending upon how busy they are —in guiding you in their use.

Let's say you slipped on the ice in front of a neighbor's home or a local shop just after a snowstorm and incurred an injury. You want to sue, but you aren't sure of your rights, or what specific steps must be taken in your jurisdiction to demand them. The law library is the place to hobble.

First thing you need to know is substantive law relating to snow and ice on sidewalks in your community. (If you live in Arizona or Florida, there may not be any, but then, chances are your fall would have been caused by a buckled sidewalk or a banana skin, and you'd find plenty of law in those categories as well.) You'll have to ask the librarian's guidance on where local statutes or codes are located. You'll find subjects listed alphabetically, but you may have to check several headings to find the one you want: snow and ice, ice, sidewalk clearing are all possibilities, and the librarian may have other finely tuned suggestions.

Once you learn that ice and snow must be cleared from sidewalks within six hours of a storm, you'll have some idea of whether or not you have a case. Obviously, if you took your tumble immediately after the last snowflake fell, you do not. If you slipped seven hours later—and can round up witnesses and other evidence to prove it—you may. If the snow and ice were cleared but not very thoroughly, you may have to read on to see if you have a chance to win a negligence suit.

That's when you start to research case law—to find out what happened to others in cases similar to yours. An encyclopedia like *American Jurisprudence* ("Am Jur" is the abbreviated reference) will give you a good initial overview of the law, with footnotes pointing to state cases and statutes worthy of further follow-up. The next step, if you really want to do a thorough job, might be to look for a treatise or text on negligence in the catalogue—which might lead you to skim Bailey's *Personal Injuries* and further case citations. There are treatises on every possible subject—on illegitimate children (Schatkin's *Disputed Paternity Proceedings*), on charities (Zollman's *American Law of Charities*), even on cemeteries (Jackson's *Law of Cadavers*).

When you get down to cases, your citation may read 12/NY2d/327—a code which is easier to crack than it looks. That simply means your case will be found in the 12th volume of the second series of New York Reports, on page 327—where the decision in question appears, and perhaps continues for fifteen to twenty pages, giving you facts and the court's reasoning, and often citing earlier precedents and referring you to similar cases. Fortunately, each case is summarized at the start, and "head notes" are provided. They are numbered to match the relevant paragraphs in the decision that follows so that you can read it selectively. It sounds complicated, but once you've read your first few decisions, you'll breeze through them like Oliver Wendell Holmes.

OK. You learn that in cases like yours where the walk was shoveled carelessly, the owner was considered negligent. Now you want to know the procedure for filing a suit, and you'll learn that in a book specific to your state, usually called the Code of Civil Procedure or the Civil Practice Act, and which describes which court a certain matter is to be brought in, the time period allowed (statute of limitations), and such things as trial procedures and the correct forms of summons, complaint, answer and reply. Many of these statute books mingle the proper forms with the text, annotating it with cases that have interpreted all the procedures. In New York, for example, we have Bender's *Forms for the Civil Practice*

Act, and I have a 22-volume set on forms of pleadings that covers almost every factual situation any lawyer might want to sue on, from negligence to a real estate foreclosure.

There is, of course, far more to legal research than has thus far met your eyes. There is the interesting process of "shephardizing"—referring to a set of Shephard's *Citations* which tell you if a case you're planning to lean on has been cited in other cases or overruled. There are "pocket parts"—small supplements periodically updating many books, slipped into a backcover pocket in each volume. But, fortunately, there are librarians who are justifiably proud of their breadth of knowledge and generous in sharing it. If you don't want to make a marathon pest of yourself, you can take a cram course in law library research in books like Pollack's *Fundamentals of Legal Research,* conveniently available at—where else?—the law library.

PART II

WHEN YOU SHOULDN'T BE YOUR OWN
LAWYER

INTRODUCTION TO PART II

Many years ago, when my leisure time was occupied with more frivolous hobbies than writing a book, I decided to build an amplifier for my hi-fi system. The kit I purchased came with detailed step-by-step instructions, all necessary components, and specified exactly what tools were needed.

I followed instructions meticulously, worked every evening for three to four hours for two weeks, and then, with wife and son standing skeptically by, plugged the amplifier into my system. It didn't work. I checked and rechecked without success. Then, on the last page of the instruction manual, I discovered a final message from the manufacturer: If, after following all procedures, the amplifier didn't work, it was suggested that the purchaser take it to an authorized service representative who, for a modest charge, would trouble-shoot the amplifier and render it operational. The rep's greater experience and sophisticated testing devices quickly pinpointed the problem—one misguided wire. My amplifier has functioned resonantly and well in the ten years since.

The preceding chapters have given you exhaustive step-by-step kits for each of a number of common legal problems. In most cases, you should be able to smoothly and successfully plug in your work. But some of us are less self-assured than others. If you're troubled by the possibility that a wire or two may have been crossed, you may feel more secure taking your product to a professional for pre-testing.

Almost any local attorney should willingly be your insecurity blanket. A phone call saying, "I'm about to file some legal papers and I wonder if I could have a short consultation with you to double-check them," should make possible the professional trouble-shooting inspection you desire. In effect, for $20 to $75, depending on the complexity of the matter, you'll have bought yourself a legal insurance policy.

How to choose and use a lawyer when you need one—whether for a brief checkup-consultation or for something too complex or serious to handle on your own—will be dealt with in the chapters just ahead.

CHAPTER 18

An Abe Lincoln of Your Own

If you lived in Springfield, Illinois, in the year 1850, choosing a lawyer would have been simple. Chances are, you'd have heard about that lanky backwoods lawyer folks said could talk the antlers off an elk. Once, after teaming with another attorney to win a case, Abraham Lincoln was so disturbed by the $250 the other man had billed for their services that he pressured him into reducing their fee. Protested a local judge: "Lincoln, your paltry fees will impoverish the profession."

He refused a collection case against a widow and her six children on the grounds that it would ruin them, and "Some things that are right legally are not right morally." And when a vindictive creditor insisted on pressing a collection case against a poor man for $2.50, lawyer Lincoln requested his $10 fee in advance, gave the debtor half of it, got him to confess judgment, collected the obligatory $2.50, and made everybody happy.

It's not easy to find a lawyer like Lincoln. It wasn't even easy then. As we've tried to show throughout this book, you can often be your own lawyer. But there may be times when that will be the equivalent of plunging a lighted match into your car's fuel tank to see if there's any gas left.

Example: Your teenage daughter phones in the middle of the night with the news that she's been arrested on a drug possession charge. The uninsured car you've been storing in your driveway slips its brakes, rumbles across the street, crashes into the wall of your neighbor's house, and lands in his bedroom, which thank Heaven, he has just left to brush his teeth. You have a once-in-a-lifetime chance to invest in a promising business enterprise on short notice, but you want to be sure the small print in the contract doesn't give you a big headache later.

These are not cases for the do-it-yourselfer. If you don't know a good attorney, your daughter may spend the night in durance vile; your neighbor—furious over your carelessness and his narrow es-

361

cape—may take you for a bundle instead of settling amicably; and you may lose your button-down shirt in the business venture (which never does succeed in manufacturing the first successful fuel pill out of discarded toothpaste tubes). For most people, even those who prefer to handle handlable things by themselves, having a family lawyer you know, trust, and can call upon in times of emergency can provide important peace of mind.

You certainly don't need to keep a lawyer on retainer until that moment occurs. Annual retainers are for businesses, for the very wealthy, or for those who wade regularly in hot or troubled waters. For most of the rest of us, it is enough to be a client who can call and pay an hourly or per case basis as a complex need arises.

But the best time to find a family lawyer—as, indeed, with a family doctor—is when you don't need one. And, whether you choose to choose an attorney in advance, when the pressure isn't on, or whether your quest begins out of the need to deal with a specific legal problem, the steps for going about your search are pretty much the same.

THE FIRST STEP:
WHAT KIND OF LAWYER DO YOU NEED?

For most matters, you're going to need a Jack-of-all-cases, a generalist who handles wills, real estate, matrimonial problems, commercial matters, as well as minor personal injury or property claims and criminal defenses. This is your family practitioner—an attorney who can keep your legal affairs in order, be on call for sudden emergencies, refer you to a specialist when necessary.

If you're involved in a serious crime, in a major tax problem, a complex patent application, a workmen's compensation case, a major medical malpractice or product liability trial, or some other matter that may require more focused expertise and experience than a general practitioner possesses, you may want an attorney who specializes in that particular area. Often your own attorney, if you have one, will refer you to a specialist he knows and trusts. I do this often, keeping involved and adding my personal knowledge of the client and his affairs to the skill of the specialist. Having done only part of the work, I end up with only a part of the fee, but I know I've done the right thing for my client.

The next ten years may see the genesis of specialty certification—an American Bar Association commission has already recommended that state groups institute specialty programs and possibly examinations—but at this writing, in most states all this is only in the arguing stages. And since lawyers enjoy nothing more than a good hot debate, they could go on for years. For the moment, recommendations from family practitioners or satisfied clients are about as good a path as any to the specialist's office door.

THE SECOND STEP:
PUTTING SOME NAMES IN THE HAT

Law schools are now turning out attorneys so rapidly (3,958 passed California's bar in December 1977, and 3,913 more New York's) that Chief Justice Warren Burger recently warned of a society "overrun by hordes of lawyers hungry as locusts." But it's still no easier to choose an attorney than when the nineteenth-century educator Edward Everett outlined the qualities of the ideal lawyer: ". . . he must fully comprehend the mighty maze of the social relations; he must carry about with him a stock of learning almost boundless; he must be a sort of god to men and communities, who look up to him in the dearest peril of their lives and fortunes; and he must, at the same time, be conversant with a tissue of the most senseless fictions and arbitrary technicalities that ever disgraced a liberal science."

Finding Everett's ideal lawyer may be about as easy as finding the ideal mate at a ten-cents-a-dance ballroom. But here are some hopefully helpful suggestions:

The blind date. Use a lawyer someone you know has used before and speaks well of. Word-of-respected-mouth is still the best place to start, asking for suggestions and recommendations from good friends, respected business acquaintances, trusted relatives. Ask enough people and the same name may come up twice, a good sign that you're on the right track. But was the area in which the attorney helped your friend the area you need help in? And try to determine if the recommendation is based on sound legal advice received, or the fact that the lawyer is your friend's tennis partner.

To eliminate possible conflict of interest, gently inquire if the recommendee is a relative of the recommendor. (Such suggestions should certainly not be *de facto* dismissed. My mother and my mother-in-law still enthusiastically pass out my cards at the slightest hint that an acquaintance may need a lawyer. I know it's not the sort of thing Cadwalader, Wickersham & Taft would approve of, but Lilyan and Charlotte enjoy it so much, how can I tell them to stop?)

You don't want to ask a friend for a recommendation because you'd rather not air your problems? Then consider your accountant, who undoubtedly knows an army of attorneys, knows you and your affairs, and can probably make a good match. If pressed, a banker may also suggest a lawyer—though bankers, being cautious by nature, are likely to offer three or four names and let you choose. They don't want you coming back later complaining, "That lawyer you sent me to was incompetent!"

Local politicians usually know enough lawyers to fill the high school gym, but they owe that many political debts, too. So their suggestions—likely to be using you as coin of the realm—must be handled with care.

The activist. You might also keep your eyes and ears open at school board and other community meetings for a lawyer who looks like (or, if you've read about him in the newspaper, sounds like) a dynamic person you'd find sympatico. The attorney you meet at a party could be the one you've been looking for, too. Strike up an acquaintance. Ask what kind of practice he has. If you like him, ask for his card. I never knew an attorney who didn't carry one. We'd as soon forget our trousers as our cardholders.

The dating service. If you can't find an attorney by recommendation, then try a service that most local bar associations provide—the lawyer referral service. Though details vary, you can usually phone for the name of an attorney and sometimes request the particular skill or specialty you need. Since names are likely to be dispensed in rotation, it's a bit of a lottery. The best referral services are those that screen or interview lawyers before listing them. It's helpful, too, when the service lists lawyers by specialties—wills, bankruptcies, matrimonial, or whatever. But you can't count on it. One brash young lawyer, fresh out of law school, confided to me: "I checked off every specialty." Clearly, bar prescreening helps.

Though some referral attorneys may be novices with great gaps in their appointment books, many are competent experienced lawyers who put their names on the referral lists both as a public service and to develop "new business." Sometimes it works, too. A client referred to me by the bar association ten years ago now owns a successful and still growing company. Referrals can play strange tricks. Once while handling the husband in a matrimonial case, I got a call from a lawyer I knew well. The bar association had referred the man's wife to him. To be completely ethical, he told her that her husband's attorney was his friend, upon which she promptly phoned the bar association for a second referral. The sec-

364

ond time, out of some 18,000 lawyers in New York City, she drew someone I knew even better.

Walk your fingers. A few communities have legal services directories, listing attorneys, their specialties training, sometimes even their fees. Check with your bar association to see if such a directory exists in your community. If it doesn't, public interest lawyer Mark Green suggests something that's easier said than accomplished: that consumers get together and publish one to fill the need.

The gazette. Since the ban has been lifted on lawyers' advertising, you may be able to find one that way. It's still a new idea and many lawyers are not ready for it. Some fear their clients might leave "an attorney who has to advertise for business." But when Tiffany's or Neiman-Marcus advertise, people understand the reason: This is a competitive world and they can't afford to stand still. My partner Paul and I joined the slowly growing ranks of lawyers who advertise because we think it's a good idea to let people know what legal services we deal in. If you like an advertisement, why not pay him an exploratory visit? Like Art Buchwald, I would run, not walk, from a law firm whose TV commercial showed a well-dressed man outside a prison saying that he'd be behind those grim gray walls right now if it hadn't been for his clever lawyers— ending the commercial with: "If you have committed a white-collar crime, or are thinking about committing a white-collar crime, call this toll-free number . . ."

People find lawyers in bizarre and mysterious ways, but sometimes the relationships work and, surprisingly, endure. I remember one client who appeared in my office when I was just starting out. Curious—in fact, close to stunned—I asked who'd recommended my name. "The elevator starter," he replied.

THE THIRD STEP:
JUDGING YOUR LAWYER

How do you decide that Family Lawyer A is a better choice to represent you than Lawyers B or C? The best way is to interview them. There may be a fee for this. Some lawyers charge for a preliminary get-acquainted consultation; others do not. If you don't like surprises, ask when you make the appointment.

If you're looking for a family lawyer, there's no better way to test how well your family will accept him than by bringing your spouse along and, if the match seems a good one, having your eldest child meet him. Statistically, they'll be the ones leaning on him most in the event of a death. It'll help if they like his style, too.

Note: I said interview "them." Even if each of your three finalists charge you $20 each for an introductory fifteen-minute visit, you'll still be way ahead if your careful screening links you to an attorney you trust and like well enough to stay with as long as you both shall live. So it won't be a total loss, bring a small problem with you for discussion. You may find that Lawyer A is great on desk-side manner, but not too quick with ideas. He stalls, seems unsure of himself. B may be good with ideas, but too brusque in manner. C may be just right. Is he dynamic? Good. But not too dynamic. If he is, he may be the kind of lawyer who is too busy talking to listen.

An even better way to go about your quest may be to invite the potential attorney to lunch. In a relaxed hour-long nonoffice situation, you'll learn far more about him, his philosophy, the kinds of cases he handles than in a quickie office visit. Possibly even more if he orders a cocktail or two. If your business relationship quickly becomes a friendship, so much the better. Whether at desk or at table, here are some of the things about him and his practice style that you should be feeding into your mental computer, through observation, direct questioning, and asking those who know him: the size of his firm, your sense of rapport, his credentials, experience, his availability, his litigiousness.

Small is beautiful. Of course, I'm prejudiced. Also self-interested. I write from the comfortable perspective of a small two-partner office, where each is his own boss and likes it. I submit that the fact that a firm has 176 lawyers does not guarantee you 176-times-better service than the solo practitioners.

There should, of course, be minimum standards. What kind of staffing does the office have? Is there a secretary or paralegal to field and screen phone calls so that conversations with your attorney—with the meter running—aren't indiscriminately distracted ("Now . . . where were we?") by phone calls and other interruptions; and so your lawyer isn't so overwhelmed by routine details and paperwork that he has too little time to effectively consider and deal with your problems? If it's a one-lawyer office, ask what, if any, coverage is offered when he's ill, or away on business or vacation. A firm with two or more partners provides this kind of coverage and generally broader expertise. In theory, the large firm offers the best coverage of all. But in practice, if the lawyer assigned to your affairs is off skiing at Aspen, about all his secretary will do is take a message. Unless your matter is truly an emergency (everybody's matter is pressing), most legal work can wait a week or more, and often does.

Very large firms may give superb legal service in their duplex skyscraper suites, but it may be impersonal and the small client can be lost in the paper shuffle. Big firms naturally tend to be more expensive, with hourly rates escalated by prestige location overhead. With all the records, filing, and indexing systems they need to keep track of their thousands of clients and tens of thousands of cases, it can cost them well over $100 just to open a "new client" file.

The fact that they are giants can on occasion be turned to advantage by small-office pygmies like myself. A year or so ago I enjoyed that opportunity when fate put me up against one such Manhattan mammoth, in a case in which my client was being sued for some $300,000 by a supplier whose contract he'd canceled because of late delivery. We felt that our defenses were strong, and the client and I decided we would fight with the very weapon that large firms often employ so effectively against small ones—bringing on all kinds of proceedings, motions, and applications calculated to generate a tremendous amount of legal work in reply. We suspected that the plaintiff (let's call him Dan Disgruntled) had chosen this prestigious Wall Street firm partly for its shock value, and that he was not so well-to-do as the firm's blue-chip clients normally are. We felt that when Disgruntled received his first bill for services rendered, he was the one who'd go into shock.

And so he did. We fired motions with the enthusiasm of a ten-year-old at tin-can target practice with his first air rifle. We had Disgruntled's attorneys in court five times in two months and so busy doing paperwork that they had to send out for lunch. Of course, I had to do a good bit of work, too, and ultimately my fee came to about $7,500. But we knew from the first moment they showed up in court—the young associate who'd researched and drafted the replies and the seasoned pinstriped partner to argue the case—that Disgruntled's legal bill was going to be easily three times my client's.

Sure enough. Shortly thereafter, my client's phone rang. "I've been thinking," said Dan Disgruntled. "All we're doing is making our lawyers rich. Why don't we get together and work out a settlement?" When the agreement had been reached—for a fraction of what he'd originally claimed—Dan told my client that he'd called after receiving a $22,000 bill for legal services rendered. "I figured," he said, "if things kept up like that, my legal fees would be more than my claim."

This is not to say that big firms don't do their job. They do for large corporations and the Rolls-Royce rich—people and companies involved in antitrust cases, massive mergers, and litigation so substantial that no matter how large the legal fee, it's hardly noticeable. Some corporate presidents do notice. Said one whimsically not long ago, "Our stock is selling at three times legal fees."

Super-firms can perform super-services. A partner may head a department of a half-dozen lawyers who will put aside everything else and work till midnight and beyond to meet an urgent deadline.

The research performed will be far beyond the scope of the small firm. Many big firms have computer terminals in their law libraries. When a salesman called on me, I thought how delightful it would be to feed in a half-dozen key words, pour a cup of coffee, and return to find citations and summaries of dozens of applicable cases awaiting me. But having priced the service—thousands of dollars a month—I had second thoughts. If I built costs like that into my fees—particularly for bread-and-butter legal work that doesn't require intensive research—my clients would depart from me quicker than a weight-watcher flees a banana split.

Some large firms make important contributions to their communities by doing a good deal of unpaid work, *pro bono publico* ("for the good of the public") lending young lawyers to poverty or environmental groups and causes. But any firm, big or little, makes mistakes, so perfection can't be expected even from the biggest.

In the *New York Law Journal*, the column "Aesop in the Courts" tells the tale of the big firm that sent a distinguished lawyer to aid a wealthy banker with an estate in rural Florida. The influential client had gotten into a furious argument with a neighbor over ownership of an egg that a colorful wild bird nesting on his land had laid on the adjoining property. With the help of two associates, the city lawyer carefully researched the law, delving deep into feudal precedents. After his presentation of the facts, the justice of the peace peremptorily dismissed the case.

"But your Honor," protested the Wall Street lawyer, "you haven't heard me out."

"Don't havta," said the justice. "You claim your client's peacock laid an egg on the defendant's property?"

"Yes, essentially that's my case."

"Well, like I said, case dismissed. Peacocks don't lay eggs. Peahens do."

Rapport: Personality's a plus. Do you feel comfortable with the attorney, or is he all business, unbending—an over-starched shirt? Does he (or she) seem to be someone to whom you can confide your most intimate feelings or problems? Does he seem intelligent, attentive, thorough? Does he sound as though he'll persistently pursue justice as far and long as necessary, not simply in pursuit of an ever larger fee? Do you think he'll do his best even on small matters, or does he seem interested only in "substantial" cases? Is he the kind of lawyer you'd like to represent you: tactful, good-humored, well-groomed?

Is there an unbridgeable age gap between you? There are many wise, understanding older lawyers—I hope to be one myself some day—but age does not automatically confer wisdom. And as one man in his late 20s said of a lawyer he went to for a divorce, "He didn't identify with my problems. He seemed to judge rather than represent me."

There are, of course, limits to what you can learn from an interview. As Judge Botein said, "One might think that the lawyer to hire is the one who, in conversation, strikes one as most inscrutable, slick, and sly. But as Dr. Johnson [remarked] . . . the moment you come from the bar you resume your usual behavior . . . a man will no more carry the artifice of the bar into the common intercourse of society, than a man who is paid for tumbling upon his hands will continue to tumble upon his hands, when he should walk on his feet."

The certificate on his wall. Ever hear of Dickinson? Or Arizona State? Well, those were the two law schools whose teams made it to the 1977 finals of the 28th Annual National Moot Court Competition. They outargued 27 other regional winners in the three-day finale judged by a panel of distinguished justices and attorneys.

So if the framed diploma on a lawyer's wall doesn't read Harvard Law, should you suddenly remember another appointment and beat a rapid retreat? The evidence seems to say, "Never judge a lawyer by his law school." The student who worked his cerebrum to the bone in a small school may be a lot better lawyer than the guy who loafed through Yale. When the big law firms are interviewing new graduates, a Harvard degree runs rings around one from Boston College or St. John's. But it's the man who makes the lawyer, not the law school.

369

A few exceptional attorneys—their ranks have thinned considerably by age—never even finished law school, but passed the bar after several years' experience as law clerks. The late Harry A. Gair, a trial lawyer who enjoyed an international reputation, never attended law school at all.

More important than educational background is whether or not an attorney keeps up. Continuing legal education, like continuing medical education for the M.D., is part of the life of every good attorney. One who thinks he knows everything and has nothing more to learn at seminars and updating courses will be defending you today with yesterday's tools and strategies.

Before you ever step into your prospective lawyer's office—or meet him for luncheon at Sardi's—you can check things like his education, his professional associations, his age, and the size of his office in the Martindale-Hubbell law directory (usually available at courthouses, bar associations, university and some public libraries; at $100 the set, not all libraries can afford it). Ads placed by lawyers (which don't look like ads but are, and quite expensive ones at that) appear throughout the directory, often listing specialties, biographical material, and sometimes even clients the firm represents.

Experience and expertise. What are the lawyer's areas of expertise, and do they coincide with your needs? How many years of experience—and how many matters—has he handled in these fields? A quick, young attorney with little actual experience but much enthusiasm can do a very good job, especially if he is in a firm with an experienced lawyer to whom he can turn for battlefield counsel. When my young associate first joined me, there wasn't much he had handled, but he could freely accept many kinds of cases in the knowledge that I would guide him through them.

Even an experienced attorney may be wrong for your particular job. Example: A woman who wanted a divorce asked a friend if he knew a good lawyer. "Sure," he said, "get Gabe Gogetter. He's a big politician. He knows every judge in the county on a first-name basis." Good old Gabe gave her short shrift in interview time, and came back with a very unsatisfactory settlement. Gogetter was a good politician, but his experience as a divorce lawyer could have been put in a walnut.

To help you determine background, a successful attorney friend suggests this scenario when, for example, you break a leg on the ski slope: "Your brother-in-law says, 'Go to Sidney Skillful—we

370

used him in a case and we loved him!' Good start. That's the kind of enthusiasm you want to hear about a prospective lawyer. But now in his office—politely, of course—cross-examine. Feel free to ask: 'How do I know you can do it? Have you handled similar cases?' If he's insulted, he's not for you. His answer should be responsive. It doesn't have to be: 'I have file drawers full of cases like this—and I've settled some of them for hundreds of thousands of dollars.' It's enough for you to have a feeling of confidence as you leave his office.''

Is he a generalist or a specialist? I'm a generalist and I have more than 1,000 law books of one kind or another on my office library shelves. Law libraries have millions. Law is too complex for any one attorney to know it all, or even to know where to look for it all. Ask your candidate for family lawyer if he ever refers a case to a specialist. "No" is the wrong answer.

As a G.P., I wouldn't think of handling a patent infringement case, or one involving serious questions of admiralty or international law. Of course, if my client requests help and can't afford a specialist's fees, I'll sometimes take on something esoteric, after making it perfectly clear that it's outside my circle of skills. A case involving a federal oil lease in New Mexico came into the office recently. Our client had taken a flyer on a land parcel, one that could be worthless but might make him rich. His card was picked in the lottery, but disqualified by the Bureau of Land Development for a technical defect. He didn't want to invest the large legal fee a Washington, D.C., specialist would demand for an appeal. I spoke to the Appeals section in Washington, learned where their decisions are published, spent some time exploring the law, and prepared what I feel was a good brief on my client's behalf. Only time will tell if it was good enough.

How busy is he? Does he appear harried? The lawyer who is always complaining about being too busy, who takes forever to return your phone calls, who is always late to meetings could be an unfortunate choice. I've seen too many clients in hot water to the hips because their attorneys—even very good ones—were too busy to give their cases the needed time. The lawyer who is always up to his ears in work may be unable to hear what you have to say.

However, as attorney Jack Horsley points out, the fact that an attorney is wall-to-wall in clients and keeps three secretaries hopping doesn't necessarily mean you've entered an office where the lawyer will be too busy to solve your problem. When, during the

371

courtroom recess, Jack asked the late Suel Arnold, a distinguished fellow trial lawyer, what he reckoned was his most important case, Arnold promptly replied, "Why, the one I'm trying now. As far as I'm concerned, it's the only one I have!"

There are incompetent lawyers, just as there are "bad apples," or drug-addicted doctors, or surgeons who'd rather cut than treat. I recently took the case of a man who'd lost his eye in an auto accident. In six years, his too busy lawyer hadn't even gotten the case on the calendar, when, in fact, it should have been on within two years and tried and disposed of in four.

How much time does he spend in court? If you need a trial lawyer, the more the better. But if every time you call a generalist his secretary tells you he's in court, his bite may be worse than his bark. It shouldn't be. In general, his goal should be the same as yours—to stay out of court whenever possible. He should know when to fight and when to compromise, and choose the course that's best for the client.

If you're involved in major litigation, you'll need an experienced trial lawyer, and often your family lawyer will refer you to one— sometimes called a lawyer's lawyer. In England, where the legal system is rigidly compartmentalized, the solicitor does the office work (and I suppose solicits the clients) and the barrister appears before the bar for trial.

Sometimes with all the well-meaning advice and advisors in the world, finding the lawyer who's just right for you is a matter of luck. When all else fails, you may find yourself doing what a magazine editor named Francis X. Wamsley did when he moved to New Jersey from North Carolina. Wamsley needed an attorney for his new house closing, but knew no one he could ask for a recommendation. For want of a better method, he fingered patiently down the "Lawyers" columns of the Bergen County Yellow Pages, starting with Abbitt and stopping with a sudden, surprised smile at Burke. Wamsley immediately phoned Burke's office in Hackensack for an appointment, explaining later: "Hell, I guess one lawyer's about as good as another. And Francis X. Burke and I will at least start with something in common—both our mothers were crazy about Francis X. Bushman, the silent screen matinee idol."

Said the lawyer later to client Wamsley: "Hallelujah—forty years I've been stuck with this name, and it finally paid off!"

CHAPTER 19

Getting the Most Lawyer for Your Money

One of poor henpecked Socrates' most quoted lines is this piece of advice: "By all means marry. If you get a good wife, you will become very happy; if you get a bad one, you will become a philosopher." An attorney-client relationship is much like a marriage. Your attorney should be friend, confidant, and counselor, and if the marriage is to be a happy one, each of you has responsibilities.

THE FIRST STEP:
BUILDING A SUCCESSFUL WORKING RELATIONSHIP WITH YOUR ATTORNEY

Here are some pointers that will help make the relationship effective for you, successful for your lawyer—some do's and don'ts that, if ignored, will force you both to become philosophers.

Don't withhold information. Level with your lawyer. Don't hold back a fact you think might be damaging to your case. It will be damaged far more if the opposing attorney discovers and uses the information first. This is true in civil as well as criminal matters. I remember a fellow lawyer at Legal Aid who made an impassioned plea to the judge for leniency for his client on the grounds that this was his first offense. The assistant D.A. cut him off brusquely with, "Your Honor, this man's record shows fourteen different arrests and six convictions."

In civil cases, I've had holes punched in my parachute by a client's secrecy more than once. So search your memory carefully. Tell your attorney everything. Let him judge the relevance of information. If he doesn't have it, he can't build a winning case for your side.

The lawyer-client relationship is one of four areas of legally privileged communication—with doctor-patient, clergy-congregant, husband-wife—so that no secret you confide to your attorney can ever be used against you. Not even a court can force him to reveal it, and the confidentiality continues permanently, even after you no longer retain him, and extends to his employees as well.

One exception: information you may give your lawyer about a crime you *intend* to commit. If a client admits to me that he has already held up a bank, I can say nothing. If he says, "I'll have your $5,000 fee tomorrow after I hold up the Second National," I must report the intended crime or be guilty as an accessory.

But don't overload your attorney with trivia. You can save his time and—at $50 to $100 an hour—your money if in a case involving heavy documentation you sift the materials carefully yourself. On a commercial matter involving breach of contract, a client recently greeted me with a suitcase full of documents, memos, and correspondence. "Here," he said, "go through this and take what you need." I spent a half-day on the stack at $75 an hour—on a job one of his assistants could have done at a fraction of the cost. Organize papers for your attorney, separating them into three piles: important, possibly important, and unimportant ("Maybe there'll be something in this pile you'll need, but I doubt it").

There are, of course, times when disorganization can be a blessing. Some years ago, when my brother-in-law Alan was a traveling salesman, he kept his receipts in a shoebox. Called down to the I.R.S. to justify his deductions, he dumped his box upside down on the agent's desk, and simply said, "Here's my proof." Aghast, the busy agent stuffed the receipts back in the box, and said, "All right, I'll take your word for it."

Don't nag, please! At the top of every lawyer's Hate Parade is the noodge—the nagging client who phones three or four times a day with a bright idea: new evidence, a new justification, a news item he saw in the paper that's sure to win his case. Matrimonials often phone breathlessly at 11 or 12 o'clock at night with: "Do you know what he just did? He locked me out of the bathroom, that's what he did!" A distant relative got too close for comfort when he became a client. He was always suing someone or being sued in return, and seemed to think my office hours were from 8 P.M. to midnight. When my teenage daughter Alison demanded a phone of her own, saying *her* friends couldn't get through because the line was always busy, I figured things had gone far enough and invited him to find a new counsel.

Believe me, no lawyer's office is so busy that he cheerfully turns away a client, but Nellie Nagg is always the first to go. My prize

374

Nellie was a woman whose neighbor, having dropped in for a cup of coffee, got into a heated argument with her, picked up a pewter coffeepot, and hit her with it. Nellie had a good case of assault and battery, and her black eye would have won any jury's sympathy. But she called several times a day. If she couldn't get my partner, she asked for me. If neither of us was available, she harangued our secretary. Finally, after many warnings, we asked her to get another lawyer. I wasn't sure I could properly represent her. I was beginning to sympathize with the defendant.

But expect to be informed. If he's to have time to work on your case, your attorney can't be expected to give you a blow-by-blow account of everything he's doing on your behalf, but you are entitled to a periodic summation of the blows he's struck, and the status of your matter. Copies of documents, too, if you request them. You should feel free to call from time to time to inquire about such progress. (A call from a client does occasionally jog me into doing something a bit sooner than I'd planned.) And you should be able to reach your lawyer in *emergencies* on weekends or evenings, but only on matters that can't wait for Monday or dawn. I'm willing to reassure a worried client now and then, but in most cases I can't do much more than say, "Take two aspirin and call me in the morning."

Be punctual. And if you change your mind and decide not to go to law, don't be embarrassed to phone and tell the lawyer's secretary you're not coming. Lawyers often run on tight schedules. We'd rather be warned than surprised. Should he be delayed in court, your lawyer owes you the same courtesy. This is not to say that he won't keep you waiting in his outer office if an urgent call comes in. But very often the wait is because someone earlier in the schedule was twenty minutes late—pushing everyone else back like a house of calling cards.

Be prepared. This is as important for legal clients as for boy scouts, because a case is only as strong as the facts it's built on. I had a matrimonial client in recently who hemmed, hawed, and maybe'd about his marriage date, a crucial point in a divorce proceeding. When a client does his homework at home, I can often save him an hour or more of expensive interview time. Sit down at home for a couple of hours, outline the facts, and think about what sort of information might help your attorney. In a personal injury case he'll want to know exact location—go back and measure it if possible—"the broken sidewalk on which I fractured my ankle is

375

in front of Brown's Delicatessen, on First Street, two feet west of the fire hydrant, as per attached snapshots." Give him the time of the accident, weather conditions if relevant, names, addresses, and phone numbers of all witnesses. That sort of thing.

I think you'll find if you furnish your lawyer with the information on the checklist that follows, he'll welcome you as the watchman welcomes the dawn—and you'll save his time and your bank balance.

CHECK LIST

1. Name, address, age and other pertinent information of all parties:
   a. Your name and address
   b. Your spouse
   c. The other parties
   d. Witnesses

2. Telephone numbers (home and office of all parties).

3. Details and facts relating to the matter:

   If accident:

   a. date and time
   b. location
   c. description—personal injuries
                     property damage
   d. physicians—hospitals—ambulance
   e. auto registration
   f. expenses incurred—medical, repairs, wages
   g. employment (time lost)
   h. police officers
   i. insurance company

   If matrimonial matter:

   a. maiden name
   b. date of marriage
   c. place of marriage
   d. name and birth date of children
   e. how long at present residence

f. date and place of birth
g. cause of marital breakup (dates and place of events complained of)

If house closing:

a. address of house (description if possible)
b. old deed
c. mortgage information
d. purchase price
e. terms
f. all personal property included in sale
g. closing date

For will or estate plan:

a. name and address of all relatives who would be entitled to inherit if no will existed.
b. complete list of all assets, including bank accounts, stocks, bonds, real estate, personal effects, household furnishings, mortgages, patents, etc.
c. in whose name assets are listed
d. life insurance
e. business interests
f. pension, profit sharing and death benefits
g. how you want estate distributed
h. when do you want minors to receive their inheritance
i. name and address of executor and guardian for infant children

Don't be a know-it-all. If you knew it all, you wouldn't need a lawyer. Lawyers appreciate knowledgeable clients. The Medical Mystique has crumbled and today patients are asking many more questions of their doctors, even politely questioning their decisions. So it is with the Legal Mystique. Clients are equally entitled to question and challenge lawyers, rather than just accept our edicts as passively as a house accepts a coat of paint.

So read the appropriate chapters in this book, leaf through the half-dozen handbooks on law for the layman you'll find in your local library. But let your lawyer make the ultimate legal decisions on how he will approach the matter. You can recommend a course of action, but if you insist and he disagrees, either give him your vote of confidence or seek another opinion.

I've had considerable help from clients over the years. About ten years ago, I was assigned to defend a man accused of the murder of a drug peddler and of possession of cocaine. He proved to be an excellent jailhouse lawyer, who spent the considerable amount of time on his hands in the house-of-detention library poring over law books. The memoranda and case citations he sent saved me a great deal of time, and some of it was useful in his defense. Unfortunately, the government elected not to try him on the murder charge—which I felt confident I could beat—and went after him on "possession," where it had an unbeatable case. Sharp as my client was, he had foolishly postponed leaving town until he could pick up his favorite suede jacket at the dry cleaners, where he was arrested with two pounds of cocaine in his shopping bag.

Don't be counterproductive. When crucial decisions must be made ("Should we settle for $25,000 or hold out for fifty?") they should be made together. Listen carefully to your lawyer's advice, or you're wasting your money. But ultimately it's for him to recommend, for you to decide. If you're still vaguely discontented and important money is at stake, invest in another lawyer's opinion. First, of course, inform your attorney of your intention. A good lawyer not only will raise no objection, but will cordially turn over the necessary documents and write an explanatory forwarding letter to your consultant.

We represented the wife in a divorce case recently in which the husband stubbornly refused to listen to his lawyer, who had recommended a settlement for $75 a week alimony to be reduced when the wife got on her feet. He furiously dissented, firing off angry counterproductive letters to her and to me, forcing the matter to court and costing him far more in legal fees and alimony than if he'd kept his pen in his pocket.

Don't talk to the other side. It's too easy to let a strategic cat out of the bag—or to be too generous in a settlement. Your lawyer doesn't have to be Mr. Nice. Let him argue over the numbers.

Don't get delusions of future grandeur. When someone has been injured in an accident and life's little pleasures have been clouded for weeks or months by pain and inconvenience, it's only human to see the lawsuit as a well-deserved sterling silver lining. "Gee," a client will say, eagerly leaning forward after gingerly putting aside her cane, "I read in the paper yesterday about that woman who

378

hurt her leg tripping on a hole in the carpet at the Americana Hotel. She got $1.2 million dollars. Will I get that much?"

Not likely. It all depends—on so many factors that when I'm asked that inevitable "how-much-will-I-get?" question, I can only shrug and say, "Anywhere from zero dollars to . . ." and I name a possible outside figure. No two people suffer the same pain, or heal the same way, though their injuries may be similar. And no two juries will award the same verdict. If a prima ballerina's broken ankle heals badly, it may well be "worth" two million dollars. A typist will recover far less.

Here's where you must rely on your lawyer's experience and sense of timing. He knows—very roughly—what value an insurance company will place on your slip-and-fall case. He'll neither advise you to settle for too little (after all, the size of his contingent fee depends upon the amount recovered) nor encourage you to demand an unrealistic sum that will force the case to trial. He knows the economic and emotional cost of a two- or three-week court battle and may recommend accepting a settlement for slightly less than he thinks he'll be able to win by going to trial.

The weaker your case, the more likely it is that he'll suggest settling. I have an auto accident case pending now where the other side has made a $150,000 offer, but my client refuses to settle. Where questions of liability exist, you never know which way the jury will go, and there is always the possibility that we'll lose and come up empty-handed. In one of my first big cases, my client sued a major broadcasting network for $250,000 for a show idea that she alleged they had pirated. They offered nothing prior to trial, but while the jury was deliberating, my adversary approached me in the corridor: "I just got off the phone with my client. I've been authorized to offer $50,000 in settlement." I was delighted, and saw myself cheerily marching into my bank to deposit a $16,667 contingency fee. But alas, my client wanted all or nothing, and an hour later, when the jury emerged, nothing was what each of us got.

Don't ask your lawyer to break the law. VISITOR: Is there a criminal lawyer in this town? RESIDENT: We think so, but we haven't been able to prove it yet.

I've been fortunate. I've never had a client ask me to do anything worse than notarize a document already signed by someone who's not there. I've been asked to do that dozens of times, but I never have—it's a crime and the penalty can be disbarment. The list of things for which a lawyer can lose his license is long enough

379

to make me nervous just thinking about it. I know a securities lawyer who was disbarred for knowingly including false information in a stock offering, and the whole country knows a half-dozen, including a former president of the United States and his attorney-general, whose Waterloo was Watergate.

THE SECOND STEP:
WHEN THE RELATIONSHIP BREAKS DOWN

Many lawyer-client relationships last a lifetime. Shared challenges and weathered crises often mellow such associations, changing them to friendships. Some of my best clients are friends. If, however, you find that you and your lawyer enjoy about as much rapport as moonshiners and "revenooers," if your attorney no longer meets your changing needs, it may be time to change your attorney.

You can feel free to discharge an attorney at any time, even while your case is in progress. Don't make a move hastily, but don't hang on when you are unhappy either. Any records or files on your case belong to *you* and you should ask for them. Exception: You owe the attorney money. In that case, he, like a mechanic or tradesman, has a lien on your papers until you pay the outstanding fees. If, on the other hand, you paid in advance for more hours than have been put in, you may well be entitled to a prorated refund.

If your case is being handled on a contingency fee, your new lawyer will have to come to an agreement with your old representative on the future division of the spoils, if any. If they can't agree, the court will decide for them, based on the amount of work each has performed.

THE THIRD STEP:
FILING A GRIEVANCE

Maybe you are discharging your attorney for more than just a clash of personalities or a difference of opinion. Perhaps you feel he's guilty of unethical conduct or of not properly representing you. Maybe he has misappropriated funds in his care, or missed a key court appearance, causing your case to be dismissed. Your next move may have a major impact on your attorney's future. It

380

may be that his error was inadvertent, or that there were mitigating circumstances.

Your first step then should be to call and ask for an appointment to discuss the problem. Try to settle privately. He should be anxious to do so; no attorney wants to face an official grievance, if he knows he's wrong. If you can't reach him by phone, write. If he still doesn't respond, send him a letter warning that your next move will be to the bar association. If he continues to ignore you, it's time to write or visit the bar's grievance committee, spelling out your complaint in detail. You may be asked to sign an affidavit attesting to the facts.

The bar association's response generally depends upon the extent of the misconduct, whether or not you've shown the attorney to be in violation of the professional code of responsibility, and the zealousness of the local bar in weeding out "rotten apples."

Steps that may be taken by the state court upon recommendation of the bar association, if an investigation establishes the justice of your cause, range in increasing severity from censure to temporary suspension to outright disbarment. Disbarment—which almost always spells "The End" to a legal career—may be automatic if the attorney is convicted of a felony. It's a harsh penalty, but it fits the crime. We are sworn in as attorneys, we become officers of the court. Like Pompeia (you remember Caesar's wife), our conduct must be above reproach.

THE FOURTH STEP:
THE CHARGE IS MALPRACTICE

Bringing an attorney up on charges before the bar may bring you satisfaction, but it will not necessarily bring a recovery of damages. Sometimes it may; as part of disciplinary proceedings, the lawyer may agree to make restitution. But ordinarily you'll have to sue the attorney because of what is often labeled malpractice (a word that makes us all tremble) but actually involves negligence, malfeasance, or breach of contract.

You can't make that accusation just because you've lost your lawsuit. In every case, somebody wins and somebody loses. To prove malpractice, you must show that: (1) the attorney acted negligently by not adhering to accepted "standards of care"—that is, he did not "exhibit such skill, prudence, and diligence as well-informed lawyers of ordinary skill and capacity commonly possess and exercise''; and, (2) if your legal matter had been properly handled, you would have won the case.

The most common reason for malpractice suits is neglecting to meet a statutory time limitation—failure to start an action or answer a complaint in time, with the result that the client forfeits his rights and his case. Some other reasons include incorrectly searched titles or failure to record mortgages leading to loss of property; the giving of erroneous advice causing financial loss; and accepting a case he was unqualified to handle and should have referred to a specialist.

The number of malpractice suits against lawyers has increased sharply in recent years—doubling between 1972 and 1975—and the rise is expected to continue.

Just as it is often difficult to find a doctor to testify against another doctor, it may be difficult to find an attorney willing to sue a colleague. Certainly, none will take the case unless convinced it's a strong one. But lawyers can be found for meritorious cases, often on a contingency fee basis. Because lawyers don't relish open trials that might damage their reputations, better than 95 percent of malpractice suits are settled out of court. Some, however, win big headlines—like Doris Day's thumping courtroom victory over her longtime attorney, for improper legal advice on tax shelter investments over a fifteen-year period: a $26 million verdict.

It was, you might say, quite a day for Doris!

CHAPTER 20

Paying the Legal Freight

Twenty-one hundred years ago, the Cincian law of Rome forbade advocates from charging any fee. But times—and rent and utility bills—have changed. Legal fees today are seldom the size of the whopping $400,000 charged by Paul, Weiss, Rifkind, Wharton, & Garrison to represent Jackie Kennedy Onassis in a countersuit against a photographer she charged with invasion of privacy.* But they are high enough to discourage many people in middle-income brackets from seeking legal services, occasionally even those in Park Avenue penthouse brackets. Runaway financier-embezzler Robert Vesco, asked why he had made a donation of $200,000 to The Committee to Reelect the President (a chap named Nixon), reportedly shrugged and replied: "It was cheaper than paying lawyers."

Cost may be a factor in which attorney you select, but it should not be the major factor in whether or not you use an attorney. In a complicated legal situation you can't handle on your own, the most expensive move you can make may be *not* to hire a lawyer. If you can't afford the legal fees typically charged in your area, and studies indicate that only 10 percent of Americans can comfortably afford such fees, there are ways of obtaining assistance either at reduced fees or, if your income is very low, at no cost at all.

The problem, judging from this old English ballad of unknown authorship, is not a new one:

> A lawyer, quite famous for making a bill
> And who in good living delighted,

---

*Jackie's husband Aristotle Onassis, though a multimillionaire, was outraged by the fee and refused to pay it. When the law firm sued for payment, he settled for roughly half: $225,000.

To dinner one day with hearty good will
　　Was by a rich client invited.
But he charged six and eightpence for going to dine,
　　Which the client he paid, tho' no ninny,
And in turn charged the lawyer, for dinner and wine,
　　One a crown, and the other a guinea.
The lawyer he paid it and took a receipt,
　　While the client stared at him in wonder.
With the produce he gave a magnificent treat,
　　But the lawyer soon made him knock under.
That his client sold wine, information he laid,
　　Without license; and in spite of his storming,
The client a good thumping penalty paid,
　　And the lawyer got half for informing
But gossips, you know, have a saying in store,
　　He who matches a lawyer has only one more.

You say you don't want that sort of thing to happen to you?
Then here are some ways to get your hand on the cost control lever
and keep it there.

Don't hesitate to ask about fees. You are as entitled to know in
advance the approximate cost of legal services as I am to know a
surgeon's fee before he cuts me. Introduce unflinchingly the issue
of costs and you'll find it's not really all that sensitive. You'll find
that most lawyers share your desire to raise it, resolve it, and get
down to the grit of your legal problem. If by the end of a first meeting a client hasn't asked the money question, I assume embarrassment is running rampant, and quickly clear the air by broaching the
subject myself. Sometimes a client will want to know my fee even
before discussing a matter. If it sounds outrageous, his motor's
running for a fast getaway.

There's absolutely nothing wrong with that, other than the fact
that the client often oversimplifies the problem. A husband will tell
me, "It's going to be an easy divorce to handle. We've got the settlement all worked out." I quote a fee for an uncontested divorce.
But it's quickly clear after I talk to the wife's attorney that the couple has had only the most general of discussions. So many rough
spots remain to be smoothed that extensive negotiations or a court
fight lie ahead, and the fee quoted is no longer applicable.

Only a few years ago, in many parts of the country, you could
have gone to a dozen law offices to get a price on a house closing,

and it wouldn't have varied a nickel's worth. That, in fact, is exactly what a man named Lewis Goldfarb discovered in Fairfax County, Virginia, a few years back, and his experience made U.S. legal history. It resulted in his bringing an antitrust suit that eventually, in 1976, reached the U.S. Supreme Court and resulted in minimum fee schedules, until then widely used and published by local bar associations, being declared illegal. With market restraints loosened, I suspect that fees now vary at least a little everywhere, that some attorneys have reduced their fees markedly, and that the consumer who shops around may get something of a cost break as a result.

Since the abolition of community-wide minimum fee schedules, some firms have published their own. You might ask if the attorney you're considering has done the same.

With minimum fee schedules gone the way of the powdered wig, attorneys are freer to decide what they—and a particular service—are worth. Many variables are fed into that decision: the part of the country you live in, the nature and extent of services to be rendered, the complexities of your case, the novelty of the legal questions, the amount of time needed, and the sum of money or value of property involved. Factored in, too, are the importance and general significance of the case (landmark law is bound to cost more), the experience, skill, and reputation of the attorney (you can't expect to command the attention of a senior partner in a major firm for much less than $200 an hour, and I wouldn't be surprised if courtroom superstars like Melvin Belli or F. Lee Bailey charge a good deal more per hour than the average man earns in a week). Good results count for something, and so does the client's ability to pay—with the rich sometimes subsidizing those less amply endowed.

There are basically four methods of paying for legal services: the flat fee, the hourly fee, the contingency fee, and a combination of them all.

The flat fee. "How much will an uncomplicated, uncontested divorce cost?" you ask. "I charge a flat fee of $600 for that," the attorney replies. Why a flat fee? Because he's handled enough divorces to know about how long one will take and thus how much he must charge. Most attorneys charge flat fees for routine services: a will, a real estate closing (often scaled to the value of the property), formation of a corporation, or a one-time court appearance, the amount to be paid partially (or entirely) in advance.

A very busy specialist may decide that he's worth more than others in his field. I know a matrimonial lawyer with a Rolls-Royce clientele who won't even book an appointment unless a potential client agrees to pay his $500 nonrefundable retainer in advance. Once he has listened to one spouse's side of the case, he is then ethically barred from representing the other. If spouse no. 1 decides not to retain him, he is effectively locked out of the case. By getting his fee in advance, he is assured of some compensation.

What to charge is a particularly knotty question for the newly admitted attorney. My partner Paul tells me that while in law school he asked his real estate professor how to set a fee for a house closing. The response goes far to explain why graduates emerge with question marks in their eyes. "You're not," said the prof, "supposed to learn that in law school."

The hourly fee. In many law offices, the meter is always ticking. In some, the charge to the client goes up at rates from $4 to $25 every six minutes. In others, fifteen-minute units are used. In some ultramodern offices, the phone may even be tied to a timing device and a computer will "time in" the moment the lawyer picks up a client's call. Charges are then automatically printed out on the client's statement at month's end. But most firms are still limping happily along on the old charge slip system. The attorney notes the length of conversation, client's name, and date and drops the slip into a charge basket on his desk.

You can't automatically assume that a young lawyer charging a low hourly rate will save you money. An experienced attorney may charge more per hour but, knowing the ropes, spend less time—your time—than the younger man. If an experienced lawyer agrees to charge you $30 an hour, on the face of it you have a good deal. I find it hard to believe that—in New York anyway—he can make a living at that rate. Deduct personal and administrative chore time from his 40-hour week and assume that it isn't possible to charge for more than 75 percent of his time (I find I can't bill for more than 50 percent). Factor in the reality that his overhead eats up roughly half his income—unless he works out of his garage and his wife does his typing—and it's possible to conclude that he is not going to make it unless he is just a trifle reckless in reckoning your time charges.

The contingency fee. In what may be the most useful legal invention since the gavel, attorneys often accept certain kinds of cases—most often personal injury, medical malpractice, product liability, and collection matters—on a contingency fee basis. In effect, they're willing to gamble. They'll work with no guarantee and nothing "up front" on time-consuming and costly litigation that few people could otherwise afford. For your part, you must agree that if the case is won, they share in the recovery on a prearranged sliding scale percentage—anywhere from 20 to 50 percent, depending on custom or law in the state and the size of the verdict or settlement. Generally, the higher the award, the lower the percentage. If you lose, your lawyer gets nothing. In a weak case he may insist that you guarantee him a small fee, or, at least, reimbursement of his court costs and out-of-pocket expenses.

The contingency arrangement, though extremely controversial because of the whopping fees earned by some lawyers, serves a useful purpose. It provides a mechanism for someone with poor financial resources and a good case to obtain justice. Some states regulate the contingency fee attorneys may charge. New York permits 50 percent of the first $1,000, 40 percent of the next $2,000, 35 percent of the next $22,000, and 25 percent of the excess—or an optional one-third of the total recovery. In a case involving a minor, an incompetent, or wrongful death, the court often rules on the percentage, rarely OKing more than one-third.

The combination. The importance of the matter and the skill of the attorney sometimes necessitate combining several methods to arrive at a fee. An apocryphal story illustrates it, about a businessman who asks his attorney's advice on whether to invest in a particular venture. Next week, he receives a bill for $5,000. Outraged, the client phones his attorney, and protests. "You asked my advice," he is told. "You made a substantial investment and will earn a large profit. $5,000 is what my advice is worth." The following week, the businessman meets his attorney in the street. "Nice day, isn't it?" he greets him. Hurriedly he adds: "This time I'm telling—not asking."

A lawyer who through his experience and ingenuity obtains a swift and satisfactory result may be entitled to more than his normal hourly rate. Assume that he recovers $250,000 by attaching some valuable paintings that were about to be shipped precipitately out of the country by an evasive debtor. He spends but ten hours on the project. Since his hourly rate is $100, should he bill the client $1,000? Most lawyers would multiply that by 10 or even 20 in a case like this. Their skill produced a quick satisfactory result, avoiding prolonged litigation that might have cost the client substantially more than the $10,000 or even $20,000 billed.

In such circumstances, few clients would argue—not even the late railroad tycoon E. H. Harriman, who once cabled lawyer John G. Johnson detailing every point of a proposed merger of several railroads and asking if he could proceed without being prosecuted under antitrust laws. Johnson cabled back a reply in four words: MERGER POSSIBLE, CONVICTION CERTAIN. He reportedly billed Harriman $25,000 per word for his expert advice.

Disbursements. Attorneys, not surprisingly, bill their clients for long-distance phone calls and travel, whether it's a flight to Paris to take a witness' deposition (a situation which, alas, arises infrequently in my office) or auto mileage for the trip to court. Clerical costs—photocopies, services of process, filing and recording documents, and even postage—may be included. It's our practice to bill and identify each item.

Ask for an estimate. "A ballpark figure" is what clients sometimes euphemistically term it, and on most matters an attorney should be able to estimate "at least — but not more than — hours at $— per hour." It's almost impossible to do this when litigation is involved. I can't predict how many mornings I'll have to sit in court waiting for our case to come up. Nor can I be sure how long the trial will last. But I can, at least, give a broad range, and a cost per day.

I'm currently handling the sale of a small business that is closing next week. I told the client a few months ago that the cost would be from $500 to $750. Turns out it's going to be relatively easy, and the client is going to be delighted with my bill: $500. When an attorney sets a fee, ask him whether the fee will be reduced accordingly if the work turns out to take less time than expected. If you ask, it may be. If you don't, no one else is likely to bring up the idea.

Fee bargaining. Every attorney would like the prospect who comes for an interview to sign up as a client, but there's nothing wrong with shopping around. Example: A patriarch died, and his children needed a lawyer to supervise the administration of his estate. The eldest son called an attorney he'd dealt with in the past and got a quotation: $100 an hour for work performed by a senior partner, $65 an hour for an associate's time, $13 an hour for a paralegal up to a maximum of $7,500. A son-in-law called a lawyer friend and was given a price of $3,000. Delighted, he tentatively accepted, but pulled out in annoyance when the lawyer called the following day to say that after sleeping on it, he realized there would be more time involved and he wanted $4,000. A daughter called a friend who said he would charge an hourly rate of $75 in his office, $100 when he stepped out of it. He estimated a possible time requirement of 100 hours—with a possible $7,500 charge. Another relative, a CPA, phoned a lawyer acquaintance who said he would charge a flat $3,500, provided the accountant did the tax returns and other financial paperwork. That offer was chosen to everyone's satisfaction—except that of one daughter who said wryly, "I'm glad we're getting a good price, but we'll be hearing from Charlie for the next five years about all the free work he did for us."

Put it in writing. No matter what the fee arrangement or method of payment, it should be in writing. (I don't *always* get around to doing this—particularly with longtime clients—but it *is* a good idea.) It should be a very simple agreement, spelling out what services will be performed, and when and how you'll pay for them. If there is a payment plan or a way of charging the fee to a credit card, that should be duly noted. Both client and attorney should sign the document, with a copy for each.

Request a score card. If an hourly rate is agreed upon, ask if you can get an accounting once a month, so that you'll always know where you stand and won't unexpectedly be hit by a blockbuster of a bill. I believe that every bill should be itemized. At one time the mammoth firms were able to get away with billing simply: "For legal services rendered in 1977 . . . $225,000." Today, even blue-chip clients want bills carefully itemized, and so should you.

The growing prepaid option. The number of Americans with prepaid legal coverage isn't growing quite so fast as the number of homes with cable TV or kitchens with microwave ovens, but it is sharply on the rise. And with young lawyers streaming out of our law schools in unprecedented numbers, looking for an office wall— any office—on which to hang their diplomas, the two trends are sure to intersect to the advantage of both.

Prepaid legal plans operate as either open groups (anyone can join by paying the premium) or closed groups (only members of a particular union, club, or area may join), and as open panels (you can choose any lawyer) or closed panels (your choice is limited to one law firm, a group of cooperating firms, or, conceivably, an entire bar association). A plan open to any member of the IBM Westchester Employees Federal Credit Union is probably representative. Any of the union's 18,000 members may agree to have $10 deducted monthly from their paychecks—as, surprisingly, only

500 have done. That premium entitles each participant to four 30-minute conferences, five hours of non-court work, and 15 hours of litigation work, with additional time, if needed, billed at agreed-upon rates. Use all your allotted time and you've got yourself quite a bargain—legal services at something like $6 an hour. Of course, among the items this particular plan won't pay for—you may already have guessed this—are lawsuits against the plan's godfather: IBM. This, then, is a closed group plan, and with legal services provided by a single Westchester law firm (which has, however, a corresponding relationship with several law firms in Connecticut and New Jersey to provide coverage where many plan members live), it is a closed panel plan as well.

If such plans continue to grow and proliferate, it's more than possible that some kind of national confederation of prepaid legal plans—a kind of Blue Shield for lawyers, or Blue Gavel—will eventually take shape. It might feature reciprocal privileges in other states, so that not only would you use your Blue Shield card to pay doctor bills after an accident while vacationing in California, but your Blue Gavel card to retain a lawyer to defend you on the reckless driving charge.

FINDING HELP WHEN YOU CAN'T AFFORD TO PAY

The goal of legal assistance for all who need it—not just for all who can afford it—is still only a light at the end of the tunnel. But at least the tunnel shows no sign of collapsing; it still offers safe passage for the poor and for some in the middle of the great American financial sandwich who are unable to pay full legal fees. Here are some of the possibilities:

Self-help law. That, of course, is what this book is all about, and with it—or other single-subject be-your-own-lawyer texts on wills and probate, divorce, bankruptcy, etc.—you can handle many legal problems on your own. Just don't get in over your head. Then there are services like "Divorce Yourself," offering follow-the-numbers divorce, wills and bankruptcy kits specifically tailored to the requirements of some states or even counties.

Here come the legal clinics. Still relatively rare, these inexpensive, accessible (often shopping center storefront) law firms can be expected to spread rapidly now that the barriers to lawyer advertising have come tumbling down. Most are privately run by groups of young, often recently graduated attorneys, but a few are sponsored experimentally by local bar associations. Legal clinics ordinarily emphasize uncomplicated legal services, post their low-low fee schedules conspicuously, and keep them low by relying on paralegals and clerks to do routine work. Their goal is to achieve high volume with few attorneys. That, legal clinic theoreticians fondly anticipate, will allow fees to remain low while the attorneys' salaries rise to approach those of lawyers in private practice.

A typical center might be sandwiched between a supermarket and a luncheonette, open evenings and Saturdays. The new client might get a free or low-cost screening consultation with a paralegal or lay counselor, with the case then assigned to the appropriate attorney, either a full-timer or a part-time consultant-specialist. The paperwork on the matter might be handled by the same screening counselor, using standardized forms, checklists, and manuals, and with the final product being reviewed by the attorney. Admittedly, the atmosphere would be assembly-line, without the unhurried personal service available from traditional law firms in the community. But the fees charged might be one-third to one-half the usual amounts—and that should make a lot of clients happy. Many private practitioners are starting to worry about the competition, but these things have a way of working themselves out. Lawyers who can't lick 'em may well join 'em—or open legal clinics of their own.

Then there's good old Legal Aid. My Uncle Sam used to tell the story of a ride he took in his office building elevator my first year out of Brooklyn Law School. As he entered the lift, returning from lunch, the operator greeted him with a warm, "Good afternoon, Mr. Kantrowitz." A Western Union messenger beside him turned to my uncle. "Excuse me," he asked, "are you by any chance related to the eminent attorney Walter Kantrowitz?" My uncle's chest swelled. "Why, yes, I am," he said. "Why do you ask?" "Because," said the messenger proudly, "he's *my* lawyer!"

People like that messenger on modest incomes can find out with a phone call if they're eligible for free legal aid from the century-old Legal Aid Society, which is not only a blessing for clients but for young lawyers as well. I worked for New York City's pioneering unit, which is the second largest "law firm" in the United States, smaller only than the Federal Department of Justice—in my first real job as a lawyer. I interviewed and advised more than 2,000 clients (some of whom, their fortunes improving, followed me into private practice), was in court almost every morning battling avaricious slumlords and hard-eyed collection agencies, and tried hundreds of cases.

Legal Aid offices are found in most metropolitan areas in the United States, sometimes with slightly different names. Their civil sections handle such matters as landlord-tenant disputes, consumer problems, adoptions, neighbor-neighbor warfare, and divorces. Demand sometimes exceeds lawyer supply, however, and clients often have to queue up. I've heard of at least one center where divorce clients have to wait a year for an appointment.

The problem is always budgetary. Money comes from government sources and donations, and there's never quite enough to go around. Clients can be generous, though. I remember an aging ex-concert violinist I helped with a half-dozen problems over the years. When I went into private practice, she became a client (with my rent only $40 a month, I didn't have to charge her very much), and the legal matter that surprised me most was the making of her will. Her assets were far greater than I'd imagined, and would have disqualified her for Legal Aid. But Lucille more than made up for all the free legal advice she'd received, when she had me list the Legal Aid Society as a beneficiary—for more than $7,000.

Some Legal Aids have government-funded criminal sections providing free assistance, (the equivalent of Public Defenders) to those accused of crime. Here, as with civil proceedings, your attorney is assigned, not chosen, and you never know if you'll draw a seasoned campaigner or an enthusiastic but decidedly nervous lawyer handling his first felony defense.

Volunteer lawyers and other friends in deed. In some areas, it's the bar association that makes free legal assistance available, with volunteers agreeing to represent indigents without fee in civil matters or to help out in matters beyond the scope of Legal Aid.

When Legal Aid or a Public Defender can't represent someone in a criminal matter because of a conflict of interest (they already represent a defendant in the same case), the judge can draw a name from a panel of attorneys in private practice who have volunteered to serve for less than their usual fees.

Still another option available to the poor in some areas are neighborhood law offices under Office of Economic Opportunity grants. Though buffeted by local and national political pressures, young poverty lawyers in these Judicare-type programs have managed to do excellent work for their clients.

There is no denying, however, the damning statistic that 90 per-

392

cent of this country's lawyers work for 10 percent of the people—which leaves a lot of big and little legal problems neglected by those in middle- and lower-income brackets who can pay the legal freight only with difficulty, if at all.

Maybe that's an opportunity as much as an indictment. Low-fee "Honest Abe & Partners" fast-law franchises on every other corner might be just the thing to provide jobs for all the bright young lemmings currently flocking suicidally into our overpopulated law schools and to deliver legal aid to those who can't afford Arnold & Porter.

It's a solution all right. But in solving the young-lawyer unemployment problem, would it create even grimmer problems for society? I can see it now: a corner "Honest Abe," with a massive burnished brass scale of justice on its roof and, flashing irresistibly over its arched entryway, a neon sign with an automatic counting device built in. Emblazoned across it, this proud boast: 2 BILLION SUMMONSES SERVED.

R.S.V.P.: An Authors' Afterword and Invitation

Now you've read the book. Soon, we trust, you'll be using it. Possibly to draft a will. Perhaps to start a business. To win a Small Claims Court case. To administer a family estate. We hope not to declare bankruptcy or divorce a spouse, but such things happen in the best of companies and families. And, just in case, the chapters are there.

Our invitation is this: If you find this book helps you, let us know. If you find a flaw, let us know that, too. We suspect there will be future editions of this book. Feedback from you—comments and experiences, even complaints (though we hope they'll be few)—will help to make them better.

So, if the spirit moves you, write us at the law offices of Kantrowitz and Goldhamer, 277 Old Nyack Turnpike, Spring Valley, N.Y. 10977. With details if you have the time. With a brief paragraph or two if you don't. In any case, with an address or phone number for us to establish contact. We thank you in advance. We are already in your debt.

INDEX

402

collecting on, 287
judgment as, 82
Life insurance, 253
bankruptcy and, 316
proceeds from, 129
Lincoln, Abraham, 361
Liquor licenses, 265–66
Loans:
bankruptcy and, 324
See also Debts; Mortgage
Lucey, Patrick, 124–25

Malpractice suits against lawyers,
381–82
Marital deduction, estate taxes and,
130, 131
Marriage counselors, 137
Marshall, Tom, 67
Miranda warnings, 344
Money:
specific bequests of, 108–9
in typed will, 113
More, Sir Thomas, 34
Mortgage:
additional charges in monthly
payments, 201
closing and, 198, 200–2
contract for sale of house and,
185–86
foreclosing on a, 286–87
obtaining a new, 194–95
recording of, 202, 203
selecting a house and, 180
taking over an existing, 193–94
Motion for Contempt for Failure to
Appear in Supplementary
Proceedings, 87
Motor vehicle bureau, finding identity
of owner of vehicle from, 35

Name:
business, 253–55
changing your, 331–36
Negligence, landlord's, 219
Negotiator, judge as, 61–62
Nichols, Ted, 258
Notary public, 340–41
Notice:
of appeal, 83

of Motion, opening default and, 85
of probate proceeding, 126

Oath, 67
Objections to evidence, grounds for,
73–75
Onassis, Aristotle, 383
Onassis, Jacqueline Kennedy, 383
Opening default, 85
Oral deposition (examination before
trial), 54, 56

Partnership, 109
agreement, 266–72
Business Certificate for, 255, 257
death of a partner and, 250, 270–71
buy-out insurance, 279
dissolution of, 269, 280
incorporation compared to, 248–53
liability and, 248–49
taxes and, 252
Perjury in civil actions, 58
Permits, business, 266
Personal injury:
amount of claim for, 36
landlord's negligence leading to, 219
Personal liability, incorporation and,
248–49
Personal property (or effects):
in bankruptcy petition, 314–15,
317–18
bequests of, 108
foreclosing on, 286–87
real property sales contract and, 186
separation agreement clause on
division of, 150
Pets, apartment leases and, 211
Police, arrest by, 342–46
Power of attorney, 336–40
Preparing for court, 49–62
clothes to wear in court, 60–61
counterclaims, 56–57
judge as negotiator, 61–62
knowing the law, 59–60
pretrial discovery, 53–54
selecting the court, 49–50
serving the summons, 51–53
summons and complaint, preparing
a, 50–51

405